BEYOND TECHNONATIONALISM

INNOVATION AND TECHNOLOGY IN THE WORLD ECONOMY

MARTIN KENNEY, *Editor*
University of California, Davis and Berkeley Roundtable
on the International Economy

Other titles in the series:

JASON OWEN-SMITH
Research Universities and the Public Good: Discovery for
an Uncertain Future

ANDREW HARGADON
Sustainable Innovation: Build Your Company's Capacity
to Change the World

MICHAEL STORPER, THOMAS KEMENY, NAJI MAKAREM, AND TANER OSMAN
The Rise and Fall of Urban Economies: Lessons from
San Francisco and Los Angeles

SHIRI M. BREZNITZ
The Fountain of Knowledge: The Role of Universities in
Economic Development

MARTIN KENNEY AND DAVID C. MOWERY, EDS.
Public Universities and Regional Growth: Insights from the
University of California

MARY LINDENSTEIN WALSHOK AND ABRAHAM J. SHRAGGE
Invention and Reinvention: The Evolution of San Diego's
Innovation Economy

JOHN ZYSMAN AND MARK HUBERTY, EDS.
Can Green Sustain Growth? From the Religion to the Reality of
Sustainable Prosperity

ISRAEL DRORI, SHMUEL ELLIS, AND ZUR SHAPIRA
The Evolution of a New Industry: A Genealogical Approach

JEFFREY L. FUNK
Technology Change and the Rise of New Industries

BEYOND TECHNONATIONALISM

Biomedical Innovation and Entrepreneurship in Asia

Kathryn C. Ibata-Arens

STANFORD BUSINESS BOOKS

An Imprint of Stanford University Press   •   Stanford, California

Stanford University Press

Stanford, California

Special discounts for bulk quantities of Stanford Business Books are available to corporations, professional associations, and other organizations. For details and discount information, contact the special sales department of Stanford University Press. Tel: (650) 725-0820, Fax: (650) 725-3457

Printed in the United States of America on acid-free, archival-quality paper

Library of Congress Cataloging-in-Publication Data

Names: Ibata-Arens, Kathryn C., author.
Title: Beyond technonationalism : biomedical innovation and entrepreneurship in Asia / Kathryn C. Ibata-Arens.
Description: Stanford, California : Stanford Business Books, an imprint of Stanford University Press, 2019. | Series: Innovation and technology in the world economy | Includes bibliographical references and index.
Identifiers: LCCN 2018033665 (print) | LCCN 2018040780 (ebook) | ISBN 9781503608757 (electronic) | ISBN 9781503605473 | ISBN 9781503605473 (cloth ; alk. paper)
Subjects: LCSH: Biotechnology industries—Government policy—Asia—Case studies. | Technological innovations—Government policy—Asia—Case studies. | Entrepreneurship—Government policy—Asia—Case studies.
Classification: LCC HD9999.B443 (ebook) | LCC HD9999.B443 A7853 2019 (print) | DDC 338.4/76606095—dc23
LC record available at https://lccn.loc.gov/2018033665

Typeset by Westchester Publishing Services in 11/15 Minion Pro

Cover design: Christian Fuenfhausen

Cover illustration: iStock | StudioM1

In memoriam
Agnes Kazuko Ibata (née Morioka)
Richard Alan Ibata

CONTENTS

ACKNOWLEDGMENTS

This book has followed a long and winding road from idea to completion. The adventure has run its course over six years, four countries, three languages, and countless planes, trains, buses, and rickshaws. Many have contributed to its fruition.

I am grateful to the editors at Stanford University Press. Kate Wahl recognized the vision for this book and encouraged me early on in the writing. Margo Beth Fleming stood by me through ups and downs, resolutely acting as a sounding board and confidant. It was bittersweet to see her move on to the other coast and to new opportunities. Steve Catalano took over from Margo as the book neared completion and has lived up to his reputation as an "author's editor." Olivia Bartz shepherded this book across the years and editors.

Introductions by colleagues were vital to accessing sources and informants in the various countries discussed in this book. Shelley Ochs, Ezra Vogel, and Frank Hawke facilitated such access in China; in India, Vinod Baliga, Guljit Chaudhri, and Kiran Mazumdar-Shaw; and in Singapore, Poh Kam Wong and Phillip Yeo. Anonymous informants in the aforementioned countries provided powerful insights into the inner workings of government, business, and politics. In Japan, the guidance of Harukiyo Hasegawa and Junichiro Kuroda were essential to transforming ideas into action on the ground.

In Kyoto, many people made it feel like my second home, including Kohei Fukumoto, Ikkei Matsuda, Sachiyo Okuda, Chikako Takanishi, Kuniko Takemi, and Taeko Tanida. In Tokyo, Mike Alfant, Jeff Char, Patricia Bader-Johnston, and James Higa offered perspectives as global entrepreneurs and venture capitalists. I am obliged to Gerald Hane, Russell and Yuko Kawahara, and Yasuko Watanabe for encouraging me to take a break once in a while to get together in Tokyo with friends for a good meal and great conversation, the ideas flowing as smoothly as the wine.

The research would not have been possible without funding, and equally important network synergies enabled as Abe Fellow, sponsored by Japan Foundation Center for Global Partnership, administered by the Social Science Research Council. In addition to generous funding for field research, fellow workshops were instrumental in germinating the seeds for this project. The same is true for the Mike and Maureen Mansfield Foundation with support from Japan Foundation Center for Global Partnership, U.S.-Japan Network for the Future Fellow Program. First under the leadership of Paige Cottingham-Streater, then Benjamin Self and faculty mentors Len Schoppa and Ezra Vogel, who each provided support and encouragement along the way. The research was also enabled by grants from the Kauffman Foundation, Japan Society for the Promotion of Science (JSPS), Fulbright New Century Scholars Program, Japan Ministry of Education, Sports, Science and Technology (MEXT), and University Research Council, DePaul University.

Research affiliations essential in carrying out the field research in Asia included the Research Institute for Economy, Trade and Industry (RIETI) of the Ministry of Economy, Trade and Industry (METI), Tokyo, Japan; Ritsumeikan University Graduate School of Management, Research Center for Innovation Management, Kyoto; and the Kyoto University Graduate School of Management. In this regard, Masaki Kuroki at Ritsumeikan University and Naoki Wakabayashi at Kyoto University were both gracious faculty hosts.

Ms. Qing Wang should be singled out for her tireless work as research assistant over a three-year period. Her patience and dedication are much appreciated. I also appreciated the energy of all the research assistants who have lent a hand throughout, at home at DePaul University and in the field: Benjamin Bui, Abbas Dahodwala, Qiqi Gao, Slok Gyawali, Liyu Hu, Naixin Kang, Keiichiro Koda, Wanlin (Mia) Lu, Lillian Hart, Mingjing He, Alka Kumar, Tejashree Prakash Rane, Alexander Shaindlin, Dolma Tsering, Shaokun Wang, Yuhang (Gloria) Xu, Kentaro Yamamoto, Chao (Ariel) Yang, Rao Yu, Robert Zelm, and Kris Zhou.

I am indebted to colleagues who provided candid feedback on early chapter drafts including Mary Bullock, Robert Eberhart, Anthony D'Costa, Feng Kaidong, Frank Hawke, Robert Kneller, Gregory Noble, Kenneth Oye, T. J. Pempel, Pankaj Sharma, Hiroki Takeuchi, Ezra Vogel, and Kouji Yamada. Two anonymous reviewers pushed me to hone the book's argument and its reflection in the country and entrepreneurial firm case studies herein. I am grateful to the biomedical scientists and entrepreneurs in this study, and their ilk worldwide, for their risk-taking vision and perseverance in bringing new products and therapies to humanity. Any errors or omissions remain my own.

Heartfelt thanks to my family, who tagged along during early field-work in Asia, then later tolerated my time away, and upon my return adjusted to my late nights writing. Fortunately, my sister, Jennifer Ibata-Fetzer, and her husband, Mike Fetzer, as well as our parents, Janie Ibata and the late Richard Ibata, helped by keeping our children, Maximillian and Elizabeth entertained. Lastly, the love of my life, Cris Arens, remained steadfast throughout. I look forward to a future full of afternoons together in our garden and evenings by the fireplace.

Kathryn Ibata-Arens
Chicago and Kyoto

CHAPTER 1 NETWORKED TECHNONATIONALISM IN THE BIOMEDICAL INDUSTRY

Mapping the Global Innovation and Market Context

IN THE TWENTIETH CENTURY, Asian countries—including Japan, South Korea, and Taiwan/Chinese Taipei—succeeded in maintaining economic growth while protecting domestic firms and nurturing new industrial sectors. The Asian developmental "miracle" was so named because rapid, high growth distributed wealth across classes while improving the education and skills of the domestic workforce. In the past, the ability of East Asian countries to develop economies that produced science and technology innovations on par with the West had been attributed to protectionist economic policies and investments into establishing internationally competitive national innovation systems (NIS). For example, scholars often cited such arguments as the developmental state thesis (Johnson 1982; 1995) when referring to Japan. Japan was also said to be technonational in that it equated national security with technology independence. In doing so, it prioritized protecting and nurturing nascent domestic industries while excluding foreign capital and foreign firms from the domestic market. These theories are reviewed in Chapter 2.

In a transnational twenty-first century, when countries must adhere to multinational arbiters of openness, including the Agreement on Trade-Related Aspects of Intellectual Property Rights (TRIPS) under the World Trade Organization (WTO), states have limited maneuverability in pursuing such trade and investment protectionism as preferential treatment of domestic firms and capital vis-à-vis foreign (Lall 2004). Instead, firms must compete within a context of unprecedented international interdependence and economic openness. At the same time, states continue to intervene in their own markets to protect domestic firms and increase national competitiveness.

Country-level economic openness has been defined as the structural orientation of the domestic economy to imports and to inward foreign direct investment (FDI). Multilateral organizations, including the Organisation for Economic Co-operation and Development (OECD) and the World Bank, track openness with various composite indices (OECD 2017; World Bank 2017).[1] The framing here is extended to include the mind-set of domestic political and economic leaders toward these inflows, as well as receptivity to the presence of foreigners (as expats, diaspora returnees, and immigrants). Measures of economic openness are discussed in detail in Chapter 2.

This book proposes a new framework of "networked technonationalism" to explain how states including China and India have adopted a quasi-open, yet fundamentally technonationalist stance in pursuing developmental goals. These countries benefit from harnessing global diaspora networks in making technology investments and entrepreneurial gains in the domestic economy. Outlined in detail below and specified in Chapter 2, it is this networked technonationalism that explains the relative success in certain countries in advancing the dual goals of improving innovation capacity and making gains in entrepreneurial activity in certain technologies. Old-style technonationalism, such as that lingering in Japan, is no longer tenable in the current international context. Neither is a fully open, global orientation fully viable, as the experience of Singapore shows.

In the twentieth century, technonational development was pursued aggressively by such countries as Japan. Some have argued that states should transition their economies into liberal, open markets with a global orientation (Corning 2016; Nelson and Ostry 1995). Yet, despite globalization, technonationalism is alive and thriving in Asia. Nonetheless, in order to survive and prosper in a global era within which reciprocal market openness is demanded, technonationalism has adapted and become networked. A new networked technonationalism (NTN) has evolved in places like China and India, with Singapore adopting a forced-by-circumstance technoglobal approach (Hobday 1995; Kaplinsky and Messner 2008; Nelson 2004). In NTN, industries are targeted as strategic components of the national interest and supported by government policy accordingly. These countries are also pursuing strategies to increase innovation capacity while promoting entrepreneurship in frontier industries. While technonationalism has been researched in depth in the Asian context, further comparative research may identify variations in other regions of the world.

In the twenty-first century, the international context has shifted in two key ways. First, competing at the technology frontier, countries can no longer depend on a clear path to guide them, as they had previously in catching up to Western technology levels.[2] The present path to technology leadership is unclear. Second, within the current international system, demands for reciprocity mean that closing borders to foreign trade is untenable. Governance structures under a WTO regime and global production networks require a degree of openness to imports and foreign capital. This book focuses on strategies employed by governments to protect firms and workers, enhance technology gains, and stimulate the creation of new products and firms—with the aim of creating systems suited for innovation and entrepreneurship at the technology frontier.

Janus is the Roman god of beginnings, openings, and doors. Open to the outside, closed and protective to the inside, the Temple of Janus was open only during times of war.[3] Likewise, Asian countries seeking to improve their innovative and entrepreneurial potential have been compelled to open to the outside world, despite the risks to the domestic economy. Today we are witnessing the retreat of the classic form of the developmental state; countries are no longer able to close their economies to foreign firms and capital in their pursuit of developmental goals (C. Wong 2012). Still, fully opening the doors to an influx of foreign investment and products may displace less competitive domestic firms and workers. This dilemma—open and exposed or closed and left behind—presents a challenge to national governments and is the central *problématique* of this book.

The world is witnessing an unprecedented shift of production capacity to Asia, led by economic transformation in such countries as China and India (Altenburg, Schmitz, and Stamm 2008). In 2014, Asia represented 60 percent of the world's population. By 2050, it is anticipated that half of global gross domestic product (GDP) will be generated in that region. At the same time, the nature of international economic competition in the twenty-first century has made prior developmental strategies in Asia, including previous forms of technonationalism (TN), obsolete (Nelson and Ostry 1995; Samuels 1994). In technonationalism, predicated on the idea that technology independence is key to national security, governments target specific industries for development. Targeted industries benefit from state subsidies and protection from foreign competition. Domestic firms operating within state borders receive exclusive support within and protection from the outside.

The NTN framework extends national innovation systems (NIS) approaches beyond the territorial borders of the state, incorporating the role of international networks (Humphrey and Schmitz 2002; Saxenian 2006). An NIS is comprised of institutions, policies, and practices and the interactions among them that produce innovations in an economy. NIS is defined and explained in detail in Chapter 2. Innovation systems have the potential to extend beyond national borders. For example, high-technology clusters within economies have been noted for their high levels of international network connectivity and the access to technology expertise and venture capital that these networks provide, thus compensating for weakness in such domestic institutions as capital markets (Hobday 1995). In this new form of technonationalism, the developmental state has been eclipsed by a networked technonational state, aiming to improve both innovation and entrepreneurial competitiveness in targeted, usually high-technology industries.

Networked technonationalism is Janus-faced. It is globally oriented on the one hand, for example, via opening to inward FDI and internationalizing its workforce (e.g., expatriate and diaspora professional networks, and domestic workers learning to compete while employed at foreign firms). On the other hand, it is nationalistic, as the players engage in technology upgrading through imitation, reverse engineering, and sometimes outright appropriation of foreign intellectual property. Further, NTN countries utilize their global diaspora networks[4] in a nationalist way by, for example, appealing to their national identity or beckoning them home to their families, real and imagined (Anderson 1983; Pruthi 2014). Other countries lacking a critical mass of global diaspora talent, though they may also be internationally connected (e.g., via research and development, R&D collaborations, or supply chains), are at a competitive disadvantage. Chapter 2 proposes a "knowledge and network" typology (KNT) for measuring the degree of NTN in an economy. This allows a standard method of measuring and comparing variations in the governance regime and structural and institutional architecture accordingly. The cases of China, India, Japan, and Singapore—representing variations in the degree of NTN—are examined empirically in terms of variation along a spectrum (classic technonational–networked technonational–technoglobal) and the historical-institutional context from which these variations emerged.

These countries were selected for comparative study based on their differences in market size and economic development. Taken together, they reflect broad variation on the model of networked technonationalism. To be sure, the findings would be more comprehensive if additional (Asian) countries were included. Other countries should be considered for subsequent analysis, especially as a way to examine, for example, the more narrow variation of technonationalism within East Asian countries. In this regard, Korea and Taiwan have been the subject of book-length analysis by Joseph Wong in *Betting on Biotech* (2011). Details on how this study builds on the aforementioned and related works are provided in the review of existing literature in Chapter 2.

In a globalized economy, countries seek international market access but prefer to protect existing domestic firms and (sometimes) nascent entrepreneurs. National governments must therefore engage in a delicate, Janus-like balance between opening their doors to foreign firms, while still supporting nascent technology sectors and enterprises. In this regard, a number of countries in Asia have targeted the lucrative biomedical industry as a potential source of competitive advantage (Bagchi-Sen, Smith,

TABLE 1.1.

Technonationalism, networked techonationalism, and technoglobalism compared

	Technonationalism	Networked technonationalism	Technoglobalism[a]
Role of state	Protect domestic firms, subsidize, export	Manage openness, subsidize, export	Regulate, promote transparency
Overall system architecture	Closed	Networked	Open
Posture to foreign participation in domestic economy	Exclude	Allow with conditions	Allow
Key actors	Nation-state, corporate conglomerates	International knowledge and capital networks, nascent entrepreneurs incentivized by state policies	Multinational corporations (MNCs) and other transnational actors
Countries	Japan	China, India	Singapore

[a]A more recent variant could be called technolocalism, focusing on local clusters of innovative and entrepreneurial activity and how these locales connect to global technology flows (Yamada 2000).

and Hall 2004; J. Wong 2005; C. Wong 2012; Koh and Wong 2005; Atkinson et al. 2012; Rasmussen 2004; Heller and Eisenberg 1998; Giesecke 2000; McMillan, Narin, and Deeds 2000; Nightingale and Martin 2004; Su and Hung 2009; Dodgson et al. 2008; Lee, Tee, and Kim 2009).

This book builds on previous work in four ways. First, referencing existing literature in innovation systems and developmental state policy, it identifies links between a set of institutional practices within innovation systems and entrepreneurial ecosystems while illustrating (Schumpeterian) dynamics of innovation to entrepreneurial transformation.[5] Is the technological rise of Asian countries predicated on similar domestic policies and institutional arrangements?

Second, it compares these dynamics in a number of countries representing a range of approaches: classic technonational, CTN (Japan); networked technonational, NTN (China, India); and technoglobal, TG (Singapore). Table 1.1 outlines these variations.

Third, this book addresses the global geopolitical context. The twenty-first-century global economic and political environment differs from earlier periods in that it is the most transnational due to advances in communications and other technologies, which enhances the power of transnational actors including multinational corporations (MNCs). Countries at different levels of economic development base growth policies on initial factor endowments, including the natural resources and domestic human capital at hand (Porter 1990).[6] Thus, governments must be mindful of domestic and international complementarities and how to parlay them into competitive advantage.

Fourth, the book's focus is on comparative growth and development in the global biomedical industry. The biomedical industry, comprised primarily of biopharmaceuticals and medical devices, has been targeted for innovation and entrepreneurship development by all four countries in this study, in earnest by each since the 1990s.[7] Seeking to lead global markets in these technologies, the countries analyzed herein have taken divergent paths, representing a range in CTN-NTN-TG as measured by the knowledge and network typology (KNT). Further, advances in biomedical innovation and new-product and new-business creation have profound impacts on human health. Existing research on innovation and entrepreneurial systems, reviewed in Chapter 2, has been focused on such industries as automobiles, electronics, and information technology (Anchordoguy 1989; D'Costa 2012; Giesecke 2000; Mazzucato 2015, 2016; Saxenian 2006). The biomedical industry has been more dependent than others on public investments, meriting comparisons across national contexts (McMillan, Narin, and Deeds 2000; J. Wong 2011). Further, R&D alliances play a unique role in biopharmaceuticals, transcending national boundaries toward the development of a global innovation system in these technologies (Rasmussen 2004). How national governments maintain domestic investments within a globally interdependent value chain might yield useful policy insights. In this regard, this book contributes to existing literature on the role of the state in building innovation capacity and stimulating economic development.

Global Overview: Competition, Innovation, and the Biomedical Industry

This book analyzes innovation and entrepreneurship in China, India, Japan, and Singapore in the biomedical industry to present a range of approaches in technonational regime governance and institutional architecture. A focus on science and technology policy since the 1990s provides an opportunity to examine government interventions that occurred over the same period in these countries, since all included the biomedical industry, in particular, as a strategic policy target for development. Investigating state interventions across these four economies provides insights that comparison of like economies would not yield. Though China is less developed than Japan, it has challenged Japan's performance in stimulating high-technology entrepreneurship. While Japan is a mature economy, China midstage, and India at an earlier stage, they each have attempted similar strategies regarding the biomedical industry—to varying degrees of success in striking the right notes in networked technonationalism, as the country case-study chapters that follow illuminate. Lastly, Singapore's city-state size allowed it to pursue national, cluster, and firm-level strategies simultaneously and is worthy of comparative analysis. These Asian countries also reflect global trends in the prevalence of state intervention when attempting biomedical industry development.

Global healthcare spending is expected to continue to increase an average of 5 percent per year through 2018, remaining above 10 percent of GDP. The overall global market size for healthcare in 2014 was $9.59 trillion (Price Waterhouse Coopers 2015). In 2014, global revenue for biomedicine, also referred to as the "life-science industry," was nearly $2 trillion. In 2014, pharmaceuticals led revenues with $1.23 trillion; medical technology (e.g., medical devices) came in at $363.8 billion (2013 data); and biotechnology, $288.7 billion (Deloitte 2015). The average year-on-year global market growth was 10.8 percent. Pharmaceuticals alone doubled from $932 billion in 2009 to an estimated $1.6 trillion in 2018.

To date, most revenue is generated in the United States and Europe, together comprising 60 percent of global revenues, followed by Asia with 26 percent (Deloitte 2015).[8] The most rapid growth in the future is expected to be in Asia and the Middle East, matching the expected expansion in private and public healthcare in those regions (EIU 2014). Leading exporters continue to be the United States and Europe, while rising market opportunities include Brazil, China, India, and other emerging markets. Between 1995 and 2010, the United States, Japan, and Europe maintained their lead in global pharmaceutical industry output but declined in their total shares. In comparison, China's total share rose from zero prior to 1995 to more than 18 percent by 2010. India's output rose slightly to 2.4 percent by 2016 (Atkinson et al. 2012; IBEF 2016). Global demand remains strong and growing for biomedical products, indicating increasing returns for investment in biomedical industry development (EIU 2014). Consequently, strong future estimated growth in biomedicine presents significant economic opportunities for entrepreneurs, existing firms, and countries alike.

Intellectual property rights (IPR) via patent protection of products resulting from research-and-development investments have acted as a barrier to entry, enabling leading firms in the biomedical industry to garner some of the highest profit margins in the world. For example, an analysis by the *McKinsey Quarterly* of seven thousand public firms listed in the United States found that pharmaceuticals and biotechnology had the highest consistent returns on invested capital (ROIC), above all other industries (Jiang and Koller 2006). As such, the biomedical industry has become an irresistible growth target for governments around the world.

The United States has led the world in biomedical innovation, with 37.2 percent of all biotechnology patents under the Patent Cooperation Treaty (PCT),[9] greater than the European Union (28.1 percent) and Japan (11.9 percent) (2010–2013 data). China's share was 3.5 percent; India's, 1 percent; and Singapore, 0.8 percent (OECD 2016b) (fig. 1.1). In terms of the number of firms and firm size, the United States remains the industry leader with 11,554 dedicated biotechnology firms. Japan is the only Asian country included in the analysis, with 552. Denmark, the global leader per capita had 134 firms (OECD 2016a, 2016b). Other estimates including pharmaceutical and biotechnology firms (2015 data) place China in first position in Asia with 7,500 firms. India followed with 3,000 firms (in pharmaceuticals alone), while Japan had 1,000 in aggregate. Singapore had 95 firms. As mentioned previously, other Asian countries, including Taiwan (850 firms) and South Korea (600 firms), have also targeted the biomedical industry for development, making for useful comparisons to the countries herein (Philippidis 2016; J. Wong 2011).

Measured in terms of bio intellectual property stock ("revealed technology advantage") as compiled by the OECD, Singapore leads in Asia (3.3), followed by India and Malaysia (1.4). China, Hong Kong, and Korea (0.6) surpassed Japan and Taiwan/Chinese Taipei (0.4). Worldwide, Chile (4.4), Estonia (3.3.), and Denmark (3.2) take the top three slots. The United States (2.0) is twelfth in this ranking (2010–2013 data). For Japan, its absolute score declined since the previous ten-year benchmark (2000–2002) (OECD 2016a).[10] Japan's performance improves with triadic patents reported in 2013 (comprised of the European Union, United States, and Japan), for example, exceeding the number of U.S. triadic patents (17,213) with 18,702. China followed Japan, rising from a mere 63 triadic patents in 1999 to 1,473. Limiting the data to biotechnology, the United States leads, averaging 4,800 between 1999 and 2004, followed by the European Union, with an average of 2,800. Likewise, Japan leads again in Asia, producing at least 1,000 biotechnology patent applications annually since 2000. Patent Cooperation Treaty (PCT) patents represent reciprocity across 152 member countries. Triadic patents as a proxy for innovation capacity are considered a more reliable measure than comparing individual country data since the substantial time and financial resources required for multiple international filings is indicative of the perceived economic value of such innovations by the investors behind them (Warner 2015; WIPO 2016). Figures 1.1 and 1.2 illustrate these trends. Overall, Asia doubled its share of world Patent Cooperation Treaty (PCT) applications between 2005 and 2015 to reach 47 percent of total world applications. Japan led with more than 45,000 filings, followed by China with nearly 43,000 (WIPO 2016, data estimates).[11]

Countries seek to increase their innovation capacity through investments into science and technology research and development. R&D expenditure has remained stable across countries, with Japan and Korea spending a greater percentage of GDP than others. Between 2002 and 2012, Japan spent between 3 and 3.5 percent of GDP on domestic R&D, while the United States spent about 2.5 percent during the same period. China's expenditure as a percentage of GDP doubled (from 1 to 2 percent), while for the years for which data was available for India, it remained below 0.75 percent. Most countries increased the number of R&D personnel

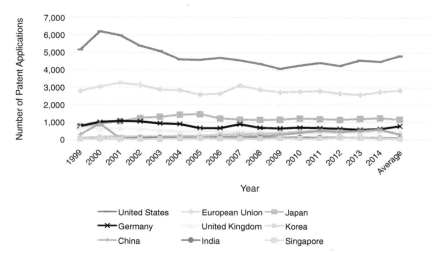

FIGURE 1.1. PCT patent applications in biotechnology (1999–2004). Source: Data from the OECD website. Patent applications filed under PCT: Biotechnology, OECD.Stat, https://stats.oecd.org/ (accessed July 10, 2017).

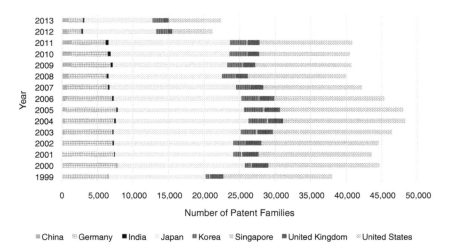

FIGURE 1.2. Triadic patent families (1999–2013). Source: Data from the OECD website. Patents by technology: Triadic patent families, OECD.Stat, http://stats.oecd.org/ (accessed July 10, 2017). According to the OECD, due to delays in reporting, the total number of patents do not appear in the data in and after 2012.

in the 1990s and 2000s. Japan remained about the same, while Korea made the most gains among Asian countries, resulting from its commitment to technology capacity improvement (C. Wong 2012). China made significant progress after 2005, doubling its per thousand of labor force in R&D (from 2 to 4 percent) (OECD n.d.a). Figures 1.3 and 1.4 illustrate these trends in global context.

If all goes as planned, government investments in R&D and human capital result in innovation capability improvements. These are certainly necessary conditions for innovation-system development. However, as the analysis herein demonstrates, a national government that mitigates openness in a globalized economy while pursuing not just developmental, but innovation and entrepreneurial goals may provide the sufficient conditions for leapfrogging over international competitors. As a point of departure, key concepts in the analysis of technonationalism in innovation and entrepreneurship are introduced below and contextualized within existing literature in Chapter 2.

Key Concepts

In Japan, considered the archetypical technonational state, *technonationalism* (*kagakugijutsurikkoku*, 科学技術立国) refers to the concept of "nation building by science and technology" (Nakayama 1991, 200; 2012).[12] With the aim of improving national security through scientific and technological independence, foreigners and foreign capital were largely excluded from Japan in the twentieth century (Samuels 1994; Johnson 1982; Mazzucato 2015). The justification for remaining closed to the outside is as follows: in a resource-poor nation, an initial goal is knowledge diffusion, which in turn increases the quality of local production capacity, thus improving efficiency over time and ultimately national competitiveness. Key features of technonationalism include trade and investment controls, importing technology while at the same time keeping out foreign products and inward foreign direct investment (Nelson 1993, 86). Government policies include negative (tax, tariff) incentives on foreign firms and positive (exemptions, subsidies) incentives aimed at protecting domestic firms. Recent government initiatives, including "Made in China" and "Make in India," reflect a resurgent

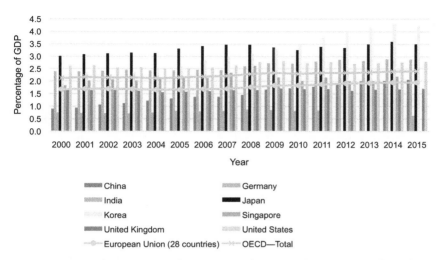

FIGURE 1.3. Gross domestic expenditure on R&D (2000–2015). Source: Data from the OECD website. GERD as a percentage of GDP, OECD.Stat, http://stats.oecd.org/ (accessed July 17, 2017). Data from the UNESCO website. GERD as a percentage of GDP, UIS.Stat, http://data.uis.unesco.org/?queryid=74 (accessed July 17, 2017). Note: Data on India were extracted from UNESCO, and some data years are missing as of July 17, 2017; data year 2015 of Singapore is not available on the OECD website as of July 17, 2017. For both UNESCO and the OECD, the gross domestic expenditure on research and development (GERD) is defined as the "total intramural expenditure on research and development performed on the national territory during a given period" (OECD 2013; UNESCO 2018).

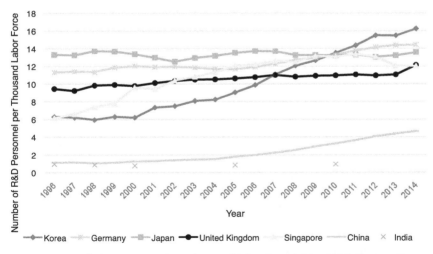

FIGURE 1.4. Total R&D personnel per thousand labor force (1996–2014). Source: Data from the OECD website. Total R&D personnel per thousand labor force (FTE), OECD. Stat, http://stats.oecd.org/ (accessed July 10, 2017). Note: U.S. data are unavailable on the OECD website; some data years for India are missing on the OECD website as of July 10, 2017.

technonationalism in those countries. These and other policies are discussed in greater detail in the next chapter and in country contexts in subsequent chapters.

During the period of capacity improvement, opening the domestic market to foreign multinational corporations (MNCs) who compete head-to-head with domestic firms and workers exposes vulnerable industries to the gale of creative destruction in which old and uncompetitive firms are destroyed and replaced, ideally, by new entrepreneurial enterprises (Schumpeter 1942). In reality, domestic actors often lack the will and wherewithal for new firm formation. In this scenario, the "creative" element of the economic transformation—new products and enterprises—remains unattained in the domestic economy.

Given international competition, to speed up the process of capacity improvements, technology must be obtained any way possible, via imitation (such as through reverse engineering) and occasionally appropriation. In Japan, in the 1980s, the then Ministry of International Trade and Industry (MITI) Very Large Scale Integration (VLSI) project driving national investments into improving computer chip memory was cited as an example of successful technonational policies (Anchordoguy 1989; 2005; Morris-Suzuki 1994). Japan was the center of debate over technonationalism in the twentieth century, and China is becoming a center of similar debate in the twenty-first century. Early twenty-first-century fears of the rise of China are reminiscent of that directed at Japan in the 1970s and 1980s (Pempel 1987). Accusations of Chinese expropriation of Western intellectual property (IP) are similar in tone to the 1982 IBM industrial espionage case against Japan (Nakayama 1991, 229).

In technonational regimes, governments assume a responsibility to intervene in markets in order to improve the technological capacity and competitiveness of domestic firms. Economic strength is the basis of national security and therefore national interest. As outlined above, technonationalism refers to the idea that in addition to state leaders (politicians and bureaucrats), knowledge producers (universities, public research institutes) and economic actors (entrepreneurs, corporate actors) are driven in part by a desire to benefit the nation as a whole and do so while pursuing their own economic interests. Referring to Japan,

Richard Samuels defined technonationalism as a fundamental part of national security. Consequently, national governments are compelled to nurture, promote, and protect domestic science and technology (Samuels 1994). Technonationalism also refers to the commonality of identity and purpose across domestic actors (Montresor 2001) that prioritizes behaviors that lead to knowledge and innovation gains for domestic actors, sometimes at the expense of foreigners and foreign firms.

Within technonational systems, a common language, culture, and institutional framework (e.g., centralized governments with national education systems) promote cohesion (Montresor 1998; 2001). This is its most benign manifestation. Political and economic leaders in these systems pursue policies and strategies that benefit the domestic economy broadly. Technonationalist policies target specific industries for improvement, using such measures as research and development and related subsidies, tax credits, import protection, export promotion, and government procurement. The goal is to build capacity to innovate in order to introduce new technology, products, and services into the economy, making domestic industry internationally competitive. Yet when technonational government policies and state-sanctioned business practices benefit domestic actors at the expense of foreign ones, countries have been accused of violating the principles of open and free trade. A half century of scholarship observing successful technonational regimes in East Asia has indicated that managing domestic actors, through incentives and sometimes cajoling, has been effective in producing gains in innovative capacity and sectoral growth (Amsden 2001; Anchordoguy 1989; Johnson 1982; Samuels 1994).

Technonationalism's antithesis is *technoglobalism*. Technoglobalism is influenced by ideas of liberalism, in that proponents argue for free and open borders to facilitate flows of trade and investment. Such countries as the United States and the United Kingdom have promoted technoglobalism. D'Costa (2012) notes, though, that the latter adopted its "free-trade doctrine" in the context of its then international hegemony and colonial regime. In other words, it was in the economic interest of the United Kingdom to open borders of countries to its exports, but not necessarily to the economic benefit of the less-developed, usually colonized receiving country. Singapore provides a cautionary tale in this regard, discussed in Chapter 6.

Networked technonationalism in contrast could be described as quasi or cautious liberalism. It is Janus-faced. That is, networked technonationalism is global minded and open to the outside world, yet nationalistic in the domestic economy. In so-called late developers (Gerschenkron 1962), the state has less leeway in the short term, unable in the search for foreign technology to close the economy to foreign competition in investment (inward FDI) and trade (imports). In the long term, openness to outside capital and foreign firms pays off if national governments invest inward flows of capital into science and technology infrastructure, labor skills improvement, and other institutional upgrading. National governments, in Janus-faced fashion, must mitigate the dangers of foreign capital making it a losing proposition for domestic firms and labor. China and India have turned to their global diaspora networks to serve as conduits to foreign technology and capital and also to draw from their professional expertise in building domestic science and technology capacity. Indeed, as explained in Chapters 4 and 5, both countries have established special ministries to court the return of diaspora talent. The role of the diaspora in domestic economies is addressed in Chapter 2.

China and India have pursued networked technonationalism with varying degrees of success, while Japan remains imprisoned by institutions created by traditional technonationalist policies.[13] Singapore's small city-state size limits its ability to be anything but technoglobal. Table 1.1 presents an overview of (classic) technonationalism, networked technonationalism, and technoglobalism across the countries of this study in terms of key actors and government posture toward foreign participation in the domestic economy.

A *national innovation system* (NIS) is comprised of a country's regulatory system, including protection of intellectual property and policies supporting science and technology research and development (Nelson and Rosenberg 1993; Nelson and Ostry 1995; Freeman 2002). Success in NIS development is measured, for example, by intellectual property capacity (patents, R&D workforce). It should be noted that science and technology capacity doesn't necessarily translate directly into new products and new business creation. This is the case in Japan. The Japanese government was effective during the twentieth century in subsidizing new product developments in existing (particularly large) firms, but did not have a direct role in the immediate post–World War II increase in the number of such entrepreneurial start-ups as Honda and Sony that grew to become global firms. It would not be until the early 2000s that the Japanese government would focus specifically on stimulating new entrepreneurial firm creation. Japan and its international competitors have since attempted to build entrepreneurial ecosystems.

Overall, a healthy innovation system is necessary for long-term economic growth, though not always sufficient for technology entrepreneurship and not always without conflict. The institutions and people that are the foundations of advances in innovative activity within public and private research organizations (such as national institutes and universities) and private firms supported by government policies comprise national innovation systems (Freeman 1995; Nelson and Rosenberg 1993). Research on technonationalism and national innovation systems has focused on national policy and large corporations, leaving the relationship between innovation and entrepreneurship underexamined. This book aims to extend an understanding of these relationships.

An *entrepreneurial ecosystem* is the set of institutions and practices conducive to new business creation. Ecosystems can be at the national or subnational (city, region) level. Entrepreneurial ecosystems are often stimulated by national government policies, including incentives for firms to invest in certain technology and strategic industries. A case in point is the Silicon Valley in the United States, for some considered the quintessential naturally occurring entrepreneurial ecosystem, which was, in fact, seeded by significant Department of Defense technology investments (Kenney and Von Burg 1999).[14] Measures of development of entrepreneurial ecosystems include numbers of new business start-ups (moving up from necessity to high-growth opportunity levels), increasing employment in new firms, and so forth.

The networked technonational approach presented in Chapter 2 and analyzed across countries in subsequent chapters explains the ways countries have pursued innovation-capacity and entrepreneurial-ecosystem development in a globalized economy, wherein a Janus-faced openness—networked to the outside to draw capital and technology, while protective of nascent industries at home—is most effective at reaping the benefits of international connection while mitigating negative effects.

Chapter Outlines

The following chapters provide a review of the theory and methods of the book, followed by country-level analyses of how networked technonationalism is cultivating scientific and technological seeds into new products and firms, ideally reaping a return on investment for economies, firms, and citizens. Each country chapter is organized around three themes: the developmental vision of the state, government policies, and entrepreneurial firm-level strategies.

First, the state vision (paradigm/ideology) is reviewed, noting the rhetoric in support of technonationalist policies. Institutional legacies of the twentieth-century technonational vision are reviewed. This includes an overview of the structures supporting, and sometimes hindering, national innovation and entrepreneurial ecosystem development.

Second, how national governments put vision into practice is analyzed through a review of policies targeting science and technology (S&T) policy, innovation, and entrepreneurship generally and the biomedical industry specifically. The presence or absence of connections between innovation capacity and entrepreneurial activity can be assessed using a knowledge and network typology, introduced above and specified in Chapter 2.

Third, after outlining characteristics of the biomedical industry, firm-level strategies in new ventures provide a lens through which to view the efficacy of state policies on the ground, where new products, new business, and employment gains emerge.

Chapter 2 reviews the intellectual history of technonationalism, focusing on the impacts of technonationalist ideas across countries and over time. The review notes key thinkers and political and economic leaders who have affected the evolution and practice of technonationalism in Asia. The conceptual typology of knowledge and networks is

TABLE 1.2.

Technonational regimes by country

	Japan	China	India	Singapore
State- and private-sector structure	*Keiretsu* production pyramid (monopsony subcontracting)	State-owned enterprises (SOEs), township and village enterprises (TVEs), "mass entrepreneurship".	Public sector undertakings (PSUs), public-private partnership (PPP or P3)	SOEs (government-linked companies [GLCs]); state–MNC–tech park nexus
Key ministries	Ministry of Economy, Trade and Industry (METI), Ministry of Education, Culture, Sports, Science and Technology (MEXT)	Ministry of Science and Technology (MOST), Torch Center	Ministry of Human Resource Development (MHRD), Department of Biotechnology (DBT)	Agency for Science, Technology and Research (A*STAR), Economic Development Board
Targeted sectors[a]	Biomedical, energy, nano	Biomedical, energy	Biomedical, IT	Biomedical

[a] Previously targeted sectors include defense-related technology.

presented, relating the networked technonationalism framework in the book to existing theories, including national innovation-systems and developmental-state approaches. The latter half of the chapter outlines how technonationalism is pursued within a certain knowledge and network (governance) regime and (structural and institutional) architecture, as a basis to compare countries.

Aggregate data utilizing public and proprietary data sets are complemented with original fieldwork-based policy analysis, firm-level case studies, and interviews with entrepreneurs, government officials, incubation managers, and investors in China, India, Japan, and Singapore, conducted in the language of each country. The conceptual framework outlined in Chapter 1 and specified in Chapter 2 provides the narrative lens through which the innovation and entrepreneurship stories of China, India, Japan, and Singapore are presented. Table 1.2 provides an outline of the main institutional features of technonationalist (knowledge and network) regimes in each country. Countries appear in the table in the order of subsequent chapters.

Chapter 3 introduces the first of the case-study countries, Japan. With its old-style technonationalism (and developmental state), Japan was the archetypical, or classic, technonationalist state in the twentieth century; emulated all over the world then, it has since become a cautionary tale in the twenty-first century. Despite Japan's rapid economic rise, its strengths in intellectual property production have since failed to translate into globally competitive new-product and new-business creation. Insular and closed institutions and business practices have created "sticky" (*ningen no nenchakusei*, 人間の粘着性) networks. These structures, while protecting weak industries from global competition, have trapped nascent entrepreneurs and undermined globally competitive human-capital development. Yet Japan remains the largest market for biomedical products and services in Asia (and second in the world after the United States). Since the 1990s, it has built on its strengths in medical devices (Ibata-Arens 2005) to expand into biopharmaceuticals. For example, since the awarding of the Nobel Prize in medicine to Kyoto University professor Shinya Yamanaka (2012), the Japanese government has invested extensively in stem-cell research. Its aging population (with ample household savings) is increasing its healthcare product consumption, making it an even more lucrative market in the future. Further, demographic pressures shrinking the size of its working population mean that future growth must be based on productivity gains. This translates into opportunities for foreign firms and investors to enter Japan, potentially improving Japanese innovation and entrepreneurial networks in the future.

Meanwhile, China has made substantial innovation and entrepreneurship gains. The Janus-faced nature of twenty-first-century networked technonationalism is evident in China and presented in Chapter 4. Features of China's NTN include aggressive science, technology, engineering, and math (STEM) education and entrepreneurship policies. Further, the biomedical industry has been identified by political and economic leaders as a "strategic emerging industry" (*zhanlvexingxinxingchanye*, 战略性新兴产业) and is a focal point of state-led economic development. In contrast to Japan's insular and closed (sticky) domestic knowledge and business networks, China's diaspora and substantial inward FDI have contributed to developing globally competitive business networks. Over time, China has been able to use its growing domestic market as a lure to foreign firms from which technology appropriation can occur. However, China's large population size and urban-rural disparities mean that egalitarian redistribution of new wealth has not been guaranteed in this system. Moreover, the introduction of Western (mostly chemical) pharmaceuticals has been antithetical to its historical strengths in traditional medicine and therapies. Meanwhile, China has invested in genomics as the entrepreneurial cases BGI and Sibiono Genetech show.

Variations in NTN in India provide interesting comparisons in Chapter 5. India offers the opportunity to examine networked technonationalism attempted in the context of an earlier stage of economic development. Decades ago, India's public and private sector invested in generic drug research and development and production capacity, complemented by advances in information technology (IT). In the pharmaceutical industry, as part of a social welfare policy meant to ensure access to reasonably priced medicines, product patents were prohibited until its 1995 joining of the World Trade Organization (WTO). By that time, India had already become a world leader in generic pharmaceuticals. From this base, such entrepreneurial firms as BIOCON have benefitted from protective government policies, enabling domestic firms to build capacity and market share in biopharmaceuticals. Meanwhile, expatriate networks of Indian professionals have contributed to new products and firms, particularly in the IT industry in India. Within India, there appears to be regional variations in the benefits of networked technonationalism and, like China, a less than egalitarian redistribution of resources.

Singapore has been paradoxically both more and less successful than India in creating an innovation and entrepreneurial ecosystem. Chapter 6 offers an analysis at its city-state level from which insights can be drawn despite its size. Singapore's developmental model had to be based within its multiethnic Chinese, Indian, and Malay population; and from its very inception as a nation-state in 1965, it was global in outlook. Lacking domestic resources, it had no choice but to become technoglobal. Nevertheless, its meritocratic Agency for Science, Technology and Research (A*STAR) tied inward FDI to domestic human-capital development and redistribution of internationally derived wealth to its domestic population. The "guppies to whales" human-capital development contributed to productivity gains through attracting the region's best and brightest STEM youth and offering them citizenship. This has also included luring stem-cell scientists from Japan to lead government-sponsored technology entrepreneurship, as the case of Celligenics at A*STAR illustrates. While the Singaporean city-state's small population has proven an impediment to establishing a critical mass of new technology entrepreneurs, open immigration policies have the potential to fast-track future development, though indigenous workers have been displaced in this process.

Chapter 7 reviews the key findings of the book, reflecting on the conceptual framework of networked technonationalism. It summarizes variations in the manner in which innovation-system and entrepreneurial-ecosystem development has been pursued in China, India, Japan, and Singapore. The book concludes with theory and policy implications of networked technonationalism for Asia and the world economy.

As a point of departure, the next chapter presents the book's theoretical framework, reviews the origins of technonational ideology in premodern Asia, and proposes a "knowledge and network" typology as a basis for analyzing the country case studies that follow.

KNOWLEDGE AND NETWORK TYPOLOGY

Comparing National Innovation Systems and Entrepreneurial Ecosystems

TECHNONATIONALISM, THE IDEA that national security depends in part on technological self-sufficiency, has guided innovation and economic development policies in many countries. Before tracing the intellectual history of technonationalism in Asia, this chapter proposes a typology for comparing economies at the national level on the continuum of technonationalism–networked technonationalism–technoglobalism through an analysis of knowledge (codified versus tacit) and network (closed versus open) regimes. This conceptualization helps explain, for example, why Japan, despite its ample scientific and technological knowledge base, has heretofore failed to generate significant amounts of high-growth startups in such emerging industries as biomedicals. Japan is living the legacies of its technonationalist policies of the previous century. Comparisons to China, India, and Singapore in subsequent chapters offer insights into the twenty-first-century networked-technonationalism variant. The chapters also assess the relative success or failure in matching ideological vision with actionable policy that results in advancements in innovation that translate into entrepreneurship.

As outlined in Chapter 1, the country cases manifest along a range of technonational approaches that have affected innovation-system and entrepreneurial-ecosystem development. At one end is the closed nature of Japan's classic technonationalism (CTN). In the middle of the spectrum is the networked technonationalism (NTN) that has emerged in China and India. Networked technonationalism, in Janus-faced fashion, is open to the outside yet fiercely protective within the domestic economy. Singapore represents the other extreme, fully open and exposed to the outside, in a technoglobal (TG) orientation. As illustrated in table 1.1, networked technonationalism offers a framework to explain how such countries as China and India—in a departure from earlier forms of classic technonationalism, as in Japan—have mitigated openness to inward FDI and imports. In their simultaneous pursuit of building domestic capacity in innovation and entrepreneurship, networked-technonational countries have harnessed such quasi-open international networks as via scientists, technologists, and management professionals in their global diaspora in making national economic gains with a return to domestic firms and workers. The networked-technonational framework and knowledge and network typology (KNT), introduced in Chapter 1, are presented and specified with hypotheses in further detail below.

Briefly, the following figures illustrate the range of binary conditions (or active versus passive orientations), as led by state policies and overall openness to the outside, corresponding to the closed–quasi-open–fully open structures of CTN-NTN-TG states of action and states of mind within economies. Classic technonationalism (fig. 2.1) sees a focus at the state level on buttressing codified knowledge and closing off the domestic market from the outside world—which some might refer to as a twentieth-century adaptation of the previous seventeenth-to-eighteenth-centuries *sakoku* 鎖国 "closed country," or national isolation, period initiated under the Tokugawa Shogunate in 1640. Observing the colonization of other countries that followed European Christian missionaries and traders, sakoku was intended to protect the Japanese from the corrupting influence of exposure to the West. The twentieth-century manifestations of closure are detailed in Chapter 3.

China and India demonstrate networked technonationalism in that tacit knowledge exchange is prioritized (fig. 2.2), seeking technology and capital gains from foreign partners through a quasi-open network structure. Initial weaknesses in indigenous codified knowledge (formal, learned from the written word) are compensated for by channeling

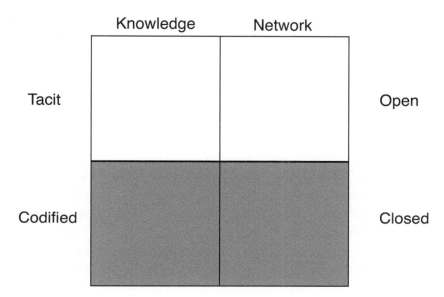

FIGURE 2.1. Classic technonationalism (CTN) (example: Japan).

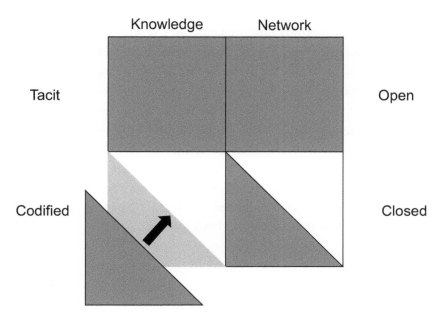

FIGURE 2.2. Networked technonationalism (NTN) (examples: China, India).

newfound tacit knowledge (informal, learned by doing) exchange such as via international collaborative R&D (e.g., as discussed in Chapter 4, evidenced in the participation of Chinese scientists in the Human Genome Project that later presented entrepreneurial opportunities for the Chinese venture the Beijing Genomics Institute). This quasi openness as a way to draw from international diaspora networks is examined in Chapter 4 on China and Chapter 5 on India. For example, India would eventually appeal to its diaspora, referred to in that country as "nonresident Indians," or NRI, through such policies as the NRI Ambassador Scheme and related programs of the Ministry of Overseas Indian Affairs, modeled on a similar program in China overseen by the Overseas Chinese Affairs Office of the State Council.

Macroeconomic gains from this openness have exacted costs on domestic stakeholders, however. Openness is mitigated, but not completely, as has been evident in the displacement of rural and lower-skilled labor in favor of returnees and foreigners in stimulating high-technology entrepreneurship. Beijing and Bangalore grow exponentially, while hinter regions in these countries see little improvement. The city-state Singapore had to adopt the other extreme on the continuum from closed to open in its technoglobal approach of actively open knowledge and network structures (fig. 2.3). Consequently, Singapore—with its Agency for Science, Technology and Research (A*STAR) guiding technology acquisition from foreign partners and overall intellectual capacity improvements—has grown at a pace rivaling the East Asian Tiger economies. Its fully open posture to foreign MNCs and foreigners in general has led in recent decades to rising resentment among native-born Singaporeans who have been squeezed out of increasingly luxury-level real estate in central Singapore and passed over in favor of foreigners in high-technology employment.

Research Methods

The methods in this book are threefold. First, aggregate statistics provide a global context for the Asian region and individual country-level findings. Second, using original-language policy document analysis, contemporary news reports, and related documents, key national policies are outlined in

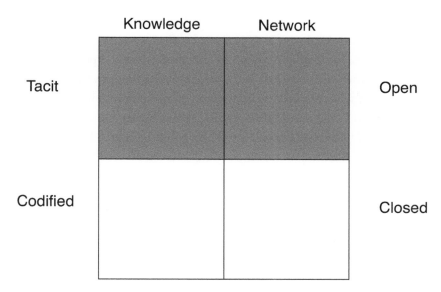

FIGURE 2.3. Technoglobalism (TG) (example: Singapore).

historical context, reflecting the sociopolitical and institutional environment preceding the pivot to biomedicals in each country. For example, government policy documents show the state's perspective, while supplemental accounts from contemporaneous news media provide nongovernmental (private sector) interpretations. Third, the findings drawn from macro-level analysis and review of policy history are supplemented by extensive original-language fieldwork in each country conducted between 2010 and 2017 with stakeholders, including government officials, academics, new venture entrepreneurs, and venture capitalists.

For example, aggregate data drawn from the Global Competitiveness Index (GCI), Global Entrepreneurship Monitor (GEM), and OECD biotechnology statistics are complemented with an original data set. The latter was compiled utilizing proprietary data sets (citation, patent, and firm level), including Dunn and Bradstreet and Teikoku Databank, as well as open-access data sets from WIPO (World Intellectual Property Organization), OECD, and Scopus and Web of Science citation data. This provides the opportunity to analyze global-, national-, and firm-level data—to identity concentrations of innovation and entrepreneurship within economies.

Semi-structured interviews were conducted with government officials, business and industry association executives, venture capitalists, and
entrepreneurs. For example, questions collected informant perceptions of
state policy (national, regional, local) as they relate to innovation and entrepreneurship. Supplementing informant perspectives with business news
reports allows contextualization within expressed issues and concerns in
contemporary business environments. It should be noted, however, that
the countries herein experience varying degrees of media censorship.[1]
Nevertheless, the inclusion of news reports reflects the public signaling
of government leaders and those in the private sector attempting to
influence government policy and promote their own economic agendas.

The knowledge and network typology provides a framework to assess
countries' relative innovation capacity and how that capacity connects
or lacks connection to and thus affects entrepreneurial activity in key
industries. Economies and their respective national innovation systems
and entrepreneurial ecosystems can be compared in terms of codified
knowledge (knowledge about things) and tacit knowledge (defined below). Measures of codified knowledge include that which comprises
innovation capacity, including patents (figs. 1.1, 1.2, and 2.5), expenditure
on R&D (fig. 1.3), and authoring scientific articles (fig. 2.4).

Tacit knowledge, or knowledge about how to do things, is unwritten
and exchanged via face-to-face interactions, such as those between
skilled professionals, technologists, and entrepreneurs. It is noncodified
and difficult to measure. Interorganizational tacit-knowledge exchange
promotes innovation across institutional boundaries. With this in mind,
the existence of tacit-knowledge exchange is implied by proxy measures,
including labor mobility, interorganizational (e.g., international) R&D
collaborations, and the like (table 2.2, upper left quadrant). Open networks in knowledge and business, particularly those occurring within
R&D focused entrepreneurial exchange, also promote tacit exchanges.

There are numerous challenges to analyzing causal relationships
between policy and industry and firm-level outcomes in such complex
systems as national economies. For example, in the absence of concrete
data, government officials might see their impact on industry as greater
than in reality. On the other hand, company executives and entrepre-

neurs might focus on the inefficiencies of government as well as how government decisions get in the way of business activities rather than the ways in which government policies contribute to institutional capacities. Further, while the author attempted to collect data from a balanced and wide variety of sources, errors in interpretation may still be present. Though the author is fluent in Japanese, reliance on interpreters in China on occasion and translations of Chinese sources may also limit the analysis. Likewise, even though English is an official language of India and Singapore, there is no doubt that nuance is lost due to the inability to engage with sources in the various indigenous languages across domestic ethnicities of these countries. Before outlining the knowledge and network typology and presenting hypotheses, an overview of the role of diaspora networks in networked technonationalism follows.

Diaspora Networks and Knowledge Diffusion

International diaspora networks have been found to play important roles in the economic development of the home country that extend beyond the ability of local native-born networks available within the borders of the domestic economy and complement other international connections, if any exist, among domestic innovators and entrepreneurs. NTN regimes have appealed to nostalgia and nation in the diaspora—appeals that would not have resonance with most foreign nationals who lack these cultural connections to "home." Developmental roles include technology acquisition, introducing business opportunity, and providing financial resources (Kuznetsov 2006; Pandey et al. 2006; Wadhwa et al. 2011; Warner 2015). For example, often initiated at the behest of diaspora executives making outsourcing decisions to invest in home country facilities, learning by doing occurs in international R&D collaborations in addition to expanding scientific and professional networks among project participant cohorts. India in particular has benefitted from its diaspora executives at technology companies in the United States in this regard, as discussed in Chapter 5. Other examples include Japan's Nobel Prize recipient Shinya Yamanaka's collaborative R&D relationships forged at the Gladstone Institute in the United States early on in his career (discussed in the next chapter).[2]

TABLE 2.1.

Number in diaspora (select Asian countries)

	China	India	Japan	Singapore
Number in diaspora	50 million	25 million	3.5 million	212,000
Year of measure	2012	2010	2014	2014

SOURCES: China, Xiang (2016); India, Greater Pacific Capital (2013); Japan, Association of Nikkei and Japanese Abroad (2015); Singapore, Today Online (2015).

Diaspora networks also introduce business opportunities, including new market niches and new product ideas, such as that of Beigene, an immune-oncology venture located in the Zhongguancun industrial district in Beijing. The district is immense in size and the number of returnee entrepreneurs (discussed in Chapter 4). Diaspora networks also link domestic entrepreneurs to financial resources, including angel investment and other venture funding. Shane and Cable (2002) note the importance of diverse networks in access to venture finance by entrepreneurs. The Indus Entrepreneurs (TiE) global network of nonresident Indians (NRI) has served as an important conduit between domestic entrepreneurs and international venture-capital opportunities, as mentioned in Chapter 5.

Knowledge diffusion and innovation are facilitated by common cultural understandings. Differences in language and culture can interfere with the exchange of tacit knowledge (as it is implicit and often transmitted verbally) more than in the transfer of codified knowledge, which is written down and accessible in documents (the use of which is often referred to as "book learning"). Studies on transnational business activities have found that sharing a common language, for example, improves economic outcomes (Ginsburgh and Weber 2011). A unique feature of NTN systems is that they benefit via expatriate and diaspora networks from cultural ambassadors, who are able to code switch between domestic and international language and cultural contexts. In China and India, these individuals tend to be science and technology professionals.[3] The large pool of diaspora talent for China (50 million) and India (25 million) presents a competitive challenge to countries lacking such international networks, including Japan, with a mere 3.5 million in its diaspora, and Singapore, having a negligible 212,000 due to its small population. Table 2.1 outlines the size of the diaspora of countries in this book.[4]

TABLE 2.2.

Knowledge and network typology

	Knowledge	Networks
Informal (network level)	Tacit Networks, patterns of interaction	Open Interorganizational flows, social capital, trust, embeddedness
	(proxy) Measures: labor mobility, employee turnover rate, start-up/ closure rates, international R & D JVs, VC deal flow, etc.	Measures: international coauthorship, international copatenting, JVs
Formal (institution level)	Codified IP stock, resource endowments	Closed Intraorganizational
	Measures: triadic patent output, high-impact scientific citations, GERD, STEM workforce ratios (OECD 2013, 2016c, n.d.a, n.d.b, n.d.c)	Measures: hiring practices, employee turnover

These transnational individuals act as conduits of knowledge transfer between international and domestic institutions. As will be examined in the chapters that follow, Chinese and Indian diaspora returnees are embraced and valued for their newfound international experience. Japanese who go abroad, however, have had difficulty reintegrating into domestic institutions and are even shunned by them, undermining labor mobility and the development of a transnational technonational class. Singapore's small population size means that its diaspora lacks scale (and thus critical mass). This has a negative effect on tacit information flows in particular. How Singapore has dealt with these insufficiencies is explored in Chapter 6.

Knowledge and Network Typology

The following typology outlines a framework to compare connections between innovation capacity within national innovation systems (NIS) and domestic entrepreneurial ecosystems. Countries are compared in terms of the knowledge and network typology, assessing the strengths and weaknesses in each quadrant (codified knowledge, tacit knowledge, closed networks, open networks). Figures 2.1, 2.2, and 2.3—introduced above—provide a stylistic view of the knowledge and network framework, while table 2.2 is a detailed version.

The knowledge and network typology (KNT) is for comparing countries at the nation-state level, under a technonationalist vision. A KNT is also manifested in countries as a regime (governance system) and often an overall architecture (structures as they relate to each other). In this study, the knowledge and network typology, manifested in a domestic institutional context as regime and architecture, is also embedded in a technonationalist developmental paradigm (a shared system of beliefs). These are all facets of how countries orient their aims for knowledge acquisition and network connection for the purposes of improving innovation capacity and entrepreneurial outcomes.[5] Hence, a note on terms is useful:

- Conceptual framework—a system of concepts, assumptions, expectations, beliefs, and theories supporting and informing research. A conceptual framework explains the main phenomena under study, identifying key factors, concepts, or variables and the relationships among them.

- Typology—classifying of characteristic groups by certain attributes whereby the elements within a type are as similar as possible, while differences between types are as distinct as possible. The purpose of a typology is in identifying patterns across cases through establishing a standard to compare countries across groups of attributes.

- Regime—a system or planned way of doing things, especially one imposed from above. It is derived from the Latin *regimen*, meaning "rule, guidance, or government."

- Architecture—the complex or carefully designed structure of something (see Lessig 2002 for innovation architecture).

- Paradigm—"the entire constellation of beliefs, values, techniques and so on, shared by the members of a given community" (Kuhn 1970, 175).

Explaining the Quadrants of the Knowledge and Network Typology
Formal or Codified Knowledge (Innovation-Capacity Base)

Measures of the capacity of economies to create new knowledge in emerging sectors include the amount invested in research and development (e.g., gross domestic expenditure on research and development [GERD]), the number of scientists per capita, growth in international citations of scientific publications, and patent output.[6] These are all measures of formal knowledge, things that can be counted (thus having been codified), such as in patents. Formal or codified knowledge is learned through reading texts and exchanged in writing accordingly, via, for example, legal contracts. Several global indices claim to compare economies in a standard fashion, while utilizing a variety of quantitative and qualitative methods. For example, the Innovation Capacity Index (ICI) is comprised of sixty factors underlying a country's ability to create an environment encouraging innovation. The ICI is built upon five pillars: institutional environment, human capital, training and social inclusion, regulatory and legal framework, research and development, and adoption and use of information and communication technologies (López-Claros 2009). Porter's diamond model (1990) of country-level competitive advantages takes a similar capacity-building approach. An extensive literature exists that examines the relative merits of codified and tacit knowledge in technology management and intellectual property rights (see, for example, Johnson, Lorenz, and Lundvall 2002; Edvinsson and Sullivan 1996; Burk 2008).

The more up-to-date Global Competitiveness Index (GCI) measures innovation capacity via six measures: quality of scientific research institutions, company spending on R&D, university-industry collaboration in R&D, government procurement of advanced technology products, availability of scientists and engineers, and PCT patents and applications per one million people.[7] The knowledge base and innovation capacity more broadly can be improved through tacit-knowledge exchange (KNT, upper left quadrant) across institutional boundaries.

Informal/Tacit Knowledge

Tacit knowledge, in contrast to the formal nature of codified-knowledge exchange, is transferred by informal, usually unwritten means. Learning by observation and learning by doing are processes through which tacit knowledge is exchanged within and across organizations (Powell 1998; Powell and Grodal 2005).[8] A proxy measure of the incidence of informal- or tacit-information exchange is labor mobility, as workers who move between firms tend to be conduits of tacit-knowledge flows. More broadly, Mowery et al. (2001) refer to *social* technologies, including customs and norms, in contrast to *physical* technologies, similar to the codified knowledge outlined above. Governments are thus challenged to promote tacit-knowledge exchange, benefitting the domestic economy, while protecting domestic actors from foreign exploitation. Historically, maintaining closed business networks has been key to protectionist national policies.

Closed Networks

The structures of dominant institutions and industrial organization that serve as the foundation of business activity ideally allow a country to adapt to the demands of international competition in new technology sectors. Closed *intra*-firm networks (KNT, lower right quadrant) are not always negative, as high levels of work-team cohesion can improve labor productivity and incremental innovation. *Inter*-firm or interinstitutional network is defined here as informal relations between individuals that transcend institutional boundaries. It is distinct from such formal inter-firm relations as contracts or other legal agreements. Mutual trust and social capital in these informal, socially embedded relations mitigate cheating and malfeasance (Granovetter 1983, 1985). Research indicates that economic growth and democratic institutional cohesion are facilitated by high levels of social trust. Scandinavian countries are often noted for their high levels of development, social cohesion, and overall trust in this regard (Levitt and Dubner 2005).

While protectionist tariff and nontariff barriers (NTBs) once insulated weak domestic firms, these policies are no longer viable on a large scale within an international trade and investment environment that demands equal treatment (e.g., under World Trade Organization [WTO] membership rules). Consequently, the practice in Japan of hiring employees and providing lifetime employment—at least in large firms—limits the flexibility of firms to adapt to external changes. Benefits to firms of flexibility in hiring practices might also harm workers due to the potential use of underemployed part-time and low-wage contract labor. Also, complete openness to the outside world (i.e., via trade and investment liberalism) without protecting domestic nascent entrepreneurs and less competitive existing firms may interfere with the development of globally competitive new industries. Countries are therefore prudent to maintain a Janus-faced type of openness, for example, through encouraging inward foreign direct investment while funneling capital into and nurturing domestic emerging industries. A way to accomplish these competing goals is opening domestic knowledge networks to the outside world.

Open Knowledge Networks
One way of understanding the level of international openness in a country's knowledge architecture (KNT, upper right quadrant) is the incidence of coauthored high-impact scientific citation and international co-invented patents (Leydesdorff and Persson 2010).[9] National governments have sought to boost their international citation rankings, and similarly university faculty have been responsive to state-sponsored funding incentives to publish more frequently. In China, for example, in the last decade, scientists have been rewarded for publishing, and as a result the number of international publications has increased significantly. (Measures of quality and originality are a separate matter, discussed in Chapter 5.)

Recognizing the positive effect on innovation, governments have encouraged international science and technology collaborations. For example, countries have increased copublishing and co-inventions with foreign partners. Between 2002 and 2012, most countries experienced a steady increase in international scholarly collaborations, as measured by coauthorship of scientific articles. European countries improved from their already strong internationalized position. By 2012 nearly half of all scientific publications by Europeans shared authors across country boundaries. Japan improved about 10 percent, while India and China remained flat (OECD n.d.b).

Between 1999 and 2014, patents with foreign co-inventors increased. Globally, China experienced the most impressive gains, of 2,259 percent.[10] India followed with 680 percent growth. Both countries had even greater growth in overall patenting activity (4,164 and 822 percent growth,

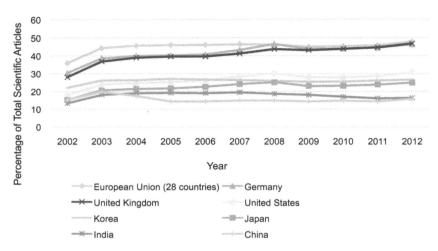

FIGURE 2.4. International coauthorship of scientific articles (2002–2012).
Source: International coauthorship is defined by the OECD as scientific articles with two or more authors from different countries. Data from the OECD website. International coauthorship, percentage of total scientific articles, OECD.Stat, https://stats.oecd.org/ (accessed May 18, 2016). Note: Singapore data are unavailable.

respectively). In copatenting, Japan grew slightly (74 percent) and Singapore (435 percent) also experienced gains (OECD 2017).[11] Overall patents for Japan grew by 387 percent and Singapore by 365 percent. Figures 2.4 and 2.5 illustrate the trends toward international research and development collaborations across economies.

Open Business Networks

The upper right quadrant in the knowledge and network typology reflects a country's ability to bridge the gaps between the institutions underlying innovation capacity with new business (entrepreneurial) opportunities. Measures confirming network openness (to the outside global economy) include strategic tie-ups, firm-level international research and development collaborations, joint ventures (JVs), and so forth.

The prevalence of inward foreign direct investment (FDI) and market access of foreign goods are measures of overall openness, as is the degree of internationalization of the domestic workforce. This is important in developing economies especially, for example, in the proportion

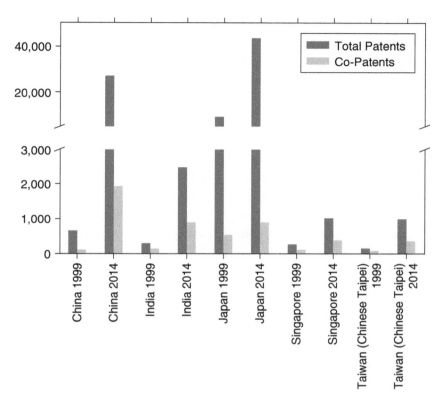

FIGURE 2.5. Comparison of total patents and patents with foreign co-inventors (1999 and 2014). Source: Data from the OECD website. Percentage of patents with foreign co-inventors, OECD.Stat, https://stats.oecd.org/ (accessed July 17, 2017).

of indigenous labor in management positions in foreign firms. Research has demonstrated that experience in a foreign multinational is an important training ground for domestic entrepreneurs (Görg and Strobl 2005). Further, these individuals become important conduits of foreign know-how and technology via tacit-knowledge flows into the domestic economy. Scholars have found that successful entrepreneurs in China (Wang, Zweig, and Lin 2011) and those remaining competitive in recessionary Japan (Ibata-Arens 2005) are likely to have executive teams with international study and work experience. Likewise, the extent to which states use foreign human capital via open immigration policies is another indicator of openness.

Determining the relative contributions to innovation capacity of institutions and policy is a complex task. At the very least, it has been established that such investments into human capital as improving science and technology skills and infrastructure (e.g., lab space, IT capacity) are important components of strengthening innovation capacity (Freeman 2002; Freeman and Soete 1997; Lundvall 2007; Etzkowitz and Leydesdorff 2000). Improving the entrepreneurial ecosystem so that advances in science and technology capacity translate into commercializable products and new business growth is an equally complex task. Likewise, looking back on the success of technonational policies to determine the relative contributions of tariffs, nontariff barriers (NTBs), tax incentives, subsidies, and the like to a country's economic growth has yielded a variety of explanations as to the relative impact of state interventions (Amsden 1994; Beason and Weinstein 1996; Evans and Rauch 1999; Johnson 1987; J.-W. Lee 1996; Segerstrom 1991). This represents a significant evolution from earlier economic assumptions that the only way to stimulate growth is either to lower nominal wages or devalue currency (Lundvall 2007). The macroeconomic environment plays an important role, including low inflation and fair access to bank and other financing. Countries must also be able to sell their products on the open market, ideally having reciprocal access to other countries within an open international trading system. Managing mitigated openness guided by a technonationalist development strategy—protecting nascent industries and firms while seeking openness abroad—becomes a delicate balancing act.

Asian countries, including Japan, South Korea, and Taiwan (Chinese Taipei), have been singled out for their technonationalism, as outlined in Chapter 1. This elicits the question of whether countries are in fact technonationalist in their vision and policy orientation. Judging by the volume of research on Asian countries in this light, it would seem that they are indeed primarily technonational in orientation, while Western countries are not generally identified as such.[12] Even so, with the exception of Japan, Asian countries have had an inconsistent record of technonationalism, and some might argue that this was a key factor in their vulnerability to Western colonization in previous centuries. This is not to say that the pursuit of national security through technology leadership has not existed in Western countries, despite the lack of scholarly research applying the concept of technonationalism. Bismarckian Germany, for example, could be said to have exhibited similar tendencies for economic nationalism.[13]

Asian cases may represent one extreme, or a model case whereby a national technonational developmental vision is supported by state policy and firm-level behavior. If it is a binary, meaning either technonationalist or not, then those countries that drank the Kool-Aid, so to speak, of Western free-market liberalism under the so-called Washington Consensus, opening their borders to "unfettered" capital and foreign exports would therefore not be considered technonationalist. It is beyond the scope of this book to identify particular countries of the latter type, but one need not look too far among postcolonial states in Africa and Latin America to find examples (T. Suzuki 2012).

The conceptual framework of networked technonationalism is grounded in advances in several fields, including policy analysis, political economy, and economic history. It is also grounded theory in that it is derived from data and evidence based on qualitative social research and fieldwork (Lundvall 2005). It contributes to existing explanations of innovation and entrepreneurial outcomes on an industry and economy level. It draws from previous work on national systems of innovation (NSI), or national innovation systems (NIS), theories of economic development (including the developmental state), and conceptions of national security (including technonationalism).

This book proposes a conceptual framework of networked technonationalism to explain the variations in Asian nation-state policy and firm-level strategy targeting frontier innovation–based new industry emergence and related entrepreneurial-ecosystem development. Using the biomedical industry as a test bed, it lays out a knowledge and network typology as a way of categorizing both the overall system of political and socioeconomic structures and governance regime (the way states attempt to guide economic activity inside their borders) within which innovation and entrepreneurial activity takes place. Next, the intellectual history of technonationalism and national innovation systems are reviewed, from which emerged the contemporary vision in state policy in the technonational origin states China and Japan.

Intellectual History of Technonationalism and National Innovation Systems

Technonationalism

The following review represents three general periods in the evolution of technonationalism in Asia: premodern or pre-nation-state, twentieth century, and twenty-first century. These periods represent a gradual evolution of technonationalism into networked technonationalism in rising global powers, including China. The three periods in the evolution of technonationalism share common beliefs on the part of government leaders, including that technological superiority is critical for national security. As modern Japan was inspired by premodern China, the ideology of technonationalism has subsequently been emulated throughout Asia and beyond. The current variant of networked technonationalism evidenced in China and India continues its evolution—responding to contemporaneous constraints and opportunities in the international environment. An example is the global WTO IPR regime targeting India's generic pharmaceutical industry, discussed in Chapter 5.

The notion of security through technological superiority has origins in ancient China in the writings of the legalist scholar Shang Yang, 商鞅 (d. 338 B.C.E.). Shang is credited with the group of ideas associating successful political unification with maintaining technological superiority. The writings of Shang, along with Han Fei and Li Si, are credited with advising a succession of Qin military leaders, enabling Qin to consolidate political power, previously one of seven nations (Chu, Han, Qi, Qin, Wei, Yan, and Zhao) vying for dominance in China. The Qin emperor is now called the "first emperor" of China.[14] Later, as Japan's early architects constructed palaces reminiscent of the Chinese palaces that preceded them, Japan's nineteenth-century Meiji leaders emulated these ideas in their own version of technonationalism at the dawn of the twentieth century. China's current networked technonationalism can be said to be both new and old as it references Japan's version of technonationalism, which in turn had been based on the latter's interpretation of historical Chinese technonationalism (Tao 2006, cited in Nakayama 2012).

Samuels (1994) reviews the ideology underlying Japanese technonationalism in the Meiji Restoration slogan of "rich nation, strong army" (*fukoku kyōhei*, 富国強兵) and notes its inspiration from political writings, including the aforementioned Shang. Emulating pre-nation-state China, the components of Japanese technonational policy were fourfold: protect domestic industries; subsidize capacity upgrading; obtain and distribute machinery to the private sector; and create state-owned enterprises, nurture them, and eventually transfer them to private hands. Likewise, as late as 2015, China was still quietly sending envoys to Japan to emulate perceived Japanese successes in technology development (Anonymous interview 2015). For example, sources indicate that the Chinese Maglev train infrastructure was copied wholesale from Japan Rail, reminiscent of the Japanese IBM espionage of U.S. technology in 1982 (Gerth 1982), though a Japanese diplomatic source says it is considered "bad form" to mention it (Anonymous interview 2016).

Nakayama (1991, 85) explains that the true source of Japan's economic "miracle" was the introduction of technocrat scientists and engineers, elevated to high status as part of the Meiji government's strategy of co-opting samurai for political expediency (just after their hereditary stipends had been cut off). Rapidly absorbing technology from the West was a main goal, and former (literati, warrior-class) samurai were encouraged to join the new science and technology disciplines. Afforded high status in Japanese society, these former military personnel became the leaders of early science and technology development in the late nineteenth century. At the same time, the samurai code of duty to clan lord was transformed into duty to nation (Nakayama 1991).

The protectionism that was key to Japan's technonationalism in the twentieth century insulated Japanese producers and nascent entrepreneurs from international market competitors but also led to unintended consequences in the twenty-first century. One of the legacies of Japanese network and knowledge insularity (discussed below) is that it has undermined the ability of domestic producers in Japan to maintain global market leadership and, worse, weakened the economic environment for producing world-class entrepreneurs. China and India, due to their lost centuries under British imperialism (China) and colonialism (India), and Singapore, a postcolonial city-state established officially in 1965, have different legacies and challenges, discussed in subsequent chapters.

Nakayama (1983) coined the English term *technonationalism*, and Samuels (1994) expanded understandings of its ideology and policy import in Japan in the twentieth century. The common thread in these works is that science and technology (S&T) leadership is key to national security. It is incorrect to assume, however, that Japanese technonationalism in the postwar period with its focus on S&T development was also equated with developing the military-industrial complex (Samuels 1994). Instead, MITI's[15] greatest accomplishment in the postwar period was that it effectively protected domestic industries from the "aggression of foreign capital" (Nakamura 2012). Common perceptions in the literature on technonationalism include the belief that the Japanese government chose large *keiretsu*[16] corporations (e.g., electronics and automobile producers) for development, in top-down fashion. Underestimated is the critical role of entrepreneurs as national champions and entrepreneurial firms as engines of economic development and growth. Further, the association of technonationalism with militarism has waned over time (Hughes 2011). Now the battle is over setting international standards and strategic entrepreneurship, discussed below (Mazzucato 2011, 2015).[17]

By the 1980s Japan's automobile and electronics manufacturers had gained increasing market share in the United States. Meanwhile, Japan remained closed to U.S. firms and products. *Kagakugijutsu rikkoku* (科学技術立国)—"nation building by science and technology" (Nakayama 1983, 2012), or technonationalism—became a slogan of the Japanese government in the early 1980s. According to Nakayama, this was in direct response to the Reagan administration moves to reinvigorate basic science in the United States while identifying Japan as a technological threat. Likewise, Japan's economic rise began to be perceived as a threat to the U.S. economy (Nelson 1993, 17). Freeman (1995) and Freeman and Soete (1997) use Japan's national prowess in guiding industry and innovation diffusion as the basis for describing an effective national system of innovation in this regard—from which the United States should take lessons. At the time, it seemed that the United States could use a little technonationalism for itself (Nelson and Ostry 1995).

National Innovation Systems

A national system of innovation or national innovation system (NIS), defined in Chapter 1, is comprised of four main subsystems, according to Freeman (2002): science, technology, culture, and entrepreneurship. In addition, the political subsystem, to the extent that it promotes innovation, enables congruence between the other subsystems (Freeman 2002). Others posit a triple helix model of collaboration between the state, universities, and industry (Leydesdorff and Etzkowitz 1996; Leydesdorff and Meyer 2006; Leydesdorff 2013; Etzkowitz and Leydesdorff 2000). As noted above, Lundvall (2007) reminds us that the origins of NIS research emerged as a response to "too simplistic" assumptions of economists as late as the 1980s that countries need only reduce nominal wages or devalue their currencies to achieve growth. As such, NIS is both a grounded theory (primarily in the country context of Denmark) and an evolutionary theory (ripe for further development and application across space and time).[18]

The capacity of national innovation systems to facilitate economic growth rests on the *social* capability for institutional change, especially high rates of technological change. In this regard, Freeman (2002) describes the capacity of knowledge transfer (by individuals via tacit exchange) from existing sectors to emerging sectors. Examples of this social capability include Britain in the eighteenth century (developments in iron- and waterworks technology leading to the capacity to manufacture textiles) and the Asian Miracle economies in the twentieth century (small-scale artisanal design and production as a precursor to advances in electronics manufacturing) (Mowrey and Nelson 1999; Chandler, Amatori, and Hikino 1997). Effective tacit-knowledge exchange requires information to flow between people freely across institutional boundaries. For this to occur, a flexible and mobile labor system is necessary. This is discussed below and in subsequent chapters.

Freeman (2002) and others argue that the most effective national innovation systems are those that maintain strong relationships between scientists and entrepreneurs. Following List (1841), in order to stimulate economic growth, the domestic institutions of science (and arts) education connect domestic and imported technology. Without deliberate, often government-incentivized active learning within these domestic institutions, opening to inward foreign investment in the aim of integrating foreign technology will not result in improvements in domestic technological capacity. Cohen and Levinthal (1990) note the importance of absorptive capacity in the innovative process, enabling a move from imitation to innovation. Nelson and Rosenberg (1993) single out the technonationalism of Asian high-growth economies, including Japan, South Korea, and Taiwan, as reflecting national action leading improvements in technological capabilities in domestic firms and therefore national competitiveness. With these innovation goals in mind, national governments have pursued technonationalism to fast-track growth.

Technonationalism and Innovation

Nelson and Ostry (1995) refer to the post–World War II technonationalism of Japan (foreign exchange controls, barriers to inward FDI and goods) that paid off by the 1980s as a challenge to U.S. hegemony. Even after Japanese government intervention weakened in that period, the authors note that "structural impediments" remained, themselves resulting from the historically close collaborative ties between government and business. In these public-/private-sector relations, cross shareholding of keiretsu and vertically integrated production and distribution networks kept foreign firms out of Japan. These once protective exclusionary networks have since become Japan's competitive undoing, as will be discussed in Chapter 3.

Criticizing Chalmers Johnson's *MITI and the Japanese Miracle* (1982), Nakayama notes that while the Ministry of Defense (MoD) and Science and Technology Agency (STA) were technonationalist, MITI (now METI) had by then become technoglobal. Further, Nakayama noted that MITI's power was already on the decline by the time the book *MITI* was published. Odagiri and Goto (in Nelson 1993) argue that Japanese government prowess was not the sole reason for Japan's rapid "catch up" to Western technology levels. However, their case studies of engineers and entrepreneurs in the Meiji era and subsequent periods tell a story of efficacious government policy in reinforcing private-sector developments. Other factors enabling Japan's catch-up included preexisting private-sector absorptive capacity, nationalism professed by nascent entrepreneurs,[19] and an established role of state policy in Japan's industrialization and economic development.

Edgerton (2007), in a review of the intellectual history of technonationalism and technoglobalism, finds no clear positive relation between national innovation and rates of growth, noting that the United States was an anomaly and that most countries grew on technology imported from elsewhere. In summarizing, Edgerton asserts that "national use of technology is hardly dependent on national innovation" (8). In other words, managed properly, foreign inflows of capital and technology can lead to independence rather than dependence. This will be demonstrated in China's new networked technonationalism, introduced in Chapter 4, after the legacies of old-school technonationalism in Japan are identified and implications discussed in Chapter 3.

Montresor (2001) argues that technonationalism and what could be called technolocality (colocation) are as relevant to nation-states as globalization in the innovative process. For example, Suzuki (2012) finds that economic nationalism in Asia in an era of globalization has mitigated inequality outcomes through, for example, policies that promote learning by doing by indigenous workers even as countries open their doors to foreign capital.

Corning (2004) argues that one result of the recessionary 1990s in Japan was the opening of a few of MITI's research programs in computers and transportation to foreign participation—reflecting an increasingly technoglobal approach, at least in that ministry in Japan. However, the post-2000 METI has faced reticence from other parts of the national bureaucracy (e.g., the Ministry of Finance, the Tax Agency) in reducing barriers to foreign firm entry. The present legacies of Japan's closed-to-the-outside-world developmental paradigm include de facto closure to inward FDI and a competitive weakness in internationalized or globally competent human capital. Japan shows that supporting the development of science and technology does not lead automatically to new firm creation or new sector emergence.

Promoting Innovation Through Industry Targeting of Biomedicals

To date, studies on national innovation systems relating to biomedical innovation and new venture business have been few (Henderson, Orsenigo, and Pisano 1999; Saxonhouse 1985). Notable exceptions include Kneller (2007a, 2007b, 2010, 2013) and J. Wong (2011). In a study of drugs approved by the U.S. Food and Drug Administration (FDA) between 1998 and 2007, Kneller (2010) found that new biotechnology companies and university technology transfer in the United States produced half of the FDA-approved drugs, dwarfing the performance of Japanese, European, and other producers. Kneller (2013) suggests that features of the American innovation system—including high levels of public funding (notably from the National Institutes of Health [NIH]), access to said funds by junior researchers, and flexible and mobile career paths—play a role in this performance. This is contrasted with Japan's low labor mobility, most importantly during the prime productive years of a scientist's career, and lack of access by junior researchers to significant research funds as reasons explaining Japan's lackluster performance. In a review of a history of the Japanese pharmaceutical industry Kneller (2013) notes, "One of Japan's fundamental problems is that too many of its great human and financial resources are locked up in old organizations doing old things" (240).

Related works have outlined the impact on university technology transfer of the post-2000 government reforms, including shifting authority to universities from the national government over ownership of university inventions (in addition to compelling universities to share more of the financial burden). Until these reforms, few university discoveries had been attributed to national funding. These reforms ended the widespread practice by university researchers in which publicly funded scientific discoveries had been misattributed to major corporate donors in order to avoid having to declare them "national assets" that would be subject to government control (Kneller 2007b).

Kneller, a researcher at Tokyo University and medical doctor (and also juris doctor) who worked previously at the NIH, in comparing the innovation systems in the United States and Japan (2007b), reflects this public research institute expertise. Due to the centrality of large Japanese conglomerates (keiretsu) to national policy and preferential access to new technology out of universities, his 2007 book on biomedical entrepreneurship is largely focused on—except for a middle chapter featuring venture business case studies—large firms and university-technology-transfer–private-sector (mainly corporate) relations. Kneller (2007b) finds that a top-down and silo "autarkic" innovation structure within large firms and universities prevents Japan from making significant gains in biomedical and other high-technology entrepreneurship. Kneller offers a detailed and thorough analysis of the limitations of the Japanese innovation system and observes an alternative approach in evidence in Japan: "tethered spin-offs" out of large companies. However, Kneller concludes that those tethered spin-offs from established companies that are for the most part controlled by their parents are unlikely to resolve Japan's low level of science and technology entrepreneurship. Further, as the book is a comparison of venture-poor Japan and venture-rich United States, the international political and economic dynamics in global and Asian regional context are not a center of the analysis. Neither is the role of diaspora networks. The focus herein extends and complements Kneller's previous findings, while Joseph Wong (2011) examines additional Asian cases (Korea, Singapore, Taiwan).

Wong (2011) contributes to an understanding of Asian country attempts to adopt the developmental state model that had been successful in following innovations from Western countries (electronics and IT) to the uncharted territory of the biomedical industry. Wong reflects on the former success of the developmental state as having relied on incremental improvements on Western innovations. He also notes similar improvements on existing Western policy and strategy models on the part of state bureaucrats and industry executives. According to Wong, in a desire to compete at the level of such Western countries as the United

States, Asian developmental states have since bet hugely and ultimately poorly on biotechnology.

Comparing Korea, Singapore, and Taiwan (Chinese Taipei), Wong finds that each has struggled to promote biomedical innovation and entrepreneurship, given a new international competitive environment that limits state choices. Domestic institutional legacies also create certain path dependencies. In Korea this means a reliance on vertically integrated research and development, production, and international marketing led by large, corporate conglomerates (*chaebol*). Lacking a domestic market, Singapore took a global approach, attempting to situate that country as an Asian hub for multinational corporations (MNCs). Taiwan's history of supporting the small-enterprise sector led it into a lower-level role in the global value chain in biotechnology.

Wong's analysis centers on state efforts to mitigate risk for new market entrants (including established firms) in an era of science-based industrialization. In this new global competitive environment, governments must seek strategic advantages at the technology frontier, no longer able to rely on followership as in previous iterations of the developmental state. Governments seek to upgrade domestic innovation capacity and human capital and often seek inward foreign direct investment to fund it. On the other hand, MNCs with the needed direct investment dollars to fuel said efforts seek instead to invest in a host economy environment having a "pool of innovative biomedical firms and research labs" producing upstream innovations that MNCs can take downstream and produce and market to the world with scale. This dynamic has been evident in the departure of several large multinational pharmaceutical firms from R&D centers in Singapore, as discussed in Chapter 6.

Wong rightly points out that China and India compensate for this lack of institutional context with growing domestic markets. These large markets serve as a lure to inward FDI that would otherwise go elsewhere. Lacking such domestic market potential, smaller economies in Asia, especially Singapore, despite billions of dollars of public investments, still lack a competitive edge in biomedical entrepreneurship. Where Wong sees a retreat of the developmental state, willful or otherwise, in such places as Korea, Singapore, and Taiwan, the chapters that follow on

China and India show a resurgence of certain developmental state characteristics, albeit in a new, networked form. These include nationalistic state rhetoric supporting not just catch-up but leadership at the technological frontier and the added strategy of appealing on nationalistic and patriotic grounds to tap into the global diaspora of talent from these countries. As mentioned previously and elaborated upon in Chapters 4 and 5, in China and India the wooing of diaspora talent has been elevated to establishing entire government units charged with identifying potential returnees and churning out incentive-laced invitations to them.

One of Wong's key insights, implied in his concluding chapter (2011) is that nation-states in the current science-innovation-based competitive environment have found it cost prohibitive to pick winners (and are loath to be called out for picking colossal losers). Instead, governments may be better positioned to create the innovation infrastructure and regulatory environment conducive to new technology innovation and entrepreneurship generally. Attempts by states to do just that, create innovation systems that link to entrepreneurial-ecosystem development, is the central focus of this book, using the lens of comparative trends in the biomedical industry to interpret broader, system-level changes within economies.[20]

The developmental state may be retreating, per Wong, or transforming into something new, as proposed herein. Wong's book provides a thorough analysis of what has gone wrong at the nation-state level in recent years. Perhaps this book's contribution to this literature is to present evolutions from the developmental state model—a new networked technonationalism, both paradoxically transnational via diaspora networks and also technonationalist—that appear to be making gains, especially in China and India, while less so in the archetypical developmental state of Japan and the city-state of Singapore.

Transnational Technonationalism?

In the twenty-first century, communications and internet technologies increasingly permeate national boundaries. Further, countries that harness such international human-capital networks as expatriate and diaspora scientists, technologists, and other professionals are able to access boundary-crossing technological developments. China has already parlayed its appealing domestic market size into technology and investment gains from foreign solar and other high-technology manufacturers (De la Tour, Glachant, and Ménière 2011; Zhang and He 2013).

As discussed above, if a country and its leading producers are able to set the global market standard for a given technology, its exporters have a significant market advantage over competitors from other countries.[21] Strategic entrepreneurship is new business creation in emerging high-value sectors, often incentivized by national government policies (Ebner 2007, 2013; Skocpol, Evans, and Rueschemeyer 1999; Mazzucato and Dosi 2006).[22] Examples of strategic entrepreneurship include (mission-oriented) internet-security technologies in the United States and semiconductors in Japan in the twentieth century (Anadon 2012). Since the 1990s, national governments have identified biotechnology for strategic investments and new venture stimulus (Lazonick and Tulum 2011; Pisano 2006; Vallas, Kleinman, and Biscotti 2015).

Embracing open markets, on the other hand, only makes strategic sense to those powers possessing dominant international standards (e.g., communications and computer technology) and therefore positioned to benefit from free and open markets for their superior products (Besen and Farrell 1994; Tassey 2000). States lacking products that set international standards are vulnerable to market entry of technology goods from dominant economies (Shapiro 2001). Consequently, newcomer economies may become relegated to a status of lower-tier producers, having to adopt the international standards or develop products that appeal only to limited, internal domestic markets (Drahos 2002; Mattli and Buthe 2003). It is a wonder then why more states have not pursued technonational policies in the aim of technology leadership at the frontier.

In the past, Asian national governments have been lauded for their developmental state policies (nurturing domestic firm growth through a combination of export promotion and protection from foreign competition). Rising competition over access to inward FDI capital and technology transfer has forced governments to be more open to foreign firms, particularly MNCs. This pressure to be open internationally affects existing firms and nascent entrepreneurs alike. For example, such international networks as those with buyers and suppliers help small, new entrepreneurial firms to succeed (Coviello and Munro 1995; Robson and Bennett 2000). In other words, technonationalism has had to become networked. It has also become entrepreneurial.

Innovative Capacity and Entrepreneurial Activity

Recent comparative policy research on the role of new firms in economies points to their significant role in innovation and employment growth (OECD 2010; Wadhwa et al. 2011). National governments, including those analyzed herein, have in the last decade placed a greater emphasis on developing the institutions and regulatory practices supportive of entrepreneurial start-ups. An entrepreneur is defined as an individual who brings new products or services to market via establishing a new firm. Van Praag and Versloot (2007), through an empirical analysis of entrepreneurship research, confirm the contributions that entrepreneurial firms make to innovation and employment relative to large firms in economies.

The link between innovation and entrepreneurship has also become a focus of scholarly work in the innovations systems literature (Waarden and Casper 2005). This relationship might be considered an innovation-to-entrepreneurship pipeline. This pipeline represents the links between innovation capacity in key technology sectors and the ability to translate this into the creation of high-growth entrepreneurial start-ups. This connection is critical for Schumpeterian creative destruction and economy-level productivity gains. The knowledge and network typology outlined above provides a basis for comparing innovation and entrepreneurship across economies. Specifically, per figure 2.2, nascent entrepreneurial firms appear to benefit from quasi-open networks that can act at once outward oriented (internationally) and also protective of domestic entrepreneurs, in Janus-faced fashion.

Entrepreneurship

Countries seek opportunity entrepreneurship due to the greater contribution to employment growth, labor skills improvement, added value, and multiplier effect on supporting sectors (e.g., vendors and service providers). Opportunity entrepreneurs are individuals who start new businesses even though they have other income earning options. High-technology start-ups are of the opportunity type. Opportunity entrepreneurship is defined by the Global Entrepreneurship Monitor as the pursuit of new business seeking return on investment. In other words, they become entrepreneurs because they desire to do so, not because they have no other opportunity to earn income. In contrast, in "necessity" entrepreneurship individuals have few alternatives to self-employment, itself for subsistence purposes. Common types of necessity entrepreneur-led businesses are low skill and prevalent in nonmanufacturing (e.g., agriculture) sectors.

An entrepreneurial network refers to informal relations between firm founders, other firms, capital, and outside resources. Research on entrepreneurial networks is well developed in business and economic-sociology literatures (Granovetter 1983; Hoang and Antoncic 2003; Street and Cameron 2007; Sigfusson and Harris 2013; Sigfusson and Chetty 2013). Less developed is research examining the role of national and other policy on the evolution and efficacy of entrepreneurial networks and, further, understanding the impact on firm-level performance (Hart 2003; Lundstrom and Stevenson 2005). International network connection is not enough to enhance technology improvements for domestic firms, particularly for developing countries, due to the need to have complementary competencies (Humphrey and Schmitz 2002). In other words, domestic firms in less-developed countries tend to share a low level of expertise and skill, while they may have unique knowledge of the domestic market and institutional context. This points to the role of government investment in improving the absorptive capacity in domestic firms, enabling local firms to develop knowledge and skills in this regard (Mazzucato and Perez 2014; Mazzucato 2015).

Internationalization in entrepreneurial firm networks has been found to be positively related to firm-level performance, including innovation and new product development and market access, particularly in such developing economies as China and India (Prashantham 2011; Yu and Si 2012; Boermans and Roelfsema 2013). However, international networks alone do not produce optimal levels of firm innovation (Patel et al. 2014) or firm survival (Bruderl and Preisendorfer 1998). A balance between strong (often local) ties and weak (international) ties enhances international market access (Coviello and Munro 1995, 1997; Granovetter 1985; Söderqvist and Chetty 2013). Further, longer-term international alliances appear to have a negative effect on firm performance (Lew and Leung 2013). Entrepreneurial firms may need international networks, but they may also benefit from prudent state policy that mitigates the exploitative effects of international exposure. The entrepreneurial case studies in the chapters that follow illustrate this point. For example, India's richest self-made woman billionaire, Ms. Kiran Mazumdar-Shaw, and her start-up Biocon, which has grown to one of the largest biopharmaceutical firms in India, benefited from foreign ownership limitations at a critical point in the firm's development. This reflects the potential of this open yet protective Janus-faced new networked technonationalism as an alternative developmental model.

Recent research has described an emergent era of international new ventures (INVs), whereby entrepreneurial firms are "born-global" upon start-up (Söderqvist and Chetty 2013; Laurell, Andersson, and Achtenhagen 2013; Rialp, Rialp, and Knight 2005). Entrepreneurs draw from social capital in their international networks obtained via relationships developed in foreign educational institutions and/or expat diaspora and ethnic communities abroad in pursing technology transfer, human-capital development, and angel investment. For example, Wadhwa et al. (2011) found that international diaspora networks have played pivotal roles in new venture investments. Others have noted the role that diaspora networks play in identifying financial resources in general (Lucas 2001).

In a study of high-technology entrepreneurs struggling to survive in Japan's recessionary "lost decade" of the 1990s, Ibata-Arens (2005) found that firms with international network connections in sales, marketing, and/or finance were able to circumvent biases in national government-supported production networks (which were created by developmental state policies and had targeted large established firms, often at the expense of the small). These internationally oriented new firms were most likely to survive and prosper into the 2000s, despite the overall economic downturn. However, internationally savvy entrepreneurial ventures have heretofore been the exception, not the rule in Japan. This is illustrated in the entrepreneurial case studies in Chapter 3, including Mujo Kim's Pharma Foods and Norio Nakatsuji and Shinya Yamanaka's stem-cell ventures at Kyoto University. Likewise, international Chinese *guanxi* (关系), personal "relationship"-based social networks, have been found to promote international trade by compensating for a weak international legal environment via community enforcement of social sanctions that deter violations of contracts (Rauch and Trindade 2002). In an increasingly global world, insular domestic inter-firm networks in Japan, embedded in vertically integrated production hierarchies, have limited the potential of its entrepreneurs.

In contrast, China and India, as well as other Asian countries, including South Korea and Singapore, though having fewer resources, have nevertheless generated increasing numbers of new start-ups—through strategic investments and policies (inward FDI and human-capital development) that have contributed to greater openness and fluidity, such as through labor mobility producing tacit-knowledge gains in (inter-firm, individual) business networks—resulting in a positive cycle of improvements in absorptive capacity and increasing global competitiveness of entrepreneurial firms.

Another way to compare countries via the knowledge/network typology is in terms of how well technonationalist policies and institutions build up capacities in codified knowledge while protecting domestic firms and nascent entrepreneurs (e.g., via semiclosed networks), while at the same time reaching innovative potential via tacit-knowledge exchange and mitigated openness to international capital and firms. BGI in China and Biocon in India, discussed in subsequent chapters, are illustrative in this regard. The cases presented in this book provide an opportunity to examine similar developmental visions and policy targets of frontier technologies within a variety of institutional environments (knowledge and network architecture). These countries have attempted to respond to similar global market opportunity.[23] While the ultimate outcomes remain unclear as of this writing, some measurable return on investment for biomedicals has been observed across each case. It may be that the reasons for falling short of innovation and entrepreneurship goals can be explained in part by the variations in knowledge and network architecture within a technonationalist vision for the state. The extent to which national governments, collaborating with private-sector actors, activate the right parts of the KNT infrastructure at the right time and to the right degree has been instrumental in the development of capacities in biomedical innovation and entrepreneurship, specifically, and national innovation-system and entrepreneurial-ecosystem development, generally. The findings represent a range on the spectrum from classic technonationalism to technoglobalism. See again figures 2.1, 2.2, and 2.3 for a presentation of these variations in the KNT infrastructure.

As mentioned previously, Asian countries, including those herein, have been studied in terms of technonationalism at a higher frequency than countries in other regions of the world. Further international comparison may be enhanced via the application of the knowledge and network typology to compare and contrast developmental vision and practice in other country contexts (across space and time). Perhaps technonationalism is in fact alive and well around the world.

Networked Technonationalism Thesis and Hypotheses

The networked technonationalism (NTN) thesis posits: national governments that mitigate openness to international investment and trade and make strategic use of open international networks, such as utilizing professionals in their international diaspora, are best positioned to pursue simultaneously the goals of innovation capacity building and entrepreneurial-ecosystem development that produce a return on-investment (ROI) for domestic firms and workers. The NTN thesis can be tested via three hypotheses:

1. Innovation capacity is necessary and sufficient for new technology entrepreneurial-ecosystem development (the lower left quadrant of the KNT).

2. Innovation capacity is necessary but not sufficient for new technology entrepreneurial-ecosystem development (the lower left quadrant of the KNT).

3. Economies might compensate for weaknesses in innovation capacity in the aim of developing a new technology entrepreneurial ecosystem through utilizing open (international) network strategies (upper right quadrant of the KNT)

   a. Interinstitutional (and international) networks facilitate (tacit) knowledge acquisition and transfer (upper left, tacit knowledge).

   b. Interinstitutional (and international) networks facilitate "born global" venture start-up activity in new technology sectors (upper right, open networks).

   c. Mitigated/managed inward-FDI facilitates innovation capacity improvements (lower right, quasi-open network architecture).

Innovation capacity and innovative capacity are distinguished as follows:

- Innovation capacity: the institutions supporting new intellectual assets and product development

- Innovative capacity: the ability by which institutions and practices in an economy are conducive to the creation of new intellectual assets and product development. Innovative capacity in the GEM surveys is a composite index of five groups of measures representing country-level endowments in R&D infrastructure, human capital, patent output, and other measures.

The notion of innovative capacity is inclusive of aspects of both the national innovation system and entrepreneurial ecosystem. The term *innovation capacity*, when employed herein, distinguishes it as the resource base upon which innovative activity occurs. Alternative explanations for the incidence of existence of and connectivity between

innovation and innovative capacity and entrepreneurial ecosystems include the economic liberalism and developmental-state theses:[24]

- The liberalism thesis: open trade and investment leads to organic
  growth (Berger and Beeson 1998; Cumings 1984; Gore 2000; Taylor
  1997; Wade 1990).

- The developmental state or classic technonationalism thesis: closed
  trade and investment protects existing firms and nascent entrepreneurs (outlined above). Further, classic technonationalism within
  the developmental state is predicated on net technology importing,
  sometimes via expropriation and espionage (e.g., Japan 1950s–1970s)
  (Johnson 1982).

The knowledge and network typology outlined above is useful in
laying out the foundations of innovative-capacity- and new-technology-
based entrepreneurial activity as well as identifying relative strengths
and weaknesses across economies in national innovation and entrepreneurial ecosystems. In other words, the KNT provides a descriptive
framework to examine underlying causal relationships between the
NTN thesis and the outcomes of innovation and entrepreneurship. This
book demonstrates that networked technonationalism appears to accel-
erate the speed at which a country is able to acquire both innovation
capacity and entrepreneurial yields.

For example, on a micro-level, new ventures are least likely to be
successful if the founder lacks prior experience in that industry (Dahl
and Reichstein 2007; Orser, Cedzynski, and Thomas 2007; Schiller and
Crewson 1997). Likewise, countries attempting to "teleport" to high-
technology, high-value manufacturing from agriculture and low-value
manufacturing should be cautioned. As the chapter on Singapore demonstrates, its current technological strength evolved from many decades
of investments into institutions and human-capital development, yet it
still struggles to achieve developmental goals.

The three stages of economic development are factor, efficiency, and
innovation. Necessity entrepreneurship is the main type of new business creation in the *factor*-driven stage and is found in agricultural
self-employment primarily. In this stage, countries compete based on

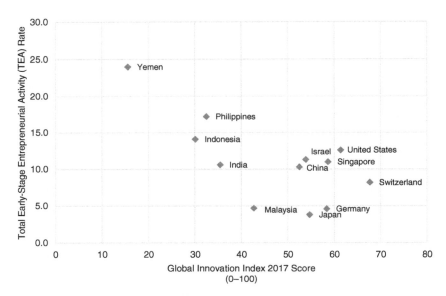

FIGURE 2.6. Innovative capacity and entrepreneurial activity. Source: Cornell University, INSEAD, and WIPO. 2017. "The Global Innovation Index 2017: Innovation Feeding the World." Ithaca, Fontainebleau, and Geneva, Global Entrepreneurship Monitor, Entrepreneurial Behaviour and Attitudes, http://www.gemconsortium.org /country-profiles (accessed August 31, 2017). Note: The TEA data was extracted from the Global Entrepreneurship Monitor website. Data for Japan and the Philippines are from 2015, while the data for Yemen are from 2009 (the latest available). Data for remaining countries are from 2016. TEA measures the percentage of the population aged 18–64 who are either a nascent entrepreneur or owner-manager of a new business.

commodities and low-added-value products. In the *efficiency* stage, ideally a transitional stage between low and high levels of economic development, countries engage in technology imitation and human-capital development, increasing the absorptive capacity (the ability to receive and invest infusions of capital and technology knowledge) of the economy. In countries demonstrating improvement in absorptive capacity, national governments deploy inward-FDI investment toward developmental goals, including indigenous human-capital and infra-structure improvements. For example, though Brazil and China remain in the efficiency stage, overall they produce far higher levels of opportu-nity entrepreneurship (an entrepreneurial surplus, given middling levels of innovation capacity). In the *innovation* stage, knowledge becomes the key input, and individuals pursue opportunities anticipating returns on investment (of capital and sweat equity).

Opportunity entrepreneurship is critical for economies, as it provides a return for public- and private-sector investments in science and technology infrastructure. Further, compared to the necessity type, opportunity entrepreneurs employ more people and have a greater multiplier effect on employment (increasing employment in support industries). Necessity entrepreneurship is most prevalent in the early stages of economic development, while opportunity entrepreneurship is expected to be active most in economies that have obtained high levels of innovation capacity. It follows that based on its innovation capacity Japan should also have high levels of opportunity entrepreneurship in such technology fields as biomedicals (hypothesis 1).[25] In contrast, despite weaker innovation capacity, China and India both demonstrate relatively stronger opportunity entrepreneurship (hypothesis 3). Figure 2.6 compares countries in terms of their innovative capacity and opportunity entrepreneurship.

Herein lies the Japanese paradox. Despite established capacity, Japan's national innovation system has an entrepreneurship deficit (hypothesis 2). Another way of describing Japan's situation is that the country has unrealized potential for high-technology, high-value entrepreneurship. This is the subject of the next chapter. Each country chapter (in the following order: Japan, China, India, Singapore) tells a story about the strategic vision that has led technonational policies and how these policies relate to improvements or lags in innovative capacity within innovation systems as well as connections to entrepreneurial-ecosystem developments. The latter is viewed through the lens of select firm-level case studies in biomedical entrepreneurship.

CHAPTER 3

CLASSIC TECHNONATIONALISM IN JAPAN

Beyond the "Miracle" and "Lost" Decades

IN THE 1980S JAPAN, the target of anticompetition accusations from U.S industry, was lauded as a so-called developmental state for its apparent prowess in accomplishing high economic growth and increasing technology capacity, while protecting domestic industry (Anchordoguy 1989; Johnson 1982). Japan's science and technology capacity remains strong even today, as measured, for example, by patents (see Chapters 1 and 2). Japan also managed to grow rapidly in the twentieth century while maintaining a healthy GDP per capita, with an egalitarian redistribution of income, growing its middle class from a destroyed economic base at the end of World War II in 1946 to 90 percent by 1970 (Momma 2017). As recently as 2017, 90 percent of Japanese surveyed still considered themselves middle class. According to Hodgson (2016), projecting to 2030, among developed markets, Japan is expected to be second only to the United States in the number of middle-income households. Japan's developmental approach is rightly respected for its relatively egalitarian distribution of wealth.

Japan's classic technonationalism also protected internationally uncompetitive small businesses through the end of the twentieth century from such big-box retailers as Walmart from market entry. The mom-and-pop store has remained deep in the hearts of Japanese, and these and other small businesses are represented by influential business associations active in lobbying the government. Further, business corruption is among the lowest in the Asian economies, and its government bureaucracies for the most part are civil servants who were hired via a rigorous and meritocratic selection process.[1] Low levels of government corruption limit the temptations for rent seeking prevalent in places like China and India (discussed in subsequent chapters) that have led to corrupt government oversight of business practices and a drag on economic development. The streets in major cities in Japan are clean and safe. A number of foreign executives have listed the aforementioned aspects of Japan as reasons they remain in Japan, despite a shrinking domestic market and struggles to obtain bank finance faced by newcomer foreign and returnee entrepreneurs (Alfant interview 2012). The economy continues to produce IT ventures with global market reach. Though the number of IPOs lags behind the rest of Asia, billion-dollar stock offerings, such as LINE in 2016, reflect Japan's still strong intellectual capacity (Martin 2016). In July 2017, *Forbes Asia* published its annual list of "best under a billion" of top publicly traded companies in the Asia-Pacific region as measured by sales, profit, and earnings growth. The list included such companies as Linical, a pharmaceutical clinical-trials firm, part of a group of thirty-eight companies on Japan's list in 2017, more than doubling 2016 performance (thirteen firms on the list) (*Forbes* 2017). Most other Japanese companies making the *Forbes* list were in internet commerce and related services. (Chinese companies led the *Forbes* list with seventy firms, down from ninety-eight the previous year.)

While Japan has been the subject of criticism since its economic juggernaut peaked in the 1980s, its innovation capacity, though not quite translating into the innovative activity that undergirds healthy entrepreneurial-ecosystem development, remains sound. Its world-class research universities, including Kyoto University and Tokyo University, continue to produce frontier discoveries in biomedicine as part of an international collaboration in stem cells (discussed later in this chapter). This is evidenced by the aggregate growth in patents shown in figures 1.1 and 1.2. Though its luster as a miracle economy has faded, its strong K–12 STEM-oriented education system has continued to provide a pipeline of young technologists who have gone on to start internet, mobile services, and software firms of global reach, including LINE, mentioned above, and Softbank. Such retailers as Uniqlo and Muji have made inroads into the global fast-fashion industry. These successes have helped to buttress the Japanese brand. To be sure, as mentioned above, Japan has maintained its technological leadership and sustained economic development, having egalitarian distribution of wealth. At the same time, discussed below, Japan has become a victim of its own success, as evidenced by the institutional legacies of its century-long strong technonational regime.

Japan's technonationalism, reviewed in the previous chapter, is centered on the belief that national security rests in part on scientific and technological independence from international competition. Technonational-vision-led protectionist policies that closed Japan to the outside were once lauded as key to its high-growth developmental state in the post–World War II period. In retrospect, Japan's high-growth developmental process in the twentieth century can be summed up as follows. First, its closed knowledge and network architecture worked for a time but was predicated on other country markets being open to Japanese exports. This era has ended. Now there are global pressures, as introduced in Chapter 1, to demonstrate reciprocity within the WTO system. The new global environment for trade and investment requires a networked technonational model of mitigated openness, but openness nonetheless. Japan, having excelled in the past, is now losing ground to those countries that have already adapted, including China and India. In essence, Japanese technonationalism was functional before; now it has become dysfunctional. Further, its deeply connected domestic institutional arrangements that served it so well in the past have since proven difficult to change.[2]

The first half of this chapter builds on the introduction in Chapter 2 of classic technonationalism and the type of knowledge and network regime that goes along with it. Before outlining what has gone wrong, the chapter reviews what went right for Japan prior to the 1990s. This sets up the background for the discussion in the second half of the chapter on the sense of urgency Japan has in targeting biomedicals for development and, more broadly, its attempts to connect its innovation system to entrepreneurial-ecosystem development.

The sections that follow have several components. First, Japan's technonationalist vision in the twentieth century is reviewed. In addition to providing an overview of the foundations of current innovation capacity, it addresses the institutional legacies of Japan's technonationalist developmentalism in terms of its closed knowledge and network architecture. Second, policy targeting biomedical science and technology is reviewed, paying special attention to attempts to connect scientists and technologists in the innovation system to entrepreneurial-ecosystem development. Third, cases in biomedical product leadership and entrepreneurial firms are presented, reflecting the role of the state in creating a system conducive to entrepreneurship at the innovation frontier (Shimizu 2013). What follows is a brief overview of the three periods of Japanese twentieth-century technonationalism in the miracle (1950s–1970s, high growth), bubble (1980s, mature), and lost (1990s and onward, decline) decades.

Technonational Vision: From Miracle to Lost

In the 1950s and 1960s, Japan's developmental miracle became a juggernaut of industrial growth thanks to aid and technology transfer from the United States, the boost to manufacturing of the Korean War, and what has been seen as prudent and effective economic policy generated by key ministries at the time. The former wartime Munitions Ministry was at the helm, then calling itself the Ministry for International Trade and Industry, or MITI.

The ideas behind Japanese postwar technonationalism centered on catching up to the West's level of science, technology, and industrial development. Japan's developmental vision was pragmatic, thanks in part to its meritocratic civil service, whose origins are in the Meiji period (1868–1912), which replaced the Tokugawa Shogunate with a modern nation-state and centralized bureaucracy. This meant that the most educated tended to seek careers in the bureaucracy.[3] During the Meiji period, former samurai transitioned from a life calling of duty to lord to life careers of duty to nation. Remnants of this honor code perpetuate even today. Japan's talented human capital set about the task of rebuilding the economy after World War II within the national government and also as entrepreneurs and industrialists (Matsumoto 2001; S. Suzuki 2001).

Japan's brand of technonationalism had three main characteristics vis-à-vis trade and investment. First, the government sought long-term international market dominance rather than short-term returns (Dore 1986; Parthiban et al. 2010). Second, it targeted exports while insulating domestic firms from competition from foreign imports as a means to develop domestic industry. This meant that the state promoted domestic (automobile and electronic) manufacturers' products abroad. Protective and supportive measures complemented this export focus. Protective measures included tariffs, nontariff barriers to entry, and exclusion of foreign firms, including service providers. Supportive measures included tax breaks, export and other subsidies, and low-interest bank loans for large corporations.[4] Third, it maintained a closed domestic market, excluding foreign products and inward foreign direct investment (FDI). In other words, its classic technonational knowledge and network architecture favored closed networks and insulation from the outside, and to the extent that knowledge exchange was open to the outside, it was in building codified capacities while underplaying the importance of tacit-knowledge exchange across institutional boundaries (see fig. 2.1). At the same time, Japan sought foreign technology, particularly from the United States, through whatever means possible (Anchordoguy 1989; Fialka 1999; Odagiri 2004; Ostry and Nelson 2000).

As a technology importer, it made sense to structure production into a vertically integrated exclusive subcontracting pyramid. Large conglomerates (*keiretsu*), which were the main beneficiaries of export and other subsidies, meanwhile used their monopsony leverage over subcontractors, reflecting the priority the Japanese state placed on keiretsu corporate conglomerates at the pinnacle of the pyramid. (These relationships were outlined in table 1.1.) This monopsony behavior included unilateral input price setting, which had the net effect of maintaining liquidity in firms situated at the top of the pyramid. Conglomerates used subcontractors as a cushion to absorb such external shocks as currency fluctuations by transferring such costs onto them rather than let their own "permanent" workers go (Ibata-Arens 2005). How these hierarchies became dysfunctional over time is addressed below.

Legacies of Lingering Paradigms

A paradigm provides a lens or worldview through which to interpret and manage new information. As the physicist Thomas Kuhn argued, a transformation or shift from one (scientific) paradigm to a new paradigm requires an existential jolt, such as disruptive technology or a crisis (Kuhn 1970). It is at these points in time that minds become open to new, alternative ways of thinking and solving societal problems. Some have argued that part of Japan's seeming incapacity to foster a radical and new way forward is because its economic decline has occurred over decades: a slow demise.

In the early 1980s, Chalmers Johnson and other scholars argued that Japan's economic prowess rested on collaborative relations between elite government ministries—including the Ministry of International Trade and Industry (MITI) and Ministry of Finance (MOF)—and corporate business (Johnson 1982), as presented in table 1.2. Johnson dubbed this elite government-private-sector-level arrangement the "developmental state." Previously, Ezra Vogel published *Japan as Number One: Lessons for America* in 1979, in which he argued that Japan's institutions, including a meritocratic state bureaucracy and large-firm-led export orientation, should be a guide to the United States in its own policies.

Others suggested that Japan's strengths in inter-firm networks were a source of its competitive advantage (Imai 1992). These ideas were echoed in works describing Japan's so-called flexible rigidities, including exclusive subcontracting within vertically integrated industrial production and supposed lifetime employment (Dore 1986). Such interpretations of Japan, lauding its economic prowess and recommending it as model for others, are indicative of the positive way Japan was viewed from in and outside during—and even after—the end of the high-growth post–World War II period through the 1980s.[5] Many of the positive features remain in Japan, as outlined above. By the mid-1990s, analyses on the Japanese economy shifted to analyzing the myriad ways Japan had lost its way. The term "lost decade" (*ushinawareta jūnen,* 失われた十年) was coined and since "lost decades" (Hayashi and Prescott 2002; Iwata and Miyagawa 2003; Fukao and Kwon 2012). Scholars have noted that the institutions of the developmental-state period became rigid over time (Lincoln 2004).

The Nakasone administration (1982–1987) embraced economic liberalism, choosing, for example, monetarist solutions over Keynesian ones. This brought on the easy money-fueled real-estate bubble that would burst in the early 1990s, ushering in the lost decades that followed (T. Suzuki 2012). Rather than encouraging the development of a new paradigm, these policy failures served to reinforce the technocrats' resolve in response to what they saw as the consequences of blind adherence to laissez-faire principles. Japan's bureaucrats have never quite adopted a Western-style hands-off regulatory approach to governing the economy—though politicians, including most recently Prime Minister Shinzo Abe,[6] have occasionally sought liberal solutions to Japan's economic woes.

Research analyzing networks of high-technology manufacturers in Japan found that the production pyramid admired by others for its "trust"-based exclusive contracting hid an underside that squeezed liquidity out of small manufacturers. After the collapse of the asset bubble, firms within the pyramid failed by the thousands, while those that managed to stay independent emerged from the 1990s successfully (Ibata-Arens 2005). Other works exposed public policy failures. For example, beginning in the 1990s, both large firms and women increasingly "exited" the social contract of caring for existing workers and giving birth (literally) to new ones (Schoppa 2006). Miura (2012) questions whether Japan ever had a welfare state. These demographic and resultant behavioral shifts have undermined Japan's ability to maintain its human-capital base. More optimistic assessments predicted that reform would take another decade to see results in terms of a rebound in economic growth (Katz 2003).

That decade passed without significant improvement, though the quantitative easing (QE) under economic stimulus policies (referred to at the time as "Abenomics" after then Prime Minister Shinzo Abe) had a modest impact by 2014. In 2016, Dr. Sayuri Shirai, a former Bank of Japan board member and early architect of Abe's monetary policies, noted that the limited effectiveness of QE could be explained by the absence of key structural reforms (also known as the missing "third arrow" in the Abenomics quiver), particularly labor market reform. For example, women, who have always been excluded from lifetime employment, are paid as little as 50 percent of the salaries of their male counterparts. Official sources in 2016 state that women made 73 percent of what men made. Economists point out that these figures exclude the large numbers of temporary workers. Even so, the 2016 figures were a significant improvement from 1990, when women officially made 60 percent (*Nikkei Asian Review* 2017). Similarly, temporary workers and those employed by small- and medium-sized firms, the latter comprising the majority of enterprises in the Japanese economy, are excluded from lifetime employment. As a result, Japan faces paradoxically both a labor shortage and falling wage rates (Shirai 2016).

No longer able to base growth on an export-oriented economy, itself built on incremental innovations (of imported technology), Japan has had the weaknesses in its historically closed economy (to foreign products, foreign firms, and foreign capital) become evident (Anchordoguy 2005). The developmental-state paradigm, led by a technonational vision—a way of thinking that prioritized export promotion and protecting domestic firms from foreign import competition—guided Japanese policy for much of the twentieth century. The favorable international environment (U.S. security backing, open export markets, liberal economies in the West) allowing Japan to pursue its exclusionary development also led to "under theorizing" about the explanatory role of this favorable global environment to Japan's twentieth-century developmental success (Pempel 2005).

Legacies of this developmental and insular paradigm linger. Old habits of mind in Japan have proven difficult to break—despite nearly three decades of stagnant growth. Japan has since become trapped in closed and insular knowledge and business networks that have limited its innovative and entrepreneurial potential—per the knowledge and network typology presented in Chapter 2.[7] As noted at the beginning of this

chapter, Japan's leading innovation capacity in frontier scientific discoveries (including stem cells, discussed below) has continued to serve
as a basis for intellectual asset strength and new product development
(per hypothesis 1 of the NTN thesis: innovation capacity is necessary
and sufficient for new technology entrepreneurial ecosystem development). What follows in this chapter supports hypothesis 2 of the NTN
thesis: innovation capacity is necessary but not sufficient for new technology entrepreneurial-ecosystem development. The country cases of
China and India, on the other hand, reflect hypothesis 3 (and its subhy-
potheses: economies compensate for weaknesses in innovation capacity
in the aim of developing a new technology entrepreneurial-ecosystem
through utilizing open, especially international, network strategies).

Economic growth, generally, is comprised of productivity gains in
existing firms and also increasing numbers of high-growth entrepreneurial new businesses. Studies in 2014 indicated, however, that Japan's
productivity had reached an all-time low following the substantial decline in total factor productivity (TFP) in the 1990s (Diamond 2014; see
also Fukao and Kwon 2004). One consequence is that its institutional
investors have continued to hold capital in risk-averse investments, ex-
acerbating the weakness in venture business capital. Japan's traditional
approaches to solving economic problems are getting old.

Demographic shifts—an aging society with low birth rates—shrinking
the size of its working population mean that unless Japan opens its doors
to millions of skilled immigrants, future growth must be based on productivity gains in existing firms and workers and new firms. Firm-level
productivity could be boosted by greater openness to foreigners and
foreign capital via measures including increased inward FDI and R&D
type joint ventures (Fukao and Kwon 2012). Japan's diaspora is small in
size, a few million compared to the tens of millions in its rising competitors China and India. This means Japan has no significant returnee
professional class to lead globally oriented ventures as presented in
table 2.1. This is addressed below and compared in the chapters that
follow.

While Japan struggles to attract international business, its Asian
competitors have already moved on to a more open, networked technon-

ationalism, improving their competitive advantage. This shift is analyzed in subsequent chapters on China, India, and Singapore. Of the countries analyzed herein, Japan maintains the strongest foundations (for now) in the cornerstone of codified knowledge per the KNT (table 2.2), serving as a building block for its national innovation system. Also noteworthy is the fact that Japan led Asian countries in bringing the standards of living of most citizens in the span of a few decades to the level of Western countries. Japan's developmentalism has since been emulated all over Asia, including in the other countries examined in this book.

Instead of a real break with the postwar technonationalists that the brief tenure (2009–2012) of the Democratic Party of Japan (DPJ) promised, the men steering the boat now (and again) descended from a long line of Liberal Democratic Party (LDP) politicians who ran Japan's technonationalist policies in the postwar period (Colignon and Usui 2001; Sakakibara 2003).[8] Unfortunately, Japan's aging and overall shrinking domestic market size makes it not especially alluring for foreign multinationals seeking market entry to Asia. (In August 2014, the BBC declared that both the world's oldest woman and the oldest man in the world resided in Japan.) These trends also present challenges to Japan's LDP governing coalition. T. J. Pempel has shown that Japan's factionalized one-party system has long hindered economic and political reform (Pempel 1998). Japan's "inverse pyramid" of predominately senior voters translates into political pressures against international openness and is against risk taking in its outlook.[9] On the other hand, Japan's aging population presents healthcare and biomedical market opportunities, which the Japanese government has been eager to promote.

Though Japan in 2017 remained the world's third-largest economy and second-largest market for pharmaceuticals, a previous national "Japan Attractiveness Survey" to executives of multinational firms (209 senior executives) indicated that a minority of 21 percent considered Japan to be a "gateway to Asia" (JETRO 2008). This reflects a continuing trend away from Japan and to other Asian countries. Japan watchers have come to call this "Japan passing," in an unfortunate reference to the "Japan bashing" that took place in its economic heyday in the 1980s, before the implosion of its asset bubble in 1991. Now Japan is literally flyover territory, as increasing numbers of Western firms establish regional headquarters in countries like China. For European firms, Japan has become a Galapagos, that country far beyond the horizon, as they land via their transcontinental flights in Bangalore, Shanghai, and Singapore. As Japan's fears of becoming irrelevant to the world economy seem realized, institutional constraints emanating from its closed and insular knowledge and business networks continue to trap its domestic human capital, undermining its ability to connect internationally.

Per the knowledge network typology, Japanese networks are sticky: closed to the outside, at once protective of domestic firms but also entrapping nascent domestic entrepreneurs (fig. 2.1). Other Asian countries, including China and India, have developed business and human-capital networks that are fluid: open and permeable to the outside (fig. 2.2). The previous chapter proposed an analytical construct for comparing Asian economies in terms of (closed versus open) network regimes. Some Asian countries have developed a unique networked capitalism that has contributed to economic growth and supported entrepreneurial-ecosystem development. As outlined in Chapter 2, international openness or closedness of Japan's business networks have important implications for domestic innovation and entrepreneurship. This conceptualization helps explain why Japan, despite its ample scientific and technological knowledge base, has heretofore failed to generate significant amounts of high-growth start-ups in such emerging industries as biomedicals. In contrast, countries like China and India, though having fewer resources, have nevertheless generated increasing numbers of new start-ups—through strategic investments and policies (inward FDI and human-capital development) that have contributed to greater fluidity in (inter-firm, individual) business networks. These dynamics are examined in subsequent chapters.

Japan's entrepreneurial ecosystem has been in the past perceived as having insular and closed and also protective business networks that have excluded foreigners. As other countries, including those described in the chapters that follow, have increasingly exploited open, international R&D networks to domestic advantage, Japan's closed system is now at a competitive disadvantage. As such, Japan suffers from a weakness of strong ties, to paraphrase Mark Granovetter (1973). As mentioned in Chapter 1, this book focuses on the biomedical industry as a way to illustrate broader trends in national innovation-systems and entrepreneurial-ecosystem development across economies. The sections that follow review in detail how the institutional arrangements that worked so well for Japan in its high-growth period have now become insular and isolated, unable to adapt to a new international competitive environment. But all is not lost. Potential remains in its entrepreneurial outliers, discussed at the end of this chapter, who are pushing the boundaries of Japan's classic technonational knowledge and network architecture.

Japan: Insular and Isolated Networks

What makes the Japanese economy closed and insular? The mentality of *intra*-institutional networks pervades the private sector. For example, Japanese (domestic) firms demonstrate low labor mobility across organizations, compared to other countries (discussed below under the section on entrepreneurial-ecosystem development). Though Japan's production hierarchies, previously led by cross-shareholding corporate conglomerates known as keiretsu, have broken down since the 1990s (many large firms have moved component production abroad), on the whole new firms struggle to find buyers among large corporate Japanese firms (Ibata-Arens 2005). This, in conjunction with such other practices as hiring by age cohorts and enterprise unionism (in which workers are forbidden by law from forming trade unions enabling them to connect to others in their craft outside their own companies), translates into sticky networks (figuratively pulling talent down, preventing them from participating in tacit knowledge exchange or open network activity), meaning that individuals are more likely to interact within various institutional boundaries (firm, school cohort) than across them. For example, case studies of Sony and Canon confirm the remarkably concentrated product R&D within the borders of Japan and, further, within certain locations within the firm (Motoyama 2012). The implications for the transfer of tacit knowledge across organizations are significant, as outlined in Chapter 2.

Exceptions discussed below that prove the rule include Kyoto University–linked ventures in regenerative medicine (using stem cells). These entrepreneurial activities benefit from international research and development relationships, often forged by individual researchers instead of government or other domestic institutions. A challenge facing Japan is how to scale these local successes to national-level transformation.

Japan's vertically integrated production hierarchies, in the past insulating large Japanese domestic firms from external market forces, became insular over time, limiting labor mobility and the tacit-knowledge exchange that goes with it, trapping nascent entrepreneurs, and leading to a dominant business network form characterized by lack of interaction with the outside world.[10] During the 1980s, the bubble economy years, too many employees were hired by large firms, resulting in an excess of middle management within what would become unfavorable labor market conditions by the 1990s. That bubble generation has since been congesting the system and preventing the rise of younger managers with potentially fresher ideas. Rather than create fluidity in knowledge and network flows, Japanese human capital has become constrained in Japan's inward-oriented networks.

Yet Japan's developmental-state paradigm lingers still, propping up Japan's giant "zombie" companies (Caballero, Hoshi, and Kashyap 2008). The legacies of Japanese technonationalism resulting in inflexible institutions and immobile labor markets stand in the way of forging productive connections between its innovation system and entrepreneurial potential (Ahearne and Shinada 2005). In the end, these supposed "flexible rigidities" (Dore 1986) were merely rigid and over time resulted in institutional stasis, an environment unfriendly to innovation and entrepreneurship (Lincoln 2004).

The Japanese government faces a dilemma in this regard. By propping up large firms, potentially massive employee layoffs are avoided, and therefore one of the so-called three sacred treasures (the other treasures are enterprise unionism and seniority-based wages) of Japan's developmental state remains intact (Johnson 1982). Its dissolution would place a far higher welfare burden on the Japanese state. So rather than encourage radical institutional change, Japan muddles through, led by senior officials accustomed to the old ways.[11]

Still, a glimmer of hope remains in Japan's overall innovation capacity.

Intellectual Capacity

Japan ranks number two after the United States in intellectual capacity (measured by patents), though various measures (discussed in Chapter 1) indicate that Japan is losing ground to China. The policy and institutional dynamics behind China's rise are examined in the following chapter. Nevertheless, the scientific and technical foundations of Japan's innovation system remain sound. Depending upon the measures used, Japan ranks at the top or in the middle of all industrialized countries in its capacity to innovate. As noted in Chapters 1 and 2, the Global Competitiveness Index (GCI) outlines factors supporting innovative capacity. The 2017–2018 GCI ranks Japan ninth in innovation. Switzerland, Singapore, and the United States take the top three spots, displacing Japan from its position at third in the 2015–2016 report (GCI 2017, 15). Also outlined in Chapter 2, innovation involves the introduction of new science and technologies and often leads to the emergence of new industries. As discussed in Chapter 1, biomedical intellectual capacity was still emerging as late as 2017 in most economies and, as such, has become a policy target in countries around the world (J. Wong 2011).

For biomedical fields, in terms of the intellectual property stock ("revealed technology advantage") as measured by the OECD, Japan ranks just above China, and both countries are at the bottom of OECD rankings (save Saudi Arabia and Turkey).[12] Denmark, Switzerland, and New Zealand take the top three slots. The United States is fifth in this ranking. For Japan, its absolute score has declined since the previous ten-year benchmark (per data years 2000–2002) (OECD 2014).[13] Including venture capital and entrepreneurship rates in these metrics, Japan sinks precipitously, as outlined in the previous chapter. So far, Japan has been unable to translate its science and technology gains into significant entrepreneurship. It seems that possessing innovation capacity has proven insufficient for Japan's goals of establishing an entrepreneurial ecosystem, thus disconfirming hypothesis 1, which states that innovation capacity is necessary and sufficient for entrepreneurial-ecosystem development.

Though composite indices often rely in part on impressionistic survey data, they are nevertheless a reference point for international business executives and investors. The 2018 Global Economic Development Index (GEDI) ranked Japan twenty-eighth in entrepreneurial performance, at the bottom tier of the thirty-one economies with leading innovation capacity, representing no change from its ranking in the 2012 report (Ács 2012; GEDI 2018; Ács and Szerb 2010). The historically big business–oriented national government policies and business practices— like slow payment to small businesses via the *tegata* payment system within exclusive subcontracting arrangements, "cost-down" monopsony unit pricing, and so-called just-in-time production that succeeded in part by exporting the cost of holding inventories onto subcontractors— had the net result in the recessionary 1990s of squeezing capital liquidity out of the majority of firms in the economy (Ibata-Arens 2005).[14] Fixed capital formation in Japan has since declined (Syed and Lee 2010). The big business–pyramid production approach has been shown to be ill suited to stimulating high-growth entrepreneurship. These structural impediments have not gone unnoticed by parts of the bureaucracy.

In 2000, the Japanese government, through the newly minted Ministry of Economy, Trade and Industry (METI) and the Ministry of Education, Culture, Sports, Science and Technology (MEXT), began investing in new business incubation facilities, technology licensing organizations (TLOs), and other incentives to encourage university start-ups (Sandelin 2005; Ibata-Arens 2014). Such efforts have been laudable, as civil servants have essentially stepped in to try to stimulate entrepreneurship, despite their lack of expertise and weak private-sector networks. Similar to the limits of QE in stimulating new economic growth in the context of maladaptive domestic economic environments, including low labor mobility and an aging workforce, Japanese bureaucrats have found themselves in the awkward position of crafting an entrepreneurial ecosystem within a rigid institutional context.

Comparing Entrepreneurial Ecosystems

How does Japan compare to other Asian countries in terms of entrepreneurial-ecosystem development, especially in the science and technology fields? Three benchmarks of national-level entrepreneurial activity include growth in numbers of new high-technology businesses, the proportion of new businesses led by opportunity entrepreneurs, and the rate of informal (angel) investment.

First, Japanese new businesses ownership rate has tended to be below both Western and Asian economies, particularly in high-tech manufacturing. An analysis of Teikoku Data Bank data (130,000 firms) in 2012 indicated that Japanese firms established in 2010 or later had the best growth in that decade, creating for the first time for Japan a number of gazelles (firms that grow 30 percent or more over a three-year period). Unfortunately, this growth has been primarily in service firms, including IT (software), rather than in biomedical and other manufacturing domains (the latter of which provide greater opportunities for employment of lower-skill workers). Services led as a percentage of GDP (70 percent as of 2015) (World Bank 2017). While the number of IT entrepreneurs had increased significantly in the previous decade, including global market ventures like LINE and Rakuten, biomedical entrepreneurs had yet to reach a significant number, compared to other countries (Ibata-Arens 2012).[15]

Second, as presented in Chapter 2, although Japan's opportunity-driven entrepreneurship rate is on par with most Western and regional economies, relative to its innovation capacity it remains quite low. As noted in Chapter 2, opportunity entrepreneurs are those who start companies as a way to be independent or increase income, as opposed to having no other source of income (necessity entrepreneurs). In 2015, according to the Global Entrepreneurship Monitor (GEM), Japan's overall entrepreneurship rate was 3.8 percent, among the lowest in the world (GEM 2015). In contrast, in the same year South Korea's was 9.3 percent, India had 10.8 percent, and China's was 12.8 percent (GEM 2017). That Japan's opportunity entrepreneurship rate is relatively strong indicates that there are possibilities to build on these foundations, with appropriate policy and other stimuli.

Third, angel investment is a critical part of venture finance for new firms. Angel investors are typically high-net-worth individuals who invest small amounts in start-ups. It is estimated that the angel investment market in the United States surpasses the capital level of formal venture capital (VC) (National Venture Capital Association 2005). Angel investors comprise a large proportion of the informal investment market, which also includes individuals of average income (Payne 2004). Japan remains the lowest in informal investment compared to other Western and Asian countries, having virtually no measurable informal investment as late as 2006. For years in which data is available for China and India, the percentage of the workforce engaged in informal investments was much higher.[16] Informal and interinstitutional networks contribute to innovation and entrepreneurship. Unfortunately, Japan's knowledge and network architecture limits potential.

Openness in Business Networks and Human Capital

Openness in social networks is an important aspect of building entrepreneurial ecosystems. While there is tremendous variation in China (e.g., urban, rural, region), and Singapore is a city-state of 5 million inhabitants, on two measures of fluidity, labor mobility and internationalization of human capital and investment, these two very different countries both surpass Japan. Availability of data on India is sporadic; still that country appears to have made better progress than Japan in recent years (discussed in Chapter 5).

First, these countries have greater fluidity in labor markets. This means individuals can move from firm to firm, seeking employment opportunities. In the *shūshokukatsudō* (就職活動) system in Japan, most large Japanese corporations hire by university graduating class cohorts—who are expected to remain in that company until retirement (lifetime employment system). Those that miss out on securing jobs soon after their graduating year are literally in peril of never obtaining a full-time position.

Japanese corporations shy away from candidates who are "different," rewarding students who have not sought international experience and also tending not to hire women (Keidanren 2011; Tabuchi 2012). This creates a system of social networks that are remarkably insular, centered on *intra*-firm relations rather than *inter*-organizational or, even less likely, international connections. In Japan's high-growth period, these organization-based networks were effective at perfecting incremental innovations on technology invented elsewhere (as well as protecting corporate intellectual property). After the collapse of Japan's bubble economy in the early 1990s, Japanese corporations hired fewer workers, and existing employees became increasingly risk averse. For example, Nakamura and Odagiri (2002) find that Japan's entrepreneurial potential in biomedicals is hampered by limited labor mobility in Japan. As previously mentioned, large Japanese corporations are burdened by a glut of mid-career managers (induced by the bubble period), burdening payrolls and limiting advancement opportunities for junior employees. As a (female) Japanese entrepreneur noted, Japan is heavy at the top with a "bunch of old men clogging up the system," which prevents real economic and political transformation (Watanabe interview 2014).

It is noteworthy that foreign firms in Japan have benefitted from the weakness in domestic labor markets. A 2007 study on labor mobility and human capital found that the skills of employees (including technical and language) were higher in foreign-owned firms and that employees felt that they had opportunities outside the firm for employment (Ono 2007). This pocket of international, mobile labor in multinational firms notwithstanding, Japan's labor market remains insular.

Japan is remarkably noninternational in its human-capital base, which exacerbates existing stickiness in networks. There are a number of measures of internationalization. For example, the level of international experience of college graduates is one indicator. Japan sends a tiny proportion of college students abroad, and those studying in the United States halved between 2004 and 2011 (Bradford 2015). Some of these students opted instead for less expensive, easier entry countries, such as China (including Hong Kong and Taiwan/Chinese Taipei). Others have opted to remain in Japan, entering "global" campuses with English-language courses and "international" academic programs. These supposedly global programs are taught almost exclusively by Japanese nationals, with a smattering of foreign faculty, "for show" as one insider noted (Anonymous interview 2017). This decline in outgoing study abroad for Japan has been only partially attributable to low birth rates. China and India continually send many thousands (Institute of International Education 2011). For example, in 2017, study abroad students from China and India totaled 847,259 and 278,383, respectively, while Japan sent 30,850 (UNESCO n.d.a, n.d.b). To be sure, the population differences partly explain this gap.

Nevertheless, countries like Vietnam, whose population is 30 percent smaller than Japan's, sent 27 percent more students abroad (53,548), while the tiny city-state of Singapore sent an impressive 22,578. This lack of international orientation has become a major source of consternation for parts of the Japanese government, concerned that Japanese society has turned inward (*uchi muki*, 内向き). This precipitated a major policy initiative in 2011 to increase the number of students studying abroad, but if nothing is done to increase the receptivity or absorptive capacity of domestic Japanese firms to "internationalized" job candidates, the impact on the economy is uncertain. For example, returnees (*kikokushijo*, 帰国子女) find themselves facing a "collective closed mind" of bullying in school, rejection on the job, and being shunned from social cohorts (Yates 1990; French 2000).[17]

In 2014, the Japanese government reported a "record" 1.2 million Japanese nationals in its international diaspora, indicating that nearly a third were living in the United States (*Japan Times* 2014).[18] Meanwhile, China and India have encouraged internationalization of the domestic workforce by, for example, embracing their diaspora networks, while Singapore was born global at its very formation as a nation-state, thus benefitting from the tacit-knowledge exchange outlined in the upper quadrants of the KNT.

Another measure of internationalization is the degree to which foreign firms invest in and establish branch offices in a country. Again, Japan has lost ground to other Asian countries in attracting foreign business. Singapore, discussed in Chapter 6, has pursued human-capital development via a proactive immigration policy whereby the best and brightest young minds throughout Asia have been enticed to Singapore with generous doctoral fellowships. Recipients are required to accept Singaporean citizenship as well as work in the country for at least three years upon graduation. Meanwhile, foreign residents in Japan still have trouble opening bank accounts, renting property, and even purchasing Japanese cell phones.

Immigration and Investment

As recently as 2017, a report noting that the "door is closed" to immigrants in Japan cited a low 1.6 percent of the population as foreign nationals. Among them were 2.23 million legal immigrants. In this regard, in 2016 Japan had allowed a mere 28 refugees out of more than 10,000 applications (Jozuka and Ogura 2017).[19] Of the 15,000 (less than 0.01 percent of the population) foreign "technical" talent identified in 2005, the latest year for which data are available, American, Indian, and Chinese immigrants were the most numerous (Yasuda 2007). The path to permanent residency (not to mention citizenship) remains fraught, though the Japan Justice Ministry announced reform in January 2017 (*Japan Times* 2017). Meanwhile, in the United States the number of foreign individuals with college degrees working in science and engineering occupations *from Asia alone* was 460,000 (Wadhwa et al. 2009). At the same time, according to a study by METI, 2010 showed a decreasing trend in foreign-owned start-ups, a trend that would continue in that decade. Such countries as Singapore, China, and Hong Kong were attracting greater numbers of leading foreign-owned companies establishing regional headquarters. Japan attracted the fewest among the countries compared in the study, and as discussed in Chapter 6, has lost scientist entrepreneurs to Singapore.[20]

Of the 1,856 firms having regional headquarters in Asian countries, a mere 75 were based in Japan. In comparison, 307 were located in Singapore, 300 in China, and 251 in Hong Kong. Among these, 330 were in manufacturing industries. Japan is clearly lagging behind developments in other Asian countries. Singapore, for example, in addition to attaining foreign scientific talent, has been particularly aggressive in courting inward FDI, as discussed in Chapter 6.[21]

The level of industrialization of an economy is related to levels of FDI. At lower levels of industrialization, countries seek inward FDI. Likewise, at lower levels of industrialization, countries do not tend to have large labor inflows. At high levels of industrialization, countries generally have both high levels of inward FDI and inward labor flows, measures of international openness and network fluidity. Japan has neither, having intentionally excluded foreigners and their capital in the past. Japan is struggling to court them now.

The Japanese national government, as part of a strategy to overcome these weaknesses and create an entrepreneurial ecosystem, has targeted three industries: IT, energy, and biomedical.[22] Since the advent of "industry-academia collaboration" (*sangakurenkei*, 産学連携) and "industry-academia-government collaboration" (*sangakukanrenkei*, 産学官連携) policies, Japanese government-led organizations have attempted to incorporate stakeholders from these sectors in policy planning. To allow for a focused, sectoral-level comparison across countries, the emphasis here and in subsequent empirical chapters is on developments in the biomedical industry. If Japan and other countries through government policy can manage to map a clear path to success for biomedicals, having great uncertainty and a long-term horizon to return on investment, then other, more clearly blueprinted industries could become future targets. Japan and its competitors have tried to chart a course of high risk and high return in the selection of biomedicals. As noted in Chapter 1, the payoffs are more than profit and include the seemingly irresistible chance to set a generation of global standards in healthcare.

Government Biomedical Policies

In Japan, the most significant national policy initiative to date, targeting new-technology-based business creation—apart from the reform of small-and-medium-sized-enterprises (SME) policy in general—has been the Innovation Cluster Initiative. METI launched its Cluster Initiative and Cluster Plan in 2000 and 2001 respectively. The plan intends to promote innovation and new business creation, particularly in high-technology industries. Related policies by MEXT are aimed at encouraging more science-and-technology-based university start-ups via two main measures: establishing technology licensing organizations (TLOs) and expanding graduate MBA programs (Harayama 2004; Myers 2005). These policies followed the findings of a special report by METI in 2001, placing biotechnology and other frontier technologies at the top of the government list of promising sources of new products and new ventures (METI 2001; Ozaki 2012).

Within the Cluster Initiative (whose main growth targets have been biotech, nanotech, environmentally friendly biotechnology, known as "eco-bio," and informatics) is an emphasis on promoting the biotech industry, particularly in the Kansai and Hokkaido regions. By fiscal year 2002, the national biomedical budget had grown to 440 billion yen (Libertas Consulting 2006; Industrial Cluster Study Group 2005). Other initiatives include the establishment of a Small Business Innovation Research (SBIR) program, modeled on the SBIR program in the United States,[23] as well as measures targeting improvements in *jinzai* (人材, personnel skills). The latter includes such activities as the National Energy and Technology Development Organization (NEDO) fellow program (now defunct due to budget cuts), which placed young scientists and other professionals in small businesses, technology transfer organizations (TTOs), and other organizations supporting new business creation, whose salaries were paid for a time by the Japanese government.

The most significant change in METI in recent years has been in-depth survey-based and quantitative benchmark analyses of how well they are doing in each target area (though some selection bias can be found in that they tend to survey firms involved, for example, as grant recipients, in METI-sponsored Cluster Plan projects) (Mitsubishi Research Institute 2005; Libertas Consulting 2006).[24] Table 3.1 outlines the main policies regarding science-based new business creation in Japan since the 1990s. Despite the national budget deficit in Japan, METI has continued to push for investments in biomedical industrial development (METI 2011).

In Japan, "biotechnology strategy fundamental principles" (*baiotekunorojii senrakutaikou*, バイオテクノロジー戦略大綱) comprised the national biomedical strategy initiated in 2002. The support for organizations for promotion of research and development and other measures was incorporated into cluster and regional policies (Office of the Prime

TABLE 3.1.

Key policy history: Biomedical innovation and entrepreneurship in Japan

Year	Name	Objectives
1995	Science and Technology Basic Law	Framework for establishment of science and technology policy in Japan.
1996	Basic Plan for Science and Technology (1996–2000)	A master plan for five years of Japanese science and technology (e.g., promotion of intellectual capital).
1998	Law for Promotion of University-Industry Technology Transfer	Promotion of transfer of university technology to a private entity.
1999	Law on Special Measures for Industrial Vitalization (1999)	Support research activities.
2000	Law to Strengthen Industrial Technology Capability, Cluster Initiative	Measures to support reinforcement of industrial technology strength, industrial clusters creation.
2001	Industrial Cluster Plan (Innovation Cluster)	Building of industrial clusters.
2001	Second Science and Technology Basic Plan (2001–2005)	A five-year master plan for Japanese science and technology (research and development under state-identified issue areas).
2003	Basic Law on Intellectual Property	Creation, protection, and utilization of intellectual property.
2004	National University Corporation Act	Turn national universities into independent administrative entities.
2005	Third Science and Technology Basic Plan (2006–2010)	A master plan for five years of Japanese science and technology (emphasis on distribution of research and development investment).
2006	Second Industrial Cluster Plan (Innovation Cluster)	Building of an industrial cluster (formation of human networks).
2009	Act on Special Measures Concerning Revitalization of Industry and Innovation in Industrial Activities	Legal changes and expansion of innovation-related industry.
2009	Innovation Network Corporation of Japan (INCJ)	Public-private partnership between the Japanese government and nineteen major corporations.
2011	Fourth Science and Technology Basic Plan (2011–2015)	A master plan for five years of Japanese science and technology (earthquake disaster reconstruction included).
2012	Program for Creating Start-ups from Advanced Research and Technology	Environmental improvement of university-led ventures.
2013	Japanese revitalization strategy	Various venture investment aid packages.
2014	Industrial Competitiveness Enhancement Act	Strengthen industrial competitive power under Abenomics.
2015	National University Corporation Act (Change)	Creation of university-led venture support fund.

SOURCES: Government of Japan 1996, 2006; Kneller 1999; Fujisue 1998; Ministry of Education Culture, Sports, Science and Technology 2000, 2001, 2004, 2005; Cabinet Office 2001a, 2001b, n.d.; METI 2006, 2016, 2017a; NPO Kinki Bio-Industry Development Organization 2006; Oba 2006; Ministry of Health, Labour and Welfare 2007, 2013; Cabinet Secretariat 2007; Office of the Prime Minister of Japan 2012, n.d.; Tamura 2014; Yamamoto n.d.

Minister of Japan 2002). With the aim of growing the domestic economy and increasing international competitiveness in biomedicine, "healthcare innovation" was identified in 2010 as key to Japan's New Growth Strategy (*shinseichōsenryaku*, 新成長戦略). The strategy was threefold and included both financial and tax incentives: core manufacturing technology for new drug designs, such as molecular targeting; strengthening Japan's reputation for high safety in drug development; and promoting open innovation through raising new ventures. However, unlike in China, India, and Singapore, the new policies lacked specific supports for biomedical entrepreneurs. A 2011 METI report acknowledged a decline in new biomedical ventures and pointed to weaknesses in the regulatory environment (METI 2011).

In 2011, support of biomedical ventures was incorporated into the government's "4th Term Science and Technology Basic Plan" (Nikkei Business Publications 2012). METI also launched a "healthcare innovation council" in that year, later renamed (in 2013) the "health and medical care national policy unit." Its structure is typical of sangakukanrenkei, with representatives from industry, academia, and government. The latter include bureau chiefs from the Ministry of Health, Labour and Welfare (MHLW), METI, and MEXT (Cabinet Secretariat 2013).

After a number of discoveries in the therapeutic use of stem cells, including the Nobel Prize–winning adult stem-cell advances by Shinya Yamanaka (discussed below), Japan began targeting regenerative medicine as the best bet within biomedicals for product commercialization. At the same time, Japanese officials were frustrated that despite their leading stem-cell research, Japan lagged behind all other countries in new product and new firm development. As of 2012, Japan had only two approved stem-cell therapies, while the United States had nine, South Korea fourteen, and the European Union twenty (Oye et al. 2016). Reprocell (discussed below) thus represents the anomaly, not the rule, of start-ups that manage to emerge within Japan's existing knowledge and network architecture. In 2012 Japan's Pharmaceuticals and Medical Devices Agency (PDMA) initiated a fast-track approval process for stem-cell-derived therapies. By 2014, this had been extended, via the "pioneering" (*sakigake*, 先駆け) strategy, to include pharmaceutical products, medical devices, and regenerative medicines generally. Typical of Japanese government targeting, (senior) researchers with Tokyo affiliations first and foremost and after that Kyoto-affiliated scholars have been the main beneficiaries of these new initiatives.

Academic centers of government investment in this regard include the National Institute of Advanced Industrial Science and Technology (AIST) in Tokyo and Kyoto University's Center for iPS Cell Research and Application (CiRA). AIST's Biomedical Research Institute focuses on research and development in biomolecules and new basic technology for drug discovery and medical therapies (National Institute of Advanced Industrial Science and Technology 2017). CiRA is dedicated to advancing stem-cell-based regenerative medicine research. The commercialization of public- and private-sector technologies is supported via the Forum for Innovative Regenerative Medicine (FIRM). The forum is led by such biopharmaceutical companies as Fuji Film and Astellas and such manufacturers as Hitachi and Olympus. FIRM, established in June 2011, aims to build consensus around the commercialization process and promote regenerative medicine techniques across various types of biomedical research and commercialization. FIRM includes a broad base of stakeholders (at least those located in Tokyo) in biomedical enterprise: new ventures, established pharmaceutical firms, and investors.

Government Budget

Despite a budget deficit, the Japanese government, through METI, MEXT, and MHW, has so far maintained its investments in biomedicine. For example, between 2006 and 2013, government expenditure was on average 182 billion yen. Unfortunately, firm-level growth has remained anemic. Part of Japan's current troubles stem from the postwar Japanese business system outlined in the first section and in Chapter 2, which created powerful disincentives (e.g., the overall domestic industrial organizational structure of vertical network integration favoring large, politically connected organizations) to risk taking and entrepreneurialism (Kneller 2007b). Other research has come to similar conclusions, based on studies specific to the university commercialization of biomedical research and development (Nilsson 2006).

Government surveys of incubation managers and start-ups identified insularity and lack of diversity in network partners as a problem for Japanese start-ups (METI 2006). A 2014 study of Japanese new business incubators found that incubation managers (many of whom are government civil servants) have reported that the closed nature of their networks limits their ability to help their tenants obtain critical resources (Ibata-Arens 2014). In sum, as argued here and reviewed conceptually in Chapter 2, Japan's sticky networks limit the potential to turn its innovation capacity into entrepreneurial outcomes. Nevertheless, market trends are creating potential pull factors for nascent biomedical entrepreneurs, potentially freeing greater numbers of individuals from the old ways.

Industry

After the United States, Japan is the second-largest market in the world for both drugs and medical devices. Due to Japan's low birth rate and aging society, medical expenses are increasing, reflected in the demand for pharmaceuticals and medical devices. By 2010, Japan was spending nearly $3,000 per capita on national medical expenditure (JETRO 2013). Growth opportunities for pharmaceuticals, medical devices, and regenerative medicine are all increasing, with the highest growth in demand expected in regenerative medicine. In this regard, the government had high hopes in 2017 for the commercialization of Japan's leading intellectual-property capacity in stem-cell discoveries.

In 2012, Japan received much international attention after the Kyoto University geneticist Shinya Yamanaka was awarded the Nobel Prize in medicine. Yamanaka's discovery was that mature cells can be made to become "pluripotent" as stem cells—iPS, or induced pluripotent stem cells. These iPS cells have applications in regenerative medicine especially, as they can potentially be used to regrow organs. Yamanaka's Center for iPS Cell Research and Application (CiRA) at Kyoto University, established as a spin-off of the Institute for Integrated Cell-Material Sciences (iCeMS) in 2010 to focus on regenerative medicine, has since developed several potential commercial products, including for the treatment of cardiac disease (Kōno 2013). The Japanese government has since doubled its funding of iPS and was expected by 2022 to spend 90 billion yen, more than half of the average spent on all biomedicals between 2009 and 2013 (*Sankei* 2013). Despite government enthusiasm for the biomedical industry, growth in the number of new start-ups has been modest.

The number of biotechnology venture businesses fell in Japan after a peak of 587 in 2006. In 2014, there were 553 biomedical companies, down from 579 in 2013. Medical treatment, health, and research support are the main fields (Japan Bioindustry Association 2015). As of 2012, there were 37 publicly listed companies, up from 22 the previous year, of which 11 were profitable. By the second quarter of 2017, there was a drop in the total number of publicly traded biotechnology companies to 12 (Bloomberg Equity Screening 2017b). In comparison, China had a total of 22 trading, while India and Singapore each had 3. Furthermore, data from Bloomberg indicated that by the second quarter of 2017 Japan and India had not announced any new initial public offerings (IPOs), Singapore had announced one, and China had announced seven (Bloomberg Equity Screening 2017a). As of 2017, the majority of public biomedical firms were in drug development, which tends to remain unprofitable in the first years after the IPO due to high R&D costs (Oikawa 2012). Previously, the market size of the domestic biomedical products and service market in 2013 was estimated at 28,144 million yen (Nikkei Business Publications 2014).

Regions

Japan is about the geographic size of the state of California in the United States. Its biomedical clusters of innovation and entrepreneurship, measured for example by patent output and firm location, are in Tokyo and the Kansai region (with Kyoto and Osaka as hubs). Across economies, due to the reliance on university and national research institutes for the basic science and technology underlying high-technology new business creation, new concentrations or clusters of entrepreneurial activity tend to be centered on such research-active locations as university towns (Audretsch and Feldman 2004; Cooke 2002; Casper and Kettler 2001; Powell et al. 2002; Audretsch 2001).

Similar to other countries in this book, Japan's entrepreneurial clusters of technology sectors, including biotechnology, tend to emerge in the capital city (e.g., Beijing, New Delhi, Tokyo) and other large cities with intellectual capacity infrastructure (e.g., Bangalore, Guangzhou, Kyoto). Relative to other domestic regions, nascent technology entrepreneurs in capital cities often benefit, on one hand, from easy and early access to information on national government funding programs and other supports. On the other hand, comparative research on high-technology clusters has found that while it is useful to have government support—ever necessary in the early stages of cluster formation (as with the Department of Defense seeding of Silicon Valley and San Diego)—it is not sufficient to foster the development of sustainable clusters. Other factors are also important, such as the presence of research-level universities with active faculty and a renewing supply of young, bright, and inexpensive graduate student researchers, as well as access to international R&D collaborations. As expected from the comparisons to entrepreneurial cluster emergence in biotechnology cited above, new firm creation in biomedicals is concentrated in Kyoto and Tokyo.

Entrepreneurial Ecosystem

Despite the network impediments outlined above, a few firms in Japan have emerged as global market leaders in pharmaceuticals and medical devices. This success rests on firm-level strategies of forging international research and development market connections through human networks. Some have been assisted by METI or MEXT via grants, though these tend to reinforce and scale firm-level progress underway at a middle stage of growth rather than as a seed fund at an early stage of the firm.

Two characteristics of firms that have established global market share in medical devices in particular are noteworthy. First, these firms have avoided from the start being lured into the exclusive subcontracting arrangements that had comprised the vertically integrated production pyramid of old. The initial adversity in not securing Japanese corporate buyers became a strategic advantage over time, whereby small entrepreneurial firms were able to balance sales portfolios between foreign and domestic clients. Some biopharmaceutical firms, including the case studies below, have freed themselves from Japan's "antiquated technogovernance regime" through launching research and development collaborations in foreign countries (Okada 2006). In this manner, successful firms encourage tacit-knowledge exchange and international network openness—the upper quadrants of the knowledge and network typology.

Second, these firms appear to flourish outside of Tokyo, where the watchful eyes of the bureaucrats are far away.[25] Further, in such places as Kyoto, a vibrant local tradition of angel investment helps to retain young, talented start-ups in the region (Ibata-Arens 2008). A number of firms in Kyoto serve as historic examples, including Horiba, Kyocera, and Murata and Omron in the medical device and technology fields (Ibata-Arens 2005). More recent success stories include Pharma Foods (est. 1997) and Reprocell (est. 2003).

Pharma Foods

Pharma Foods (IPO 2006), one of the small number of Japanese biotechnology ventures to IPO, was founded in Kyoto by Mujo Kim, who holds a doctorate in agriculture from Kyoto University. Pharma Foods develops and brands products using plant- and egg-derived ingredients for the biopharmaceutical market. Its products are focused on promoting immunity, antiaging, and nervous system function. Products include OVOPRON (egg-yolk-derived antibodies) and GABA (lactobacillus).

Kim's postdoctoral work experience at the University of California, Berkeley in the 1980s and family ties in Korea enabled his start-up to be international from the beginning. For example, in 2008, the firm established a joint venture in New Delhi, India, resulting from a decision in 2005 to be one of the first Japanese firms to test the waters in India's new international opening that had accelerated in that decade. (This opening is discussed in Chapter 5.) The JV focuses on sales and service to the Indian subcontinent.

Since going public, Kim has found it both more challenging and easier to build a global company. He says that when Pharma became a publicly traded company, for a time it was as though "a flower in full bloom was made to harvest all its petals" to service the investors. Meanwhile, with greater name recognition, it has been easier to attract top talent to the company. In 2014, sales were up 5.9 percent on the previous year (1,614 million yen, about 12 million dollars). The future is bright for Pharma Foods, Kim, and his daughter Mirei Kim, who is being groomed to take the helm of the firm and currently leads its international operations. In November 2014, the company announced a new product launch of a peptide effective in promoting hair growth. This product targets the Japanese 70 billion-yen hair tonic market. Pharma has since expanded its North American sales and established R&D and sales offices in China, Korea, and Taiwan, as well as in Egypt and the United States. It had fifty-three domestic employees in July 2015, while its revenues had risen to 2.1 billion yen (Bloomberg 2015).

Looking back on the early days of Pharma Foods, the senior Kim says that it was the human networks forged both within and outside Japan that led directly to the firm's current success. Kim notes that none of these relationships show up on an internet search of the company, since they are mostly informal. This reflects the firm's embracing of international openness, maximizing the opportunity for tacit-knowledge exchange and foreign opportunity. For example, Pharma Foods' first angel investor— when the company was a bootstrap start-up of merely three people—was Yoshihiro Otaki of Bio Frontier Partners. Kim had met Otaki at a conference and introduced himself and his concept of nutraceuticals based on his research advancing plant- and biological-based medicinals. Kim found that the conversation turned into an interview of sorts. Otaki, who built an international investment portfolio while working abroad for Nomura Securities and later on his own over twenty years, is known for the consistent return on investment of his funds. Venture investments from others followed. Years later both METI and MEXT provided modest research funds (between 2000 and 2006). It should be noted that this is an indication of Japanese government followership rather than successful "targeting" of winners. Instead, this reflects a standard pattern of government funds being offered to proven—that is, having products with established sales—ventures. This is similar to the role that midstage VC funds have in accelerating existing growth in established firms.

Kim has been quick to point out that it was his understanding of the market need that helped him to develop and pitch his product ideas—a tacit understanding that was gained over time by working for another company for a decade before starting out on his own. In contrast, according to Kim, most university ventures in Japan start with the research interests of the professor with little regard for the market need. Furthermore, it need not be said that most university faculty tend to lack significant experience in doing business. This lack of experience and market orientation may explain in part the low number of products and IPOs coming out of government sponsorship (e.g., government funds for "university ventures" [*daigakuhatsu benchā*, 大学発ベンチャー]) thus far. Faculty, ever in search of research funds to support their scholarly work, not to mention cadres of graduate research assistants and expensive lab equipment, are willing to create "paper companies" to fill that checkbox on government grant applications. Kim also attributes his ability to develop strong international networks to his and his leadership team's multilingual ability, reminiscent of what Kim learned through years of research and work in Berkeley, California, in the United States, and Korea. The Kims strive for a multicultural operation via, for example, encouraging hiring that maintains a balance of about one-third each of foreigners, women, and men. Through promoting tacit-knowledge acquisition and structuring the firm to maximize network openness, Pharma Foods creates a firm-level knowledge and network architecture that compensates for the macro-level institutional limitations in Japan.

As will be shown in the next chapter on China, Japan lags in government support of internationalization in new technology research and development, commercialization, and firm creation. Given Japan's aging and shrinking workforce, the national government should be doing a lot more to promote international connectivity for its promising new industries and firms. This means encouraging talented foreigners to settle in Japan. One way to support a more open KNT architecture would be to incorporate English as a primary language into the special economic zones (SEZs), in regions including Kyoto's Kansai (encompassing Kyoto, Nara, and Osaka), and dual-language curricula in education nationally.

The Japanese government and especially its leading ministries METI and MEXT have the policy purview to stimulate frontier sector-based innovation and entrepreneurship. They are best positioned to take bold steps, working with politicians in the national legislature and business leaders in the private sector to incentivize the creation of a new organizational structure and industrial organization for Japan—one that is open to the outside and embraces talent and risk taking by nascent entrepreneurs.

On the whole, bureaucrats and the private sector have worked less closely toward shared developmental goals than they had in the heyday of the Japan's miracle high-growth period. One explanation is the increasing competition between senior bureaucrats for the dwindling number of postretirement *amakudari* posts, which used to be aplenty in large firms. As of this writing, there have been rumblings across the ministries indicating that junior career bureaucrats have more confidence in challenging the traditional order (e.g., exclusionary corporate governance). In this regard, to jump-start innovation and entrepreneurship, Japan could do with more bold risk taking at the top of its elite ministries. It should be noted that in light of the degree of rent-seeking corruption in India on the part of bureaucrats (less so in China), Japan's minor bureaucratic deficiencies are benign in comparison.

At the same time, Kim worries about the "Galapagos problem" facing Japan as a whole, in part because government bureaucrats just cannot get a handle on the "soft" assets critical to entrepreneurial firms, including the development of international human networks. Kim argues that METI funds could be used to support hiring new, multilingual, multicultural talent both in and outside Japan to speed up progress (Mujo Kim interviews 2004, 2010, 2012). Another biomedical venture, Reprocell has had better luck in obtaining Japanese government funds for internationalization. All it took was for one of its researchers to win the Nobel Prize.

Reprocell

Norio Nakatsuji, the founding director of Kyoto University's Institute for Integrated Cell-Material Sciences (iCeMS) (est. 2007), is also a cofounder of Reprocell. Founded in Tokyo and now located next door in Yokohama, iCeMS was seed funded by a special Japanese government grant as part of Japan's biotechnology development policies and is the center of Japan's iPS cell-related patenting, currently directed by Shinya Yamanaka (Elliott and Konski 2013). Nakatsuji was an early adapter of a global model to running a university lab in Japan. First, from the outset, the lab's operational language would be English. Second, iCeMS would aim to be a truly international lab, with lead (principal investigator) researchers from all over the world, including China, England, and the United States. Nakatsuji's approach to the concept of iCeMS was based on the idea that scientific breakthroughs occur in an international collaborative, interdisciplinary environment: "Every frontier of the life sciences is now moving rapidly in a cross-disciplinary direction, in which we must work together and connect with each other in order to achieve novel and even higher-impact progress" (Nakatsuji 2012). This orientation reflects the tacit knowledge and open network orientation of its R&D architecture.

Nakatsuji (born 1950) received his doctorate in developmental biology from Kyoto University (1977). He is a pioneer in embryonic stem-cell (ES) research. He has had significant international experience, serving postdocs in Sweden (Umeå University), the United States (George Washington University, Massachusetts Institute of Technology), and the United Kingdom (Nakatsuji 2012). After success with generating monkey embryonic cells (2000), his lab successfully developed human ES by 2003, the same year that he founded Reprocell. Meanwhile, Nakatsuji (scientist-entrepreneur, professor emeritus, and occasional online blogger) was enthusiastic about Yamanaka's research and its potential to bypass the obstructions to scientific research posed by the then stringent limits on ES research in the United States (Nakatsuji 2007). Though these restrictions put in place by U.S. president George W. Bush in 2001 were lifted in 2009 by President Barack Obama, a deficit of nearly a decade of federal funding had no doubt put a damper on what would otherwise have been rapid R&D progress in the United States and created a space for other countries, a space that Japan and China (discussed in the next chapter) have sought to fill.

Yamanaka, the Nobel Prize recipient (2012) and director of iCeMS, and then subsequently its spin-off CiRA, at Kyoto University played a video of an experiment conducted by his lab. It showed a pulsating, fleshy blob. In fact, these were induced pluripotent stem cells (iPS) that had been "activated" to become heart cells. Yamanaka's discoveries, reported for the first time in 2006, enabling adult stem cells to behave like embryonic stem cells had led to this and many other potential human health applications.

Born in 1962, Yamanaka received his medical degree at Kobe University (1987) and later earned his PhD from Osaka City University (1993). After spending three years (1993–1996) at the Gladstone Institute at the University of California, San Francisco, he returned to Osaka. Yamanaka's time at Gladstone was formative, and he maintains an internationally staffed research lab at Gladstone today. Yamanaka said that these kinds of international collaborations are critical to advances in scientific research (Yamanaka 2013). According to his mentor, the founder of the Gladstone Institute, Robert W. Mahley, internationalization per se is not the point. While at Gladstone, Yamanaka learned to embrace failure and also to learn from it. In fact, the iPS discovery followed on the heels of a "colossal" failure in Yamanaka's postdoctoral experiments at Gladstone in the mid-1990s. At Gladstone, Yamanaka had been researching cholesterol reduction in the liver. To his horror, the test cells became cancerous. Rather than give up, Yamanaka was encouraged to investigate the mechanism of this transformation. This exploration of the mechanisms of the failure led directly to the breakthrough in iPS (Mahley interview 2016). Upon returning from the United States in 1996, Yamanaka joined the City University of Osaka and, in 1999, the Nara Institute of Science and Technology (NAIST), where he began the research that would eventually earn him a Nobel Prize. At NAIST, Yamanaka aimed to induce adult (at the time using mice) cells to "return to their embryonic pluripotent state" (2013). Yamanaka had brought this tacit knowledge and international research and development network gained at Gladstone back home to Japan.

In 2006, Yamanaka had identified a combination of four genes that transformed the adult skin cells of mice back to their embryonic state. Within a year, this success was replicated with human cells to "grow" skin and other human organ cells. With this innovation, the potential for regenerative medicine reached a new level. Yamanaka and his research team soon began to apply for a series of patents relating to their iPS innovations, which had complementarities to Nakatsuji's work. Nakatsuji's Reprocell aimed to develop and commercialize these and other stem-cell technologies. The company has licensing agreements with the University of Tokyo and Kyoto University and became the first company to commercialize human iPS cells. Reprocell faced a challenge when a U.S. venture established in 2006, CDI (Cellular Dynamics International) in Madison, Wisconsin, was granted international rights to use Yamanaka's patent portfolio from Kyoto University's specialized technology licensing organization iPS Academia. This university technology transfer made CDI a direct competitor to Reprocell. CDI, acquired for $307 million by Fuji Film in 2015, had built a global market share of $16.7 million by that time, with 155 employees. This points to the interference of government policies intending to promote commercialization but limiting the rights of academic inventors to the exclusive use of their inventions. Unintended consequences of government policies targeting commercialization also appear in the entrepreneurial stories of India and Singapore, discussed later.

Undaunted, Reprocell went public in 2013 with a record-setting IPO, earning it $21.7 million, nearly five times is offer price and the best performing first-day Japan IPO of an above $10 million offering since 1999 (Kitanaka and Kawano 2013). While Kyoto University remains a core source of its technologies (Yamanaka directs iCeMS and CiRA), Reprocell has compensated for its nonexclusive licensing arrangements through strategic acquisitions. For example, in 2014, Reprocell acquired Reinnervate in the United Kingdom and BioServe and Stemgent in the United States. Yamanaka and others have said that one of the challenges of being an academic scientist and entrepreneur is feeling the pressure of supporting hundreds of graduate students, postdocs, and employees. By 2015, products included heart, liver, and nerve cells with applications in, for example, toxicology and drug discovery (Hildreth 2015). Though now competing with global MNC backed CDI, in 2016, Reprocell had seventy-three employees on revenue of 1.07 billion yen. This progress is a testament to its international R&D connectivity and a powerful signal that an upstart firm can stand up to big firms like Fuji and survive. Whether this would be possible without a Nobel Prize–winning scientist on the team is debatable.

Fortunately, Yamanaka's research has been supported generously by such local foundations as Inamori and Takeda. The CiRA lab at Kyoto University, created by Yamanaka in the model of Gladstone, has the same open approach to lab space and also international research collaborations. For example, Mahley explained that to encourage interaction at Gladstone, the lab space has an open architecture of few walls, and lab spaces are designed to be shared. Gladstone has also been international in outlook—hiring researchers from all over the world. Since the beginning, Mahley sought to have a mix of cultures present in the lab. For example, in 2016, Gladstone had a number of Chinese researchers. In the early years, Israelis and Italians comprised the majority of foreign postdocs. To this day, however, thanks to the generosity of two individual donors, Gladstone keeps its main international partnership with Yamanaka and Japan. The open human-capital network architecture of Gladstone into which Yamanaka was invited in 1993 had been replicated by Yamanaka in Japan; and the tacit-knowledge exchange continues. This includes a dedicated lab space and funding for postdoctoral researchers to support Yamanaka's ongoing research (Mahley interview 2016). CiRA, iCeMS, and Reprocell indirectly have also benefited from the support of private donors, international R&D collaborations, and grants from the Japanese government (including from MEXT), the latter especially after Yamanaka received the Nobel Prize. By February 2017, CiRA had expanded to three buildings of research and lab space on the Kyoto University campus, with nearly three hundred full-time research staff (CiRA 2017). This is good for iCeMS, its 2010 spin-off CiRA, Reprocell (and competitors), and for future generations of Japanese academic entrepreneurs. CiRA's success has been emulated in India, as will be shown in Chapter 5. Whether this reflects an overall development of an entrepreneurial ecosystem in Japan is another matter.

Despite the exceptional case of Kyoto University and the region more broadly, Japan has not quite managed to scale this local-regional-global model to the national level. Kyoto and its Reprocell-like activities remain the exception that proves the rule. Fumiaki Ikeno, who in 2016 directed the Stanford Japan Biodesign program, which is helping to encourage biomedical entrepreneurship in Japan, has said that despite well-known successes such as those outlined above, on the whole, Japan still lacked an entrepreneurial ecosystem (Ikeno 2016). Seeking to assist would-be Japanese biomedical scientist entrepreneurs, Ikeno and colleagues were leading an effort to create a new bilateral entrepreneurship-focused university—the Silicon Valley Japan University (SVJU), whose viability was yet to be determined as of this writing (Ikeno 2016).

Conclusion

The analysis in this chapter has shown that despite Japan's capacities in codified knowledge, with its closed KNT architecture under a classic technonational regime, due to institutional rigidities and stickiness in its human-capital networks, it has heretofore failed to reach its potential in generating new business start-ups in frontier sectors like biomedicals (thus disconfirming NTN hypothesis 1). In contrast, countries with less knowledge capacity, as measured by patents and citations in knowledge domains, such as China, have nevertheless stimulated new business creation in these industries. This phenomenon in China is examined in the next chapter. Implications for policy point to potential developments in understanding the comparative competitive potential of Asian economies and the framework of networked technonationalism presented in previous chapters.

Japan has made modest progress creating system-level conditions—such as labor mobility and human-capital development—and even less so fostering entrepreneurial business. This points to the challenge of developing entrepreneurial ecosystems that free domestic individuals and firms to forge international connections, build social capital, and harness the resources obtained via international networks for investment into the future of their economies (the upper quadrants of the KNT). Adding network nuance to Japan's technonationalism may take it one step toward greater entrepreneurial activity building on the progress in 2017 of its "best under a billion" start-ups in other industries. Suggestions to make Japan more attractive to foreign talent include designating English as the official language of the special economic zones (SEZs), creating special long-term pathways to permanent residence visas[26] and citizenship, and incentives to attract inward FDI, in addition to the other incentives in place, all of which are good for economic growth and stability. China, the subject of the next chapter, offers interesting comparisons with its new brand of networked technonationalism.

CHAPTER 4   NEW NETWORKED TECHNONATIONALISM IN CHINA

Diaspora and "Mass" Entrepreneurship

AS OUTLINED IN CHAPTER 2, the origins of technonationalism in China can be traced back as far as the pre-nation-state Qin Dynasty (221–206 B.C.E.). For example, in addition to Shang Yang (mentioned in chapter two), the writings of Han Fei on political strength through capacity building inspired the first Qin emperor as Qin united and governed early China. Later, Emperor Wu of the Han Dynasty (156–87 B.C.E.) would advocate (state) strength through technological superiority.[1] The ancient Chinese civilization would go on to be at the forefront of technological developments in the premodern world, inventing and perfecting technologies in a variety of fields, including paper production and navigation (e.g., the compass). In this regard, the colonial period of the nineteenth and early twentieth centuries during which it was subject to British imperialism can be seen as a brief interlude in the evolution of Chinese technology leadership. This chapter focuses on China's networked form of technonationalism, which emerged during the post-Mao period (late 1970s to present), while contextualizing the legacies of Mao period policies on the economy and society of China.

The Mao Zedong period began in 1949 with the formation of the People's Republic of China. While China would take another half a century in structuring an economy conducive to innovation and entrepreneurship, investments into military and other technology became the basis for subsequent institutional and human-capital development. In the Mao period (1949–1976) military technology was prioritized, as the state invested in projects of strategic interest. These included military technology and weaponry developed by a cadre of scientists and engineers. These individuals would later be known as China's "techno-warriors" (Feigenbaum 2003). In the 1960s, technological progress was sidetracked by the Cultural Revolution, particularly in terms of national-scale training, technology development, and capital formation (Suttmeier and Yao 2004). By the 1990s, China had expanded its industrial targeting to include nonmilitary-related sectors in which the West had not yet assumed a clear lead (in part for this reason), including biotechnology and biomedicine.[2]

Referring to China, Feigenbaum (2003) coined the term "techno-warrior" as a metaphor for the central role of Chinese military leaders in the vision and implementation of strategic investments leading to technological development after 1949. According to Feigenbaum, China's techno-warriors operated under a Mao-inspired technonationalism that focused in the initial years on weapons-related research and development. For this reason, the role of particular military leaders, including Nie Rongzhen, also called Marshall Nie after his military title, would take a central position in the new nation-state China's science and technology bureaucracies. Feigenbaum's near exclusive focus on sources from a single leader (Nie) would be criticized: "the book relies very heavily—perhaps too heavily . . . on the memoirs and official histories" (Suttmeier 2004). Nevertheless, the author's extensive use of archival data in the original language paints a picture from the perspective of a visionary technological leader who made undeniable contributions to the modernization of China's technonationalism—decades prior to the contributions of Deng Xiaoping.

Nie was credited for taking the Chinese Academy of Sciences (CAS)—established the same year as the new republic (1949)—into its biggest expansion in size and scope, especially vis-à-vis science and technology development. For example, Nie and others at the helm of CAS forged an "institutionalized means to facilitate co-ordination between the military and the Academy" (Feigenbaum 1999, 305), which would lead to the professionalization of the Chinese technocracy. In 1949, CAS had been founded with two hundred employees, and after Nie joined in 1958, he led the expansion in the number of bureaus and significant growth in staff. For example, in 1960 the New Technologies Bureau was established (code-named 04 Bureau), which added tens of thousands of staff, at least a third of which were said to engage in research and development activities (Feigenbaum 2003). Another innovation under Nie at CAS was to create mentoring programs for the technical training of junior staff in all the major strategic-weapons programs, a model that would be followed as the organization entered new technology fields (Feigenbaum 2003). National security would come to be defined more broadly than in military technology alone, laying "the foundation of a truly systematic high technology industrial and science base that would promote China's overall industrial, scientific, and institutional development" (Feigenbaum 2003, 16).

Nie had been the head of the strategic-weapons program under Mao and went on to serve in various positions after the revolutionary period. For example, educated in Europe and the Soviet Union, Nie served under Mao in the People's Liberation Army. Having studied Chinese culture and history before embarking on a military career, in the 1960s Nie criticized what he saw as "excesses" of the Cultural Revolution (criticism that led to his purging until after the death of Mao in 1976) (Lew and Leung 2013). In this fashion Nie's trajectory was similar to the political fortunes of Deng, who upon returning from his own exile from the Chinese Communist Party (CCP) would usher in the next era of China's technonationalism, adding an internationally networked architecture.

China's political and economic transformation after the Mao period occurred in three phases. First, the Open Door Policy in 1978 signaled an *initial opening* to the outside world characterized by the sending out of Chinese, initially senior scholars and soon thereafter students, for doctoral study in science and technology fields at Western research universities, as well as courting inward FDI. This initial period lasted through the 1980s. Second, in the 1990s, state policy and private-sector actors increased *international collaborations* in production at first and then eventually in research and development (see hypothesis 3a, pertaining to interinstitutional and international networks facilitating knowledge acquisition and tacit-knowledge transfer). In the third phase, in the 2000s, China reached a developmental stage, enabling it to pursue greater *indigenization* in innovation capacity, as well as exporting Chinese standards of technology management to a new generation of developing economies.

Phase 1: Initial Opening to the Outside World (1980s)

China's Open Door Policy—courting inward FDI while simultaneously attempting to upgrade innovation capacity—illustrates the challenges so-called late developers have in protecting domestic enterprises and workers from foreign exploitation. Unlike previous late developers, who devised a main bank system to channel investments in capacity upgrading (Gerschenkron 1966), lacking domestic capital liquidity in the initial phases, these later developers (or "late, late") have instead opened their doors to inward FDI. (See Chapter 2, hypothesis 3c on mitigated inward FDI as facilitating innovation-capacity improvements.)

While the turning point is ascribed herein to the decade of the 1980s—once the Open Door was in full swing—several years earlier Deng had initiated a new focus on improving China's science and technology capacity. This had begun in 1977 with "winning back the goodwill of scientists" (Vogel 2011, 200), who had been alienated during the Cultural Revolution. Deng understood that the Maoist attacks on intellectuals had delayed modernization by weakening science and technology capacity. In 1977, Deng initiated talks with leaders of the Chinese Academy of Sciences and called upon them to identify top scholars, who were then provided with better research facilities and living conditions, in the aim of allowing them greater focus on their work. Overtures to overseas Chinese scientists also began, welcoming them back home. Programs for students to study abroad were created. In this manner, China's diaspora was identified early on as an important national resource. This is contrasted with Japan's overall lack of engagement with its diaspora and India's delay in tapping into these networks.

Further, under Mao, university entrance had prioritized an applicant's politics over academic ability, for example in proper (peasant, worker) "class" and "political thinking." Under Deng, entrance would be (again) earned through academic merit, as measured by the reinstated entrance exam. Under Mao, even basic research scientists were required to spend much time on "political education" activities. Under Deng, scientists would be encouraged to spend at least 80 percent of their time conducting research. The State Science and Technology Commission, which had been abolished under Mao, would also be reinstated. Deng sought to expedite the technology learning of new generations of Chinese. In 1978, he urged a delegation of U.S. scientists, led by then president Carter's science advisor Frank Press, to immediately accept seven hundred Chinese students, followed by tens of thousands thereafter (Vogel 2011). This was a major change in China's internationalization. Previously, in 1968, fewer than two hundred Chinese students were abroad (Guruz 2011). By 1984, there would be an estimated nineteen thousand Chinese students studying abroad in the United States (Vogel 2011; Worden, Savada, and Dolan 1988). During this period, Chinese American scientists in particular began to make important contributions to the restarting of science and technology policy in China. This dynamic would be repeated decades later with technologist-entrepreneur returnees.

According to a Kauffman Foundation report, returnee entrepreneurs in India and China shared similar reasons for return, including contributing to home country, family ties, and government incentives (Wadhwa et al. 2011). Both Indian and Chinese returnees considered economic opportunities as one of the major reasons for returning, while Chinese professionals were more likely to cite economic opportunity over other reasons. Chinese returnees also valued significantly the professional and family networks in China. In the same survey, Indian respondents valued highly family ties as a driving force for return.

By 2011, the *Economist* estimated that more than 3.46 million overseas Chinese were in the United States, of a total of 42.2 million worldwide.[3] Between 1978 and 2010, it was estimated that 1.9 million Chinese had studied abroad, and 632,200 had returned (Guruz 2011). China's largest biomedical research park, Zhongguancun or Z-Park in northwest Beijing, boasted in 2016 to have benefitted from thousands of returnees at the helm of new venture businesses and technology collaborations. This is discussed later in this chapter.

With the aforementioned moves toward internationalization, Deng initiated institutional reforms so that those on the inside would become readier in terms of absorptive capacity to exploit the inward flow of technology, people, and capital from the outside (fig. 2.2). The Open Door Policy of Deng Xiaoping initiated privatization and renewed modernization on a national scale.[4] The Open Door Policy was applied cautiously in the initial years, as Deng said, "crossing the river by feeling the stones." As outlined in table 1.1, under China's NTN regime, limited market access was granted to select Western firms in exchange for inward technology transfer (Zheng and Pan 2012). The first regions selected as areas for government investment—allowing greater autonomy for the private sector—were those that had the nearest proximity to the Chinese diaspora in Hong Kong, Macau, and Taiwan. These included, initially, Fujian and Guandong Provinces and the cities of Shenzen, Zhuhai, Shantou, and Xiamen. From the beginning, the Chinese internationally networked variation of technonationalism was designed to draw investments from Chinese expatriates through these international diaspora networks (Zheng and Pan 2012).[5] The knowledge and network architecture of NTN, illustrated in figure 2.2, shows how China would manage its openness to the foreign with an open yet protective orientation. The state would structure interactions with MNCs and their much-needed capital so that their presence in the economy would be managed substantively and spatially (as in SEZs). In this manner, inward FDI would be channeled into innovation-capacity improvements (the lower left quadrant of the KNT).

Early on, in 1979, Guandong and Fujian were established as "special zones" later to become special economic zones (SEZs). These SEZs represent the first attempt by the Deng Xiaoping regime to utilize diaspora networks to attract inward FDI, targeting Chinese abroad with ethnic ties to these regions. In a bold policy move at the time, the SEZs, with national government support via tax benefits and infrastructure building, would (in theory) be regulated primarily by the market. Further, these regions were encouraged to experiment and try new approaches in business. Politics still loomed large. This experimentation was limited to economic activities, and this is why the 1979 designation as "special zone" was changed in the 1980s to "special economic zone," at the prompting of Chen Yun. Chen was an important member of the first (Mao) and second (Deng) generation of leadership of China. Chen was a financial conservative, main leader of financial and economic policies of the People's Republic of China and vice premier of the State Council (1954–1965). A native of Shanghai, Chen also refused to allow his home region to become an SEZ, due to what he viewed as the "comprador" mentality of this historically cosmopolitan city of deferring to the will of foreigners. There would be no mitigated opening to the outside for Shanghai under China's NTN regime. So, in part resulting from Chen Yun's influence, the national gamble was on less-developed, more provincial regions in the southeast.

The bet on SEZs paid off. Between 1979 and 1995, two-thirds of inward FDI to China would be concentrated in these "Southern Gate" areas (Vogel 2011). The success of this regional experimentation—fund-raising from the estimated 8 million Chinese (or more) at that time from Guangdong and Fujian in Hong Kong and Southeast Asia alone—was eventually expanded to the national level. At the same time, the period was more than a door opening to the outside world. In Janus-like fashion, domestic actors, shielded from international market competition by the state, were learning to compete in a capitalist world.

Nevertheless, legacies from the Mao period (1949–1976) remained, undermining innovation-capacity development. The Cultural Revolution under Mao Zedong was aimed in part at ridding China of "technological elites" (Lakhan 2006), who were supposedly carriers of Western ideology. This decommissioning of sorts affected even China's so-called techno-warriors (Feigenbaum 2003), who fiercely protected China from attempts by Western industries to impose their standards and therefore products on China. For example, in the 1940s, Chinese technologists fought the Westinghouse-backed lobbying by the U.S. government to change China's 220-voltage system to the U.S. 110/120 voltage (K. P. Tan 2017). While the bulk of the science and technological class was suppressed and generally neglected through the defunding of research (a number had fled to the Southeast Asian countries later targeted by the Open Door), a few scientists, especially those with connections to the military, were protected. For example, the 2015 Nobel Prize recipient in medicine, Tu Youyou, who worked for one of the few traditional Chinese medicine research institutes that remained active under Mao, was protected because during the Vietnam War, the Chinese military— losing scores of soldiers to malaria—was keen to develop a cure.

Further, the 1949 Communist Revolution had brought basic health-care to rural areas via affectionately named "barefoot doctors," among whom the use of traditional Chinese medicine (TCM) was prevalent (Stanford Biodesign 2013). At the time, China faced a shortage of doctors, and initially, traditional Chinese medicine and its practitioners were supported by Mao's desire to bring basic healthcare to all Chinese people. With the 1980s reforms, healthcare shifted from a state-welfare to a for-profit model. Not surprisingly, the provision of TCM declined, in favor of more lucrative Western treatments and pharmaceuticals (Wei and Brock 2013).

A number of scholars have pointed out that given the purge during the Cultural Revolution of vast numbers of intellectuals across a number of disciplines, one collateral effect of the Open Door Policy was to further reinforce the political power of bureaucrats, who expanded their influence and personal enrichment as profitable opportunities emerged (Beeson 2009; Bruche 2009; Vogel 2011). For example, scholars have observed in China that business success hinges on political connections (Yeung and Chung 1999) or is hindered by them due to the significant amount of time diverted from more productive activities in nurturing political relations (Cao et al. 2011). Political corruption has been endemic within China's marketization process whereby bureaucrats act as gatekeepers to business opportunities and enrich themselves in the process (Lin 2001).

Cole et al. (2009) suggested that the areas that were more effective in preventing corruption in China tended to attract higher levels of FDI. This result is consistent with the previous discussion of the positive correlation between the presence of IPR protection and increasing inward FDI in China. Jiang and Nie (2014) found that firms circumvent perceived government regulatory inefficiencies through corrupt behaviors in their goal of making a profit. Consequently, in regions where regulations are numerous, corruption and, paradoxically, profit were also high. However, profits derived via corrupt practices may not serve national developmental goals. The central state has thus sought ways of channeling private-sector economic activity in support of technonational goals.

The 1980s featured two important policy shifts: tax and economic structural reform via the 863 Plan. In 1985, fiscal reform led to the decentralization of the tax system. (In comparison, this had yet to happen in Japan as late as 2017.[6]) Provinces would have greater autonomy in the distribution of tax revenues and also greater responsibility. In 1988 the China Torch policy began.[7] Numerous policies in China target the biomedical industry. A historical overview of key policies is provided in table 4.1. For example, the National Eleventh Five-Year Plan for Science and Technology (2006–2010) included measures for promoting basic

TABLE 4.1.

Key policy history: Biomedical innovation and entrepreneurship in China

Year	Name	Objectives
1978	Open Door Policy	Modernize the country, ensure that the Communist Party is always in the forefront.
1985	Fiscal and Financial Deregulation	Enhance the vitality of enterprises, emphasize economic leverage through the establishment of a rational pricing system. Implement separation between government from enterprises, expand foreign and domestic economic and technological exchanges.
1996	The Ninth Five-Year Plan (1996–2000)	Establish a modern enterprise system, cultivate a unified and open market system, strengthen the government's macro-control and regulatory capability, open further to the outside world, and make education a priority.
2001	The 863 Program under the Tenth Five-Year Plan (2001–2005)	Boost innovation capacity in the high-tech sectors, particularly in strategic high-tech fields. Strive to achieve breakthroughs in key technical fields, and to achieve "leap-frog" development in key high-tech fields.
2006	National Long-Term Science and Technology Development Plan	Confirm the development of biotechnology medicines as key objective in China. Strive to become a pioneering country in biotechnology with a focus in functional genomics, proteometrics, stem cells, and therapeutic cloning, tissue engineering, and bioconversion technologies.

TABLE 4.1. (*continued*)

Year	Name	Objectives
2006	The Eleventh Five-Year Plan for the Biology Industry (2006–2010)	Outline the principles and goals for the development of biotechnology in China. Confirm the development of biotechnology medicines as the key research area. Initiate projects on drug innovation, modern Chinese medicines, and biotechnology.
2007	National Eleventh Five-Year Plan for Science and Technology (2006–2010)	Confirm the development of chemical and biotechnology medicines as the key research area, with specific goals in drug invention, filtering, and safety measures. Develop thirty to forty patented drugs with competitive edge, and advance in drug and vaccine development. Develop scientific prevention and treatment programs using Chinese and Western medicines.
2007	The Eleventh Five-Year Plan for the National Science and Technology Support Program (2006–2010)	Focus development of select digital medical devices and Chinese medicines for major diseases. Advance in twenty to thirty target technologies. Develop ten to fifteen conventional equipment and core components.
2007	Guidelines for Key Projects of the 863 Biology and Medical Technology Applications in 2007	Establish and improve biotechnology systems. Enhance competitiveness of the Chinese biotechnology and pharmaceutical R&D sectors. Focus development programs around identified major diseases. Improve the use of biotechnology applications in clinical practice and industry. Provide guidance to the development of the Chinese biotechnology sector, and increase contribution of biotechnology and pharmaceutical R&D in the national economy.
2011	The Twelfth Five-Year Plan for the National Science and Technology development program (2011–2015)	Enhance the ability of independent innovation, technological competitiveness, and international influence. Develop a well-structured and efficient national innovation system. Achieve a significant breakthrough in technologies, and innovation capacity ranking should improve from 21 to 18.
2012	Opinions on the science and technology system reform to improve the construction of innovation system	Strengthen the dominant position of technological innovation, establish the dominant position of enterprises in technological innovation, and better integrate science and technology with economy.
2013	The Twelfth Five-Year Plan National Indigenous Innovation Capability Construction Plan (2011–2015)	Enhance capability of indigenous innovation of academic institutions and corporations. Encourage high-skilled personnel to have ideology of innovation. Strengthen IPR creation, utilization, protection, and management.

(continued)

TABLE 4.1. (*continued*)

Year	Name	Objectives
2014	Beijing Technological Innovation Action Plan (2014–2017)	Improve investment and financing policy. Foster market environment for new technologies and new product applications. Gather and train a group of high-skilled personnel in technical, scientific technology transition, and project management. Create an environment of innovative dynamics. Develop the biopharmaceutical industry by leaps by improving innovation-driven policies. By 2017, biopharmaceutical industry should strive to become a pillar industry.
2014	The Strategic Action Plan of In-Depth Implementation of the National Intellectual Property (2014–2020)	Strengthen the management of intellectual property of technological innovation, financial support from the government, and improved intellectual property funding policies. Expand international cooperation in intellectual property and promote international competitiveness of Chinese intellectual property.
2015	Made in China 2025	Improve the innovative design capabilities and national manufacturing innovation system. Strengthen the building of standardized system and the use of intellectual property rights, and promote the commercialization of scientific and technological achievements.
2015	The State Council Suggestion on Mass Entrepreneur and Innovation Policies and Measures	Improve the market environment of free competition and enhance entrepreneurial IPR protection. Support the entrepreneurial activities of scientific researchers, university students, and overseas professionals in China. Promote mass entrepreneurship and innovation.
2015	Suggestions on Making the Thirteenth Five-Year Plan from CPC Central Committee (2016–2020)	Accelerate the breakthrough of core technologies in fields including biomedicine. Enhance the autonomy of universities and research institutes in innovation, and promote the transition of government functions from R&D management to innovation service.
2015	The Development Plan of National Standardization System Construction	Standardize the development standards for biotechnical industries, including genetic engineering, biomedicine, and biomedical engineering. Promote significant improvement of biotechnological indigenous innovation capability. Add key technologies with indigenous intellectual property into the standards of corporations and groups.

SOURCES: Ministry of Science and Technology of the People's Republic of China 2006a, 2007a, 2011; State Council of the People's Republic of China 2006, 2012, 2013, 2015a, 2015b; Development and Reform Commission 2007; Zhang 2008.

research and industrial promotion. Concerning the latter, a particular focus was to stimulate "breakthroughs in key technology industries to foster high-tech and emerging industries, to enhance the core competitiveness of high-tech industry, to optimize the industrial structure" (Development and Reform Commission 2007). Within the plan, the 863 Program was an important milestone. Founded by four senior scientists from the strategic-weapons development program from whence the original techno-warriors emerged, 863 was propelled by a technonationalist vision of catching up and overtaking the West's dominance in these technologies. Biomedicine was an early target for development under these state policies.

863 Program: Torch

In March 3, 1986, life sciences and biomedicine were listed in the National High Technology Research and Development Program (or 863 Program, referring to the launch year, 1986, and month, March) as key areas to be funded, which led to significant new investments in biomedicine in China.[8] The 863 Program objectives included improving China's innovation position by closing technology gaps with foreign competitors, encouraging science and technology human-capital development, and forming new high-technology industries. Key to the plan was to develop biotechnology for diagnosing, treating, and curing a number of infectious diseases and cancers (863 Program Document 1986).

Between 1986 and 2005, the government had invested 33 billion RMB ($3.8 billion) for the 863 Program. By 2013, more than 150,000 researchers had collaborated under the auspices of 863. These researchers represented three hundred colleges and universities and nearly a thousand enterprises. According to government statistics, by the third decade after its launch, 863 Program beneficiaries had published more than 120,000 articles and issued approximately 8,000 domestic and foreign patents (State Council of the People's Republic of China 2013).[9] In 1985, China had enacted its first patent law to protect intellectual property rights for domestic inventors. A concomitant system of incentives to Chinese scientists began, including cash bonuses and the right to highly sought residence permits (*hukou*, 户口) in the urban centers. However, Chinese attorneys have reported that Chinese Patent Office bureaucrats have been paid bonuses for approving more patents. One consequence is that the high quantity of Chinese patents disguises a number of patents based on work of dubious quality (*Economist* 2010).

A more accurate measure of innovation in China is triadic patents (as outlined in Chapter 1, especially fig. 1.2), representing those granted in each of the United States, European Union, and Japan—that is, patent approval in multiple international markets that have rigorous standards is a more reliable measure of quality. Even so, China has made significant improvements in this regard. The OECD found that between 2003 and 2013, China and India had an average growth in the number of triadic patents of more than 17 percent and 12 percent a year, respectively (OECD n.d.c).

During this period, in addition to reaching out to international diaspora networks in seeking inward FDI, networks became the institutional medium of domestic economic activity, accelerated by the devolution of the central state role. Interactions within these interpersonal networks (guanxi) of scientists and business professionals have been governed by relational norms rather than contractual obligations (Jansson, Johanson, and Ramstrom 2007). These interactions not incidentally reinforced tacit-knowledge exchange. These social networks are exponentially more international in scale than, for example, in Japan, through connections to innovation and entrepreneurial networks elsewhere. For example, in Silicon Valley in the United States, Chinese and Indian ethnic entrepreneurs lead in the proportion of new high-tech business creation (Payne 2004), thanks to the extensive global Chinese diaspora.

An example of this is the World Chinese Entrepreneur Association, claiming to have nearly twelve thousand returnee Chinese entrepreneurs as members in Beijing alone. (In comparison, the Indus Entrepreneurs, the Indian diaspora network of angel investors, has an estimated thirteen thousand members worldwide.) Between 1978 and 2014, about 3.5 million Chinese students had studied abroad. By 2014, it was estimated that 1.8 million students had returned (State Council of the People's Republic of China 2015e).

By 2015 the Zhongguancun Park (Beijing), Z-Park, was host to a reported fifteen thousand returnees, 79 percent of whom had advanced degrees, and 3,000 start-ups (Y. Huang 2015). In a 2016 meeting with Z-Park officials, the author was told that its Life Science Park had 384 firms (Zeng interview 2016). Overall, Z-Park had produced more than 300 listed companies, a third of which were also listed overseas.[10] Upon mention that this researcher would visit another Life Science Park in Beijing, one official (Zeng) commented that the other was "quite small." The supposedly smaller park, Beijing Yizhuang Biomedical Park (BYBP), an eight-square-kilometer campus, was replete with ample lab facilities and housed 160 firms (2016), rivaling the size of, for example, the Scripps Research Institute in San Diego in the United States. Its head of operations in 2016 said that they are fortunate to have returnees who have studied biomedicine and engineering at such universities as Harvard and MIT "helping out," after they have worked for a company in China to gain experience (Anonymous official, interview, Beijing Yizhuang Biomedical Park, July 1, 2016). In 1988, in the first decade of the Open Door Policy, Zhongguancun had been designated as an SEZ—after a cluster of electronics start-ups had emerged along a boulevard not far from the Peking University main campus. The first of these were side businesses "in the street," often set up by university faculty (Zeng interview 2016).

Concerning the Z-Park's success in becoming a central part of China's ecosystem of innovation and entrepreneurship, Zeng said that by 2016 it had grown to more than twenty thousand companies comprising 2 million employees generating revenue of about $700 million. "To achieve it was not easy," by any measure, according to Zeng. Further, thus far, among Z-Park's companies, its software developers have been getting "lots of VC" while the biopharmaceutical and medical device start-ups have a much more difficult task. This includes the need for access to quality lab space, not to mention raw materials and highly trained bench technicians. Further, biomedical space in general is highly regulated, and so far government institutes, including the Chinese Academy of Sciences (CAS), have been the main sources of new technology research and development.

The area also houses the CAS and the Academy of Engineering (Y. Huang 2015). The district, in addition to enjoying the tax benefits and government subsidies that come with SEZ designation, in recent years has also benefitted from the Thousand Talents program, recruiting twenty-nine professionals, twenty-seven of whom were said to have started entrepreneurial businesses. Engaging with the diaspora was coupled with large inflows of inward FDI. At one point, according to Zhao and La Pira (2013) inward FDI-driven business activities comprised 40 percent of GDP, 55 percent of overall import/export, and an astounding 87 percent of high-technology exports.

This represents a serendipitous, while unintended, consequence of the Cultural Revolution purge of intellectuals that led directly to massive outmigration of technologists and other professionals into the global Chinese diaspora. That is, the Chinese Communist Party–led government would later embrace the very same Chinese professional class of the original diaspora into subsequent national innovation strategies. Previously, in an effort to draw investment capital, Qing Dynasty–era China had enacted in 1909 a jus sanguinis nationality law embracing all ethnic Chinese worldwide as citizens (Khanna 2007). India, the subject of the next chapter, would until recently be jus soli, while Japan has been jus sanguinis and jus soli in its treatment of its diaspora. In 1949, under Mao, China's Overseas Chinese Office (OCO) had been established for similar (jus sanguinis) reasons. During the Cultural Revolution, however, Mao would pull away from the diaspora, fearing it as a source of potential political opposition. Tellingly, one of the first initiatives under Deng was to reinstate the status of the OCO in 1978. Additional programs targeting overseas students would be created in the 1990s (C. Li 2004; Liu and Dongen 2016). China has since become the model for a networked form of technonationalism (see table 1.1 and fig. 2.2).[11] The openness to diaspora networks in the 1980s laid the groundwork for greater international connections in the 1990s.

Phase 2: International Collaborations (1990s)

In 1992 Deng took his symbolic "Southern Tour," in which China's leader traveled to Wuchang, Shanghai, Zhuhai, and Shenzhen to signal China's new openness to inward foreign direct investment in special economic zones. As mentioned above, these zones were placed in the southeast intentionally in order to attract Chinese diaspora capital and business interests. The year 1995 was a key year in the second phase of China's new networked technonationalism, with the creation of the 863/Torch Program (Fan and Watanabe 2006; Xie 2010),[12] the indigenization of innovation and setting standards initiatives (Suttmeier 2005; Wilsdon 2007; *Taipei Times* 2004), and the positioning internationally of a new "brand" of Chinese nationalism (Gerth 2012). Figure 2.2 illustrates the dynamic relation between knowledge and network openness and state goals of increasing innovation capacity in codified knowledge.

Torch Program

The Torch High Technology Industry Development Center has pursued the strategic goals laid out by the five-year plan (economic policy in China is segmented by five- or ten-year increments) as follows: cultivating tech-based small- and medium-sized enterprises (SMEs), establishing development innovation clusters, and building an innovative environment for science and technology development and subsequent commercialization and new business. The Torch High Technology Industry Development Center (Torch Center) was established in 1989 in Beijing and has been a key ministry within China's NTN regime. Through Torch, the State Council of China aimed to develop high-technology industries. For over a decade, the Torch Center had formulated and implemented a series of policy tools, such as science and technology industrial parks (STIPs) and technology-based incubators (TBIs). In the 1980s, aiming to translate its expanding innovation base into commercialized products in existing and new businesses, China created a variety of innovation development clusters, including STIPs.[13]

In 1991, the State Science and Technology Commission (SSTC) deputy director Li Xu'e said, "Torch had been established on the basis of nongovernmental mechanisms" (Feigenbaum 2003, 195), in reference to the eventual loosening of the theretofore tight coupling between the central state, national labs, and state-owned enterprises (SOEs). At the time, the Torch concept was intended to draw in foreign technology and investment at the local level, within designated technology development zones. According to Feigenbaum (2003), Torch projects sought also "to pry undisciplined firms away from their grasping holds on the state's purse" (196).

Since the first STIP approved by the China State Council in 1988, more than fifty-four additional STIPs had been established by 2008 throughout mainland China. By 2006, these national STIPs were comprised of nearly forty-six thousand tenant companies employing 5.74 million people. According to Chinese government sources, the total output of industrial value added from these STIPs in 2006 accounted for 9 percent of the national total, and they contributed to 5 percent of the national GDP and one-third of the country's R&D expenditures (Torch High Technology Industry Development Center 2013). By 2005, it was estimated that the government of China was spending more than $600 million per year on biotechnology research and development (Chervenak 2005), much via the STIPs. To foster "going global," the Torch Center had taken specific measures, including the establishment of nine International Business Incubators (IBIs) and seven overseas science parks, including in Singapore, Maryland (United States), Cambridge and Manchester (United Kingdom), Russia, Austria, and Australia (Torch High Technology Industry Development Center 2013).

Compared with developed countries, China has a short history of developing novel biopharmaceuticals with intellectual property (IP) rights, despite its deep history in producing medicinals. Chinese traditional medicinal firms, including Tong Ren Tang (established early in the Qing Dynasty), He Nian Tang, and Ye Kan Tang (established more than six hundred years ago), are a few examples of this medicinal lineage. Shanghai start-up Hutchison China MediTech (Chi-Med) is unique in that it distributes and sells TCM and also has a pipeline of in-house oncology drugs developed with foreign partners, including Eli Lilly and Astra Zenica, in clinical trials (Ward and Waldmeir 2016; Wee 2018). The Chinese government regards the stimulation of the development of new ventures in biomedicine as the one of the most important strategies in its industrial development plan—and policies are underway to provide finance and tax incentives for biomedical start-ups. Excess production capacity and a shortage of pipeline products are requiring biotechnology companies to seek foreign partnership opportunities. With support from local government and cooperation with international institutions, Chinese biomedicals have developed broad-based international collaborative research and strategic business networks, allowing China to play a more important role in the global biomedical industry.

Healthcare reforms in the 2010s and the central government's push for biomedical development were expected in 2017 to boost growth by as much as 30 percent, making it one of the leading growth markets within China's healthcare industry. The Ministry of Science and Technology (MOST) and National Development and Reform Commission (NDRC) have generated the bulk of biomedical-related policies. Specific policies are discussed below and outlined in table 4.1. The government has enforced several policies to better regulate the biomedical sector and has also instituted reforms to create a unified regulatory framework, reducing uncertainty in the market.

The central state would eventually loosen the reigns on its control over small-scale producers. Zhu Rongji, the fifth premier of the People's Republic of China from 1998 to 2003, indicated that government policy would "grasp the big, let go the small" (Beeson 2009, 28). In other words, moving forward, small business should be allowed to flourish, while state efforts would be focused on the so-called commanding heights of strategic high-technology high-growth-potential industries.

Meanwhile, marketization had expanded to include workers. During the Mao period, upon graduation from university, students had been assigned to their jobs. Top level PhDs in the sciences, for example, were assigned to national research institutes and SOEs (State Council of the People's Republic of China 1990). By the 2000s, the economy had transitioned to a free-choice system where graduates could be recruited and select their employer independently of approval by Communist Party functionaries. This newfound freedom led to high labor mobility, which, as discussed in Chapter 2, enhanced the transfer of tacit knowledge and innovation potential across institutional boundaries (the upper quadrants of the KNT, table 2.2). A 2010 survey found that 42 percent of university graduates from the class year 2008 had changed jobs at least once, in marked contrast to the low labor mobility in Japan that has proven a drag on tacit-knowledge exchange in that country (*China Education News* 2012).

In 2009, China established tax benefits for the biomedical industry. These tax incentives included tax credits for new product R&D investments and up to a 15 percent reduction in the corporate tax burden for approved enterprises. In theory, private firms would have equal access to these tax and other benefits, in an open and transparent fashion (State Council of the People's Republic of China 2009). Unfortunately, domestic politics and intra-party competition has often intruded on the functioning of the market. Glowing reports by high-ranking state officials about China's strides in improving innovation capacity have often masked a conflicting narrative.[14] Preventing public disclosure of intra-party rivalry partly explains China's tendency toward censorship, discussed below as it relates to innovation-system development.

Phase 3: Indigenizing Innovation (2000s)

During the Tenth Five-Year Plan period (2001–2005), Chinese government estimates boasted that during that period R&D expenditure in biomedicine increased four times, the number of academic papers published in foreign countries increased sixfold, the number of clinical medicines had increased eight times, the number of patent applications had increased tenfold, and the added value growth in the biomedical industry was over 30 percent. China has become particularly active in genomics, proteomics, and SARS vaccine research, as discussed below in the entrepreneurial case studies. China has in fact increased its number of international scientific publications, a proxy measure used to reflect innovation capacity. Responding to government financial and promotion incentives, Chinese scientists, who are largely civil servants, have increased their publication frequency. However, the emphasis on quantity—driven by the national government's aims to report growth in these measures—has undermined quality. This includes a number of cases of plagiarism. For example, in 2009, an international scientific journal had to retract 120 papers from Chinese scientists; more than half had been submitted by a single university (Jinggangshan University in Jiangxi Province) (Lim 2011). Other IP-related policies include attempts to increase the total number of patents that are used in such global-innovation ranking indices as the GII (see Chapters 1 and 2).

As mentioned previously, Chinese patent officers had been paid bonuses for approving more patents. Such Chinese firms as Huawei would acquire external technology to improve its own technology on products (Chen, Chen, and Vanhaverbeke 2011; Shim and Shin 2016). Under the new indigenization of innovation strategy, the government thought that the enforcement of IP protection would encourage R&D activities in China. For example, according to Ang, Cheng, and Wu (2014), high-tech firms in the provinces with better IP rights have access to more inward FDI. According to Dang and Motohashi (2015), the government patent-subsidy programs that subsidized filing and examination fees, which was meant to stimulate and encourage patent filing, resulted in an increase in low value-added patent applications. However, Xibao Li (2012) has argued that this subsidy program will not result in a bubble of patent growth as long as the examination process is not affected, but it was expected to have the collateral effect of increasing the complexity and workload for government patent examiners.

By 2003, the number of national biomedical companies grew to more than seventy-three hundred; of these twenty-eight hundred have "modern" biomedical (excluding China's large TCM market) as their core business. According to estimates, China's modern (which is often referred to as Western) biomedical industry's annual output value reached 60 billion RMB ($7.25 billion), while traditional (e.g., TCM) biomedical industry's annual output value reached 300 billion RMB. Traditional medicine still dominates in China, though recent studies have indicated the rising prominence of Western medicine, particularly in provinces in or near former colonial territories (Chung et al. 2011).[15] In this third phase of new networked technonationalism, indigenization, China had graduated from its focus on outward innovation network linkages within the diaspora to enticing ethnic Chinese STEM graduates home to rejoin the domestic innovation workforce. The Eleventh Five-Year Plan (2007–2012) was aimed at boosting China's international rankings in patents and scientific publications, particularly in biomedicals. Table 4.1 outlines the five-year plans in the context of other policies related to biomedical innovation and entrepreneurship in the twentieth century. Two policies dominated China's networked technonational approach in the 2000s: indigenizing innovation through its The Thousand Talents Plan and stimulating entrepreneurial-ecosystem development in high-technology industries via Innofund.

The Thousand Talents Plan

The Thousand Talents Plan (also referred to as "1000 Talents Plan") launched in 2008 encouraged overseas Chinese science and technology professionals (referred to by a homonym of "overseas Chinese," *hai gui*, 海龟, or "sea turtles") to return to China with the support of government funds (Hao and Welch 2012). The plan also targeted high-quality foreign scientists with expertise in targeted technologies. Since the start of the plan, the government claims that more than four thousand R&D class returnees have supported indigenization in key technologies. According to a government employment database surveying returnees, the highest proportion (25 percent) are engaged in biomedical R&D activities, followed by information science and technology (16 percent) and engineering and materials (15 percent). In addition to the benefits to innovation of tacit-knowledge transfer across organizational boundaries, these international scientists bring their guanxi innovation networks (Hao and Welch 2012; Hao et al. 2015). The plan is not without its critics, as a few foreign scientists have complained that the supposedly earmarked funds to support their research activities had been diverted to other expenditures, such as unrelated equipment purchases (Hvistendahl 2014). Nevertheless, the government has been able to snag a few big fish (or "turtles"), including accomplished biomedical (e.g., life science) leaders home, mainly from their posts in the United States.

Rao Yi, prior to his return to China, had been a researcher at U.S. universities, including Northwestern University (2004–2007). In 2007, he became the dean of Peking University's School of Life Sciences. Rao would lead reforms in education and management styles in Peking University to allow students to "achieve their full professional potential" (Rao, Lu, and Tsou 2004) In a controversial article in 2004, Rao did not hesitate in criticizing weaknesses in China's innovation system (Rao, Lu, and Tsou 2004). Two other scholars who returned to China from the United States and joined higher-education institutions and have kept a lower profile, avoiding public criticism of the way things are done in China, are Shi Yigong (who returned from Princeton University to become the dean of life sciences at Tsinghua University in Beijing) and Wang Xiaodong (who returned from the National Academy of Sciences of the United States) in 2008 and 2009 (Xie, Zhang, and Lai 2014). Shi Yigong also mentioned the cronyism in the grant and funding selection process in a coauthored editorial published in *Science* with Rao (Shi and Rao 2010). Rao's experience shows that even highly positioned returnees face consequences if they run afoul of the CCP regime. Rao Yi was denied entrance to the CAS in 2011, despite his stellar credentials. According to anonymous sources, the reasons behind this snub by the government were clearly the result of Rao's outspoken criticism of China's corrupt academic system (Sharma 2011).

In comparison, as discussed in the previous chapter, Japan was found to have comparatively low levels of R&D labor mobility in the biomedical industry (Nakamura and Odagiri 2002), save occasional temporary "secondment" between organizations. This innovative weakness in Japan lingers, despite the twenty-first century having been declared by the Japanese government as its "life science" century. India, the subject of the next chapter, like China, facilitates tacit-knowledge transfer through tapping into its diaspora networks, albeit at a pace behind that of China.[16] In this most recent phase of China's networked technonationalism, the biomedical and other high-technology fields have also been targeted for entrepreneurial-ecosystem development. Innofund, in China, is one such attempt at connecting the innovation system to an emerging entrepreneurial ecosystem.

Innofund

In China, to lower the individual risks and costs of innovation activities for tech-based SMEs, a funding system leveraged by Innofund, or the Tech-Based SMEs Venture Capital Introductory Fund (Ke Ji Xin Zhong Xiao Qi Ye Chuang Ye Tou Zi Yin Dao Ji Jin, 科技型中小企业创

业投资引导基金), was set up initially in 1999 by the State Council as a central government investment program (Ministry of Science and Technology of the People's Republic of China 2007b). Innofund targets small firms registered in China whose business is R&D intensive, as well as engaged in production and services in new and high-tech industrial technology-based SMEs (Innovation Fund for Technology Based Firms n.d.). After IT (40 percent), biotechnology (21 percent) is the second-largest recipient of funding under this program.

The ultimate goal of Innofund is to leverage other financial capital for innovative start-ups. Mindful of the need to create institutions providing support for new business creation, Innofund works in tandem with new business incubators that are also run by the state. As important generators of innovative technologies, as well as accelerators of technology-based enterprises, technology-based incubators (TBIs) have contributed to China's economic development and industrial restructuring by nurturing the development of a reported 15,931 successful enterprises in the past twenty years, of which 50 had gone public by 2006 (Torch High Technology Industry Development Center 2013). The Chinese government claims that Innofund, since its establishment, has received more than 30,000 applications and has provided a total of 5.3 billion RMB to almost 8,000 projects in various technology sectors. Further, the Chinese government claims that seventeen times more funds have been leveraged by Innofund from local governments and the private sector (Torch High Technology Industry Development Center 2013).[17]

As of 2010, there were 614 TBIs across the country, 197 of which have been identified by MOST as state-level TBIs, with a total incubation space of 22.7 million square meters and housing 44,750 tenant enterprises. These tenants were reported to have total business income of 262.19 billion RMB with 25,214 patents applied for and 23,394 enterprises graduated cumulatively. By 2014, there were a reported 1,700 technology incubators (TBIs), a total incubation area of 68 million square meters, 80,000 incubated enterprises, and 1.75 million jobs provided, including for nearly 150,000 college students (Ministry of Science and Technology of the People's Republic of China 2015). Ibata-Arens (2014) has compared incubation policy and practice in China with other countries in Asia and found that China has been the most interventionist (aggressive) in terms of state backing of virtually all incubation infrastructure in that country.

China joined the WTO in 2000. A decade and a half later, in February 2016, China had become the belle of the ball at the World Economic Forum meeting in Davos, Switzerland. China's vice president, Li Keqiang, announced that China's 900-million-person workforce had created 70 million enterprises (including self-employed), and China's future was now a gold mine of "mass entrepreneurship and innovation" (Li K. 2015).

With the goal of building a "modern production structure and to enhance core competitiveness," the Twelfth Five-Year Plan (2011–2015) included measures aimed at "cultivating and promoting strategic sunrise industries." Core to the plan, as in previous five-year plans, was high technology, including "new generations of information technology, new energy technologies, biotechnology, high-end equipment manufacturing, new material, and new energy cars" (Hong 2011). For the biomedical industry, the Twelfth Five-Year Plan offered a blueprint in order to strengthen innovation capacities specific to biomedicine. By the Twelfth Five-Year Plan (2011–2015), biotechnology had taken center stage as one of seven strategic "pillar" industries receiving significant government investment.[18] For example, $11.8 billion was pledged for biotechnology innovation by the Ministry of Health (Greenwood 2013). The net result was a planned $1.5 trillion boost into strategic industries, including biomedical (Lim and Rabinovitch 2010), revised upward to $1.7 trillion in the Twelfth Five-Year Plan period, including $1.5 billion for new drug development (Cao 2012). While experts doubted the reality of such large expenditures, others interpreted this as powerful signaling by the central government that biomedicals would remain a key policy target for the foreseeable future. An overview of policies aimed at increasing innovation capacity and entrepreneurial development in biomedicine and other frontier technologies appears in the policy history in table 4.1.

In 2015, the Made in China 2025 policies included new measures to stimulate indigenous innovation as part of the new China brand strategy and consistent with its move up the value chain in a number of manufactures. The expressed aim of Made in China 2025 is to make China an innovation-based manufacturing powerhouse by 2049, the centennial of the founding of the PRC. According to China State Council documents, the plan would be market oriented and be characterized by institutional reforms and financial support (Xinhua News 2015). China has also invested in overseas infrastructure.

Made in China 2025 was inspired by the Industry 4.0[19] initiative from Germany, launched in 2013 in that country. The German model provided inspiration in part because of its emphasis on "connected industry" reflecting forward and backward linkages, which could be locales for innovative activity (Wübbeke and Conrad 2015). China also wanted to build a partnership with Germany to close the technology gap faster. Thus, Made in China 2025 aimed at transforming China's manufacturing industry to be innovation driven, technology heavy, and efficiently utilizing the contribution of the human talent (State Council of the People's Republic of China 2015d). A departure from previous strategies, the Made in China 2025 initiative focused not only on the top-tier technology of the production in China but the whole production chain. It planned to optimize the manufacturing industry with emphasis in such specific fields as biopharmaceuticals and advanced information technology. Chinese sources indicated that, distinct from the Indian initiative with a similar title, Make in India, which focused on the importation of industry instead of products and technology transfer to India, China's initiative would focus more on the holistic transformation and escalation of the production that was already occurring in China. Comparison of the policy documents behind the two initiatives indicates that the focus of Made in China 2025 was to comprehensively upgrade Chinese industry so as to move away from low labor-cost production to high value-added manufacturing in priority sectors (Kennedy 2015). Make in India on the other hand focused on increasing inward FDI in manufacturing within the borders of India, with an emphasis on technology transfer across a wide range of twenty-five "priority" sectors, including biotechnology, pharmaceuticals, and chemicals (Department of Industrial Policy and Promotion 2017).[20] This difference follows from its lagging behind China in opening its knowledge and network architecture as discussed in the next chapter.

Further, China's vast global network of scientists and technologists in the Chinese diaspora has led to a tactical advantage in connecting the national capacities in innovation to entrepreneurial-ecosystem development. Returnees bring more than their technological expertise (Wang, Zweig, and Lin 2011; Liu 2012). As mentioned previously, they also bring their international (guanxi) business networks in other countries, including sources of angel investment.[21] Though the southeast of the country remains a center for international business connections, other regions in China have expanded their innovation and entrepreneurship capacity. While the discussions below of the biomedical industry, regions, and individual case studies reflect China's overall success in crafting an NTN regime of mitigated, Janus-faced openness, its archetypical NTN image has not been unblemished. Government censorship and corruption, as mentioned above and revisited in the next chapter on India, have placed a drag on innovation-system developments.

Further, the Chinese government had been utilizing online technology to control the flow of information related to sensitive political issues. This blocking of information and website accessibility has been referred to as "the Great Firewall of China" (GFW, *zhong guo guo jia fang huo qiang*, 中国国家防火墙). The coining of the term *GFW* has been attributed to an article by Charles R. Smith in 2002 (Bu 2015). GFW was part of a Chinese network-security project launched in 1998 called the Golden Shield Project (*jin dun gong cheng*, 金盾工程) as a response to the perceived threat to the CCP brought by the Democracy Party of China (DPC) in that year. The application to officially register the DPC in Hangzhou in 1998 had been denied by the government. The CCP feared that the DPC could become a real political threat because they could reach the public through the internet and therefore be harder to control. The founders were later arrested (Goldsmith and Wu 2006). The GFW project was managed by the Ministry of Public Security of the People's Republic of China at a cost equivalent to $800 million dollars from the year 1998 to 2002 (Whiting 2008). In terms of the content, the GFW was limited to blocking and filtering information on events that were thought to be the ruminations of collective action. At the time, individual critics of Chinese politics and events had not been a focus. (King, Pan, and Roberts 2013). To circumvent these limits on freedom of expression, many Chinese have used technologies like virtual private networks (VPNs) to bypass the GFW. One result was that the Xi government announced in 2017 that access to all VPNs would be completely banned starting from February 2018 (Haas 2017). In addition to squelching personal expression and putting a number of Chinese VPN start-ups out of business, Chinese scientists warned of the detrimental effects on innovation.

At a high-level national government S&T conference in 2016, an anonymous Chinese scholar was quoted as saying that government censorship of online information exchange was harming innovation in China (Beech 2016). Ironically, at the very same conference (the National Conference on Science and Technology on May 30, 2016), Chairman Xi gave a speech encouraging Chinese scientists to make breakthrough discoveries core to China becoming "the world's major S&T power" (Xinhua News 2016). Meanwhile, in Kafkaesque fashion, the principle architect of the GFW that had shut down information flow was himself unable to access information online; in other words, he had been blocked on the internet by his own invention (Beech 2016; Campbell 2016).

The CCP-led Chinese government further restricted the open flow of information preceding its Communist Party Congress (CPC), which is held every five years. In addition to generating policy initiatives, the CPC selects its supreme leader, who traditionally serves a five-year term, until the next CPC. The crackdown prior to the October 2017 CPC included sweeping restrictions of what could be stated in public (e.g., online) discourse and suspensions of television program broadcasts that might compete for viewers' attention during the CPC and its culminating three-and-a-half-hour speech by the reappointed supreme leader, Xi Jinping. His statements regarding innovation and China's "new role" were telling.

At the nineteenth Communist Party Congress in 2017, President Xi Jinping spoke at length about China's increasing role in a new global era. This role would be built, according to Xi, on a strong economy; he pointed out that China already led the world in outward foreign direct investment, trade, and foreign exchange reserves (Z. Huang 2017). Innovation was a main theme of the speech. Xi noted the need to have a market-driven system that would enable private-enterprise-based technological innovation. Xi also referred (via triple-helix structure) to the joint role of enterprise, universities, and research institutes in working together toward shared innovation goals (CGTN 2017). In a tone reminiscent of Western leaders of previous generations calling for open markets, Xi also spoke about how China "will foster a culture of innovation, and strengthen the creation, protection, and application of intellectual property" (Z. Huang 2017). The speech was also remarkable in the inclusion of references to the "rule of law" and the aim for "the great rejuvenation of the Chinese nation," which had previously received scant mention in CPC presidential speeches (CGTN 2017). In this regard, China's bet on biomedicals had seemingly paid off by the 2010s.

Industry

China has become a world leader in gene therapy and stem-cell research, in part resulting from Chinese government support (Chen 2010). Part of this rapid growth is due in part to its being unhindered by Western bioethics concerns that have led to severe restrictions on research involving (embryonic) stem cells in certain Western countries, including the United States, as well as weak protections for human test subjects (Sleeboom-Faulkner and Patra 2008). While in theory complainants have the right to petition the government for restitution, China's rule of law remained a work in progress as late as 2017, with few of those affected receiving compensation. Similarly lax regarding the rights of test subjects, India was compelled in 2013 by the Supreme Court of India to tighten regulations on clinical research involving human subjects, as discussed in the next chapter. Compared to Japan, government and business corruption is much more pervasive in China and even more problematic in India. For example, the venture Gendicine (discussed below under entrepreneurial case studies) apparently benefitted from expedited approval of its patents by the China Food and Drug Administration. Its director was later accused of taking bribes and executed (Cha 2007). The next chapter, on India's biomedical industry development, will echo the way in which corruption interferes with establishing a quality innovation system.

The medical device market in China is much smaller than biopharmaceuticals, though growing rapidly. In 2016, the market was $18.8 billion and already the second largest in the world, after the United States (LD Investment 2017). Domestic producers remain small scale and at lower tiers of the market, for example in products including syringes and wound care (Stanford Biodesign 2013). Consequently, China's entrepreneurial-ecosystem development in biomedicine has so far been centered on its biopharmaceutical industry. This experience in biomedicine reflects system-level developments in stimulating entrepreneurship.

An early success in biomedicine for China was Interferon a1b, or Ia1b, discovered by researchers at the National Institute for Viral Disease Control and Prevention (formerly known as the Chinese Academy of Preventive Medicine, Institute of Virology) in 1987. Ia1b is effective in viral infections and cancer. Ia1b is one of a number of examples of modern biomedicines derived from traditional medicines and pharmacopeia. The modernization of traditional Chinese medicine, including the isolation of active compounds, could be a source of future competitive advantage for China. TCM has been perfected over thousands of years, and these compounds have potential curative properties for everything from chronic respiratory conditions to a variety of cancers.[22] A 2012 analysis of venture capital deals by sector (Daverman and Yeo 2012) indicated that mergers and acquisitions (M & A) in pharmaceuticals had overtaken service deals, an indication that China had arrived at advanced-industrialized-nation status in these technologies. Around the same time, the SOE Sinopharm China had made inroads in gene therapy, cholera vaccines, and targeted stem-cell-based cancer treatments (*South China Morning Post* 2008). Publicly traded Chinese healthcare–related companies continued strong sales, profits, and earnings, and the health market in China is expected to grow substantially into the 2020s (*Forbes* 2017). Meanwhile, as discussed in the next chapter, India is still building on its process innovations in biosimilars (generics). These improvements in biomedical industry capacity have been, not surprisingly, in Southern Gate and other regions.

Regions

In 2012, China had more than three hundred biomedical-focused, mainly biopharmaceutical, research parks and new business incubators. These state-planned innovation and entrepreneurship clusters are spread across four main regions: northeast (Beijing), central east (Shanghai), central west (Chongqing, Chengdu), and south (Guangzhou, Shenzhen). An industry source calculated that just these four clusters had produced more than seventy-five hundred life science companies and thirty-two hundred novel drug patents and employed 250,000 people (Nastro 2015).[23] The Chinese biomedical industry has emerged as a global player, as a whole and through novel therapies developed by entrepreneurial firms, discussed below under case studies.

Another reason why the Chinese government is so keen to nurture biomedical and other high-technology manufacturing industries is that, according to Zeng Xiaodong, head of Beijing's Z-Park, even if China has 100 million people in technology-intensive work, 1.4 billion people need to eat. It is unrealistic to think that all of China's working population can become high technology. However, manufacturing is more likely to employ at the lower end than all the "app firms" that seem to be getting all the international VC thus far (Zeng interview 2016), noting that, while India is "thirty years behind China in infrastructure," it nevertheless excels when compared to China in the capacity of angel investors to understand new technology. That is, China's angel investors have earned their money in traditional industries so lack the content and also the international expertise needed to build global companies. China's government leaders have been looking to returnees to fill the gaps, and they have served as critical sources of international skills in language, education, business acumen, culture, and understanding of the regulatory frameworks governing potential export markets (Zeng interview 2016). Feng Kaidong, a research faculty member at Beijing's prestigious Peking University, who has served as policy consultant to the government on science and technology matters, in summing up China's approach, notes that the central issue with the Chinese government is that it knows that domestic producers have not been familiar at all with biotechnology in general or the rules of clinical trials specifically. Consequently, the state has been mindful of the mismatch of policy goals with the reality on the ground. Compensating for weaknesses in the local innovation system, the state has been very good at connecting the national innovation system via diaspora networks to overseas Chinese investment (Feng interview 2016). For Feng, the region to watch is Shenzen, which has so far demonstrated the capacity to lead "structural transformation" within China's national innovation system, as the ultimate effectiveness of national policy relies on the behavior of local actors including city governments. Within Shenzen, its high-IPR-producing Nanshan District has a start-up culture rivaling Silicon Valley. Shenzen, after all, managed to lure BGI away from Beijing (discussed below).

Entrepreneurial Ecosystem

State-owned enterprises (SOEs) during China's high-growth period continued to receive advantageous government support and priority attention from policy makers. Private entrepreneurs, in contrast, had been virtually invisible to the state (Zhao and La Pira 2013) and, when noticed, often passed over in favor of SOE-linked enterprises. For example, Lin (2001) shows that marketization of business was matched with a parallel political marketplace in which firms have had to trade favors with powerful state bureaucrats and their local functionaries. It goes without saying that the quality of a firm's political connections mattered more than business acumen and product quality. This situation is reminiscent of Japanese high-technology entrepreneurs' dealings with government funding sources, such as the Ministry of Economy Trade and Industry (METI) in that country's economic growth decades earlier (Ibata-Arens 2005).

Likewise, it is not unusual to have sham SOE institutional links created so that small entrepreneurial firms are able to access critical resources, including bank loans. These ties include fake joint ventures, fictional "red hat" (nominally state-owned) incorporations, and "subcontracting" from SOEs. In these arrangements, the SOE bureaucrats signing off on these marriages of convenience profit alongside the entrepreneurs actually doing the productive work. For the Schumpeterian juggernaut of creative destruction, these politico-bureaucratic arrangements with private-sector firms represent an unproductive drag on entrepreneurial activity. The scale of corruption in India has had more far-reaching impacts on its economic development, discussed in the next chapter.

Meanwhile, private small- to medium-sized enterprises had limited access to bank funds, as the major banks, in conjunction with the state (erstwhile suppressing the RMB exchange rate), service mainly SOEs and large firms.[24] China has yet to express a Schumpeterian innovation dynamic—since organic creative destruction is all but forbidden in state-led funding and policy support of SOEs and politically connected private-sector firms. Zhao and La Pira (2013) argue that China, by continuously funding state enterprises, which in turn purchase products and services from private-sector enterprises, has in effect found a Keynesian solution to the Schumpeterian problem of economic development. Others have argued that entrepreneurship in China evolved from below through trial and error on the part of nascent entrepreneurial communities. In this sense, the devolution of the central state's use of SOEs, to an opening for township and village enterprises (TVEs) (see table 1.2) has been a more radical transformation in state-private-sector relations than elsewhere in Asia. In this research, rather than benefiting from state largesse, firms disconnected (or excluded) from state networks developed alternative, market-driven, and international network forms (Nee and Opper 2012). In this manner, and reflective of the similar struggle in Japan's entrepreneurial-ecosystem development of previous decades, the nimble and quick survive in the long term, perhaps as much thanks to as despite neglect by the central state.

Nevertheless, Chinese manufacturers in particular still struggle to move up the value-added chain. The most connected to the global value chain tend to be private firms in the southeast regions, via the aforementioned diaspora networks. However, the value added remains below international market brands. Typical for original equipment manufacturers (OEMs), as they are component producers for branded clients, product improvements tend to be based on technical specs from an MNC rather than learning to respond to market needs and customer preferences. Organizational learning at the private firm level is limited in this manner.

Further, organizational learning capacity is often focused on maneuvering the unique institutional relationships with the state—a network, yes, but a politico-bureaucratic thicket, itself limited to the domestic economy. These institutional arrangements become irrelevant when competing with less politically constrained firms from other countries in international markets. That is, intimate knowledge of the domestic political context does little to support small entrepreneurial firms learning from foreign market practices. It is no surprise that China's most successful cases of internationalization (Ali Baba, etc.) are private and not state owned. Even so, few of these can say that they never benefitted from state largesse. Further, though compared to Japan, China has created an angel investment base, it has yet to reach a critical mass as in the United States.

Lack of early-stage venture capital means that otherwise talented firms must generate cash flow from noncore activity, such as service or distribution, which distracts from time spent on new product development (Chervenak 2005; Sandra Rotman Centre for Global Health 2008). Despite these institutional limitations, leaders in biomedicals have emerged in China. Firm-level case studies that manifest the state-private-sector dynamics outlined above include Beigene, BGI, Sibiono, and Sundia. BGI is one example of harnessing the diaspora.

BGI (Beijing Genomics Institute)

In late 1997, BGI's cofounders positioned China early on as the only (at that time) developing country to be a part of the Human Genome Project. Each of its three main cofounders had significant international doctoral or postdoctoral research expertise. Cofounder and president, Wang Jian, had been inspired to pursue genomics-related research as a teenager in his home province of Hunan. At the age of fourteen, he had been "sent down to the countryside" (*xiaxiang,* 下乡) a euphemism for the practice of sending intellectuals and often their children for service (and re-education) in rural communities. Wang had been sent to the mountains of his birthplace near Xiangxi, Hunan. While in Xiangxi, he noticed the high number of birth defects in the local population. In his opinion, he thought it must have something to do with the high prevalence of intra-family marriage in the community. Wang would later learn that the effect must be genetic in origin (Wang J. 2015). After completing his master's at the Beijing University of Chinese Medicine, in the early 1990s Wang studied at the University of Texas and became a researcher at the University of Iowa and University of Washington. He joined the Human Genome Project in 1997 and began working with BGI cofounder and later chairman, Yang Huanming. Yang had completed his PhD in Copenhagen as well as held postdoctoral research posts in France and the United States. Together with Yu Jun, who had a PhD in biomedical sciences from New York University and had served as a genomics researcher at the University of Washington, and a fourth founder, Liu Siqi, the group joined the Human Genome Project as the Chinese team. Their operation was affiliated at the time with the Chinese Academy of Sciences and ran out of an apartment in Beijing. It need not be mentioned the significance of this global network connectivity for maximizing tacit-knowledge exchange, with an academic scientist entrepreneurial executive team that might as easily have launched in Boston or San Diego.

Having established BGI in 1999, the Chinese research team distinguished itself early on in 2001 by completing its assignment to map 1 percent of the human genome. They were two years ahead of schedule. The team went on to help develop an antigen to the deadly SARS virus, which had erupted in 2003 in Guangdong (the megacity Shenzen is in Guangdong) and killed scores of people. Thanks to their rapid mapping of the SARS coronavirus genome and their open-source approach to sharing their research findings internationally, the team distinguished itself as lead innovator (even posting results on the social media platform Twitter). Part of the reason that BGI had left the CAS years prior was that they had been deemed "too independent" for that large state-run institution (Wang, quoted in Specter 2014). An anonymous academic was quoted as saying that BGI's move to Shenzen, far from Beijing ,was due to the politicized climate in Beijing: "It is very political.

You have two choices, either to leave China and thrive or get to the point where you don't need Beijing's money" (Anonymous interview 2017).[25] As late as 2014, however, BGI still managed to obtain $1.5 billion in loans from the China Development Bank. Other sources of funds included the Silicon Valley VC Sequoia Capital. In 2013, BGI employed an impressive four thousand people.[26]

In 2007, BGI established its research facility in Shenzen, the same year that the firm was recognized in the journal *Science* for its completion of the first "Asian genomic map." By 2010, BGI had research and other offices in the United States and Europe, reflecting its chairman's (Yang) oft-quoted acknowledgment that genomics research must be collaborative to be innovative and make progress in curing all sorts of human diseases. As early as 2010, their outside-the-box approach to innovation, including sharing results widely and in an open-access environment, attracted the attention of Bill and Melinda Gates. The Gates Foundation followed with funding and an invitation to collaborate on the cancer genome project. This international partnership helped BGI solidify its capacity in pursuing new drug discoveries based on its in-house data mining and computational power in DNA sequencing (Sender 2015). At the same time, the cofounders agree that China is poised to lead the future of genomics research, unencumbered by the regulatory hindrances within the United States and other Western systems. Company president Wang sums it up by saying: "You [the United States and the West] feel you are advanced and you are the best . . . and have all these protocols and regulations. You need somebody to change it. For the last 500 years you have been leading the way of innovation. We are no longer interested in following"[27] (Specter 2014). Beigene, a more recent biopharmaceutical start-up, has kept its relations with the Chinese state much closer.

Beigene

Beigene, an immuno-oncology biopharmaceutical start-up located in the Life Science Park of the sprawling Zhongguancun industrial district in Beijing, has been more explicitly sponsored by the Chinese state. The firm was established in 2010 by Wang Xiaodong and American Ou

Leiquang. Wang was born in Xinxiang, Henan Province, in 1963. Wang was an early beneficiary of the Open Door Policy of sending out talented young STEM students for training in Western research institutions. Having graduated from Beijing Normal University in 1980 with a degree in biology, he studied at the Southwestern Medical Center (SMC) at Texas University. Wang joined the faculty at SMC and later became a researcher at Howard Hughes Medical Institute. After being tapped by the Chinese government in 2005 to establish the National Institute of Biological Sciences in Beijing, he returned to China. In 2004, at the age of forty-one, Wang was honored by the Chinese government as the first of the Chinese Open Door students to reach the career milestone of selection into the American Academy of Sciences. Asked why he left the ivory tower of pure scientific research, Wang said that having witnessed so many family and friends stricken with cancer, he decided that "theories and concepts cannot cure disease." As a result, he decided that it was incumbent upon him to invent anticancer medicines. Wang has been driven to speed up the ability to deliver curative medicines to patients and insists that it should not matter if the best drugs are developed in China or outside China—as long as Chinese patients benefit from these innovations (Zhao 2015). Consequently, Beigene's international R&D collaborations included one with Merck for the joint development of oncology drugs (Ward and Waldmeir 2016).

By the time of its IPO in 2016, Beigene had 215 employees, 149 of whom were engaged in R&D. These researchers collaborated across the firm's research and development facilities in China, Australia, and the United States. The firm also had manufacturing operations and offices in other Chinese cities, including Shanghai and Suzhou. Its 2016 IPO raised an impressive $158 million for the start-up. Shanghai is also home to other internationally minded start-ups, including Sundia.

Sundia

Shanghai's Sundia, established in 2004, was founded by a group of returnees with a vision of starting not on the domestic market, as they observed most other returnee-led start-ups doing, but instead on the global market potential. Sundia is a contract research organization

(CRO) working with clients in Japan, Europe, and the United States, the brainchild of Wang Xiaochuan, who had been educated at Jilin University, in Chanchun, Jilin Province. In 1984 she won a UNESCO fellowship to pursue her doctoral studies at the University of Chicago. For most of her career, Wang worked in the U.S. pharmaceutical industry, gaining valuable expertise in R&D management as well as acumen for business development. In 2003, Wang was recruited by a Chinese CRO to serve as its vice president. By 2004, she had left to start Sundia, noting that "entrepreneurship was more suitable for me" (McKelvey and Bagchi-Sen 2015). Wang was able to draw from her decades in developing personal networks in the United States and China to obtain in 2004 10 million RMB in angel investment to seed fund Sundia. By 2008, Sundia had raised tens of millions of dollars from investors in China, Japan, and the United States. Soon the company was recognized by the global consulting firm Deloitte in its Fast Tech 500 ranking (2008–2012). By 2015, Sundia, located in Zhangjilang Hi-Tech Park, Shanghai, had grown to six hundred research staff, among which 8 percent were reported to be overseas returnees (McKelvey and Bagchi-Sen 2015), and 70 percent of its employees had advanced degrees.[28]

Sibiono Genetech

Sibiono Genetech, established in 1998 in Shenzen, whose blockbuster drug, Gendicine, an adenoviral agent effective in head and neck cancers, is an example of the work done by an overseas returnee enticed back home by lucrative government support. Its founder, Peng Zhaohui, had experience working for a San Diego–based U.S. biotechnology company and had studied biochemistry and genetics at Chiba University in Japan and later at UCLA. Between 1998 and 2003, Peng had used $6.25 million in government funding to attract highly qualified research professionals. Among its workforce, 10 percent were returnees like him. Between 2004 and 2008, its Gendicine gene therapy was used to treat five thousand patients (Frew et al. 2008). Thanks in part to the government support, by 2005, a year after the launch of Gendicine, Sibiono had reached breakeven (a healthy pace for a biopharmaceutical start-up, where fifteen-year returns are not unusual). The company was acquired by a subsidiary of Brenda Pharmaceuticals in 2006 and continued to develop its global market share. The speed from bench to market did not go unnoticed by its competitors in the gene therapy space. In 2007, it was accused by the U.S. biopharmaceutical company Introgen of stealing their technology, which at the time had been under development for fifteen years (Cha 2007). Peng was quoted as saying his Gendicine research had been initiated much earlier, in 1989. By 2009, Sibiono had entered a joint venture with a Canadian company to develop gene therapy and treatment centers in North America, Europe, and the Philippines. The firm was still receiving government funds as late as 2013.[29]

Conclusion

State initiatives including the Torch Program and the National Economic and Social Development Twelfth Five-Year Plan have undoubtedly played an important role in signaling national-level support of technological innovation in state- and private-sector enterprises and encouraging the development of the biomedical industry in China. As noted at the beginning of this chapter, policy support for innovation-capacity building in the strategic-technology sector and such industries as biomedicals (as well as subsequent entrepreneurial-ecosystem development) has been divided into three phases: an initial opening of the door to inward FDI and the technology that came with it (1978–1980s), engaging in international collaborations in R&D (1990s), and seeking to indigenize innovation (2000s).

As the entrepreneurial case studies show, macro-level structural institutional reform has played a significant role in the opening of China to innovation and entrepreneurship. Policies having the greatest impact include the initial connection to diaspora networks via the geographic proximity of the Southern Gate under the Open Door Policy, as well as the significant return on investment from STEM returnees from Western research institutions. These returnees have brought much more than tacit and codified knowledge and scientific training. They have also brought business partners, informal and formal investment, and international market access. Taken together, these outcomes confirm hypothesis 3 and its sub-hypotheses outlined in Chapter 2, including compensating for weaknesses in innovation capacity through utilizing (Janus-faced) international network strategies. As mentioned previously, as of 2008, 10 percent of China's workforce engaged in informal investment, while the number for India was nearly twice that. Indian and Chinese entrepreneurs can also rely on international expatriate social networks to a much greater extent than their Japanese counterparts. China's leaders are quick to embrace this international and open orientation. At the 2017 World Economic Forum annual meeting in Davos, Switzerland, in an unprecedented appearance by a Chinese president, Xi Jinping noted in his keynote speech to the assembled global capitalist elite: "Pursuing protectionism is like locking oneself in a dark room. While wind and rain may be kept outside, that dark room will also block light and air. No one will emerge a winner in a trade war" (Xi 2017). India presents useful comparisons in its own similarly Janus-like technonational opening.

CHAPTER 5   FROM CLOSED TO OPEN IN INDIA

Import Substitution, IITs, and
Liberalization

THE PURSUIT OF TECHNONATIONALISM in China and Japan in the twentieth century had been embedded in authoritarian political systems. Japan's de facto single-party state and China's one-party communist state have been insulated from certain pressures common in democratic systems—namely, having to respond to demands from citizens and firms. This is not so in India. The world's largest democracy in terms of population, India is a pluralist political system with numerous groups representing a vast array of interests.

India's technonational regime in the twenty-first century has focused on biopharmaceuticals, driven even before its independence from Britain, by goals to bring adequate healthcare to its 1.3 billion people. India has since sought to become a world leader in biomedicine. It took many decades to get to this point, however. The structure of this chapter mirrors that in previous country chapters. First, the developmental and technonational vision of India is reviewed. Second, historical periods in India's innovation system and entrepreneurial-ecosystem development are explored in terms of policy targeting in its three developmental periods following its independence from Britain in 1947: the closed-door *Swadeshi*[1] *movement* (1947–1966), characterized by classic technonationalism in which self-reliance was sought; the *Indian Institute of Technology (IIT) institutionalization* (1967–1990)[2] of a university system independent of government dictate, focused on technology education; and the open economic liberalization of its *Videshi Outlook* (1991–present), during which time its networked technonational focus emerged. Thus, India is unique among the cases herein in that it has pursued both classic technonationlism, like Japan previously, and later networked technonationalism, following China (see table 1.1). Third, the biomedical industry in India is outlined, with particular attention given to its increasing leadership in biopharmaceuticals. Lastly, the geographical regions and entrepreneurial firms in India where innovations and entrepreneurship are concentrated are presented. The chapter concludes with reflections in comparative perspective.

Vision

India's modern technonationalist vision emerged as a response to its experience as a colonized country (D'Costa 2012). Due to India's two centuries of imperial and colonial subjugation, its independence post-1947 was characterized by a pendulum swing to the extreme of statism and isolation from the world economy (Mazumdar 2012). In 1947, India embarked on a forty-plus-year import-substitution model of economic development. This, among other policies, would deter inward foreign direct investment. Deprived of capital that might have been invested into domestic institutional development, India during that period was slow to develop an innovation capacity base (Amsden 1992; Lall 1992).[3] As explained in the previous chapter, China in 1947 was at a similarly low level of per capita income. Yet China has since, due to its networked technonational strategy, far surpassed India's present-day level of economic development (Rajan and Sen 2002). While the post–World War II period was certainly nationalist, India's modern technonationalism has been less aggressive than that found in China and Japan (see also Parayil and D'Costa 2009).[4] Discussed below, India would eventually tap into its diaspora under a new NTN paradigm, gradually opening its knowledge and network architecture to the outside. In other words, India would shift from a closed KNT like Japan to a networked one. In doing so, India would follow China in moving from a codified and closed knowledge and network architecture to a tacit, somewhat open system (see figs. 2.1 and 2.2).

Nevertheless, the accelerated growth that occurred after 1991 is partly attributable to prior investments in upgrading domestic absorptive capacity, including significant investments into human-capital development, particularly in the IT sector.[5] These investments were made possible, despite a closed economy, in part due to the expansion of household savings and subsequent capital investment into machinery, transportation infrastructure, and public utilities, itself enabled by a national state-owned banking system established under Prime Minister Indira Gandhi in 1969 (S. Sen 2017; Khanna and Kaushal 2013).[6]

Nationalism in India did not end with its opening to liberalization in the 1990s. Rather, it took a new form, replacing protectionism with managed openness, like China before it, including overtures to its tens of millions in the global diaspora. This is discussed in detail below. Over time, India's technonationalism became networked like China's. The new economic nationalism that emerged with liberalization has sought to fast-track economic development by courting inward FDI for domestic technology gain (as outlined in Chapter 2). At the same time, the Indian state sought to delay alignment with international trade standards, particularly in intellectual property rights, discussed later in this chapter.

It should also be noted that within the liberal economic opening of India, while empowering a new class of technology entrepreneurs (Sengupta and Vijayraghavan 2016), it has struggled to redistribute wealth across its population—namely, its poor villages and lower castes. Compared to China's twentieth-century development, and Japan's before it, India has lagged in bringing comparable proportions of its population into the middle class (data presented below)—a process integral to sustained economic development and greater social stability (Sridharan 2004; Salve 2015).[7] As D'Costa puts it, "the glitzing of India rests on a gritty India" comprised of a citizenry that has yet to reap the benefits of economic reform (2010, 7). What follows is a review of how this technonationalist vision translated over time into three key policy periods in India: the closed door of swadeshi, IIT institutionalization, and the open door of videshi.

Closed Door of Swadeshi (1947–1966)

In 1947, India's newly independent government was keen to throw off the yoke of British colonialism. The first step in the minds of its political leadership was to decouple from the global economy, within which India had endured centuries of exploitation. India had been colonized by the British East India Company, which, after the similarly named Dutch business interest, was a preindustrial version of a multinational corporation (backed by the British military). The British East India Company's rule of India ended in 1857, after which the territory was controlled directly by the British crown.

The term *swadeshi* is derived from Sanskrit and means "of one's country," or the domestic. The concept of swadeshi was integral to the independence movement of Mahatma Gandhi. Swadeshi became an economic strategy aimed to remove the British Empire from power and nurture Indian nationalism. The Swadeshi Movement involved boycotting British products and the attempted revival of domestic goods and services that had been destroyed under British colonization.

Gandhi entreated each Indian to avoid dependence on the foreign and defend against anything that could make the "village community" vulnerable. He believed that Indians should recognize their own genius and not copy Western culture. For Gandhi, who had experienced discrimination firsthand while living in South Africa under the British, Western culture was simply a tool of colonization, designed to deny Indians their national identity. For Gandhi and his followers, swadeshi was a program for the very survival of the Indian nation. This is referred to as India's Swadeshi Movement and relates to Gandhi's prioritization of the villages of India's idyllic past, akin to Mao's focus on the peasants, in China. Gandhian values promoting the agricultural sector generally and rural villages in particular had considerable influence in the height of the independence movement in the 1940s. Eventually, however, the small-scale village community institutions inspired by Gandhi had little influence on the subsequent national technology policy regime. India has since moved on from the limitations of a rural agriculture focus to technology independence—a key characteristic of technonationalism.

India, led by Gandhi and then followed by Jawaharlal Nehru, the first prime minister of independent India, sought to bring basic healthcare to the bulk of the Indian populous, who were and remain mostly rural peasants (Aspalter n.d.; Sibal 2012; Thakur 2010). India's southern Asian geographic location means that tropical diseases endemic to that region afflicted millions of people. These include tuberculosis and malaria. India's initial decades after partition and independence would be nationalist, to be sure. Political rhetoric, while not explicitly technonationalist would aim to bring basic human health and welfare to its large population, prioritizing the health of Indians above protecting foreign patented technology. Fledgling domestic pharmaceutical and other firms also benefitted.

Under Nehru, the government adopted the concept of five-year development planning from the Soviet Union. India developed a close relationship with the Soviet Union and sent a large number of technocrats there for training. Under the Swadeshi vision, the First Five-Year Plan after 1947 aimed for complete self-reliance across all sectors of the economy. The government would have complete control over all the major sectors, such as transportation (airlines, railroads), communication services (postal, telephone, radio, and TV broadcasting), education, and healthcare. Unfortunately, the five-year plan also led to the institutionalization of the License Raj (or Permit Raj) problem. The term *License Raj* refers to the complicated and detailed system of regulations and licenses overseen by bureaucrats at all levels of the economy. It gave birth to an excessive red-tape culture, slowing down all aspects of decision making and administration. Collectively, those impediments are known as the License Permit Quota Raj problems (for simplicity, License Raj), as various government bureaucracies jostled for authority and control over business activities (Sinha 2004; Das 2006; Weede 2010). Protection of domestic firms, particularly SOEs in India called *public sector undertakings* (PSUs), was emphasized, for which high tariffs were imposed on an array of import products. India's PSUs would endure into its NTN era. India's state-private-sector structure under its version of networked technonationalism (which would manifest in that country by the 1990s) was outlined in table 1.2.

Despite bilateral ties with the Soviet Union and limited MNC presence (e.g., Monsanto, mentioned below), on the whole India closed its doors to the outside world in the initial decades after independence. This period was characterized by an inward-facing technocracy, concerned with establishing an independent, self-reliant system. In its attempt to decouple from the global trading system, India focused on import substitution and domestic market development. During this period, India's KNT was like Japan's classic technonationalist architecture. The state took a defensive posture, protectionist in its market and wherever possible closed to Western interests. In a departure from Japan's approach, which had focused on exports, India would pursue import substitution under the Swadeshi Movement. India would take some decades to shift to NTN and a quasi-open architecture, a shift from technonationalism to networked technonationalism.

Further, under Nehru's leadership, the allocation of R&D funds was limited mainly to "mission-oriented," meaning military defense and related science and technology, agencies (for reactors, rockets, etc.) while agriculture and medical research saw negligible growth. During the Nehru-era (1947–1967) development of science and technology, elite scientists (such those who were heads of prominent science institutions) were made a part of the bureaucracy and were given the same prestigious status as those of administrative officers. This was a great honor in India's hierarchical, meritocratic civil service. With this, India became a modern technocracy. Further, India's Planning Commission vice chairman reported directly to the prime minister.

Within the technocracy, policy making was overseen by these elite scientists. For example, in 1958 the Indian parliament approved the first Scientific Resolution Policy (SRP). This document is still an important landmark, as it has been repeatedly used to justify the funding and expansion of all aspects of science and technology. This period also witnessed the creation and expansion of numerous science and technology departments and such agencies as the Department of Atomic Energy (DAE), the Council of Scientific and Industrial Research (CSIR), the Defence Research and Development Organization (DRDO), and the first five Indian Institutes of Technologies (IITs). By 1967, the government was forced to shift focus in order to resolve food and other shortages caused by rapid population growth.

Initially, the policies denying intellectual property protections for Western pharmaceutical products were placed in this light—as the only way to bring self-sufficiency and basic human healthcare to the majority of the population, manifested over the years in the intellectual property regime and patent laws (discussed below). Inward-facing bureaucrats led a regime of license and permit permissions (the License Raj introduced above) in which they were the only gateway to economic opportunity for old and new firms alike. This inward-looking policy regime would continue more than a decade longer than in China, which had opened by 1978. Due to the vast human health needs, India's initial quasi-openness to biopharmaceuticals laid, in Janus-like fashion (defensive to outside, protective to inside), the foundations for later strategic investments in that industry.

Biomedical Policies

The initial foundations of capacity building in biomedicals and efforts in the development of the pharmaceutical sector by the government of India can be traced back to the Industrial Policy Resolution of 1948. At the time, due to the healthcare needs of the populace, the country was open to medicines made by foreign companies, though overall the country remained closed to foreign firms. Instead, India adopted a liberal position toward multinational pharmaceutical corporations and permitted them to establish plants without requiring licensing agreements. Despite the rapid growth of the sector, foreign companies had the typical offshoring production structure of maintaining high added value in their home countries, with low-level assembly plants in India (*Economic and Political Weekly* 1954).

The government responded in its Industrial Policy Resolution of 1956 (Department of Industrial Policy and Promotion 2017), making it mandatory for foreign multinational companies in their Indian plants to produce drugs from the R&D stage to end products. Moreover, the pharmaceutical industry was targeted due to the "high social value" of medicinal products. During this period, numerous domestic companies also entered the market as state-owned firms (PSUs).

Five-Year Plans

Key policies governing intellectual property rights and inward FDI in India were part of larger schemes targeting the economic development of the economy as a whole, while seeking to improve the basic welfare of its large population (in 1947 already 330 million).[8] India initiated a series of five-year plans, starting in 1951 and continuing to the present (with a few hiatus periods, often due to shifts in political leadership). Prior to liberalization in the 1990s, the plans focused on attaining self-reliance in agriculture initially and later industrial development. The review here focuses on aspects of the plans through the current period that have addressed innovation-system and entrepreneurial-ecosystem development, paying close attention to those that targeted the biotechnology industry. Just as India was slow to embrace foreign firms, the country eschewed the international intellectual property rights regime for most of the twentieth century.

The Science and Technology Plan (1974–1979) made explicit reference to the development of indigenous capacity and was framed in terms of reducing dependence on foreign sources. Unlike the export-oriented Asian Tiger economies (South Korea, Singapore, Hong Kong and Taiwan), Indian policies aimed at import substitution. Import substitution in India was driven by the desire to industrialize through creating a domestic-heavy capital-goods sector, building on India's large domestic market and existing domestic capitalists. From its independence through the plan period, India would remain focused on the bottom half of the knowledge and network architecture—closed to the outside world's business networks and attempting to go it alone to upgrade its technology base (see fig. 2.1).[9]

By the mid-1980s, the government of Rajiv Gandhi (the seventh prime minister of India, 1984–1989) announced a new policy on Technology Missions. At the time, the government began to recognize the extent to which India benefited from its diaspora networks, which until this time had been ignored at best. An early example of this albeit limited warming to the diaspora included Rajiv Gandhi relying on Sam Pitroda, a non-resident Indian and leading technology expert with a patenting record. He was the key person behind the creation of the Center for the Development of Telematics, which helped to develop India's first rural digital exchange and laid the foundations of India's telecommunications revolution. However, the rise of new technologies (including microelectronics, information technologies, and biotechnologies) and their institutionalization led to rapid urbanization and problems with absorption and development in rural communities, meaning that the majority of the Indian population remained excluded from these technology advances. Meanwhile, a group of technocrats had been working to increase the skills of future generations of Indians.

Human-Capital Development

The concept of the Indian Institute of Technologies (IITs) was envisaged even before India won independence from the British. After the end of World War II, the Viceroy's Executive Council was formed, while India remained under British rule. Previously, in 1944, as the first head of the Department of Planning and Development in India, Ardeshir Dalal believed that the future of India would depend more on technology than capital. From this vision emerged the initial blueprints for the Indian Institute of Technology (Francis 2011).

In 1946, Sir Jogendra Singh, who was member of the Viceroy's Executive Council appointed a twenty-two-member committee, led by Nalini Ranjan Sarkar. The Sarkar Committee was concerned initially with improving India's human capital, especially technically trained workers. The committee also concluded that in view of the geographic size of India and the location of industries across the Indian subcontinent, a regional distribution of higher education institutions for technical training would be needed. In the initial recommendation, the Sarkar Committee also suggested the expansion and development of existing and new technical institutes so that students from poorer, rural communities could take advantage of these world-class institutes without having to travel long distances.

Two members of the Sarkar Committee were trained MIT engineers, who recommended the establishment of five "higher technical institutions" across India. Further, the institutes were modeled on the structures of the MIT, as MIT's education involved teaching engineers the practical and theoretical sciences along with humanities.

The first Indian Institute of Technology (IIT) was launched in May 1950 in Kharagpur, West Bengal. The government, following the recommendations of the Sarkar committee, established IIT Bombay (1958), IIT Madras (1959), IIT Kanpur (1960), and IIT Delhi (1961). The Sarkar Committee Report, however, did not address how to fund the establishment and maintenance of the IITs. As a result, India sought aid from the outside, especially technical expertise and finance. While originally India obtained aid from UNESCO, the institutes would eventually be funded by the Indian Ministry of Human Resources Development.

These technical institutes served as a basis for building up the technoindustrial environment. Other technical and management institutes were established, including the Birla Institute of Technology and Science, Pilani (BITS Pilani) and the Indian Institutes of Management (IIMs) (Chopra and Sharma 2009). While the vast scale of India's education system and history is an important part of India's economic rise generally, it is beyond the scope of this chapter to attempt to present it. To wit, one author indicated that "Indian higher education seems like an enigma enveloped in contradiction" in that pearls of superb teaching and research were surrounded in a sea of substandard colleges (Altbach 1993a, 4). The IITs, however, are noteworthy due to their status as the first of their kind in India. The IITs are autonomous bodies governed by their own act of parliament. In contrast, under the affiliated university system, other Indian universities are governed by a regulatory body called the University Grants Commission.

Through the IITs, India asserted two things. First, it sought the independence of the nation from foreign technology (though, as mentioned above, India was not so closed as to refuse the advice of foreign experts or foreign technological know-how). Second, the change in the education system via the IITs enabled India to train its own scientific workforce. The parliament of India under the Institute of Technology (Amendment) Act of 1963, declared the IITs as an "Institution of National Importance" (Indian Institute of Technology 1963). As of 2017, there were twenty-three IITs offering BS to PhD degrees in all STEM fields. From their origins in the visions of Western-educated Indian technocrats in then colonial India, the first IITs came to fruition soon after independence. By the 1960s, they were on their way to becoming an integral part of the Indian higher education landscape.

IIT Institutionalization (1967–1990)

The second period after India's closed-door Swadeshi Movement can be called the institutionalization of the Indian Institutes of Technology, or IIT institutionalization phase. It was characterized by progress toward building absorptive capacity in the education system and nurturing human capital, particularly STEM students. India spent several additional decades building its cornerstone of codified, formal knowledge capacity, notably in the creation of the IT-focused IITs. The success of the IIT approach to educating a STEM workforce was forged over decades of attempts to improve the quality of the education system (Altbach 1993a; King 1984; Yusuf and Nabeshima 2007). Though in the initial iterations, IITs were focused on building technology capacity in military (like China, responding to its historical experience of foreign expropriation of domestic resources, focused on military technology, in the aim of buttressing defenses against potential foreign usurpers).

In subsequent decades, India moved into telecommunications, information technology, and most recently biopharmaceuticals. The IITs were the first to be established, followed by regional engineering colleges and other training institutes (Chopra and Sharma 2009). Though the most independent from government, the IITs have received the largest share of government funds (42 percent in 2002). The IITs have succeeded in training the technological workforce in India and providing industry with some of the best minds in the country with technical expertise. IIT graduates have achieved success in a variety of professions, resulting in the globally recognized IIT "brand." However, the IIT brand is not unblemished.

For example, some have complained about the government initiative to bring a "reservation" system to university entrance for 50 percent of applicants (setting aside this proportion for lower castes) in an affirmative-action-style admissions process. In addition, though the number of IITs has grown considerably over time, investments into infrastructure have not kept pace with this growth. Consequently, the quality of research and teaching facilities has declined. Chopra and Sharma (2009) note that such industry associations as the National Association of Software and Service Companies (NASSCOM) (India's premier IT trade association) have complained that as few as 25 percent of Indian engineering graduates are employable. However, the biggest criticism of IITs is that IIT-trained personnel often leave the country to work for large MNCs all over the world, which offer them better opportunities in terms of salary, work environment, and quality of life. Further, many top IIT students leave India to pursue higher education overseas (e.g., the United States, England, Australia). This brain drain has undermined the very intention behind the creation of IITs (Saravia and Miranda 2004). Even so, the fact that India has developed an educational system to create globally competitive human capital, considering the point from which it started, is impressive.

In 1950, there were 50 engineering institutes in India; the number increased to 1,668 by 2007, and in that year, the number of graduates had risen to 20,000 per year (Chopra and Sharma 2009), though others estimate the number to be much higher (Gupta and Gupta 2012). By 2012, it was estimated that India had the largest higher education system in the world, with more than 26,000 institutions, including 504 universities and 25,951 colleges. The education market was estimated to be $40 billion per year. State universities comprised 48 percent of all universities (Gupta and Gupta 2012). During the IIT period (1967–1990) while India was turned inward, building up the absorptive capacity in its technically trained workforce, it also moved away from what India saw as a foreign-controlled global intellectual property rights (IPR) regime.

Patent Act of 1970

The IPR regime in place in India as of 1947 had been inherited from the British colonial administration. For example, the British-imposed Patent Act of 1911 remained effective until 1970 (Bagchi, Banerjee, and Bhattacharya 1984). As a poor country, India lacked the intellectual capacity at the time for product innovations, so the protective benefits of IPR accrued to foreign firms. By 1959 leading legal scholars had laid out proposals for a new legislation to replace the 1911 law, arguing that the social costs of the diffusion of existing inventions (e.g., curative medicines) were low, while the private costs of inventing a marketable product were prohibitively high in India, not to mention other less developed countries. Aiming to bring affordable medicines to India's majority poor, rural population, the 1970 act reduced the number of years of IP protection from sixteen to as low as seven in the case of food, drugs, and medicines.

The Patent Act of 1970 also intended to shift the benefits from the first innovators in the West to the second innovators in India via offering only "narrow" protection on patents (Ramani and Maria 2005). Narrow protection would be provided on the condition that the materials did not include "living entities of natural or artificial origin." Entities no longer protected under the new law included viruses, genes, bacteria, algae, and other biological materials that would serve as the basis for India's biopharmaceuticals, the core of its fledgling biomedical industry. Instead, second innovators in India could acquire knowledge on these products without having to enter into licensing agreements or pay royalty fees to the original researcher, usually located in Western countries (Department of Industrial Policy and Promotion 2003). This open yet closed knowledge and network architecture, drawing in foreign technology (upper right quadrant of the KNT) while building up domestic capacity (lower left quadrant of KNT), would be the basis for India's subsequent growth.

Indian pharmaceutical companies soon began producing essential drugs like antibiotics at such low prices that India quickly became an exporter in this space. Thus, in addition to supporting development in Indian pharmaceuticals' export capacity, the gains for human health and welfare at the lowest levels of income were noteworthy. However, this came at the cost of the withdrawal of many foreign firms from the Indian market (Bagchi, Banerjee, and Bhattacharya 1984). Further, the generally weak innovative capacity of most Indian firms, along with an underdeveloped domestic market for foreign goods, prevented India from reaping the maximum benefits from the 1970 law. As discussed in the previous chapter, unlike India, China was able to use the lure of its domestic market to extract concessions from multinational corporations via technology-sharing agreements (and occasionally through the expropriation of foreign-firm IP). Likewise, Japan, which offered patent protection much later than British India, had continued to outpace patent growth by India. The reason was that Japan under its classic technonational stance virtually excluded all foreign firms from the domestic market at the time, while still being able to build on existing innovation capacity via technology importing from its main security partner, the United States (in its own version of an open yet closed KNT).

India's lower level of economic development led the government to delay compliance to international standards as long as possible. Many events beyond what is covered in this chapter occurred between India's Swadeshi period (launched in 1947), its IIT institutionalization after 1967, and 1991. Nevertheless, 1991 was a crucible point for India. The balance-of-payments crisis in 1991 precipitated radical reform and (some would say forced) liberalization at the hands of an IMF bailout. Sputtering through the early part of the 1990s, the Eighth Five-Year Plan (1992–1997) dealt mainly with recovering from the account deficit. The Ninth Five-Year Plan (1997–2002) emphasized education and labor skills improvement. Other five-year plans, as well as policies supporting development of biomedical innovation and entrepreneurship, are listed in table 5.1. When India finally opened to the outside world, it did so because it was compelled by foreign entities—namely, the IMF. In 1991 India would open its Janus temple to face the outside world.[10]

TABLE 5.1.

Key policy history: Biomedical innovation and entrepreneurship in India

Year	Name	Objectives
1958	Scientific Policy Resolution (SOR)	First science policy in independent India.
1990	Industrial Policy: Policy Measures for the Promotion of Small-Scale and Agro-Based Industries and Changes in Procedures for Industrial Approvals	To attract foreign technology and allow investment up to 40 percent of equity. 100 percent export-oriented units and units to be set up in export processing zones.
1991	Statement on Industrial Policy	Liberalizing the industry from such regulatory devices as licenses and controls.
1996	CSIR (Council of Scientific and Industrial Research) 2001 Vision and Strategy	Aims to establish CSIR as a model organization for scientific industrial research: a global R&D platform providing competitive R&D and high-quality science-based technical services worldwide.
1996	Establishment of Technology Development Board	Accelerating the development and commercialization of indigenous technology. Seek to support entrepreneurs through financial assistance (equity, loans, grants). Support industry-university-government coordination. Foster innovative culture through contract and cooperative research.
1999	The Patents (Amendment) Act	Bring India's patent regime into compliance with the WTO TRIPs agreement: especially product patents in the areas of drugs, pharmaceuticals, and agrochemicals.
2002	Tenth Five-Year Plan (2002–2007)	Biomedical sector highlighted, provisions to better enhance human health, and aims for more effective regional targeting.
2003	The Science and Technology Policy (STP)	R&D system for creating a national innovation system.
2005	Special Economic Zones (SEZs) Act	Establish economic zones to attract inward FDI, foster technology commercialization.
2007	Eleventh Five-Year Plan (2007–2012)	Sustainable economic development especially in rural regions and with minority communities.
2012	Twelfth Five-Year Plan (2012–2017)	Inflation control and human-capital development.
2013	Science, Technology and Innovation Policy (STI)	Seeks an inclusive development of the people, expanding private-sector participation in R&D technology and innovation activities, establishing an ecosystem for innovative abilities, and achieving gender parity through international cooperation and alliances.

(continued)

TABLE 5.1. (*continued*)

Year	Name	Objectives
2013	Science, Research and Innovation System for High Technology (SRISHTI)	Science-led solutions for sustainable and inclusive growth.
2014	Make in India	Transform India into a global design and manufacturing hub.
2015	Skill India—National Skill Development Mission	Convergence across sectors and states in skill training activities. Expedite decision making across sectors to achieve skill-based training at scale with speed and standards.
2016	Start-up India	Foster entrepreneurship and promoting innovation by creating an ecosystem that is conducive for growth of new firm start-ups. Become a nation of job creators instead of job seekers. Build on success in IT to grow potential in other areas, including education and manufacturing. Expand efforts from a focus on tier 1 cities to tier 2 and tier 3 cities, including semiurban and rural areas.
2017	Innovate in India (i3)	Collaborate with World Bank to boost India's biopharmaceuticals by accelerating the translation of research concepts into viable products, supporting an entrepreneurial ecosystem, and enabling networks for industry-academia collaboration.

SOURCES: Council of Scientific and Industrial Research, Ministry of Science and Technology 1996; Ministry of Law, Justice and Company Affairs 1999; N. Sen 2003; Planning Commission 2013; Press Information Bureau 2013, 2017; Department of Industrial Policy and Promotion 2014; Planningcommission.gov 2014, n.d.; MSME 2017; Chand n.d.; Skilldevelopment.gov n.d.; Startupindia.gov n.d.

NOTE: The Ministry of Finance classifies cities as X, Y, or Z based on the basis of a grading structure rather than tier 1, tier 2, tier 3. There are eight X cities, including Delhi, Mumbai, Kolkata, Bangalore, Pune, Chennai, Ahmedabad, and Hyderabad. The Reserve Bank of India uses a different classification system based on population. Tier 1 includes any city with a population greater than 100,000, and tier 2 includes any city with a population between 50,000 and 99,000.

Open Economic Liberalization of the Videshi Outlook (1991–Present)

The third period in India's evolution of networked technonationalism and concomitant knowledge and network regime, initiated in 1991, is considered India's most significant postindependence economic transformation. In that year, India opened its doors to the outside world and (like contemporaneous China's "gearing with the world" under its international collaboration period initiated in the 1990s) embraced economic liberalization and globalization (Mukherji 2008).[11] Above all it sought to build capacity in frontier technology-based innovation and entrepreneurship. During this period, the Indian government courted inward foreign direct investment and multinational corporate partnerships like never before. This period is often referred to as India's Videshi Outlook. The term *videshi* derives from Sanskrit, "not of one's country," or foreign.

After 1989, a series of internal and external events, such as the collapse of the Soviet Union, the Gulf War, runaway inflation, and depleted foreign exchange reserves in India, led the Indian government to shift its approach from the previous Swadeshi Movement to the Videshi Outlook (Richardson 2002). In other words, the door to the Indian economy was swung open—for the first time since colonization—to trade and investment with the rest of the world (Richardson 2002). This meant the rapid privatization, liberalization, and globalization of the Indian economy. It would take at least another decade, however, before India was ready to accept international IP standards and to fully embrace its diaspora, under a newly assertive networked technonational regime. This lag behind China would continue to have economic consequences for India into the 2000s.

China, discussed in the previous chapter, began steps under Deng Xiaoping toward liberalization, leading to the Open Door Policy in 1978. India's later opening was precipitated in part by the financial crisis in 1991, which enabled reformers in the government to overcome vested domestic interests, who had until that time resisted reforms (D'Costa 2005; Mukherji 2008).[12] The economic liberalization was led by a new administration, which was formed in June 1991, under India's tenth prime minister, P. V. Narasimha Rao. The main thrust of the new economic reforms was the introduction of the New Industrial Policy (NIP) in that year. Nehru-era technocracy continued to persist but was confined mostly to the areas where technocrats were entrenched, including atomic energy, defense, and space research.

The 1990s saw dramatic change in all other areas. The emphasis in the postliberalization phase was in building new science and technology policy regimes. Private-sector representatives assumed a greater role in industrial policy making. Further, with the entrance of MNCs and increased inward FDI, Indian companies (most of which were family owned and whose revenue stream relied on political contacts, similar to China decades earlier) had to reorient themselves to a privatized and internationalized market in order to survive.

The 1991 industrial reforms related to the IMF bailout were undertaken primarily to remove licensing-related barriers to entry that had been preventing the manufacturing sector to take advantage of economies of scale. To facilitate the flow of FDI, the foreign equity holding limit was increased from 40 percent to 51 percent. The 1991 liberalization and concomitant economic reforms of the Indian economy gave an impetus to entrepreneurial activities. The increase since in new firm start-ups has been attributed to that. For example, in 1995, first-generation companies accounted for 9.78 percent of Group A–listed firms.[13] In 2011, they constituted 15.08 percent (University of Pennsylvania, Wharton School, 2012). Since liberalization, India has had to compete for inward FDI with its neighbor to the north, China. Between 1992 and 1998, India was able to obtain $12 billion in foreign investments. In the same period, China had twenty times that at $240 billion (Rajan and Sen 2002).

The Patent Amendment Act of 1999 was put in place during the Ninth Five-Year Plan, after the signing on of India to the WTO TRIPS. The 1999 act was the first step in a series of measures expected to bring India up to the "standards" of TRIPS, the creation of which had been the result of intense lobbying on the part of the pharmaceutical giant Pfizer and others—who had India in its sights (Burris, Drahos, and Shearing 2005). At the same time, the 1999 act included more protections to the biotechnology industry, such as pharmaceuticals and agrochemicals. The Indian government, meanwhile, signaled to domestic firms that the initial implementation would be limited, and it intended to delay full implementation until the end of the ten-year probation period, whose clock had started ticking back in 1995 when India signed on to TRIPS (Kumar and Tiku 2009). The government would remain true to its word. The closed-door policy of the Swadeshi Movement had undoubtedly helped to develop the domestic pharmaceutical industry in India. Even as the clock ticked down to India's TRIPS compliance deadline, the government would persist in protecting its domestic industry on humanitarian grounds.

Biopharmaceuticals were the subject of renewed focus as recently as 2017, as targets for investment under the Innovate in India (i3) program launch. Government statements at the time indicated the "national Biopharma mission" as key to India's future competitiveness (Press Information Bureau 2017).[14] Its focus on bringing basic welfare services to rural peasants would lead its technocracy to engage in technology acquisition in medicines wherever possible. This meant denying patent rights to foreign pharmaceutical firms for many drugs, including antibiotics and treatments of diseases endemic to the Indian subcontinent. These measures were embedded within India's five-year economic growth plans.

India's young, English-speaking population and international professional diaspora is younger than China's, highly technical in its training, and increasingly entrepreneurial abroad and at home (Wadhwa et al. 2007). This could be a source of competitive advantage in the coming years. It remains to be seen whether India's robust democratic political system—in contrast to the authoritarian and orderly states in East Asia—will be a boon to its entrepreneurial-ecosystem development. Even in India's isolationist period, it supported domestic entrepreneurs (Khanna 2007).

Entrepreneurial Ecosystem

Policy documents from as early as the 1960s noted the importance (and necessity) of entrepreneurship and small business in general (Mukherji 2009). At the time, the Indian economy had yet to develop its intellectual property capacity and institutions to support opportunity entrepreneurship. This would take decades to establish. Consistent across the decades was the government use of five-year economic development plans based on the Soviet model, as mentioned above and discussed in policy context below.[15]

When entrepreneurship was eventually promoted after the 1960s, it was initially in support of family-run businesses, which depended on connections within government agencies. Further, part of the measures supporting the goal of self-reliance meant that tight restrictions keeping out imports of consumer goods and FDI shielded domestic companies from foreign competition. These measures were in place for all sectors of the economy. So, from the 1950s to 1980s, the main aim of private firms was to get government licenses rather than focusing on improving the quality of goods, capturing markets, funding R&D, and developing innovative technologies, integral to building innovation-system capacity (Kohli 2006). In sum, India's entrepreneurs would undergo a period of protective isolation from the outside world, while government bureaucrats would become the sole gatekeepers to economic opportunities. Nascent entrepreneurs and existing firms, in order to survive and prosper, would have to become oriented toward currying political favor with government officials, similar to China's politico-economic model of state bureaucrats as economic opportunity gatekeepers (Lin 2001).

Such institutes as the National Science and Technology Entrepreneurship Development Board (NSTEDB) and Science and Technology Entrepreneurs Park (STEP) were created in 1982 and 1984 respectively. The NSTEDB is an institutional mechanism to promote self-employment in the country and to match underemployed science and technology workers to jobs. NSTEDB promotes STEP and other mechanisms of high-technology entrepreneurship. STEP aims to provide a comprehensive approach to innovation and entrepreneurship involving education, training, research, finance, management, and government. As mentioned in the previous chapter, the focus of Made in China 2025 was to comprehensively upgrade Chinese industry, so as to move away from low labor-cost production to high value-added manufacturing in priority sectors as part of its indigenization of innovation strategy (Kennedy 2015). Make in India on the other hand focuses on increasing FDI and encouraging national and multinational companies to manufacture in India, with an emphasis on technology transfer in twenty-five priority sectors, reflecting its earlier stage of development (Dasgupta 2016).

At the same time, the government has not been as insulated as other Asian economies from the demands of various domestic groups. These pressure groups hail from India's heterogeneous business community, class and caste constituencies, and a variety of citizen's organizations, who make numerous demands on the Indian state. Some would argue that, for India's government, while seeking inclusive development, responding to these demands has instead led to anti-innovative policies. Though it is beyond the aim of this chapter to explore in depth the scale and scope of the sociopolitical embeddedness of economic activity, the impact of corruption on economic development is one example.

China and India have both had endemic government corruption. One reason India lags in developmental progress when compared to China is that Chinese government officials down to the local level have responded to incentives to increase the size of the economic pie. In India, in contrast, skimming off the top on the part of government bureaucrats has occurred without adding value, which has slowed progress in that country (Khanna 2007). For example, findings indicate that economies that reward non-rent-seeking entrepreneurial activities grow faster than those that do not (Murphy, Shleifer, and Robert 1991; Warner 2015, 75; Ács and Varga 2005). This is reflected partly in the lag of India's entrepreneurial ecosystem behind that of China's.

Even though the Eleventh Five-Year Plan (2007–2011) targeted waste and corruption to reduce the drag on innovation capacity and FDI, India continues to perform poorly. According to the World Bank's Doing Business 2018 report, India ranked 100 compared to China at 78, Singapore at 2, and Japan at 34 (World Bank 2017). India's ranking in barometers like "Dealing with Construction Permits" and "Enforcing Contracts" is even worse at 181 and 164 respectively. According to the report, India ranked 131 in 2016 and 130 in 2017.

Access to even basic services—utilities, police service, public schools, public health, courts—is difficult without greasing palms across the web of India's red tape (e.g., the License Raj system). According to Transparency International's[16] 2017 Global Corruption Barometer report on the Asia-Pacific region, the bribery rate in India was highest in Asia at

69 percent, compared to 26 percent in China and 0.2 percent in Japan. The survey showed that an astounding seven in ten people in India had paid a bribe to access basic services, including healthcare. India fared better than China, however. The survey also found that China had the highest percentage of respondents who perceived that corruption had worsened since 2014 (73 percent). Only 41 percent thought so in India, while 28 percent thought so in Japan (Pring 2017).

The role of corruption in disrupting investments is not limited to the level of corruption but also the predictability of corruption. The more unpredictable the corruption, the worse the impact on investments (Campos and Lien 1999). The unpredictability of corruption in India is made worse by the fact that India into the 2010s still lacked legislation dealing with antigraft policies in the private sector.

Embracing the Diaspora

The Indian government took much longer than China to recognize the asset to the domestic economy of its diaspora, potential returnees who had developed important skills in foreign education institutions and international companies. Its diaspora (comprised of NRIs and persons of Indian origin, POIs) would be generally neglected until nearly the twenty-first century. Meanwhile, the country has benefitted from among the highest global remittance incomes in recent decades, mostly from lower-skilled NRIs in Gulf countries (Kapur 2003; Khadria 2006). In 2011, for example, remittances totaled $64 billion (Rajan, Kurusu, and Saramma Panicker 2013). India's diaspora in the postcolonial period differed from China's. For example, India's NRIs were more likely to have lower education and skill levels than the professional class that had left China after the Communist Revolution.[17]

As of 2010, 25 million ethnic Indians were residing outside India. About a third resided in Southeast Asia, while the next largest percentage were located in Gulf countries. These migrants tend to be semiskilled workers. Of the skilled migrants to developed countries, the United States attracts nearly 80 percent (Khadria 2006). The Indian diaspora is mainly in the United States (3.2 million), followed by Saudi Arabia (1.79 million), the United Arab Emirates (1.7 million), Malaysia

(1.91 million), and Sri Lanka (1.6 million). By 2011, Britain had more than three times the number of ethnic Indians (1.5 million) as Chinese (300,000). The number of ethnic Indians residing in Japan was negligible, while China had more than half a million living there (*Economist* 2011a; Greater Pacific Capital 2013).

Through the 1980s, while China was engaged with its international diaspora and incentivizing their return in an open jus sanguinis posture—India kept a standoffish policy of jus soli, making it clear to all in and outside the country that only resident Indians were worthy. According to one scholar, the prolonged exclusion of critical human capital from the developmental agenda of India "must rank as among the most egregious cases of mismanagement of a national resource" (Khanna 2007, 181). Observing the relative technology and entrepreneurial accomplishments of Indians in the United States is indicative of the depth of this underutilized resource. For example, studies on the Silicon Valley innovation and entrepreneurial cluster found that Indian nationals led a high proportion of technology start-ups; and the now well-known TiE network brought Indians of all ethnic and regional backgrounds together (Saxenian 1999). India finally warmed to its diaspora after the 1991 liberalization, though it took more than a decade after that to see significant policy changes to encourage returnees.

By 2004, India had created an entire ministry devoted to engaging with the Indian diaspora, the Ministry of Overseas Indian Affairs (Khanna 2007). China's equivalent, the Overseas Chinese Office, had been reestablished in 1978 nationally and in every municipality. After the dot-com bubble burst in the United States in the year 2000, India received 35,000 professional returnees—though in comparison a tiny fraction of the number of Chinese returnees who were leading existing and new firms. Nevertheless, India's new embrace of its diaspora would be consistent with the NTN thesis (upper right quadrant of KNT) in that the government began to tap into its international networks of NRI professionals and a growing number of returnees in pursuit of developmental goals. Overtures to the Indian diaspora increased after 2014, when the Bharatiya Janata Party (BJP) rose to national power.

Hindu Nationalism and Liberalism

The BJP has been considered to be closer to the diaspora than its predecessor, the Congress Party. For example, the BJP government launched the Pravasi Bharatiya Divas (Non-Resident Indian Day) in 2003. Prime Minister Atal Bihari Vajpayee (1998–2004) formed the High Level Commission to the Indian Diaspora—whose foundational report, published in 2002, continues to be the guiding framework for India's engagement with its diaspora. The committee was composed of mostly senior BJP parliamentarians and foreign service officials.[18]

According to the historian Ramachnadra Guha (2014), in the preindependence era, under the leadership of Mahatma Gandhi, the Indian National Congress (INC) sought to establish the party's relationship with NRIs. In fact, in 1922, the INC had also prepared a document called "Publicity Work in America: A New but Permanent Plan." According to Guha (2014), the plan sought to "create and control public opinion in foreign countries at [India's] own expense in order to safeguard the interest of her sons and daughters, and to let the world know of India's ideals." However, after independence in 1947, the INC's engagement with the diaspora was limited. This aloof posture maintained into the 1990s. Rather, after liberalization in 1991, it was the BJP and not the INC that sought actively to build and maintain a link with the diaspora (Guha 2014). Since the BJP's Narendra Modi took office as prime minister in 2014, the inflow of FDI reflects how the diaspora community and international investors have responded to the renewed FDI-friendly policies. Inward FDI in education and R&D, for instance, increased from $107 million to $394 million between 2013–2014 and 2015–2016 (Reserve Bank of India 2017a).

During the fourteenth Pravasi Bharatiya Divas (Non-Resident Indian Day) held in Bangalore in January 2017, the India prime minister called on the NRI community to invest in India. In that speech, he added, "To me, FDI means First Develop India through Foreign Direct Investment, the norms of which have been fully liberalized for non-resident Indians and persons of Indian origin" (*Hindustan Times* 2017). For instance, from 2015 investments made by Indians in the diaspora and their descendants from their rupee-denominated accounts in India would not be treated as foreign investment. Still, "fully liberalized" was an exaggeration as sectors including insurance and defense still maintained caps on inward FDI. Nevertheless, investments by overseas Indians would be considered domestic, encouraging more inflows (Reserve Bank of India 2017b). He added that his government was trying to turn "brain drain into brain gain" and that it would be possible with the help of the overseas Indian community (*Hindustan Times* 2017). This was an extension of what Modi highlighted during his first official visit to the United States in September 2014. In a letter titled "An Invitation to Make in India," in the *Wall Street Journal*, Modi wrote that "India will be open and friendly—for business, ideas, research, innovations and travel." His letter also put an emphasis on the enduring importance of the Indian American community, "a metaphor for the potential of our partnership, and for the possibilities of an environment that nurtures enterprise and rewards hard work" (Modi 2014).

Executive-Class Indians in the Diaspora as Bridges

The networked technonationalism of India has also drawn in the network of Indian executives in MNCs and used them as leverage into inviting more expertise and investment into India. The likes of Kanwal Rekhi (Novell) (IIT-Bombay, 1967), Alok Aggarwal (IBM) (IIT-Delhi and Johns Hopkins), Rajat Gupta (McKinsey) (IIT-Delhi, 1971, and Harvard Business School, 1973), and Ashwini Gupta (American Express) (IIT-Delhi, 1974, and Columbia University, 1977) are but a few examples. For example, it was Rajat Gupta who led McKinsey to be a pioneer in subcontracting research services in India and also helped to establish the Indian School of Business Hyderabad.

As mentioned above, the economic liberalization of the 1990s stimulated interest by foreign investors in the Indian market. Venture capital and private equity have entered India at a steady pace since. By 2000, with the aid of the boom in IT and communications, India received $1.16 billion in investments, with an average deal size of $4.14 million. Though this trend fell slightly between 2001 and 2003, it has since risen, both in terms of overall investments and the size of the investments. One of the key players likely to invest in early-stage companies in India in the mid-2000s were entrants from the United States, which include Sequoia Capital India, Oak Investment Partners, Artiman Ventures, Norwest Venture Partners, and Austin Ventures, all whose key principles were people of Indian origin (Evalueserve 2006). Inward FDI has also been facilitated by the Make in India, Digital India, and Startup India campaigns and the implementation of the goods and services tax, allowing 100 percent FDI in limited liability partnerships and the easing of regulations for setting up offices. The OECD (2018) reported that inward FDI to India was up to $44.458 billion by 2016. Between 2014 and 2017, the inflow to drugs and pharmaceuticals averaged $1.036 billion (Department of Industrial Policy and Promotion 2017).

A 2014 study found that Indian entrepreneur returnees relied on the strength of local business and family ties, in addition to their international networks. The study also found that filial piety was a powerful pull for returnees (rather than government policies), as many had moved to be closer to their parents (Pruthi 2014). Thus, India's economy would benefit (per hypothesis 3, increasing innovation capacity through utilizing open network strategies) from increasing levels of international network connections. A 2013 study forecasted significant growth in the number of Indian returnees, as a result of expanding economic opportunity in India, up to 300,000 by 2017 (Rajan, Kurusu, and Saramma Panicker 2013; Biswas 2014). The uptick in returnees resulted also from the environment in the United States, which had become less welcoming to foreigners, coupled with a tightening of immigration policies in that country.

These numbers had yet to compensate for the ongoing brain drain affecting the biomedical industry unfortunately. N. Buga and J.-B. Meyer found that about 90 percent of engineering and biotechnology graduates had moved to the United States after completing their degrees in India (cited in Greater Pacific Capital 2013). One interviewee noted that the healthcare industry suffers from this brain drain. The "best Indian doctors are found in the United States," as the pay and living conditions in most of India are lacking. The Tenth Five-Year Plan included measures to improve the entrepreneurial environment for biomedical start-ups, some that could be led by returnees and funded by investors in the diaspora.

The Tenth Five-Year Plan (2002–2007): Biomedical Industry Takes Center Stage

A number of advancements vis-à-vis biomedical technology capacity were initiated by the Tenth Five-Year Plan. Consequently, more aspects of the tenth plan are covered herein than of previous plans. Within the plan years, for example, the Patent Amendment Acts 2003 and 2005 were the final stages of the full implementation of the WTO agreement on TRIPS. In addition, the 2005 Special Economic Zones Act—enacted twenty-five years after similar legislation in China—created biotechnology parks in regions across India. In 1991, there were two MNC-backed research and development centers. By 2002, India had sixty (Richardson 2002).

In the Tenth Five-Year Plan, launched in 2002, scientific discovery and commercialization in biomedical technology would be justified as the best way to alleviate poverty, increase employment, and improve the overall quality of life for all Indians (Vajpayee et al. 2002). India was aiming to become a global center of pharmaceutical manufacturing. For the first time in India's postcolonial experience, the economy was poised to seek leadership in frontier technologies. As late as the 1980s, biotechnology was mentioned rarely in policy documents. In 2002, it was integral to the plan document. Biomedicals had become core to the policy mission of the Indian government.

In previous plans, biomedical development had been limited to agriculture and aquaculture. Part of the new focus was to stimulate demand for millions more knowledge workers. The Department of Biotechnology was charged to create a national facility for virus diagnosis, echoing developments in the 1990s in China establishing a program on genomics. Improvements in human capital were also a center of the new policy. Universities throughout India would receive support to expand capacity in biotechnology education.

The macroeconomic environment within which overall investments into biotechnology were implemented proved favorable for the private-sector absorptive capacity of these new technologies. Interest rates stabilized in the period, while inward FDI experienced rapid growth, especially as of 2006. The former would be favorable to entrepreneurial firms while the latter would benefit large and small firms alike. Since the 1980s, India had been plagued with high interest rates. On average, interest rates in India were twice those of China. This limited the affordability of bank loans to new firms and consequently firm growth. However, thanks in part to the regulatory reform IP protections, the Tenth Five-Year Plan period would see inward FDI double from less than 1 percent of GDP to greater than 2.

Embracing IPR

The Patent Amendment Acts of 2002 and 2005 would signal to potential foreign investors that new product R&D conducted in India would be protected under an IPR regime that adhered to international standards. The 2002 Patent Amendment Act was a first step. The act continued to prohibit patenting of plants or animals, in whole or in part, or any naturally occurring substance or entity. At the same time, the act extended the range of patentable inventions to include biochemical, biotechnological, and microbiological processes (Kumar and Tiku 2009).

With the Patent Amendment Act of 2005, India met the TRIPS standards fully—and just in time for the ten-year deadline for full implementation. Patent protection would now be valid for the broadest set of products since the 1911 British version of the Patent Act: inclusive of "all fields of technology, including food, drugs, chemicals and biotechnology" (Kumar and Tiku 2009). In India's large democracy, domestic legislation would finally catch up to national government promises to the outside world. Foreign firms responded in kind. Net FDI inflows would rise to greater than 3 percent of GDP by 2006. Overall private-sector research and development had risen from 41 percent of total R&D in 1985–1986 to 63.5 percent in 2002–2003 (Department of Science and Technology 2006).

The Patent Amendment Act of 2005 also incentivized Indian companies to engage in new product innovations. In the past, Indian pharmaceutical companies used reverse engineering processes on patented drugs to produce cheap generic drugs on a mass scale. Due to low prices compared to Western pharmaceutical firms, India became the main supplier of essential medicines for developing countries (though it has not been without quality concerns over the years). For example, as late as 2012, UNICEF had procured from Indian companies $558 million worth of services and supplies (UNICEF 2012).

After the 2005 Patent Amendment Act, Indian pharmaceutical companies have recognized that R&D in new chemical entities (NCE) could be the basis for long-term growth. Such Indian companies as Dr. Reddy's Laboratories, Ranbaxy Laboratories (acquired by Sun Pharma in 2014), Nicholas Piramal India, and Sun Pharma have each established separate divisions for NCE activities. At the same time that India instituted an IPR regime conforming to international standards, it created incentives to foreign firms to invest in India.

The 2005 Special Economic Zones (SEZs) Act aimed to attract inward FDI, build infrastructure, and facilitate the commercialization of new technologies in existing and new firms. One of the most serious barriers to new firms was the red-tape culture of the License Raj and other ways in which government bureaucrats would stifle innovation and entrepreneurship, as mentioned above. The new SEZs would streamline—and ideally cut out bureaucrats on the take—through establishing a single window of regulatory approval. The Indian government also established a legal framework to encourage inward FDI (Dohrmann 2008). Fiscal incentives included income tax exemption on profits and gains for the first five consecutive years, 50 percent exemption for an additional five years, customs duty exemptions, and the like (Nagayya and Rao 2010). Much of this investment in SEZs has been concentrated in already developed regions with existing FDI inflows, as well as centered on the IT industry (Bhatt and Bhatt 2012). Further, SEZs in India have been criticized for accelerating internal displacement and thereby limiting inclusive development (Sampat 2008, 2010). Another intent of India's SEZs was to provide spaces for networking effects—discussed in Chapter 2—to emerge in particular industries, especially in biotechnology.

The Eleventh (2007–2012) and Twelfth (2012–2017) Five-Year Plans also sought to improve the environment through investments into clean air and water technologies. As of 2016, the population in India had grown to over 1.3 billion. A Pew Research Center study (Kochhar 2015) found that while both China and India were successful in reducing poverty in the past decade, China did a better job of bringing people into the middle class. The study found that while 18 percent of Chinese had reached middle-income status, only 3 percent of Indians had done so. (Even so, this is about the combined total populations of Canada and the United States.) The remainder of Indians still lived in low-income or poor conditions. Nearly a billion people in India have yet to catch up to the standards of living in the developed world. Though beyond the scope of this chapter, part of the reason why distributive benefits of economic growth have been limited in India is the caste system.

In the Eleventh Five-Year Plan (2007–2012), the Planning Commission went after what it saw as excessive red tape, waste, and corruption. This included problems in bringing healthcare and education to rural regions, such as excessive "absenteeism" by doctors and teachers in these areas (Etienne 2009; Rogers 2005). The Twelfth Five-Year Plan (2012–2017) would be even bolder. It called for a paradigm shift in the deployment of innovations. Between 2010 and 2012, plan documents noted the average growth rate of 14 percent in the publication of Indians in scientific journals outpaced the global average of 4.1 percent during the same period. Ambitious targets included increasing the number of full-time R&D personnel from 154,000 to 250,000, doubling the number of patents granted, and boosting the number of publications of basic research to 5 percent of the global share (from 3 percent). Research and development expenditure would rise to 2 percent of GDP (from the 2012 level of 0.9 percent). This would include adding another 10,000 R&D personnel to established research centers.

While the Department of Space would receive the largest share of research and development funds, the Department of Biotechnology would receive funds to build five new research centers. 1,204 billion rupees (using 2016 exchange rates, about $17.7 billion) would be allotted for the Twelfth Five-Year Plan, compared to 750 billion (using 2016 exchange rates, about $11 billion) in the Eleventh Five-Year Plan.[19] In tune with India's culture of educational attainment and recognition, the

Twelfth Five-Year Plan aimed to improve India's global rankings in a number of measures, in addition to scientific publications and patents. This included moving up in the global rankings of SCI publications, Patent Cooperation Treaty (PCT), and Innovation Index and university rankings. At the same time, the plan would aim for "inclusive growth," meaning that rural communities should receive more attention, especially in basic infrastructure (Planning Commission 2013).

The Indian government, as late as 2014, continued to court inward FDI by increasing the FDI cap in pharmaceuticals and other industries. FDI policy allows 100 percent FDI in investments in new pharmaceutical ventures and 100 percent FDI upon government approval in existing pharmaceutical companies. Additionally, in July 2016, the government decided to permit up to 74 percent FDI automatically in brownfield pharmaceuticals (Press Information Bureau 2016). In the 1970s, foreign ownership had been limited to as low as 30 percent in such industries as pharmaceuticals. Even while courting this inward foreign investment, the government has been mindful of distributing benefits to its impoverished population. This has led to a series of measures to reduce the cost burden on low-income Indians. In 1970, the Indian government imposed the Drug Price Control Order and administered it through the creation of the National Pharmaceutical Pricing Authority (NPPA). The NPPA was mandated to ensure the affordability and availability of medicines. Its authority includes obtaining refunds from manufacturers found to overcharge for their medicines. In 1995, as part of moving toward adherence to WTO TRIPS, the list of price-controlled drugs would be reduced by half (Chaturvedi and Chataway 2009).

A second Drug Price Control Order was instituted in 2013, with mandated price controls on drugs listed in the National List of Essential Medicines (NLEM). The list was even shorter than in 1995. Still, one unfortunate consequence has been a decline in R&D investments and market share in India for drugs on the NLEM list. Between 2007 and 2015, the market share fell from 78 to 70 percent (Silverman 2015).

In addition to intellectual property reform via the Patent Law Amendments, India has also implemented a number of policies in science and technology, identifying specialized "innovation" universities and regulatory measures. The emphasis has been to initiate India's growth via science and technology through indigenous start-ups and entrepreneurship. In the mid-1980s, the government had created the Department of Biotechnology (DBT) and allowed it some autonomy through granting its own budget. The major achievement of the DBT has been its contribution in the creation of postgraduate and doctoral programs. The DBT has played a role in creating training programs that help India compensate for its historical lack of biomedical scientists, who span the disciplines of biology and engineering. In India's education system, the biology (usually premed), chemistry, and engineering tracks have been fragmented. Several seasoned biomedical entrepreneurs interviewed for this study noted that in the early years of their industry, it was virtually impossible to find chemists who could do the disciplinary boundary-spanning biochemistry. The few that had been trained in India in that generation were lured to Western countries by better wages and living conditions, as mentioned previously. The DBT has tried to train new generations of Indian biomedical workers who would remain in India. Singapore has taken a similar tack but also included recruiting foreigners into the technology class and offering them permanent residency and citizenship, which would have broad impacts on the economy, explored in the next chapter.

The Indian Bio Design Innovation Centers are just such an initiative by the DBT. The aim is to promote innovation in medical technology, biosciences, and bioengineering. The main purpose of this initiative is to connect the Indian medical system and its resources with engineering systems and also a basic science system for need identification (medical) with prototype development (engineering) and product validation (medical regulatory and engineering). There are five Indian Biodesign Innovation Centers initiatives by the DBT.

One of the initiatives is the Stanford-India Biodesign (SIB) Programme. SIB, which began in 2001, is funded mainly by the DBT, the Ministry of Science and Technology, and Stanford University. It is a collaboration between Stanford University, the Indian Institute of Technology, Delhi, and the All India Institute of Medical Sciences (AIIMS), Delhi, in partnership with the Indo-US Science and Technology Forum (IUSSTF). The SIB was conceptualized in the year 2000 at Stanford University by Stanford faculty Paul Yock and Paul Rajiv Doshi. The program focuses on training medical technology specialists with an understanding of the Indian institutional context, through offering postgraduate fellowships. The first SIB center started in India in New Delhi in 2008. The program also hopes to establish New Delhi as a hub of medical technology innovation. Though as of 2016 the results have been mixed (Anonymous interview 2016),[20] the SIB intends to boost the healthcare start-up ecosystem in India. Further, in 2006, in collaboration with UNESCO, India announced the creation of a Regional Center for Biotech that would serve to train biotechnology experts in India and the developing world.

Further, in terms of the amount invested, R&D that is not "mission-oriented" (military defense) has been of lower priority in India, other than biotechnology used in agriculture, known as bioagriculture, or bioag. This has led to a neglect of research in higher education. India has since created innovation capacity in its 16 Indian Institutes of Technology, 30 National Institutes of Technology (NITs), 162 universities awarding about 4,000 doctorates and 35,000 postgraduate degrees, and about 40 research laboratories run by the Council of Scientific and Industrial Research (CSIR). Additional labs were planned around the country. These CSIR labs were supposed to conduct applied research and raise their revenue/partial support by working with industry. Only a few success stories have emerged, and only a few labs have produced measurable results, despite progress in patenting since 2000 (Ajay and Sangamwar 2014). Consequently, the working business model of these CSIR labs has since been questioned (Sharma, Nookala, and Sharma 2012). There has been an important ideological shift from basic research to technological innovation. At the same time, India has struggled, despite its opening to international standards, to have even a single Indian university recognized in various global top 100 university rankings. With this in mind, the DBT has been actively seeking international partners to fast-track building domestic institutional capacity in biomedicals.

Also, SMEs employ close to 40 percent of India's workforce. Yet they contribute only 17 percent to India's GDP. The explanation for this lag behind other countries is twofold. Firstly, SMEs in India have relatively low productivity and weak technology adoption. Secondly, many Indian small businesses prefer to remain unregistered and unincorporated in order to avoid taxes and regulations. The "inclusive growth" and innovation promised by recent five-year plans are possible only when this sector of the economy is integrated more effectively.

In 2014, the government launched the India Inclusive Innovation Fund (IIIF) under the Public Private Partnership (PPP) model, but the government committed support for a mere 2 percent of the total budget. Not surprisingly, private investors have been lukewarm about participating in the fund. Other funding programs include the Bio Innovation Growth Fund (Burrill 2014). In 2015, India launched a five-year National Biotechnology Development Strategy (NBDS) in conjunction with the Start-Up India program, initiated in January of that year. The goal of the NBDS was to grow the India biomedical industry to $100 billion by 2025 (Philippidis 2016).

Guljit Chaudhri, an Indian biopharmaceutical entrepreneur and cofounder of the biotechnology entrepreneur association ABLE, remarked on the success of Indian government policy, noting that with a population of 1.3 billion, national policy of any sort is unlikely to reach most people. Even in places like Bangalore, which are now world famous as IT and biotechnology clusters, the reality is that it was actually private companies like Biocon (discussed below) that seeded the biomedical cluster (Chaudhri interview 2016). With this in mind, the following sections provide an industry overview, a regional overview of innovation and entrepreneurial activity in biomedicals, and select case studies.

Industry Overview

The Indian biotechnology market is divided into biopharmaceuticals, bioservices, bioagriculture (bioag), bioindustrial (biomanufacturing), and bioinformatics. Biopharmaceuticals is the largest sector contributing about 62 percent of total revenue, followed by bioservices (18 percent), bioag (15 percent), and bioindustry (4 percent). Bioinformatics is still emerging, contributing just about 1 percent of total revenue (Panchal, Kapoor, and Mahajan 2014). An estimate put the size of the Indian biotechnology market at $11.6 billion by 2017, having reached $7 billion in 2015 (IBEF 2016). Still, the biomedical industry contributes a few percent to GDP, compared to services (56 percent in 2014). As outlined above, it remains a key policy target due to its importance in improving human health in India and elsewhere, in addition to its potential for high added value, new products, and new business creation (Shapiro and Mathur 2014).

The biotechnology industry in India was seeded by the government investments into PSUs. In 1925, the Haffkine Institute began production of vaccines in Mumbai and later with the Pasture Institute of India. During this time, India depended on foreign companies to meet the country's demand for basic medication because of epidemics associated with its rapid population growth. In the 1960s, many companies were established for the production of vaccines, and subsequently later the focus on biopharmaceutical products shifted to the enzyme market and such companies as Biocon became the first Indian company to manufacture and export enzymes to the United States and Europe (Varma 2009). In the 1960s, the Indian government set up bulk-drug manufacturers as PSUs, the Hindustan Antibiotics Ltd. (HAL, est. 1954), and the Indian Drugs and Pharmaceuticals Ltd. (IDPL, est. 1961) locally to compete with MNCs' overseas bulk-drug operations for supplying local formulation plants.

HAL was established to manufacture such antibiotics as penicillin with the assistance of the WHO and UNICEF. The IDPL, with the support of the Soviet Union, produced surgical instruments and synthetic drugs. The Indian government created a number of research institutes under the guidance of Indian Council of Medical Research (ICMR) and the CSIR to promote technological advancement of the country. However, these research institutes have been criticized over the years for lacking commercial orientation (Sharma, Nookala, and Sharma 2012). Other state-private-sector initiatives with foreigners have had better results, including so-called reverse pharmacology.

The use of what Prahalad and Mashelkar call "reverse pharmacology," integrating effective formulations used at patients' bedsides back into the R&D process, is an example of this innovative system (Vaidya

2014). Instead of the costly move from laboratory to a clinic, Indian policy makers and scientists reverse the process. For instance, in 2000, Lupin Pharmaceutical started to use a traditional branch of Indian medicine called *Siddha* to find a cure for psoriasis. Siddha's origins can be found in the folk medicine of the southern Indian state of Tamil Nadu, while the first Siddha text is dated between the fifth and eleventh centuries (Scharfe 1999). Lupin Pharmaceutical collaborated with dermatologists, using such quantitative measures as the Psoriasis Area and Severity Index to assess the success of its formulations. In 2003, the Indian government offered to fund the project and encouraged a partnership with two state-owned research organizations, the Central Drug Research Institute and the National Institute of Pharmaceutical Education and Research. Likewise, reverse pharmacology was able to push down the price of drugs. The U.S.-based company Pfizer was thus compelled to sell the cholesterol drug Lipitor at $0.90 in India because the Indian company Ranbaxy's was selling Atorvastatin for $0.90. At the time (2010), the price in the United States was $2.70 (Prahalad and Mashelkar 2010).

Until 2013, a number of overseas companies (including contract research organizations) considered India a key destination for clinical trials of drugs, as the cost of conducting clinical trials was often reduced 50–75 percent below Western trial costs. However, the Indian biomedical industry suffered a setback in 2013. Unnamed Western drug companies were found guilty of sloppy human-test-subject protections in clinical trials in poor, rural communities in India in which a number of test subjects died. The Indian Supreme Court ruled that the Ministry of Health must increase rigor in the process of approvals of new clinical trials. This rightful win for the protection of test subjects has had negative collateral effects. Several biopharmaceutical entrepreneurs complained that clinical trials approvals since had all but halted. The Supreme Court ruling was a wake-up call for India's pharmaceutical industry that there needs to be better self-policing (Gurpur interview 2016).

The cofounder of the Association of Biotechnology Led Enterprises (ABLE) and founder of the biogenomics start-up STRAND Life Sciences, Vijay Chaundru, noted that in the absence of proactive self-regulation, when inevitable mistakes occur, the Indian government goes into re-action mode, which "gums up the innovative process." A venture capitalist leading a biopharmaceutical fund, with prior experience at NASSCOM, recounted the story of one of his investments. The com-pany was founded by two NRIs from the United States who had been encouraged to return to India to start up their venture, in part because of the then fast-moving clinical trials approval process. After the 2013 Indian Supreme Court ruling, the firm struggled for a few years, still waiting in the application queue. It recently gave up and returned to the United States, where it was quickly able to obtain West Coast VC. The entrepreneurs have no plans to return to India (Chaundru inter-view 2016). Other sources confirm the negative impact of the slowdown in approvals of new clinical trials has had on venture business. A legal scholar noted that the Ministry of Health does not want to be on the wrong side of questions about the protection of human test subjects, so it is easier to simply "leave applications in the queue indefinitely" (Gur-pur interview 2016). Despite these kinds of setbacks, India has created clusters of innovation and entrepreneurship in the biomedical industry in several regions.

Regions

Bangalore, Hyderabad, and Mumbai have become centers of biomedi-cal industry development, particularly in pharmaceuticals. Bangalore is home to a vibrant local IT cluster, and this institutional capacity helped seed an emerging biomedical cluster. Hyderabad, which calls itself Genome Valley, was seeded by PSUs, including Indian Drugs and Phar-maceuticals (IDPL). Mumbai, a historical trade entrepôt, has been an international business hub for many decades. Sharma, Nookala, and Sharma (2012) studied the challenges and opportunities of India's na-tional and regional innovation systems. They identified several clusters where the majority of educational institutions, industry, research/technology parks, and business incubators are colocated, thus contrib-uting to regional economic development. A key challenge observed among Indian educational/research institutions and corporations is the insuf-ficient quality of education in India. The Indian educational system, established during the preliberalization era and despite the success of the IITs, focused on memorization rather than factual understanding and critical thinking.

The following case studies in entrepreneurship—CIPLA, Biocon, and Shantha Biotech—illustrate how far the Indian economy has progressed in building innovation capacity necessary to support technology and entrepreneurship and yet how far the country needs to go to create a critical mass of biopharmaceutical entrepreneurs and entrepreneurial-ecosystem development generally.

Entrepreneurial Case Studies

CIPLA

CIPLA is one of India's oldest pharmaceutical companies. In 1935, Khawaja Abdul Hamied established Chemical, Industrial and Pharmaceutical Laboratories (CIPLA). The firm was founded in Mumbai under then British rule. At the time, India was dependent on expensive imported medicines. In 1939, Mahatma Gandhi asked Hamied to supply medicines to Britain for World War II. In return, Britain had supposedly promised independence to the Indian nation. India eventually won independence, but CIPLA still struggled under the tough patent laws (Life Science World n.d.). In response, Hamied and others established the Indian Drug Manufacturers Association (IDMA) to press for change (S. Singh 2012). It would take many decades for this to happen.

The Indian Patents Act (1970) was brought about partly as a result of the lobbying efforts of the IDMA. After this, CIPLA helped the Indian pharmaceuticals industry to bring in drugs from overseas and sell at affordable prices. CIPLA revolutionized access to HIV/AIDS medicines, by making generics and thereby reducing prices around the world. At the time, Hamied said, "We are being humanitarian. But we are not doing charity. We are not making money, but we are not going to lose money either" (CBS News 2001). In 2012, CIPLA upended world markets again by slashing the prices of six cancer drugs by 76 percent. In 2014, the market capitalization of CIPLA was $8 billion, on annual revenues of $163 million. Leading revenues were from South Africa (13.2 percent), Europe (5.7 percent), and North America (6.8 percent). The rest of the world contributed 24.5 percent (CIPLA Annual Report 2014). While CIPLA represents the founding generation of Indian pharmaceutical firms, Biocon is a next-generation biopharmaceutical venture, having moved into the branded-product market.

Biocon

Biocon is India's leading biopharmaceutical company. It was established in 1978 in a Bangalore garage by Kiran Mazumdar-Shaw as a joint venture with Biocon Ireland. Presently, Biocon and its subsidiaries, Syngene and Clinigene, together employ over seventy-three hundred personnel drawn from a number of fields, including biology and engineering. More than half of employees have postsecondary degrees.

Mazumdar-Shaw's father was a brewmaster at United Breweries. Following in her father's footsteps, she completed her studies and qualified as a master brewer from Ballarat University, Australia, in 1975. It was an uncommon career choice for a Brahmin family belonging to the alcohol-prohibiting state of Gujarat (Kalegaonkar, Locke, and Lehrich 2008).[21] After finishing her brewmaster studies, Mazumdar-Shaw was unable to find a paid job in this male-dominated industry. She had been working as an intern—the only "job" she could obtain—when she met Leslie (Les) Auchincloss, the owner of Biocon, the Irish biotechnology company. Auchincloss, a serial entrepreneur, had traveled to India in search of local business partners.

The Irish firm made industrial enzymes for the brewing industry. Auchincloss had been introduced to Mazumdar-Shaw by one of her classmates. Upon meeting Mazumdar-Shaw, given her background and training, Auchincloss determined that she was the perfect partner to bring Biocon Ireland to India. Soon Auchincloss appeared at Mazumdar-Shaw's door in 1978 with a business proposition (S. Singh 2016). Auchincloss wanted to manufacture a papaya enzyme called papain, which is used in clarifying beer, among other applications. India had provided a low-cost source of the raw material for the manufacture, an alternative to Japanese brewing enzymes, which were of higher quality and therefore price. In India at the time, still under the self-reliance ideology of its nation's independence movement, foreign ownership was limited to a 30 percent share—in a prudent quasi-openness to the outside world, while providing the space for nascent entrepreneurs like Mazumdar-Shaw. Thus Biocon Ireland needed a majority equity Indian partner to move the business forward (Masterson and Tandon 2014).

Mazumdar-Shaw immediately moved to Ireland and spent six months learning about enzyme production techniques. Soon thereafter Biocon was founded in India with an investment from Auchincloss of $1,200. The early years were a constant struggle for Mazumdar-Shaw, in large part because of gender discrimination. Bankers refused to lend money, vendors refused service, and she was often shunned at business meetings. It was through her social relationships that she was able to get a real start.

Mazumdar-Shaw faced many other obstacles. Recruiting people to work for her was difficult. She convinced a friend to fill in as her secretary. The first accountant she had hired left as soon as he found another job opening. Landlords were not willing to rent space as they assumed that as a woman she would not be able to pay. Braving these adversities Mazumdar-Shaw started producing two enzymes, mass papain and isinglass, from a garage in a rented house in an undeveloped part of Bangalore.

Mazumdar-Shaw persevered. Papain was the first product of Biocon India. By the late 1980s, Biocon was a profitable venture that made $1 million per year. In 1989, Auchincloss sold his 30 percent interest to Unilever (30 percent remained the maximum foreign ownership allowed under Indian law at the time). Buoyed by the existing legal protections on percentage of foreign ownership, Mazumdar-Shaw kept her 70 percent and stayed on. As part of Unilever, Biocon started producing enzymes for Unilever's food business. Unilever had brought process improvements to production, particularly in sanitation methods. (In Biocon's early years, supplies that would have been disposed of after use in the United States and Europe were routinely reused in resource-poor India.) However, Mazumdar-Shaw was exasperated under Unilever's top-down management style and started to look for other business opportunities for her team.

Biocon's chief scientist, Shrikumar (Shri) Suryanarayan, visited Japanese factories to learn their methods for the solid-state process of fermentation and developed a pilot plant in 1989. By the mid-1990s, there was a need for a bigger plant, so Shri and his R&D team built a unique and subsequently patented fermentation reactor. They called it the PlaFractor, which cut down the fermentation process and created greater control, thereby reducing waste and inefficiency. Mazumdar-Shaw understood that she could leverage the technology she developed for enzymes to begin manufacturing biopharmaceuticals.

In 1994, Biocon decided to start a new business venture, Syngene. Syngene provided its clients with bulk volumes of target molecules, reagents, and custom molecules for early-stage drug discovery and development. In 1997, Unilever sold its specialty chemicals division (which would have included Biocon) to what Biocon executives said was the "paint company" ICI (Imperial Chemicals Inc.), which knew zero about the biopharmaceutical industry. Fortunately, under Mazumdar-Shaw's original contract with Unilever, she had preemptive rights, which she enforced. The catch was that Mazumdar-Shaw had to come up with $2 million for the buyback. Fortunately, her fiancé, John Shaw, a former textile executive, was just selling his London home to make the move to India with his bride. John Shaw now heads international business development for Biocon and owns 25 percent stock.

In 2004, Biocon went public, making it only the second company in Indian IPO history to reach a first trading day high of $1 billion. Biocon then launched Biocon Biopharmaceuticals. Biocon Biopharmaceuticals has since built India's largest multiproduct biologics facility at Biocon Park, Bangalore. Mazumdar-Shaw is always looking to the innovation horizon, saying, "If you fix yourself in one spot, I don't think you will do justice to your entrepreneurial potential" (Kavlekar 2012). Biocon is unique in India's generics-dominated pharmaceutical market in that the company is not content to coast on generics-/biosimilars-based profits. Instead, like a few other Indian pharmaceutical firms, it has followed a pattern of risky R&D investments aiming at breakthrough innovations through international partnerships maximizing tacit-knowledge exchange and tapping into international human-capital networks (Kurup, Chandrashekar, and Muralidharan 2011). In 2014, Biocon revenues were mainly in biopharmaceuticals ($284 million), followed by research services ($116 million). In that year, branded formulations added a modest $64 million to the bottom line. By 2016, its market capitalization was $2.4 billion, and its shares reached an all-time high based on progress on R&D for the anticancer drug Pegfilgrastim, developed jointly with the U.S. company Mylan (*Times of India* 2016).

In 2016, *Forbes* listed Mazumdar-Shaw as among the top 100 most powerful women in the world, with a net worth of $1.6 billion, making her India's richest self-made woman entrepreneur (*Forbes* 2016). Biocon, with Mazumdar-Shaw at the helm, plans to extend its global reach in seeking research and development collaborations in key markets around the world. Reflecting India's networked technonational knowledge and network architecture, at once open to the outside while protective to that within, Mazumdar-Shaw and Biocon have so far been able to draw from international connections within a national context that has protected domestic entrepreneurs. Shantha, a start-up of the post-1991 liberalization generation shows how much has changed in India's innovation and entrepreneurship ecosystem, presenting challenges to Western pharmaceutical firms.

Shantha Biotech

Hepatitis B infection has caused many deaths in India and was the driving factor behind the establishment of Shantha Biotech. Attending a WHO conference in 1992, K. I. Varaprasad Reddy was shocked to see the severity of the hepatitis B problem in India and elsewhere in the developing world. He saw the solution would be in an inexpensive generic vaccine. Reddy initially approached a Western pharmaceutical firm, asking for a licensing agreement on humanitarian grounds. He was rebuffed by a company representative who is reported to have said, "India cannot afford such high technology vaccines. India does not require vaccines, and even if you can afford to buy the technology, your scientists cannot understand recombinant technology in the least" (Chakma et al. 2011, 3). Incensed by this blatant condescension, Reddy saw this as a call to action. He had a new mission.

Reddy was trained as an electrical engineer, and admittedly, he had no knowledge of biotechnology R&D. What he had was motivation and a belief that he could delegate what he lacked to a team of experienced scientists. When he decided to set up the firm, he found it difficult to raise funds as no financial institution was willing to fund early-stage start-ups that had no revenue. Instead, he bootstrapped. Reddy raised $1.2 million by selling off his father's property and by pulling together funds from the typical sources for early-stage entrepreneurs—friends and family. To compensate for his lack of expertise, he contacted numerous NRI scientists and managed to convince two "of the lot" to join him in his mission to bring affordable vaccines to India (Chakma et al. 2011). Shantha Biotech was established in 1993 in Hyderabad.

Shantha was incubated in Osmania University, but the company eventually left the campus, tiring of the intrainstitutional politics typical of universities. Shantha was on its own. By 1995, Shantha had exhausted its initial capital and was on the verge of bankruptcy. It was then that Reddy met, fortuitously, H. E. Yusuf Bin Alawi Abdullah, the foreign minister of the Sultanate of Oman. Alawi Abdulla's country needed an affordable vaccine for his own citizenry. With this confluence of interests came the next capital infusion of Shantha Biotech (Chakma et al. 2011). Oman injected $1.2 million in return for a 50 percent stake in the firm and preferred access to the vaccines. This new investment allowed Shantha to move into a new facility at the Centre for Cellular and Molecular Biology in Hyderabad.

Eventually, Shantha found success with Shanvac-B, which was derived from *Pichia pastoris*, a yeast different from that used in the existing patented hepatitis B vaccine. It would take time before public health agencies in India would have a mandated vaccine schedule (and thus guaranteed pipeline of customers). Thus, initial sales of Shanvac-B were financed almost entirely by the private sector. Building on this success, Shantha became the first company to be prequalified by the WHO. Shantha also established partnerships with the U.S. National Institutes of Health, Bill and Melinda Gates Foundation, and Johns Hopkins

University. In 2009, the French pharmaceutical company Sanofi had purchased a majority of Shantha and by 2013 had acquired the company, infusing it with more than $109 million in capital by 2017 (Department of Industrial Policy and Promotion 2017). The company invests a lot of money into its international marketing campaigns, because, as Shantha's executive director Khalil Ahmed has noted, now "everybody and their cousin have started a biotech company in India" (Chakma et al. 2011).[22] At the same time, one study estimated that up to 65 percent of Indian start-ups flee the red-tape License Raj structure and move out of India, usually to Singapore (Philippidis 2016).

Conclusion

India has watched closely the success stories of other Asian economies. Indian policy makers cite postwar Japan and other Asian high-growth economies as the inspiration for this ideological shift from the Swadeshi Movement to the Videshi Outlook (M. Singh 2013; Dawra 2015). India has become a destination for international clinical research and manufacturing activities, though recent clinical trial mishaps, discussed above, led to an Indian Supreme Court ruling that has slowed the pace of research and development. As this chapter has shown, in addition to the well-known story of Indian IT entrepreneurs, such biopharmaceutical entrepreneurs as Hamied of CIPLA, Mazumdar-Shaw of Biocon, and Reddy of Shantha have led the growth in that industry while expanding access to vaccines and improving human health around the world. India now has developed intellectual capacity allowing reductions in cost and time for developing and marketing new drugs. For example, India can outsource components of the drug-development process to its now established domestic contract research organizations.

Since the 1991 liberalization, the government of India has introduced several economic reforms and schemes for promoting science-and-technology-based innovation and entrepreneurship. This has been one of the key factors in shaping India's economy today. However, India's opening of its doors in 1991 to the global economy was initiated more than a decade later than China's (1978). Due to this lag, as well as the absence of a centrally cohesive authoritarian state able to implement policy while insulated from the demands of citizens, the country has struggled to catch up, despite an indigenous culture historically supportive of entrepreneurs. Nevertheless, India's since established capacities in biopharmaceuticals—coupled with its young, STEM-educated, English-speaking, often internationally educated professional workforce—position India for competitive advantage in the future. India's state-led technological development was less insulated from societal pressures than either the Chinese or Japanese and, therefore, comparatively slow in its growth trajectory (Mukherji 2009).

Its pluralist innovation and entrepreneurial-ecosystem model may, however, prove to be a competitive advantage in the future, owing to the higher levels of labor mobility and institutional flexibility (the upper quadrants of KNT). In other words, what India has lacked in the codified knowledge core of the knowledge-network matrix (lower left quadrant), it makes up for in its quickly adapting and international diaspora-enabled networks. The subject of the next chapter, Singapore, demonstrates that what it lacks in the scale of China and India, it has in part compensated via strategic investments by the state.

CHAPTER 6   BORN GLOBAL IN SINGAPORE

Living the Janus Paradox

THE TROPICAL CITY-STATE of Singapore is about seven hundred square kilometers (about three times the size of Washington, DC), or slightly larger than the sprawling Z-Park in Beijing discussed in Chapter 4. Singapore is one of the busiest port cities in the world, measured by tonnage (Central Intelligence Agency n.d.). The nation-state of Singapore was once a part of a greater Malay nation, a land colonized by Great Britain. After emerging from colonial rule officially in 1963, it became clear, according to its first prime minister, Lee Kuan Yew, that Malaysia's political leaders "were intent on a Malay-dominated Malaysia" (Friedberg 2010, 261; see also Lee K. Y. 1998). By 1965, Singapore's multiethnic enclave had been cast out from a *bumiputra* (sons of the soil) vision for the Malaysian nation-state (Friedberg 2010).

The founding principles for Singapore, in part descending from its history as an international trade entrepôt on the southernmost end of the Malay peninsula, were also a direct response to having been excluded from the new nation-state of Malaysia in part due to their multicultural ethnicities. Instead, Singapore would be founded on the "four-M" conception of nationhood: multiethnicity, multiculturalism, multilingualism, and multireligiosity. In later years, observers would refer to Singapore as the "4Ms, plus M," for meritocracy, reflecting the integrity and overall lack of corruption in the state (Sidhu, Ho, and Yeoh 2011). These central precepts of embracing multicultural identities have guided the national identity and policies of the government. From its inception as a nation-state, Singapore was international in outlook. The majority of Singapore's population is ethnically Chinese, followed by Malay, Indian, and other, mostly Asian ethnicities. While Singapore has four official languages (Malay, Indian Tamil, Mandarin, English), the administrative language, including in schools, is English.

The entrepôt model was less successful for the Singapore economy after its 1965 independence as it no longer had access to the Malaysian market; and other Asian countries were pursuing postcolonial nationalist-movement inspired import-substitution policies. Singapore needed a new model for its economic survival. Its small size meant that it had little choice but to be open to the outside. Thus, the city-state became technoglobal in outlook, as outlined in table 1.1. This included embracing the presence of MNCs in the domestic economy despite the risks, for example, to domestic workers and state autonomy. This devil's bargain, so to speak, would continue to challenge Singapore's ability to act in the interest of its citizens, a theme recurring and increasing with intensity over time, as noted throughout this chapter.

This openness to the outside was complemented, as mentioned above, by a strict meritocracy.[1] From the very beginning, talent regardless of ethnicity or citizenship was embraced.[2] This translated into a knowledge and network regime that was open to international human-capital networks (see fig. 2.3), though Singapore's small population of then fewer than 4 million meant that scale would prove elusive. In 1965, Singapore was a swampy, undeveloped spot of land with little infrastructure outside of the shipping docks in the port areas. What industry there was would drain its effluent into the canals. No significant sewer system was in place. Karan Thakral, the chair of the Singapore chapter of the angel venture-capital network the Indus Entrepreneurs (TiE) and local entrepreneur, remembered that back in those days despite the sweltering summer heat, his mother would not let him swim in the canals with his friends, due to the pollution (Thakral interview 2010). Given its modest resources, for Singapore to be both technonationalist and global at the same time would be some feat.

Vision

Lacking domestic market size and overall scalability in its small economy, Singapore would lack the ability to sustain a portfolio of high-tech industry, for example, as part of a diversified menu that had been possible in China, India, and Japan. After independence, Singapore built manufacturing capacity in a few industries, such as electronics. By the 1990s, it would put all of its chips in on an exclusive bet on biomedicals, as outlined below. Singapore's vision to emerge as Asia's leading biomedical science hub would require a multifaceted approach. Despite Singapore's small size, the number of ministries, agencies, and advisory and other boards tasked with promoting biomedical innovation and entrepreneurship have been many and varied over time. The analysis herein focuses on key actors and agents in creating a knowledge and network regime conducive to connecting Singapore's innovation-capacity upgrading to entrepreneurial-ecosystem development. Singapore has aspired to be like Finland, which despite a similarly small population size has an "innovation system that emphasizes entrepreneurship and technology creation" with a strong network among stakeholders to maximize transfer of both tacit and codified knowledge (Koh and Wong 2005, 281; see also Lundvall 1992). There are three key periods in Singapore's policy history in this regard. First, after independence in 1965, the city-state spent decades building basic *manufacturing capacity*. Singapore had a globally open knowledge and network architecture from the outset. Second, the 1997 Asian financial crisis prompted a new strategic focus on the *biomedical industry*, which had previously been one of several industrial development foci. Third, political infighting by 2006 brought *bureaucratic reform* and subsequent unintended consequences.[3] If Singapore's gamble fails, it will not be for lack of trying.

Policy

Singapore, along with Hong Kong, South Korea, and Taiwan (Chinese Taipei), has been called a Tiger economy, due to its rapid and sustained economic growth. Since its founding as a nation-state, the average growth rate has been 8 percent. The initial emphasis was to improve manufacturing capacity through increasing the presence of MNCs, rather than innovation per se. At the same time, Prime Minister Lee Kwan Yew was careful to discourage Singaporeans from "aping the West"—instead seeking to develop a unique multicultural yet steadfastly Asian national identity (Gopinathan 2001, 24; see also Lee K. Y. 1998). Singapore's lack of natural resources other than its people meant that economic development policy would emphasize improving its human capital through education. In a country with multiple indigenous languages, the use of English, though the colonial language, as the medium for education, helped to unify the populous. Originally, the education system was divided starkly along class lines: English-speaking professionals at the top and Malay and other unskilled laborers at the bottom. The government would deal with improving the school performance of all citizens in earnest.

Education

Singapore's education policy can be divided into three main periods: 1959–1978, 1978–1997, and post-1997 financial crisis. Between the 1960s and 1990s, the developmental goal was to improve manufacturing capacity, so the emphasis was on teaching Singaporeans to be good MNC employees. Between 1979 and 1991, four major policy initiatives shaping education would be in place: ability-based streaming (1979); ethnic "self-help" education to help ethnic Malay citizens "to help themselves" (1981); establishment of schools independent from government dictate (autonomy earned based on their high performance), similar to the Indian IIT system but inclusive of precollegiate levels (1986); and provision for ten years of general education (1991) (Gopinathan 2001).[4]

Since 1959, when the ruling People's Action Party (PAP) came to power in pre-independent Singapore, like India it has used education policy as a key instrument to bring forth socioeconomic development (Tan and Gopinathan 2000). After Singapore declared its independence from Malaysia in 1965, the education system focused on what Prime Minister Lee Kuan Yew said should "produce a good man and a useful citizen" (OECD 2010b; see also Lee K. Y. 1998). In the first phase (1959–1978) of the new educational policy, the government emphasized education for all under a national system of public education, growth of the number of schools, adoption of a bilingual approach, and intense recruitment of teachers. But economic globalization and the loss of competitive advantage in Asia's low-skilled, labor-intensive industries necessitated fostering an education system that emphasized critical thinking and innovation. In 1978, then deputy prime minister Goh Keng Swee was tasked with investigating what by that time had been identified as problems in the education system. His recommendation of creating a more flexible educational system became the source for the 1979 New Educational System. This change coincided with Singapore's transition from a low-skilled to a high-skilled economy. Streaming, based on student's academic ability, was introduced. Streaming created multiple tracks of education for students in accordance to their academic interest and (test-based) ability. It created three types of schools: academic high schools that prepared students for college, polytechnic high schools for advanced occupation and technical training with college-bound potential, and technical institutes that focused on occupational training for the lowest 20 percent of students. Also introduced was the Curriculum Development Institute of Singapore, which was tasked to produce high-quality textbooks and instructional materials for the different streams (OECD 2010b).

After the 1997 Asian financial crisis, it was determined that the future of economic growth would be driven by the global knowledge economy (OECD 2010b). The new focus was to be on innovation, creativity, and research. In 1997, under the stewardship of Prime Minister Goh Chok Tong, the Thinking Schools, Learning Nation (TSLN) program was initiated. This was meant to create "a nation of thinking and committed citizens capable of meeting future challenges, and an education system geared to the needs of the 21st century" (Ministry of Education, Singapore, n.d.). From the early 2000s, the state shifted to creating a knowledge economy that could produce innovations at the technology frontier and also support technology entrepreneurship. Education policy adapted accordingly, emphasizing teaching Singaporeans to be entrepreneurial and cosmopolitan in a global world.

After the TSLN program began, every few years the government would introduce new initiatives aiming for an education system that promoted innovation and critical thinking over rote memorization. In 2017, for example, the government decided that it would do away with strict grades and changed the structure of exams in primary schools. Additionally, at least a tenth of admissions to universities are now based on Early Admission Exercise (EAE) aptitude test scores rather than (rote memorization–based) test results, and the public service will no longer classify officers by their educational qualifications (Zaharia and Ungku 2017). This might reflect an attempt to reduce the bias in government hiring of National University of Singapore (NUS) graduates over other local universities, including Nanyang Technical University (NTU), as one observer noted (Anonymous interview 2017).[5]

According to the 2018 Global Innovation Index (GII), a report co-published by Cornell University, INSEAD, and the World Intellectual Property Organization, Singapore ranked fifth (up from seventh in 2017) with a score of 59.83 on a scale of 0–100. China, India, and Japan ranked seventeenth, fifty-seventh, and thirteenth respectively. The one area where Singapore lags behind, however, is in education, where it ranks forty-second (though up from seventy-sixth in 2017). (This index measures such indicators as expenditure on education, pupil-teacher ratio, secondary- and tertiary-level inbound mobility, and gross expenditure on R&D, among others.) The report notes that though Singapore is still number one in Asia, other countries, including Vietnam, the Philippines, and Thailand, are catching up. The report also ranks Singapore thirty-fifth (down from thirty-second in 2017) in overall creative output (which measures the creativity of intangible assets, creative goods and services, and online creativity) (Dutta, Lanvin, and Wunsch-Vincent 2018).

Despite initiatives since 1997, there has also been criticism that the educational system does not provide space for critical thinking and innovation. In a U.S. Chamber of Commerce survey (2017) of executives with offices in the ASEAN region meant to determine U.S. business perception, Singapore scored low on analytical and problem-solving sections (25 percent versus 44 in other ASEAN countries) and communication and cross-collaboration (27 percent versus 41 in other ASEAN countries) (U.S. Chamber of Commerce 2017).

Scholars have argued that in Singapore the private sector must be the engine of growth in innovation and entrepreneurship, but for this, they also need an efficient public sector. This efficiency has come at a cost—it has captured much of the local talent within the high-status meritocratic public sector while creating a shortage in the private sector needed for promoting innovation and entrepreneurship at the system level (Chew and Chew 2003).

Seeking to increase Singapore's global standings, seen from the outside, its policy makers and leading academics may seem obsessed with various global indices, such as the World Economic Forum global competitiveness rankings. An interview with a government official is almost guaranteed to include some citation of Singapore's ranking in this or that global index. While Singapore has been able to create an education system over time characterized by both centralization and decentralization (e.g., "white spaces" for schools to determine curricula), research has raised doubts that the system, as structured as recently as 2015, is suited to the level of creativity and innovation necessary to sustain a knowledge-based economy (Tan and Dimmock 2015).

As a city-state economy, Singapore's extreme exposure to the currents of international trade and investment has made its leaders keenly attuned to potential international (e.g., political) opportunities to exploit to its own national advantage. For example, in the 1980s, the U.S.-Japan trade rivalry heightened. At the time, the United States was concerned about falling behind Japan's then perceived technonationalist policies that had led to its S&T advances, as discussed in Chapters 2 and 3. Referring to a 1983 budget statement by Tony Tan, then minister of trade and industry, outlining a new emphasis on improving value-added capacity in emerging industries, including biotechnology, a local news article at the time quoted Tan: "We can do no worse than to take advantage of the current adversity to lay our own foundation" (Gelfert 2013). In addition to attempting to focus energies and budgets into their best guess as to which areas of biomedicals would pay off for Singapore, government bureaucrats had clear expectations of tangible results in technology commercialization. At the same time, dependent on MNCs for inward FDI, Singapore has had to be nimble and adaptive in dealing with foreign firms as it attempts to build its own innovative capacity (Khorsheed 2016). An early shake-up involved the appointment of Vincent Yip in 1984 to the executive directorship of the Science Council as the result of dissatisfaction that the council had so far done little to advise in strategy and until that point had merely "organized seminars and exhibitions."

In 1985, Yip warned that it was important to identify a few niches within bio that Singapore could realistically pursue, making sure that "the large sums of money we spend are not thinly divided over several fronts" (Gelfert 2013).[6] In that year, Singapore laid the foundations for future biomedical technology development with the establishment of the Institute of Molecular and Cellular Biology (IMCB) (Finegold, Wong, and Cheah 2004). The institute was launched at the National University of Singapore (NUS) to cultivate Singapore's biomedical R&D capabilities. Sydney Brenner, a South African molecular biologist, awarded the Nobel Prize in 2002 for his advances in gene research, was a critical bridge between the "mismatch in expectations" between government bureaucrats leading biomedical industrial policy and the academic scientists conducting the fundamental research. The significant investment into the quasi-autonomous IMCB was for Brenner "an entrance fee for Singapore into the world of biotech" (Gelfert 2013). In his view, the government bureaucrats had to cede some autonomy if they wanted to see innovation flourish in Singapore's public-sector institutions.

In addition to the oft-cited political leadership of the nation's founder, Lee Kuan Yew, a small number of names crop of repeatedly as key stakeholders, considered founders of the biomedical industry in Singapore. In addition to Sydney Brenner, Tony Tan and Phillip Yeo have led a sometimes-contentious rivalry in this regard. In such a small place as Singapore, each leader tends to take on broad and multiple responsibilities, potentially encroaching on the territory of others. From the outside, this may appear as personalistic policy leadership that occasionally has led to bureaucratic rivalry. Viewed in a positive light, this rivalry has resulted in variations in approach to accomplishing shared developmental goals. Different ideas have been piloted over the years, with enough personnel shuffling among government ministries and boards to encourage tacit-knowledge exchange (at least within the central state bureaucracy).

Singapore's bet on the biotechnology industry has been attributed to the ideas of Phillip Yeo, then chair of the Economic Development Board (EDB), within the Ministry of Trade and Industry (MTI), an organization with a mission to promote economic growth akin to METI in Japan. Established in 1961, the EDB oversees the goal of establishing Singapore as a global business hub to obtain and channel inward FDI to local economic development. The EDB had been instrumental in attracting several biomedical MNCs to Singapore, including GlaxoSmith-Kline, Merck, Roche, and Siemens Medical Instruments (PR Newswire 2010), though the ultimate success has been mixed (discussed below). The EDB has offered many tax incentives for foreign firms investing in Singapore (Singapore EDB 2014).

Yeo has been credited as the architect of the country's biomedical sciences initiative. He was a revolutionary of his time, if this can be said about a technobureaucrat working within a state bureaucracy. Yeo, having assumed the chairmanship of the EDB in 1986, courted David Lane, a Scottish genomics researcher, and Brenner to join the effort to establish Singapore's biomedical industry. Wanting to see a nimbler approach to building capacity in biomedicine and biotechnology that would eventually serve to seed industry development, in 1991 Singapore formed the National Science and Technology Board (NSTB). Yeo intended to carve out a new niche separate from the existing Science Council, which for Yeo had been overstaffed with senior university officials. However, the Science Council and NSTB continued to falter, for example in pursuing what Yeo and Brenner saw as a dead-end investment in agrobiology (Friedberg 2010). By 1988, a national committee of stakeholders from government, legislators, and academic scientists had been created and tasked with drafting a development plan for the biotechnology industry. Again, due to Singapore's small size, it lacked the government funds needed to pursue a diversified investment approach.

According to Yeo, the real architects of Singapore's venture into bio-medicals were three academics: John Wong, Tan Chorh Chuan, and Kong Hwai Loong (Yeo interview 2010). As of 2017, John Wong was the Isabel Chan Professor in Medical Sciences at NUS and chief executive of the National University Health System. Tan Chorh Chuan was a founder of Singapore's Biomedical Sciences Initiative. Tan was in 2017 the president of NUS and previously served as dean of the NUS Faculty of Medicine from 1997 to 2000. Kong Hwai Loong played an important role in the establishment of Biopolis. Kong served as the executive director of the Biomedical Research Council (BMRC) and deputy man-aging director for A*STAR. Meanwhile, Yeo led the EDB in senior posi-tions of the MTI including as EDB chair 1986–2001. Yeo oversaw the EDB Biomedical Science (BMS) group and A*STAR's BMRC in the 2000s (until 2007). The role these organizations played is outlined below.

Why Biomedical? The Gang of Four

Under the leadership of Phillip Yeo and Tony Tan, among others men-tioned below, and on occasion seeking the counsel of Brenner, Singapore embarked on a series of policies that have resulted in its leapfrogging to global economic status, at least in terms of manufacturing and modest innovation capacity, if not quite an entrepreneurial ecosystem per hy-pothesis 3 (concerning open network strategies as a factor behind tech-noentrepreneurship despite capacity weaknesses). The first official science and technology policy began in 1991 (Koh and Wong 2005). At the time, Singapore was investing less than 1 percent of its GDP into its entire education system and less than that on research and development (Gopi-nathan and Lee 2011). Though biotechnology was mentioned as an area on which to focus, electronics and chemicals remained the primary targets of government policy. The amount invested in biomedicals at the time was negligible.[7] The Asian financial crisis in 1997 changed everything.

1997 Asian Financial Crisis as Crucible

As a globally connected city-state–sized economy, Singapore has been especially vulnerable to international market volatility. For example, the domestic impact of the 1997 Asian financial crisis[8] prompted the Singaporean government to pursue market diversification. At the same time, the government sought to position Singapore as a regional, if not global, hub for technology. A 1998 economic assessment by the Committee on Singapore's Competitiveness (CSC) called for Singapore to become a knowledge economy (Ministry of Trade and Industry Singapore 1998; Poh 2016). A knowledge economy for Singapore meant that economic growth and development should be based on research-and-development-intensive industries. Based on the report, the CSC identified the biomedical science sector (BMS) as a key building block toward a knowledge economy.

Philip Yeo, then executive chairman of A*STAR, said that the focus on biomedical as one of the key pillars of knowledge-driven growth was the need to diversify the economy "to become like a table with many legs." The Biomedical Sciences Initiative (BMSI) was intended to be the fourth key pillar (or table leg) of Singapore's economy, alongside electronics, engineering, and chemicals (Ministry of Health 2012).[9]

Yeo planned the growth of the biomedical sector along with aforementioned scholars Tan Chorh Chuan, John Wong, and Kong Hwai Loong—a group Yeo refers to as the "biomedical sciences 'Gang of 4.'" The BMSI was prepared in an all-night session in the year 2000 by the four of them and submitted to the government, which after some hesitation gave the go-ahead (Epps 2006). In the same year, John Wong and Kong Hwai Loong, along with Tan Chorh Chuan, were instrumental in setting up the Singapore Genomics Program, with the support of Yeo, which later became the Genome Institute of Singapore in 2002—a flagship public program of the BMSI.

In phase 1, the focus was on building a strong foundation of biomedical research within Singapore. This led to investment in such infrastructure projects as the construction on Biopolis in One North and the expansion of biomedical research institute capabilities. They also invested in recruiting international talent who would mentor younger scientists. Tan Chorh Chuan and John Wong were appointed to the executive committee in phase 2 (2006–2010) of Singapore's BMSI, which was chaired by Phillip Yeo. Part of the effort then was to establish

Singapore as a leader in medical research and also to translate that into medical tourism and industry development (A*STAR n.d.b, n.d.c). Tan Chorh Chuan went on to become A*STAR's deputy chairman.

The Agency for Science, Technology and Research, or A*STAR, created in 2002 to centralize, fund, and oversee biomedical industrial development, is an economic agency under the auspices of the MTI (Friedberg 2010). A*STAR was formerly known as the National Science and Technology Board, which had been established in 1991. In the goal of creating a knowledge-driven economy, A*STAR sponsors mission-oriented and translational research. A*STAR leads eighteen research institutes and consortia, more than half of which are dedicated to biomedical research (A*STAR 2010). Table 1.2 outlined the state-private-sector structure in Singapore, within which A*STAR is key.

In 2004, the IMCB became an autonomous research institute of A*STAR and moved to the biomedical R&D center, Biopolis (A*STAR n.d.a). While other countries such as China and Japan have included the biomedical industry as one from among a menu of strategic sectors for development, Singapore officials have targeted the BMS sector almost exclusively (P.-K. Wong 2007). The government has attempted to leave as little to chance as possible and has put the full force of the state behind growth targets, focusing the efforts across government ministries at the onset with A*STAR playing a central role.

A*STAR and the EDB are statutory boards responsible for implementing policy targets. These government bodies enjoy a greater level of autonomy than their parenting executive ministries. Statutory boards are managed by boards of directors, in the Japanese public-private-university collaboration model: comprised of private-sector professionals, industry experts, and senior civil servants. In a departure from the Japanese model, these boards include several foreign experts. With this openness, Singapore's knowledge and network architecture centered on leveraging inward foreign direct investment and a unique "guppies to whales" strategy of engaging international human-capital networks.

Human-Capital Development

When asked about the policy for which he is most proud, Yeo reflected on the "guppies to whales" human-capital development strategy that had allowed Singapore to move rapidly up the value chain in technology manufacturing. This strategy embraced foreigners in an open knowledge and network architecture in an attempt to engage not only in technology importing but also in importing science-and-technology talent (fig. 2.3). In addition to Yeo's strategy of attracting Nobel Prize–level senior scientists (whales) to serve at the helm of newly established research institutes (e.g., Brenner at IMCB), he also sought to increase the incoming flow of junior scientists by luring precollegiate high-scoring STEM youth (guppies) to Singapore. The first National Science Scholarships began in 2001. For Singaporean high school graduates, only the perfect scoring need apply. These students would be compensated handsomely with fellowships and scholarships for undergraduate and graduate degrees. In fact, seeking an advanced degree was part of the scholarship requirements (Friedberg 2010, 270–71). Policy leaders were mindful of the possibility that they would merely be providing a free ride to "nomadic (techno) entrepreneurs, promiscuous in their relations and affiliations" (Sidhu, Ho, and Yeoh 2011, 32). Phillip Yeo was quoted at the time noting that he was well aware that scientists know of no national duty. Rather their only loyalty was "to their science" (Yeo quoted in Holden and Demeritt 2008). Yeo would be later criticized for broadcasting the names—in what could be viewed as an attempt at public shaming—of those guppies who had reneged on their contractual obligations to work in the service of Singapore after completion of their degrees. Singapore would likewise have strict views toward its own diaspora.

Diaspora

Seeking employment opportunities, the first wave of Singaporeans to emigrate abroad in the 1970s and 1980s were treated with indifference by the state, amid government perceptions that these sojourners had been disloyal to the young Singaporean nation. However, the internationalization of the Singaporean economy and the need for human capital compelled the government to incorporate the inclusion of its diaspora into its economic strategy. As a result, Contact Singapore was set up in 1998. The original mandate of this government agency was to find highly skilled foreigners for Singapore, but in addition it was also tasked with networking with overseas Singaporeans in the diaspora.

In 2001, in a speech by Prime Minister Goh Chok Tong at the inaugural Raffles Institution Lecture on National Issues,[10] he spoke of the need to balance the exposure of Singaporeans to "world-class companies and foreign top-rate minds and talents" and ensuring that the talent comes back home (Goh 2001). He added that in the era of this highly mobile generation, if Singapore continued to lose its top minds, it would be a hotel and not home—this lack of "sense of ownership will lead to Singapore's decline" (Goh 2001). The same year, Goh also reignited the narrative around the diaspora, calling Singaporean's who had emigrated abroad as "quitter[s]," because they had supposedly turned their backs on the county. In contrast, those who remained in the country working for its development were lauded by the honorific "stayer" (Naruse 2013).

However, the government of Singapore, acknowledging the need for its diaspora in an increasingly knowledge-based economy in 2002, launched the Mejulah Connection. (The name derives its significance from the country's national anthem "Majulah Singapura" ["Onward Singapore"].) It was the networking body for Singaporeans in the diaspora to ensure they maintained links to their home. But the government struggled in its diaspora strategies in pursuing often-conflicting goals of being a global city while retaining the postcolonial nation-building project (Ho and Boyle 2015). Though limited in number, the Singaporean diaspora has since been expected to play the role of "bridge" between Singapore and their new home. For example, in 2004, the constitution was amended to enable Singaporeans born overseas to pass on Singaporean citizenship also to their children born abroad (Ho and Boyle 2015).

Further, in 2006 the Overseas Singaporean Unit (OSU) was established under the Prime Minister's Office to reach out to overseas Singaporeans and facilitate return migration. The OSU is also responsible for organizing professional networking activities and an annual festival known as Singapore Day across the globe (Ho and Boyle 2015). These governmental attempts to create nationalism within the diaspora and a sense of social service by returning home are made explicit through the production of the *Conversations on Coming Home* booklet by Contact Singapore, which publishes stories of those Singaporeans whom Contact Singapore helped bring back to a place "they can truly call home." These and other network opportunities have been limited strictly to Singaporean citizens and those having permanent residency (and thus serving obligatory military service). A long-term foreign resident of Singapore recounted being banned at the door of a 2016 Contact Singapore event held at his Ivy League university in the United States because he lacked the "proper papers" of Singaporean citizenship (Anonymous interview 2017).

Complementarities with the aforementioned human-capital development schemes would be found in the 1998 World Class University program aiming to internationalize the National University of Singapore. Singapore has two major universities, NUS and NTU. NUS has had historically close ties with the central state, while NTU (in part resulting from neglect by the state) charted its own independent path. Subsequent Global Schoolhouse programs would be established as part of the education policy goal to transform Singapore into a knowledge and innovation hub by establishing networks and collaborations with foreign universities. The first such partnership would be created by Tony Tan, with his alma mater MIT. Others would follow, in which the Singapore government sought to uplift its global brand by seeking out partnerships with top (research active) international schools, including Stanford University. These programs are illustrative of new expressions of economic nationalism under conditions of globalization in that Singapore is trying to draw global talent into the service of Singapore through putting up major funds to support international collaborations (Sidhu, Ho, and Yeoh 2011).

At the same time, local experts have cautioned that state leaders should remain mindful of the reasons why so-called top schools like Yale and MIT might agree to partner with Singapore. A fallout with Johns Hopkins University in the 2000s illustrates these concerns. A

Johns Hopkins administrator who was not involved in the split acknowledged that the word on campus in Baltimore was that the Johns Hopkins University departure from Singapore was acrimonious indeed, souring relations thereafter (Anonymous interview 2017). That is, foreign universities have their own goals that, while facilitated by Singapore government funds, may not always coincide neatly with the aims of Singapore (Gopinathan and Lee 2011). Further, Singaporeans and international partners alike have bristled at the minute level of government oversight ostensibly to monitor school quality, inclusive of everything from test scores to the number of overweight students (Tan and Gopinathan 2000). Meanwhile, government and industry leaders in Singapore have lamented the lack of creativity and critical-thinking skills among students and the workforce.

Singapore 21 and the NUS Overseas College program have been similar attempts to nurture a class of technoentrepreneurs by sending groups of undergraduate students to global technology clusters, such as in Silicon Valley, Boston, Shanghai, and Bangalore, on yearlong experiential learning via internships with tech start-ups and course work to develop an "entrepreneurial mind-set." The intent was also for these students to develop international social networks (the upper right quadrant of the knowledge and network typology) (Wong, Ho, and Singh 2007). Poh Kam Wong, an NUS faculty member who has led many entrepreneurship initiatives, said that in order to compensate for the lack of critical mass in the overall number of local start-ups, it was time to start helping NUS students build international social capital via the social networks that are created through experiential learning opportunities abroad (P. K. Wong interview 2010).

NUS would subsequently roll out a case-study/mentor/mentee approach whereby their students would shadow a biomedical entrepreneur in one of several biomedical clusters in the United States, Sweden, China, and India. Wong says that students return from these experiences with a hands-on understanding of the start-up process, from which innovations can emerge that would not otherwise, including new product ideas and personal networks in these global technology clusters to obtain seed funds. If a student returns to Singapore with an executable venture idea, even better. NUS is situated to provide matching funds and offer incubation space. For Wong, as many other government and academic architects of Singapore's innovation and entrepreneurial ecosystems in this study, it is all about changing the mind-set of future generations of Singaporeans and creating an ecosystem that has a natural "idea flow." Wong, who had primary responsibility for technoentrepreneurship at NUS, said, "The goal is to get myself out of a job . . . to establish a vibrant venture support ecosystem, so that we are no longer needed" (P. K. Wong interview 2010). In essence, these policies have been an attempt to reengineer citizenship and create an ideal type of citizen, with the intellectual and social capital to contribute to Singapore's vision for a knowledge economy with global network reach. Lacking a critical mass of indigenous Singaporeans to carry out this task, the strategy since the 1990s has been to import foreign talent to staff the upper levels of innovation activity as well as initiate international learning networks. Despite these large-scale programs, funded by government largesse, NTU, with far fewer resources, would upstage government-favored NUS in both technology and entrepreneurship.

NTU

NUS is a comprehensive university while NTU is dedicated to science and technology. Since its inception in 1991, NTU has tried to create a spirit of entrepreneurship and innovation and has dedicated entrepreneurial units. For instance, Nanyang Innovation and Enterprise Center Office, established in 2000, helps in the commercialization of NTU research. NTUitive Pte Ltd. is the university's innovation and enterprise company and supports the university's mission to develop an innovative ecosystem to encourage innovation, foster entrepreneurship, and facilitate the commercialization of research. Another unit dedicated to nurturing links between scientific research and business is the Nano-Frontier, which provides business support and incubation services to nanotechnology research at NTU (Mok 2013). Despite its relative exclusion from lucrative government programs (compared to its neighbor NUS), NTU managed to produce a number of bootstrapped start-ups in the technology space. The Singaporean government finally warmed to NTU in the 2010s, leading to new collaborations. In this regard, Singapore mirrors practice in Japan. That is, the state ignores institutions outside its existing networks until such upstarts prove their mettle. Then, the state offers midstage support.

Commenting on the government largesse to NUS over NTU, an entrepreneur with experience in Japan observed that this is akin to Tokyo University, in that tradition and legacy led eventually to institutional stasis between the Singaporean state and NUS. NUS had always been the center; therefore, it continued to be by default into the late 2010s. It was not until NTU succeeded on its own (discussed below under the Celligenics case) that the technoentrepreneurial university on the western edge of the city-state seemed to have finally appeared on the government's radar. After all, like Tokyo University, the personal networks of NUS alumni in high-ranking posts in government ministries run deep and wide. The national economic and political decision makers have been, with few exceptions, NUS graduates.

By the late 1990s, Singapore was sensing rising competition from China, in that other regional locales began to compete with Singapore for global talent and capital. Singapore's leaders decided that it needed to close the gap between its existing innovation capacity and the technological frontier. Typical of Singapore's studious approach, soul-searching policy research ensued, resulting in a pivot to biotechnology (Koh and Wong 2005; J. Wong 2011). Since the 1980s, Singapore's impressive economic growth was due largely to efficient electronics-sector performance. Competition from low-wage emerging economies in the region provided the impetus for this biomedical initiative (Chuong and Ang 2008). As discussed above, the 1997 Asian financial crisis precipitated a quick policy shift. In 1999, the government announced a billion-dollar investment to establish Singapore as a biomedical hub. Infrastructure investments included the Tuas Biomedical Park and Biopolis. Biopolis is on the One North campus, itself budgeted initially at S$500 million (then US$285 million) (JTC Corporation 2007).[11]

This biomedical research hub was intended to situate Singapore as Asia's "premier" biomedical cluster. Biopolis was modeled on biotech clusters including that in San Diego (Parayil 2005). The Biopolis campus is just down the road from NUS, and nearby are also Singapore Polytechnic, the Institute of Technical Education, the National University Hospital, the Singapore Science Park, and the Ministry of Education. In addition to Biopolis, Fusionopolis (an R&D complex) and Tuas Biomedical Park (a manufacturing hub) serve as physical reminders of Singapore's ambitions for creating a knowledge economy. Biomedical hub creation was initiated in tandem with programs (outlined above) intending to make Singapore a regional education hub aspiring to attract nonlocal students who might eventually settle in Singapore. By 2002, in addition to launching Biopolis, A*STAR had established six biomedical research institutes. Additional research institutes would be established into 2017. However, political infighting led eventually to changes in the way innovative activity was managed.

In June 2000, Singapore launched the BMSI (Ministry of Trade and Industry Singapore 2011). The initiative was to be overseen by the Biomedical Initiative Executive Committee and advised by the BMSI Advisory Council. This long-term initiative was designed to develop local biomedical innovation (Waldby 2009). The BMSI has been divided into three five-year phases. Throughout the first phase (2000–2005), Singapore focused heavily on the development of biotechnological capabilities. National biomedical research institutes were created, and Singaporean universities were provided funds to develop BMS programs, R&D capabilities, and local BMS talent. The second phase (2006–2010) addressed developing translational and clinical research capabilities. The third phase (2011–2015) continued to address the need to develop translational and clinical capabilities, while also promoting the emergence of local industry through mission-oriented programs, including biotechnology, pharmaceuticals, and medical technology (Ministry of Health 2012). Investment per phase was approximately US$4–5 billion (Kaufmann 2013).

Along with BMSI, to assist in the coordination across agencies and with the private sector, the Biomedical Research Council (BMRC) was also created in 2000. The BMRC has played a central role in supporting the development of Singapore's innovation system for biomedicals. The BMRC acts as an operating arm of A*STAR and supports and coordinates public-sector biomedical R&D in Singapore. Reflecting the open knowledge and network approach of Singapore, it aims to facilitate international research collaborations for indigenizing innovation capacity. An example of intra-agency collaboration, the BMRC works with the EDB and the Ministry of Health's National Medical Research Council (NMRC) to oversee and support Singapore's biomedical R&D initiatives. Internationally, BMRC entities partner with international universities and public and private firms to advance biomedical R&D (A*STAR 2011b). The BMRC further targeted five specific, or niche, industry clusters, building on its success in biologics and pharmaceuticals (Biomedical Research Council 2013). These would include bioprocessing, genomics and proteomics, molecular and cell biology, bioengineering and nanotechnology, and computational biology (A*STAR 2017). By 2003, Singapore was spending 28 percent of its total public R&D on biomedicals (J. Wong 2011, 50).

Attracting inward FDI to fund biomedical industry development became central to Singapore's development strategy in the 2000s (Finegold, Wong, and Cheah 2004). The Singaporean state has leveraged inward FDI through a combination of scholarships, grants, incubator schemes and other incentives (Kaufmann 2013). However, Singapore's policies, while attracting numerous multinational pharmaceutical companies, had in 2017 yet to develop the scale necessary for a biomedical entrepreneurial ecosystem. Meanwhile, a report analyzing Singapore's progress in the early 2000s, found that basic research, clinical trials, commercialization, and SME support systems remained undeveloped (Wong, Ho, and Singh 2005).

In 2006, Singapore made a significant shift, whereby decision-making power and funding became more diffuse, keeping the EDB and A*STAR while creating additional oversight, mainly in the form of the newly established National Research Foundation (NRF). Some observers attribute this split to an ongoing personal rivalry between Tony Tan and Phillip Yeo,[12] who had over the years differed on how to go about pursuing shared developmental goals.

The boards receive policy targets from their respective ministries, which after 2006 based their initiatives on macro-level strategies and

TABLE 6.1.

Key policy history: Biomedical innovation and entrepreneurship in Singapore

Year	Name	Objectives
1987	The Institute of Molecular and Cellular Biology	Biomedical manufacturing capacity building. Create innovation culture. Nurture high-tech talent in Singapore. Promote basic research in biomedical fields.
1991	The First National Technology Plan	Demonstrate the importance of R&D activity in economic development. Create incentives and provide funds for R&D activities. Include the medical sciences as target technologies (though minimally funded).
1996	National Science and Technology Plan (NSTP) 2000	Attract five thousand researchers and scientists in the allotted period to meet the demand of skilled human resources. Enhance technological capability and make R&D activities accessible.
2000	Biomedical Research Council (BMRC)	Target fields including bioprocessing, genomics, cell biology, bioengineering, nanotechnology, and computational biology. Encourage interdisciplinary research in biomedical fields aiming at enhancing human healthcare. Improve human-capital development and social awareness of biomedicine.
2001	Science and Technology 2005 Plan	Develop infrastructure to attract more talent to Singapore. Provide technology entrepreneurs easier ways for financing. Invest in top international firms for them to set up regional headquarters in Singapore.
2002	Agency for Science, Technology and Research (A*STAR)	Formerly known as National Science and Technology Board. Expand the influence of open innovation. Oversees eighteen research and scientific institutions in Singapore. Nurture high-tech talent.
2003	Biopolis	Establish world-class biomedical research hub, including the entire chain of biomedical activities from R&D to manufacturing. Attract top-level talent from all over the world. Include biomedical field and medical technology. Support the biomedical industry as fourth pillar in Singaporean economy (along with electronics, engineering, and chemicals).
2006	National Framework for Research, Innovation, and Enterprise (NFIE): Schemes, Grants and Programmes—Singapore	Established to enable growth of innovation and entrepreneurship in Singapore. NFIE enables this by setting up startup companies, and they encourage institutions to commercialize their research and technology to bring their products and services to the market.
2006	Science and Technology 2010 Plan	Establish the Research, Innovation and Enterprise Council (RIEC). Promote R&D with S$14.5 billion investment. Increase the share of private sector in R&D. Strengthen connection between technology and enterprise.

TABLE 6.1. (*continued*)

Year	Name	Objectives
2011	Research, Innovation and Enterprise 2015 Plan	Demonstrate knowledge as the base of innovation and attract researchers to Singapore. Provide better and competitive funding environment for both public and private researchers. Implement research on economic outcomes and commercialization of socially beneficial products.
2011	Science, Technology and Enterprise Plan 2015	Promote R&D activities to increase the GERD to 3.5 percent of GDP. Implement the sustaining of talents, commercializing of R&D. Research and international collaboration of scientific ideas.
2016	Research, Innovation and Enterprise 2020 Plan	Develop based on the results of the RIE 2015 Plan. Encourage more interdisciplinary scientific research and provide more competitive funding to build an efficient scheme to select the best idea. Promote more value creation that would benefit the economy.

SOURCES: Koh and Wong 2005; Ministry of Trade and Industry Singapore 2006, 2011; A*STAR 2011b, 2013, n.d.b; National Research Foundation 2017; INTER-CEP n.d.; Pharmaceutical-technology.com n.d.
NOTE: Five-year plans in Singapore are delineated by end years.

goals prepared by the NRF. The NRF operates as a bureau under the Prime Minister's Office. In the same year, the NRF was founded to support the Research, Innovation and Enterprise Council (RIEC). The prime minister chairs the RIEC. Members of the NRF board and RIEC include senior bureaucrats, business executives, academics, and foreign officials. The NRF sponsors programs that enhance local talent. It also implements initiatives that support industry growth and enterprise.

From 2011 to 2016, Singapore's government allocated $19 billion for R&D, 40 percent of which was earmarked for BMS R&D. Table 6.1 outlines Singapore's efforts to promote biomedical innovation and entrepreneurship. From a negligible amount invested in biomedicals in 1991, the year of the first five-year science and technology plan, the Research, Innovation and Enterprise 2020 plan (launched 2016) would spend ten times as much, S$19 billion. How these policies have translated into innovation and entrepreneurship gains is addressed below.

Funding Research and Development

According to latest figures published in 2016 by A*STAR, gross expenditure on R&D was S$9.5 billion, an increase of 11.8 percent since 2014.

While there has been a concentrated push by the government to promote the biomedical industry, the story concerning business expenditure is a bit different. For instance, public-sector funding grew for
biomedicals from S$1,156.1 million in 2014 to S$1,311.2 million SD in
2015—compared to S$935.2 million in Infocomm Media (ICM),[13] and
S$300.3 million in 2015 to chemicals. Despite the largesse of the state,
the private expenditure in R&D for biomedicals lags behind the spending in electronics and ICM. In 2015, electronics and ICM received
S$3,500 million in private investments. Biomedical sciences grew by
14.3 percent to S$726.7 million in 2015 from S$636 million in 2014
(A*STAR 2016).

Nurturing Scientists

Singapore has sought to increase the number of domestic and foreign
research scientists. In 2015, Singaporean and permanent-resident researchers and engineers numbered 23,764, up from 18,277 in 2005. The
jump in the number of nonpermanent-residential foreign research scientists and engineers is even more impressive with a growth from
3,061 in 2005 to 11,224 in 2015 (A*STAR 2016).

This growth has been supported through initiatives like the Singapore Translational Research (STaR) Investigator Award. Established in
2006, STaR is designed to recruit and nurture world-class clinician scientists to undertake translational and clinical research in Singapore as
part of the second phase of the BMSI (2006–2010). It also launched the
Clinician Scientist Award (CSA), which provides research funding and
salary support to enable medical researchers to devote more time to research. Other initiatives to grow this base of clinician scientists include
the Translational and Clinical Research (TCR) Flagship Programme, established in 2007, having a five-year budget of S$25 million. The pur-
pose of the program was to be a platform for researchers and clinician
scientists to collaborate in solving scientific problems and translate their
research into developing quality healthcare solutions for patients (bench-
to-bed solutions). Recognizing that human-capital development under
various disparate programs was not going to have a game-changing impact on Singapore's labor force, the government stepped in, again.

Under the Nanny State: MOM

As Singapore transformed into a knowledge-based economy, it needed to update its labor-management strategy to keep pace with its overall economic strategy. As a result, in April 1998, it formed the Ministry of Manpower (MOM). The ministry was tasked with the need to create a national action plan "to build a globally competitive workforce that would power Singapore into the 21st century knowledge economy." The report "Manpower 21: Vision of a Talent Capital" was drafted after consultation with educational institutions and industry leaders (Ministry of Manpower 1999).

Another area of concern has been maximizing learning opportunities for workers through employment at foreign firms. For example, analyzing the reasons why employees stay with or leave MNC subsidiaries in Singapore, Reiche (2009) found that in Singapore a firm's reputation in the end market may be a form of "external prestige" that contributed to a member identification in MNC subsidiaries and thus positively affects their desire to stay. Other positive factors include international assignment opportunities. Meanwhile, international staffing policy that privileges expats over locals is seen as a reason to leave an MNC (Reiche 2009).

MOM also collects annual data to study the trends of employment and what skills are missing. In the highly mobile labor market in ASEAN, Singapore is a net importer. In Singapore, the 1.2 million foreign workers represent a massive 35 percent of the labor force, of which 14 percent are skilled workers. In 2010, Singapore also hosted 92,000 foreign students. The increase at the time in inviting foreign students and workers is based partly on the rising median age of the Singapore labor force, which grew to forty-three years in 2016 from forty years in 2006 (Manpower Research and Statistics Department 2016). But the increase in foreign employment pass (EP) holders precipitated concern by domestic Singaporeans about unfair hiring practices. As a result, in 2014 MOM implemented the Fair Consideration Framework, tightening immigration policies (Smit 2016).[14] For instance, employers would be compelled to advertise job vacancies on the government Job Bank for at least fourteen days before they apply to hire an EP. Even more stringent policies were enacted in 2017, thought to be targeting the then large population of Indian guest workers (Bhattacharya 2017). Discussed below under entrepreneurial case studies, new ventures have since had difficulty hiring foreign talent. The impact of these immigration restrictions on Singapore's fledgling entrepreneurial ecosystem remains to be seen.

Social Conservatism of the PAP and Its Impact on the Economy

Scholars have argued that as Singapore has become further entrenched in the (neoliberal) globalized economy a deep crisis has emerged. The PAP can no longer take credit for economic success while blaming external forces for its economic failures, as an ever-connected citizenry has access to alternative narratives. The sudden boom of economic growth coupled with increased inequality, rising expenses, and a liberal immigration policy since 2006 has led to an increase in xenophobia (K. P. Tan 2017). The PAP has tried to maintain the balance between addressing the growing aspiration of Singaporeans while still remaining open to its policy of technoglobalism with policies like the Fair Consideration Framework, which does not privilege Singaporeans but ensures a fair opportunity of employment in all companies working in Singapore.

Policy Output Measures

Singapore has since made significant gains in the innovation half of the innovation-entrepreneurship goal. Government agencies and programs have worked in tandem to transform Singapore into a recognized biomedical science cluster. Similar to India, Singapore has built on a foundation in biologic and pharmaceutical manufacturing. The number of workers in the pharmaceutical and biologics manufacturing industries between 2009 and 2015 increased by 36 percent (3,992 to 6,269) (Department of Statistics Singapore 2017). No other industry saw similar growth in the number of workers. Total output peaked in 2012 at S$25 billion (Department of Statistics Singapore 2017). By 2015, however, total output had declined to S$17 billion (Department of Statistics Singapore 2017).

As outlined above, various ministry statutory boards, Prime Minister's Office councils and bureaus, and government facilities have developed schemes that promote BMS R&D. In addition to the newfound focus on technology-cluster-based economic development, the state after 2000 was determined to change the mind-set of people to increase creativity and entrepreneurialism. However, since the establishment of Singapore as a nation-state in 1965, the government had oriented its entire human-capital system to create a "tight labor control regime" to ensure a compliant workforce for MNCs investing in Singapore (Holden and Demeritt 2008). Also, by 2015 nearly one-third of Singapore's research community was foreign, having unintended consequences outlined below (Poh 2016). Although Singapore has made gains in improving innovation capacity, resource limitations have limited progress in entrepreneurial-ecosystem development.[15] According to Shigeki Sugii, founder of stem-cell venture Celligenics, "NTU has been recognized by the world. It may not have much government support but it is doing well by making use of international talent" (Sugii interview 2017). This is discussed in the Celligenics case, below.

Entrepreneurial Ecosystem

Government-Industry-University

Singapore has been on an ambitious mission to create a biotech industrial cluster. It has moved from a paternalistic model with a dependence on adopting and adapting foreign technologies to a "value-adding manufacturing base dependent on export-led development as its passport to economic growth" (Parayil 2005, 54). In the case of Singapore, Parayil distinguishes between a national innovation systems (NIS) framework and a triple-helix framework. The triple-helix concept presented in Etzkowitz (1993) and Leydesdorff and Etzkowitz (1996) is based on the principle that the university has equal status with government and industry, as a leading institutional sphere that fosters innovation in knowledge-based societies (Ranga and Etzkowitz 2015). Parayil (2005) argues that in Singapore, though, the triple-helix model is a variant of an NIS framework, which is more useful in understanding the research-intensive biomedical cluster where there is an emphasis on the important role "for the academic sector in the innovation milieu" (51).

There is growing recognition that if government, industry, and university work together to promote innovation, enterprise, and entrepreneurship in Singapore, the academic sector will be given more autonomy. Consequently, in 2006, both NUS and NTU were transformed into corporatized, autonomous universities, like Singapore Management University. The same year, the government also started the National Framework for Innovation and Enterprise (NFIE), a national program established to enable innovation and entrepreneurship in Singapore. The NFIE supports Singapore universities in commercializing their research and establishing technology-based companies.[16] At the same time, Singapore's strong government presence in all aspects of the economy and society mutes public critique and limits network flexibility. That is, penalties for leaving the social compact in Singapore are "very, very, harsh" (Anonymous interview 2017). A long-term resident of Singapore observed that he felt that once distanced from the city-state, one might never return (Anonymous interview 2017).

While Singapore has undoubtedly improved its value-added position within high-technology manufacturing, including in biomedicals, critics have noted that it still falls short in translational capability—that is, the capability to translate fundamental research into commercially viable products and services. For example, while India under its networked technonationalism has decreased its dependency on MNCs, Singapore, under technoglobalism, has not. Singapore has thus struggled to make the transition from technology importer to innovator in its own right (Mahmood and Singh 2003).

Unintended Consequences

One challenge Singapore has faced in attempting to create an entrepreneurial ecosystem has been the unintended consequences of government policy. For example, following a 2002 report by the Subcommittee on Entrepreneurship and Internationalization, it was found that encouraging public research institutes (PRICs) to spin off high-technology ventures under the Technoentrepreneurship 21 Program, or T21 (as the NSTB had done in the 1990s), had unintended and unwelcome consequences. The PRICs were found to be hoarding promising technologies that might otherwise be licensed to existing firms, resulting from PRIC staff aiming to profit from equity ownership in their own venture companies (Koh and Wong 2003). Restructuring followed, whereby the government transferred authority over T21 from NSTB to the EDB.

Further, in 2011, several "whales," or leading international scientists, announced their departure from Singapore. Observers in Singapore worried that this was a harbinger that the bureaucratic mentality was edging out the scientific vision. For example, the state began to impose "key performance indicators (KPIs)" on scientific output that according to experts "don't actually measure scientific performance" but nevertheless tie eligibility for government grant monies to these measures and are also dependent on mandatory "industry collaborations." This reflects the "impossibility of tightly programming scientific discovery as an economic deliverable" (Catherine Waldby, quoted in Gopinathan and Lee 2011, 297). How this has played out at the biomedical industry level and firm level in Singapore is reviewed next.

Creating an Entrepreneurial Culture

There are two main drags on entrepreneurship in Singapore (similar to those in Japan): the public sector attracts the most talented people, and Singapore is a risk-averse society. Recognition by the state of the need for an "entrepreneurial culture" dates to the mid-1980s when the government set up the Subcommittee on Entrepreneurship Development. The subcommittee found that the government's development policies indeed had consequences on the entrepreneurial ethos of Singapore. It found that the focus on MNCs and large government-linked companies stymied local entrepreneurship. Further, rapid development coupled with high employment levels, high salaries, and job security had made Singaporeans used to the comforts of being employed, in turn sapping the incentive and the desire to venture into their own businesses. In 2016, according to the Hudson Report, which surveyed 636 employers and employees, only 3 in 10 employees in Singapore thought they were encouraged on the job to take risks (Hudson Global Resources 2016).

Limited by its population size and lack of indigenous resources, Singapore has relied on mobilizing domestic talent and importing international talent to develop its economy. Population growth fueled by immigrants has led to strains in domestic society. For Singaporeans, the pressure is on from both sides: high-skill, high-net-worth, often foreign-born individuals pushed property prices upward, while lower-skilled labor from neighboring countries limited the rise of middle-class incomes (Pesek 2017). According to Palatino (2013), this growing socioeconomic gap led to an increasing sense of alienation from the political process and rise in xenophobia against foreigners despite Singapore's diverse, multiethnic domestic population.

On the other hand, pursuing economic nationalism in a fully open and liberal economy when the latter brings with it foreigners who compete with domestic workers for jobs and housing has proven a delicate balancing act for the nation's political leadership. Its authoritarian single-party state (PAP), unlike in pluralist India, has afforded Singapore's leaders a degree of insulation from societal demands. Media censorship means that discussions of the underside of globalization in terms of the burden borne by the indigenous population remain muted. While as of this writing the PAP has maintained its parliamentary majority, since 2011 a slow creep of opposition party representation has continued. Opposition politicians have appealed to resentments against foreigners.

Indigenous Singaporeans have complained and even organized against both an influx of the exorbitant lifestyles of the "rich and famous" (e.g., film stars Jackie Chan and Jet Li have estates) and also the perceived poor hygiene and behavior of low-skill foreign workers (Chong in D'Costa 2012). After about doubling the number of foreigners, which include noncitizens and permanent residents, every decade, by 2010, 1.8 million of the about 5 million residents in Singapore were persons of foreign origin, whereas by 2017 of the 5.6 million residents there were 2.2 million people of foreign origin (Department of Statistics Singapore 2010, 2017). Foreign residents have contributed to inflation in housing

prices and have been criticized for pushing the indigenous population out of the private housing market. Meanwhile, the public housing system has led to the further separation of newcomers from the rest
of Singaporean society. Public housing, in the form of Housing and Development Board (HDB) flats, has been reserved exclusively for Singaporean nationals and permanent residents and, in addition, governed
by ethnic residency quotas. Thus, Singapore has had to balance the support of its indigenous citizens with the goals of promoting economic
growth and development through new industry creation.

Industry

By the 2000s, in addition to the attempts to indigenize innovation outlined above, Singapore was rushing to embrace creative destruction and
encourage technology entrepreneurship. The MNC-based export-led development strategy of the prior three decades had run its course and
was no longer viable in the face of the rising initially low-wage and now
skilled-labor competition from China and India and declining market
opportunities in the mature markets in the West (Gopinathan and Lee
2011). To address these issues, Singapore established the Singapore Management University (SMU) to focus on technology management and
entrepreneurship education. Though Singapore, as of this writing, has
invested billions of dollars into establishing so-called entrepreneurial
universities, observers have argued that Singapore lacks some of the
critical ingredients. Namely, in newly industrialized countries such
as Singapore, the state has had to establish and fund major educational
institutions, including universities. Dependent on the state for their
budgets, most universities in Singapore have not functioned independently of government dictates. In contrast, continental European and
U.S. universities have evolved over centuries into relatively independent
entities. Second, Singapore's latecomer status means that university
training has prioritized the absorption and diffusion of innovations
from outside. This has limited the emergence of a risk-taking and entrepreneurial way of thinking. Japan, the subject of Chapter 3, still struggles to emerge from this mind-set. Third, the shift toward a knowledge

economy at the innovation frontier requires a high degree of absorptive capacity in the private sector for university inventions—but this capacity is lacking in Singapore (Wong, Ho, and Singh 2007).

In addition to the loss of senior scientists mentioned above, perhaps a bigger blow has been the exodus of major pharmaceutical firms via the closure of Singapore R&D facilities. This includes Novartis announcing in 2016 that it would be moving out of Biopolis to Emeryville, California (Min 2016). Meanwhile, Novartis had also built an R&D campus in Shanghai, China, where costs were lower, and there was access to large numbers of STEM university students. In preceding years, Biopolis had lost Eli Lilly (2010) and GlaxoSmithKline (2014), while its neighbor Raffles Hospital bid farewell to Pfizer (2013). An industry observer noted that these departures resulted from R&D productivity decline and also that the promise of new products had never materialized. Singapore has since made a modest pivot to medical technology, such as devices, while still trying to support its fledgling biopharmaceutical ventures.[17] The Singaporean state is at once wholly supportive and omnipresent in the lives of biomedical start-ups, as the cases below illustrate.

Cases

Clearbridge

By 2014, Johnson Chen had licensed three technologies from NUS (NUS Enterprise 2014). Chen, a serial entrepreneur, had previously led companies (including two successful exits) in the healthcare sector. Between 2009 and 2011, three Clearbridge companies had been founded. Chen, with Professor Lim Chwee Teck of NUS, sought to commercialize technology that trapped tumor cells circulating in blood. In 2009, Chen and Lim founded BioMedics. After moving from prototype to commercial product, the duo launched the ClearCell System. Chen didn't need to look any further to find his next two investments. Lim's bioresorbable and biocompatible nanofiber also proved commercially viable. Clearbridge NanoMedics was founded to apply this technology to cosmetic and wound-management solutions.

Also from NUS, Lian Yong's ultralow-powered electrocardiogram (ECG) chip led to the establishment of Clearbridge VitalSigns. In 2013, Clearbridge BioMedics reported raising S$9 million in Series B financing.[18] Clearbridge firms relied on the NRF's Technology Incubation Scheme (TIS). As of 2017, Chen sat on the board of directors at Clearbridge Accelerator (CBA). Established in 2010, CBA is supported by the NRF's TIS. In 2012, CBA was selected to participate in a SPRING Singapore accelerator coinvestment program. Yet another government entity, SPRING is Singapore's Technology Enterprise Commercialisation Scheme. Clearbridge Biomedical Science Accelerator (BSA) was set up to manage the S$40 million fund. Clearbridge BSA identifies, profiles, and finances Singapore-based medical technology start-ups.

Despite the success of Clearbridge in harnessing university technology, a significant portion of IP in Singapore remains untapped (D. Tan 2013). Clearbridge's success was due to the productive collaboration between a serial entrepreneur with significant international experience and entrepreneurial academics. According to a World Bank study, only ten out of seventy start-ups in Singapore received follow-on funding from private investment (Worsley 2013). This evidence suggests a deficiency in translating its still fledgling innovation capacity into entrepreneurial-ecosystem development. Other partnerships between business-minded and scientific-minded tehnoentrepreneurs supported explicitly by the state include HistoIndex and Invitrocue.

HistoIndex

HistoIndex (est. 2013), a spin-off from the A*STAR Institute of Bioengineering and Nanotechnology, manufactures optical medical-imaging equipment. In 2004, HistoIndex's founder, Gideon Ho, joined the institute. Ho holds a PhD in bioengineering from the University of Strathclyde (in Glasgow), having studied engineering at NTU and the University of Glasgow. Ho was interested in the accurate detection of liver fibrosis. Upon returning to Singapore after his doctorate, Ho taught at NTU while also working in various intellectual property management and commercialization capacities at A*STAR. In 2010, A*STAR invested in

Dr. Ho and his idea for HistoIndex. In 2011, SPRING helped Ho to build a working prototype (SPRING 2016).

Initial trials at the time showed that HistoIndex's laser-based medical-imaging system was 85 percent accurate, 20 percentage points more so than the traditional staining method (65 percent). The system was also faster, producing reports within one hour. In contrast, the staining method took days. In addition to liver fibrosis, the HistoIndex system assesses the severity of cancer in tissues. By 2016, its imaging system reached 95 percent accuracy with results available within minutes. The potential of HistoIndex to displace existing technologies reflects the aim of Singapore's entrepreneurial state to lead creative destruction in the biomedical space. The key role of the central state in technology entrepreneurship reflects the core argument of this book that even in an increasingly globalized economy, states pursuing a technonationalist, mitigated openness have attempted to ride the wave of globalization to the ultimate benefit of their own economy and its citizens. The fully open knowledge and network architecture in Singapore (see fig. 2.3), while enabling the country to obtain substantial MNC investments in initial decades, has since constrained the government's ability to generate new technology start-ups. The government has tried to make up for these weaknesses by providing infrastructure, investment, and human capital wherever possible, utilizing A*STAR as a central conduit.

In 2012, after about two years of product development and fundraising, with the support of A*STAR's commercialization arm, Exploit Technologies Pte. Ltd. (ETPL), HistoIndex made its first sale in China. The decision to go global right from the start was deliberate: the high-end nature of the technology required a market with big demand, and the start-up felt it was crucial to have international recognition for the technology. HistoIndex grew from five employees (2012) to fifteen in their Singapore and China offices by 2014.

HistoIndex was able to venture into the Chinese market through a grant from International Enterprise (IE) Singapore (SPRING 2016). According to Ho, IE did more than provide seed funds. They also made connections for the fledgling firm, set up meetings with investors, and assisted in negotiating the agreement. This involvement netted Histo-

Index an investment of more than S$2 million and a wholly owned subsidiary in Hangzhou (SPRING 2016). These initial moves into China led HistoIndex to arrange a 2016 joint venture with Joinscience Medical Group, a major Chinese medical equipment distributer. China's high level of liver disease (estimated by some at 10 percent of the population) makes this a crucial partnership for HistoIndex's growth in the Chinese market. Other product applications in the works include an endoscopy device (SPRING 2016). Reviewing how HistoIndex and Clearbridge have built their international market presence, the entrepreneurial biomedical start-ups of Singapore can be seen as wholly owned subsidiaries of the state. InvitroCue is no exception.

InvitroCue

InvitroCue is also an A*STAR spin-off, this one from the NUS-MIT partnership. InvitroCue develops in vitro cell-based imaging technologies with applications in digital pathology. Its cofounders, Steven Fang and Hanry Yu, have numerous international science, technology, and business degrees. Their effusive praise for the support they received from the Singapore government to get their start-up off the ground reads like a veritable promotional ad for Singapore, Inc., saying that the state has "put in a lot of effort to support local startups financially, as exemplified by our company—the technology was developed in house at A*STAR IBN [Institute of Bioengineering and Nanotechnology], incubated under ETPL and spun off in 2012. With strong financial support from the government, there will be a growing number of biotech companies that aim to go global in the future" (Biotech Connection Singapore 2016). This intensive state support has induced foreign entrepreneurs to settle in Singapore.

Celligenics

Celligenics is an example of the kind of foreign scientist entrepreneur class that had been attracted to Singapore as a result of biomedical cluster policies. The genesis for Celligenics came from Shigeki Sugii's work on a project to create a device isolating induced pluripotent stem cells (iPS) from fat tissue ("adipose-derived"). Sugii founded Celligenics in

2016 with the help of an angel investor, Kurt Wee. Wee, who also served, as of 2017, as president of the Singapore Association of Small and Medium Enterprise, took over the day-to-day operations of Celligenics as CEO. Sugii remained on as silent partner and scientific advisor, a division of labor that allowed Sugii to continue his scientific research. As part of his regular job as a research lab director at A*STAR, he uses stem cells from fat tissue to study such metabolic diseases as diabetes. In late 2017, Celligenics was in the proof-of-concept stage in the development of a device that can quickly isolate stem cells from fat tissue. Through liposuction samples, their team found a way to quickly isolate samples and were collaborating with engineers to make a medical device. In this way, the revenue model is twofold: banking fat samples from liposuction (akin to cord blood banking) and developing a device that would extract stem cells and treat patients. The former has a short-term ROI (less than two years), while the latter has a five-year return scenario. Not surprisingly, Sugii says his investors are keen on encouraging the former.

From Shizuoka, Japan, Sugii earned a bachelor's degree in agricultural biochemistry in 1996 from Kyoto University. He then went to the United States as an exchange student focusing on agricultural chemistry at the University of California, Berkeley (1996–1997). Sugii recalls that, at the time, he had no idea how to apply to graduate school. While at Berkeley, he figured it out, having embedded himself in an ideal environment in the San Francisco area (like the Japanese stem-cell scientist and entrepreneur Shinya Yamanaka years prior). Within the year he embarked on doctoral study at Dartmouth, where he began studying metabolic diseases. Upon completing his PhD in biochemistry (2003), Sugii spent seven years as a postdoctoral fellow at the Salk Institute for Biological Studies and Howard Hughes Medical Institute (HHMI) near San Diego.

During his time at Salk/HHMI, he observed the effects of drug called TZD, which is a popular drug for diabetes and a product for GlaxoSmithKline. It is often thought of as a "blockbuster drug." However, this drug increased the chances of heart attack. GlaxoSmithKline would eventually be subject to a number of lawsuits. At that time, Sugii began to "realize the limitations of the pharmaceutical approach" (Sugii inter-

view 2017). This experience led Sugii to explore other less toxic treatment methods, including stem cells. He also began to study the various
tissues of the body that had potential as rich sources of stem cells, including fat tissue.

Around that time in 2010, he became aware that Singapore had increased investments in stem-cell research. Sugii also learned that top
stem-cell scientists had been attracted to Singapore by the lucrative funding available there. The chance to run his own lab drew him to the
country in 2011. His primary work in 2017 was at A*STAR, and he also
taught for the Duke-NUS medical program. Within A*STAR's twelve
biomedical institutes, Sugii works primarily in the bioimaging sector.
While his specialty was not bioimaging per se, his lab research related
directly to his work as a scientist-entrepreneur in the imaging-device
space. He was also asked by NTU to teach in their newly established
medical school and since became an adjunct professor there. It is worth
noting that in Japan this type of interinstitutional affiliation and thus
boundary-spanning networks are discouraged under that country's
siloed innovation system (see Chapters 2 and 3).

According to Sugii, NTU is rapidly progressing and has done well
in commercialization. He also mentioned that NTU, as of 2017, featured
on a number of "best" international university rankings. According to
Sugii, NTU faculty and students "have lots of energy." By the mid-2010s,
thanks to the university's proven success in commercialization that had
generated significant licensing revenue, the government took notice.
Government leaders have since recognized that NTU has "a good ROI"
(Sugii interview 2017).

NTU's organic growth continued, enabling it to establish a medical
school. The first school of medicine in Singapore was established by NUS
and then the second with Duke-NUS. Both collaborate with SG General Hospital. The third school of medicine was established in 2013 by
NTU. This third school of medicine is operationally independent, has
independent resources to use, and is not a "shared" hospital like the previous two.

Previously, in 2001, the biomedical program was launched at NUS.
During the first decade, they wanted to focus on capacity building and

were looking for good scientists to be a part of the program. Sugii said that after 2010, around the time that he was recruited to join A*STAR, the focus seemed to shift to encouraging entrepreneurship. Its stem-cell institute is already in one hundred clinical trials worldwide for applications in inflammatory diseases, arthritis, heart diseases, and diabetes.

Sugii mentioned that the Ministry of Trade and Ministry of Education have different opinions (not unlike the situation of interministerial factionalism in Japan). As a Japanese national, Sugii noted that the national leadership in the Singaporean Prime Minister's Office has tried to avoid a *tatewari* system, referring to the siloed structure of Japanese research institutions. Instead, the Singapore government has been trying to avoid "go it alone" structures and is perceived by some to be "forcing" funding agencies to collaborate (Sugii interview 2017). One result is that no one in the A*STAR management held just a single position at any one time (reminiscent of the need for one person to serve in various developmental roles at the same time). Instead A*STAR employees are expected to serve concurrently in other capacities elsewhere.

Despite this, unproductive bottlenecks remain, especially in the reporting requirements imposed on firms by the government. For example, the NMRC is equivalent to the NIH in the United States. The NMRC and A*STAR work together to provide funding. Accepting government funds means a researcher is then subject to sometimes onerous and time-consuming reporting requirements, on top of other bureaucratic paperwork. (Similar complaints are voiced by researchers in Japan.) "How can a junior researcher advance a career when they have to do so much administration?" asks Sugii (Sugii interview 2017). Working in a government lab like A*STAR's involves complex administrative work, and everyone—even bench scientists—is expected to help with administrative work.

In response to a question about the 2017 announcement that work visas would be more difficult to obtain and fewer in number, Sugii said that he hasn't encountered personally priority given to Singaporean citizens, "but in general, hiring foreigners is getting harder" (Sugii interview 2017). Nevertheless, as of 2017, Sugii said he was excited to stay and keep working in Singapore, noting the benefits of living in a truly multicultural metropolis. He said it would be hard to find such diversity even in the United States. Sugii added that the competition for funding in stem cells in the United States has been fierce, so it had been nice to be a big fish in a small pond for a change.

He mentioned that biomedical policies have changed in the past ten years. While the policies were focused on building up the industry initially, now the biomedical industry is driven by the private sector. At the same time, Sugii acknowledged that the top-down approach in Singapore is what brought the country to this point. However, like Silicon Valley (itself seeded by significant Department of Defense money), in order to establish an entrepreneurial ecosystem, Singapore needs to allow scientist-entrepreneurs, in bottom-up fashion, to feel free to try new ideas. In this regard, NTU may have contributed to entrepreneurial-ecosystem development (and echoing similar patterns in Kyoto, Japan, and Shenzen, China, as discussed) precisely because it was neglected by the central state. Compelled by its frugal circumstances, NTU made its own way, bootstrapping its science and technology commercializations and growing organically. NTU, as of 2017, was doing so well that it seemed to have quietly become a key part of Singapore's entrepreneurial cluster.

According to the NTU 2010 annual report, the university received grant funds totaling more than S$163.5 million, primarily from the government (Nanyang Technological University 2010). By 2017 NTU received more than twice as much, S$374.6 million in grant money (Nanyang Technological University 2017, 28). In comparison, in 2010 NUS had received more than S$1 billion in governmental grants (National University of Singapore 2010, 70). In 2017, NUS received slightly less, about S$702.3 million (National University of Singapore 2017).

Indicative of its rising fortunes, according to a press release on June 8, 2017, NTU reported that it had jumped from seventy-fourth best in 2010 to eleventh in June 8, 2017, on the Quacquarelli Symonds scale (QS), an internationally recognized index reflecting academic reputation (Nanyang Technological University News Release 2017).[19] Furthermore, in 2018, NTU was the highest-ranked Singapore university, thus surpassing its city neighbor to the east and heretofore government favorite, NUS

(QS World University Rankings Asia 2018). NTU was placed at the top of four hundred universities in Asia. The QS Asian ranking is comprehensive as it includes the "proportion of inbound and outbound of exchange students, and as well as examining an additional bibliometric measure of research papers per faculty" (Nanyang Technological University News Release 2017).

NTU has also analyzed the international impact of its engineering program, for example, tabulating articles that were cited in international-refereed journals with an impact factor greater than four for the period 2001–2011 (Nanyang Technological University 2011). More than six thousand articles by NTU faculty had been cited, placing NTU as the sixth-most-cited institution in the world in 2011, after the University of Illinois, MIT, CAS, Stanford, and UC Berkeley (Nanyang Technological University 2011). NUS ranked tenth, after the University of Michigan. By 2015, the government had funded S$38 billion to establish the National Additive Manufacturing Cluster (NAMIC) at NTU, matched by S$2.8 billion by private companies (Junn 2017). Reflecting its strengths in engineering, "NTUitive" start-ups (including Endomaster) were making inroads. Founded at NTU in 2004, after inventing and beta testing a robotic surgical device, Endomaster would raise by 2017 S$14.6 million in venture capital. It was considered one of the top ten best funded start-ups in Singapore and had plans to launch its product in 2018 (T. Lee 2017).

The 2014 Global Entrepreneurship Monitor (GEM) revealed some changes in Singapore's entrepreneurial environment. Compared with twenty-five other innovation-driven economies (and Malaysia), Singapore performed relatively well in the "fear of failure" category. Among Singaporeans surveyed, 38.6 percent reported that fear of failure would prevent them from starting a business. This is the best result so far in Singapore, better than proportions in Japan (44.4 percent) and Finland (42.1 percent). The United States (32.8 percent) and Switzerland (34 percent) posted better scores (Chernyshenko et al. 2015). The GEM report also reveals that despite the very well-publicized and lauded government-led support system for start-ups in Singapore, perception of entrepreneurs and entrepreneurship in general from 2011 to 2014 had remained unchanged (Chernyshenko et al. 2015). Another start-up ecosystem report from the same noted that it takes approximately 17 percent longer to hire an engineer in Singapore for start-ups than it does for start-ups in Silicon Valley (Compass.co 2015). Despite ranking tenth in the world overall in this particular report (first in the Asia-Pacific region), Singapore ranked twentieth in the "talent" category (Compass.co 2015). In sum, Singapore has the will to establish an entrepreneurial culture. At the same time, its small population and market size mean that it is lacking in the wherewithal to pull it off on a mass scale, compared to China and India. For this reason, local venture capitalists have suggested that Singapore might succeed instead by starting as MNC employees and then leaving to become suppliers to that MNC within the established global "food chain" (*Malay Mail Online* 2015).[20] As discussed above, Singapore has been vulnerable to MNC exit as these global companies move on to more lucrative markets and lower wage rates elsewhere in Asia.

Conclusion

By the 2000s, Singapore had developed into a pristine, shining metropolis of technology parks and five-star hotels. Under Singapore's techno-global openness, even though indigenous Singaporeans have priority access to education and housing, perceived gaps between the foreign "haves" and the indigenous "have nots" had increased. Singapore's delicate balancing act between attracting and retaining foreign talent and firms and providing for its domestic workforce had faltered.

It seems that moving up the value chain from manufacturing to innovation and entrepreneurship at the technology frontier has so far proven beyond Singapore's human-capital capacity. Citing a fallout with international R&D partner Johns Hopkins University, Joseph Wong (2011) sums up Singapore's technology conundrum. The need for foreign funds and foreign technology has limited the ability of the state to manage its own private sector to nationalist ends, as "in the end, Singapore's biomedical future hinges on the decisions of [foreigners] whose interests may not align with the city-state's aspirations" (106).

Lacking a large domestic market (to entice and cajole foreign partners) and a critical mass in domestic human capital, Singapore maintains few innovative ventures that could be sources of new technology ideas and acquisition targets for MNCs. (A critical mass of biomedical ventures is one of the reasons why the United States has been able to maintain its leadership at the technological frontier.) Singapore has struggled to mitigate openness in its knowledge and network regime as it pursues a technoglobalism necessitated by its specific circumstances. Networked technonationalism has heretofore not been a viable option for the city-state due in part to its lack of diaspora networks from which technoentrepreneurial returnees can be drawn. Its top-down authoritarian policy state has tried to adapt the education system to nurture a mind-set more conducive to creativity and entrepreneurship at the technological frontier. However, Parayil (2005) demonstrates that the state still exerts too much control over innovation policy. Echoing Japan's lingering legacies of its developmental-state paradigm, the challenge remains in getting people to think for themselves, when all these years the state has been doing it for them.

CHAPTER 7 CONCLUSION

*Variations in Technonationalism
Compared*

Networked Technonationalism in the Twenty-First Century

In the imaginary economic world, action is taken while making assumptions of "all other things being equal." In reality, policy is never implemented within a vacuum for which all contingencies and variations are accounted. Instead, as the experiences in each of the countries herein show, policy was attempted both within a preexisting domestic institutional context and situated within an international trade and investment environment placing limits on maneuverability. Seeking capital and technology from the global economy forces countries to play by certain rules, such as reciprocity imposed by the WTO.

The narrative arc of the country case studies of this book has presented variations in the model of technonationalism as it guides government policy, from the most closed (Japan) to the most open (Singapore). Middle cases, representing a Janus-faced mitigated openness in knowledge and network regimes, are found in China and India. Each of the countries of this book has targeted the biomedical industry for development, led by a technonationalist vision of how to encourage innovation and entrepreneurship at the technological frontier. In the past, developmental states could make incremental innovations on existing technology following the lead of Western countries in such industries as computers and information technology. At the innovation frontier, the way forward is less clear, and the path to success is undefined. As such, countries like China, India, Japan, and Singapore have placed an enormous gamble on biomedicine, given the relatively high costs of research and development. The payoffs could be substantial, including global market leadership and the ability to set international standards, further solidifying first-mover advantages.

As outlined in table 1.1, in classic technonationalism, such as the approach taken in Japan, technology independence was perceived as a key foundation for national security. In technonationalism, nascent domestic industries are protected from global competition through exclusionary markets and closed business networks. State-owned enterprises and large firms are prioritized by state policy. In Japan, under its legacies of lingering paradigms, the economy has struggled to shake off the yoke of the vertically integrated production pyramid, at the apex of which sit keiretsu conglomerates together with government bureaucrats. Legacies of the hierarchical and insular knowledge and network architecture in Japan limit the potential for internetwork connection. For example, Japan has heretofore failed to incorporate its diaspora talent into developmental policies.

China, in contrast, began a devolution of the central state's stronghold on the domestic economy through expanding opportunity since the launching of the Open Door Policy in 1978. This initial opening was followed by the creation of spaces for innovation and entrepreneurship in SEZs and embracing its diaspora in economic opportunities, especially in its Southern Gate region. Entrepreneurial case-study examples include BGI and Beigene. India has followed China's networked technonational lead and similarly embraced its global diaspora as a way to pursue mitigated openness to foreign capital and firms in its own journey from developing economy to technology leader. The experience of Biocon's Kiran Mazumdar-Shaw is one example of the benefits to domestic startups of protective and mitigated openness to FDI.

NTN, such as that practiced in China and then India, draws from international resources, including diaspora networks that serve as an effective bridge between domestic economies and global markets.

Further, entrepreneurialism is encouraged in these systems. Networked technonationalism is Janus-faced. That is, NTN is global minded and open to the outside world yet at the same time nationalistic within the domestic economy. In these systems, national governments seeking inward FDI mitigate the dangers of foreign capital, ensuring that economic growth is also a winning proposition for economic development within existing domestic firms, with nascent entrepreneurs, and for labor. Technoglobalism has been pursued typically by advanced industrialized countries, including the United States. Seeking inward FDI and rapid technology transfer to the domestic economy, the city-state Singapore also adopted a technoglobal orientation. This has left the Singaporean state vulnerable to the whims of MNCs, whose (profit) interests may not align with the (developmental) interests of host countries. As a result, Singapore has to some extent subordinated the nation-state to foreign firms.

The book has argued that countries that pursue networked technonationalism have been effective in upgrading innovation capacity and also encouraging entrepreneurial activity in targeted industries. Countries have been compared in terms of a knowledge and network typology, manifested in economies as governance regimes and structural-institutional architectures. In brief, codified knowledge comprises information about things (e.g., book learning). In contrast, tacit knowledge is about how to do things and is not written down. Knowledge is also exchanged between people within networks. These networks exist person to person and also between firms and other organizations. Networks can be closed and insular or open and interactive, as outlined in table 2.2 (KNT). The KNT offers a way to compare strategic orientation and developmental vision of the variations on technonationalism (table 1.1). The book has presented comparisons of the characteristics of each variation on the technonational continuum in terms of key actors, role of state, and posture to foreign participation in the domestic economy, from most closed on the left (classic technonationalism, or CTN) to most open on the right (technoglobalism, or TG).

In other words, while the conceptual framework of variations on technonationalism offers a broad-strokes presentation of state strategic orientation in the pursuit of developmental goals, the KNT adds granular detail on the specific ways nation-states go about implementing these strategic developmental goals via specific open or closed knowledge and network architecture policies. These are pursued at formal and informal levels of the economy. Examples of the institutional locale of the manifestation of technonationalism through system architecture include intellectual-capacity-related resource enhancements and building interorganizational networks. Critical to the functioning of networked technonationalism on the ground, in firms and entrepreneurial individuals, is tacit and other knowledge exchange that transcends institutional borders. How the KNT is structured across CTN, NTN, and TG economies is illustrated in figures 2.1, 2.2., and 2.3.

A knowledge and network architecture tends to be either codified and closed or tacit and open in the aim of supporting innovation and developing an entrepreneurial ecosystem (the set of institutions and practices that are conducive to new firm formation). Likewise, a knowledge and network regime encompasses the political leadership and state policies that attempt to guide innovation and entrepreneurial developments, which in turn influence the structure (e.g., inward or outward orientation) of knowledge and network architectures.

Key to the new networked approach taken by China, in particular, has been the orientation of the domestic knowledge and network regime toward inward foreign direct investment, foreign technologists, and their own international diaspora, affectionately referred to as "sea turtles," under a jus sanguinis foundation. India followed some decades later, initially under a jus sanguinis and jus soli model (much like Japan's remains today). Since the rise of the BJP in the 2000s, displacing decades of Congress Party–led inward-looking politics, inspired initially by Mahatma Gandhi, appeals to the diaspora became more overtly Hindu nationalist in orientation. In contrast, Japan historically shunned its diaspora. A Janus-faced mitigated openness maximizes the benefits of openness to the outside while limiting the domestic costs borne by firms and workers. As introduced in Chapter 1, China, India, Japan, and Singapore each began to target the biomedical industry for first-mover development in the early 2000s, having laid the foundations of innovation capacity in preceding decades.

Successful network technonationalist states such as China do so in a similar manner: pursuing developmental goals through mitigated openness to the global political economy and relying in part on international diaspora human-capital networks to facilitate innovation in the domestic economy. In contrast, previously successful but now dysfunctional technonational states such as Japan have heretofore failed to adapt domestic innovation systems to a new international reality. In the old-school technonationalism of the twentieth century, these countries were situated within an international system that tolerated their closed domestic markets and allowed them to engage in net technology importing through followership of frontier innovations in Western economies.

Both China and India have focused their efforts on attracting inward FDI, incorporating foreign technologists into domestic research and development, and appealing to their own diaspora possessing science and technology talent. Both had established high-level government units devoted to engaging with their diaspora in the aim of enticing them to become returnees in order to contribute to fast-tracking development in domestic innovation and entrepreneurial ecosystems. Overtures have included substantial financial incentives, as in the Thousand Talents Plan initiated in China in the 1990s and more recent tax reform in India to attract (NRI) FDI, referred to by Prime Minister Modi as "For the Development of India." The archetypical technonationalist state in the twentieth century, Japan has since struggled to free itself from the legacies of its own success, trapping nascent technology entrepreneurs within a closed knowledge and network architecture. Despite these limitations, Japan has managed to maintain some level of technology leadership through riding the wave of prior decades of technological success evident in its support for advances in stem-cell research. Singapore has pursued its own form of technonationalism with the most global veneer among the cases studied, though the lack of scale in the domestic economy limits entrepreneurial outcomes, and after the mid-2000s, it lost numerous MNCs, mainly to China. Table 2.2 provided a typology to compare the orientation of knowledge and network architectures across country contexts.

Knowledge and Network Typology Revisited

The conceptual framework of networked technonationalism introduced in Chapter 1 was specified in Chapter 2, relating the networked technonationalism framework in the book to such existing theories as national innovation systems and the developmental state. The conceptual framework of networked technonationalism through the knowledge and network typology provides the narrative lens through which the innovation and entrepreneurship stories of China, India, Japan, and Singapore are examined. The firm-level entrepreneurial case studies reflect variations in the national systems of innovation and overall knowledge and network architecture across economies. The classic technonationalism of Japan presented in Chapter 3 was followed in Chapter 4 by the archetypical networked technonationalism of China. Further variations are evident in Chapters 5 and 6 on India and Singapore.

The knowledge and network typology (KNT, table 2.2) provides a basis to assess the degree to which countries pursue new networked technonationalism rather than fall back on classic patterns of technonationalism. In classic technonationalism (fig. 2.1), such as in Japan, the domestic knowledge and network architecture is geared toward amassing codified knowledge and maintaining protective, closed business networks. Industries and markets targeted for development are well defined, thanks to other advanced economies acting as first movers in technology. The objectives are twofold under this system: first, draw technology from more advanced countries, and second, protect domestic firms from foreign competition. As discussed above, in the twenty-first-century global "WTOified" world, this closed and insular approach is no longer viable, due to global demands for reciprocity.

Networked technonational countries, including China and India (fig. 2.2) pursue developmental goals by having a domestic knowledge and network architecture comprised of open networks and human-capital flows. This includes domestic labor mobility and inward diaspora networks that facilitate tacit-knowledge exchange. In Janus-faced mitigated openness, the state incentivizes foreign investors with access to growing domestic markets while encouraging foreign technologists and diaspora talent to contribute to domestic research and development. The diaspora is lured home with financial incentives and also filial piety to family, by blood and by nation.

On the continuum from technonationalism to technoglobalism (table 1.1), the most global-oriented type is reflected in Singapore. Singapore's small domestic market and population size limits the ability of the state to act in a strictly technonational manner. Though its vision is consistent with technonational ideals of national security through technology leadership, Singapore, like more advanced economies in the West, has had the closest approximation to technoglobalism in practice. Thus, Singapore's knowledge and network architecture has been built to seek innovation and entrepreneurial returns to the domestic economy via open borders and human-capital networks conducive to tacit-knowledge exchange critical for innovative activity. Around the world, as the economic-development role of transnational diaspora networks, including technologists, entrepreneurs, and investors increases, perhaps the technoglobal approach over time will reap greater domestic returns for Singapore. Figure 2.3 illustrates the knowledge and network architecture of technoglobalism.

This book has examined the relationship between the technonational vision guiding state economic-development policy and the knowledge and network regime in the domestic economy, facilitating and sometimes hindering the developmental process. The country case studies have attempted to test several hypotheses in this regard.

Networked Technonationalism Thesis and Hypotheses

To reiterate from Chapter 2, the networked technonationalism thesis purports the following: states that mitigate openness to international investment and trade and make strategic use of open international networks—such as utilizing transnational diaspora human networks—are best positioned to pursue simultaneously the goals of innovative-capacity building and entrepreneurial-ecosystem development, reaping a return on investment to domestic firms and workers. Due to the complexity of potential explanatory factors, it makes sense to break the thesis down into constituent hypotheses, in turn grounded in the afore-mentioned conceptual typology, or matrix of knowledge and network governance regime and institutional architecture:

1. Innovation capacity is necessary and sufficient for new technology entrepreneurial-ecosystem development (not supported by data) (lower left quadrant, KNT)

2. Innovation capacity is necessary but not sufficient for new technol-ogy entrepreneurial-ecosystem development (Japan's insular and sticky networks, Singapore critical mass problem) (lower left quad-rant, KNT)

3. Economies might compensate for weaknesses in innovation capac-ity with the aim of developing a new technology entrepreneurial ecosystem through utilizing open (international) network strate-gies (China, India) (upper right quadrant, KNT)

    a. Interinstitutional (and international) networks facilitate (tacit) knowledge acquisition and transfer (upper left, tacit knowledge)

    b. Interinstitutional (and international) networks facilitate "born global" venture start-up activity in new technology sectors (up-per right, open networks)

    c. Mitigated/managed inward-FDI facilitates innovative capacity improvements (lower right, quasi-open network architecture)

Alternative explanations, reviewed in Chapters 1 and 2 include the lib-eralism thesis whereby open trade and investment should lead to organic growth, based on so-called comparative advantage. However, policy leaders in the countries analyzed in this book have recognized that this would leave developing economies at the bottom of the value chain, sell-ing commodities like bananas and coffee to world markets while—lacking domestic capacity to produce higher value-added goods—thus compelled to buy the capital goods exports of advanced industrialized countries.

In the twentieth century, the developmental state of closed trade and investment borders was seen as a pragmatic, nonideological approach to economic growth and development, within which political and economic elites eschewed Western liberal economic ideology. Developmental states could get away with insulating the domestic economy from foreign competition within the Cold War aim of keeping communist expansion out of emerging Asian economies. That was then; this is now.

The twenty-first-century context is far different. Most Asian economies are trying to compete at the technological frontier, no longer able to rely on the security interests of Western countries of containing communism to cloud economic interests. The Soviet Union no longer exists (notwithstanding a resurgent Russia), and China's CCP might as well be referred to as the Chinese Capitalist Party. Chapter 1 introduced the concept of networked technonationalism and placed it on a continuum between the closed classic technonationalism (Japan) and fully open technoglobalism (Singapore). China and India, with their mitigated openness (to, for example, MNC inward FDI) are networked technonational because they are able to structure their KN architecture drawing especially from international diaspora networks. As presented in table 1.1, each country has certain key actors, roles for the state, and postures to foreign presence in the domestic economy. A summary of country-level comparison of the variations in the knowledge and network approaches to pursuing technonational goals follows.

Limits of Classic Technonationalism and Potential for New Networked Technonationalism

Japan: "Miracle" to "Lost"

Japan has been considered the archetypal technonational state and for this reason was the first country case study presented in this book. Under a classic technonational vision, the Japanese state excluded foreigners, their capital, and foreign products from access to the domestic economy. Pursuing developmental goals of nurturing and protecting domestic technology commercialization, central state bureaucrats worked closely with corporate conglomerates (keiretsu) in a tightly integrated vertical production pyramid. Technology gains were made at the expense of foreign firms, but also excluding potentially entrepreneurial ventures. To be sure, Japan made significant technology gains in electronics and automobiles by perfecting existing science and technology, especially that from the United States. Meanwhile, Japan's shunning of its diaspora exacerbated the insular nature of Japanese networks.

Despite the decimation of its industrial base at the end of World War II in 1945, by the 1950s it had already entered its high-growth miracle period, which it rode until the 1970s. By the 1980s, the economy had matured, and its then capital-rich investors fueled rampant real-estate and other asset inflation during its so-called bubble economy period. By 1991, the same year that India entered its liberalization period, the asset bubble had burst, leading initially to the lost decade of the 1990s. Japan's failure since to create a critical mass of entrepreneurial technology start-ups, its paltry amount of VC funds in key industries, and overall stagnation lingered still in its third lost decade as late as 2018.

The closed and protective knowledge and network regime (fig. 2.1) that was instrumental in its rapid economic growth after World War II has since constrained Japan. Japan eventually caught up to the United States, becoming the lead economy in many high-value products, with strengths in intellectual property production. Japan's high economic growth beginning in the 1950s and peaking in the 1980s was attributed to its meritocratic developmental-state bureaucrats in ministries, including METI and MEXT, leading pragmatic policy choices in collaboration with willing private-sector partners. This developmental ideal has been emulated in other Asian countries. As discussed in Chapters 2 and 3, in the aim of catching up to the West, the classic technonationalist developmental approach centered on technology importing while eschewing inward foreign direct investment and maintaining closed protective domestic markets. It also rested on an institutional architecture of vertically integrated domestic-production structure that ensured that players lower on the keiretsu chain (i.e., smaller and more entrepreneurial firms) often at their own expense were in compliance with Japan's corporate conglomerate interests.

The burst asset bubble in the 1990s ushered in the lost decades of stagnation, and Japan has heretofore failed to produce significant new business creation in frontier industries. Insular and closed networks and business practices, albeit protecting weak industries from global competition, have trapped nascent entrepreneurs and undermined human-capital development. A glimmer of hope was evident in that the Japanese state encouraged international science and technology collaborations starting in the 2010s, which may be a potential first step to broader internationalization and open networks. Further, Japan's corporate governance norm of long-term market share over short-term profit, though weakened in recent decades, may translate into competitive advantage in the future. This of course assumes that Japan will counteract its dwindling working-age population (before it is too late).

Over time, the knowledge and network architecture in Japan became dysfunctional as the world economy around Japan changed, and other Asian countries moved up the value-added chain and became direct competitors. Of the number of dysfunctions discussed in Chapter 3, two stand out. On the one hand, Japan remains an economy largely closed to foreigners, and further, talented returnees from its diaspora face employment discrimination. The other side of this is the lack of labor mobility within most Japanese academic and private-sector organizations, reinforcing insularity through age-cohort-based intraorganizational networks. Japan's workforce becomes siloed from a young age, undermining potential tacit-knowledge exchange critical for creativity and innovation, an important foundation for the emergence of entrepreneurial firms.

With this institutional backdrop, Japan has targeted the biomedical industry for development, in its cluster and subsequent policies initiated in the 2000s, as well as the establishment of an industry-academic-government healthcare innovation council more recently (2011). Japan's biomedical industry benefited when Shinya Yamanaka of Kyoto University received the Nobel Prize in medicine for his advances in stem-cell research. The Japanese government responded by investing billions of dollars into that field of biomedicine. Upon closer inspection, however, the discoveries in iPs for which Yamanaka is lauded had been generated not within the Japanese innovation system but previously while a postdoctoral fellow in San Francisco in the United States. Reprocell and other Japanese biomedical entrepreneurial cases, including Pharma Foods, illustrate Japanese government followership rather than leadership in state biomedical policies.

In other words, the successes of these biomedical ventures have rested on circumventing Japan's closed knowledge and network architecture while establishing internationally connected human-capital networks and enhancing tacit-knowledge exchange. The Japanese government has since followed these outside-the-box examples and provided ample R&D and commercialization funds for stem-cell research in particular. Unfortunately, incentives for the commercialization of university assets have counterintuitively undermined nascent entrepreneurship in Japan, as reflected in the case of Reprocell vis-à-vis its Fuji Film–backed foreign competitors.

China: Open Door to Indigenization of Innovation and "Mass" Entrepreneurship

If Japan is the classic technonational state, China has become a new archetype for networked technonationalism. China's CCP led its central state, in the words of Deng Xiaoping, to pursue cautious openness to the outside world under its developmental vision, "crossing the river by feeling the stones." Per Table 1.1, under NTN, China would manage openness to foreign firms, allowing them access to the domestic economy under certain conditions, including initially to SEZs in regions posing minimal threat to the established Communist Party–led political order. Openness to inward FDI would be mitigated by subsidizing initially SOEs and then quasi-private and then eventually fully private firms as nascent producers of products for international markets. It would leverage international knowledge and capital networks, facilitated by embracing its tens of millions of professionals in the global diaspora. It is noteworthy that, like their counterparts from India, Chinese nationals are successful entrepreneurs in places like Silicon Valley in the United States.

Following its initial opening in the 1970s, China officially launched the Open Door Policy in 1978. By the 1990s, China would scale out these efforts with a renewed focus on international R&D collaborations. These would place China by the 2000s in a position to indigenize strategic biomedical technologies at all stages of product development, from bench to market. Its *hai gui* (sea turtle) returnees from its diaspora would eventually lead thousands of new technology start-ups, including BGI and Beigene, evident in the entrepreneurial case studies in Chapter 4.

Through a Janus-faced quasi-open knowledge and network architecture, as illustrated in fig. 2.2, China activated tacit-knowledge exchange and open networks in stages. This included sending out students for training in the West but limited these opportunities to students having the "right kind" of politics (i.e., Communist Party) and patriotism in the 1970s. As discussed previously, China engaged early on with its global diaspora. China also remained closed in that foreigners had access to the domestic economy only within clearly identified spatial boundaries in Southern Gate SEZs. On the knowledge side of the KNT, China would continue to funnel inward FDI in conjunction with government funds into not only manufacturing capacity improvements but also strength in codified knowledge, including mission-oriented science and technology and eventually biomedicals, particularly genomics.

Its quasi-open knowledge and network architecture emerged by the mid-1970s and was in place on a national scale by 1978, with its Open Door Policy. China's NTN invested in STEM education and encouraged entrepreneurship. Among the countries of this book, China was the first to embrace its global diaspora of talent and has made the most relative innovation gains as a result. Meanwhile, in addition to mission-oriented military investments, the biomedical industry was identified as a "strategic emerging industry." In contrast to Japan's insular and closed (sticky) domestic knowledge and business networks, China's expatriate communities and active inward FDI have contributed to evolving globally competitive business networks. China has used its large domestic market as an incentive to attract inward FDI.

From the outside, China has been viewed as a closed communist economy. However, even before the 1978 Open Door Policy, its strategic vision had shifted to greater openness, and the state began sending Chinese students abroad on scholarships, especially to the United States.

Its Open Door Policy under Deng Xiaoping ushered in a period of mitigated openness of encouraging foreigners with capital and technology expertise to join China's developmental journey. Less discussed in existing research has been the other side of openness—that is, the aforementioned sending out of Chinese scientific talent for training. China's developmental process was also helped by its embrace of Chinese in the diaspora. While Japan had been known in the twentieth century as the archetypal technonationalist state, in reality, the very concept of technonationalism had emerged two millennia before, in pre-nation-state China, under the Qin Dynasty (221–206 B.C.E.). What would eventually become the modern nation-state of China advocated that political leaders seek strength through technological superiority.

In China's targeting of the biomedical industry under twentieth-century CCP-led policies implemented by the Ministry of Science and Technology (MOST), its knowledge and network architecture had been designed to compensate for a weakness in the construction of indigenous codified technical knowledge, through embracing its talented returnees, from among its global diaspora of 50 million (as of 2017). Tacit-knowledge exchange is facilitated through high domestic labor mobility, following government reforms in the 1990s, whereby college graduates would no longer be assigned to positions by the state. Domestic labor mobility is complemented with an influx of returnees, themselves responding to financial and infrastructural incentives (e.g., free incubation space) to pursue their technoentrepreneurial dreams "at home."

Symbols of the seriousness of the effort to create a strong innovation to the so-called mass entrepreneurship pipeline include the sprawling biomedical-focused Zhongguancun Park (Z-Park) in Beijing—housing a reported 15,000 returnees and 3,000 start-ups, as of 2015. In comparison, all of Japan's returnee entrepreneurs would fit comfortably together inside a small café. China's Torch Program (est. 1989) led China's expansion into inward FDI attracting SEZs. China has parlayed its open network architecture into advances in biopharmaceuticals, especially in gene therapies and genomics. Its Beijing Genomics Institute (BGI), founded in 1999, had its first hit in 2003 with developing an antigen to the deadly virus SARS, based on the firm's ability to rapidly map the SARS coronavirus genome. BGI's returnee cofounders had been educated abroad and served as team members of the U.S.-initiated Human Genome Project. BGI eventually left Beijing's ample government-supported infrastructure for the southern city of Shenzen, in a bid for greater independence. It still managed to be enriched by government largesse afterward. Other biomedical start-ups, including Beigene and Sundia, show the way in which returnee entrepreneurs have benefited from the open knowledge and network architecture initiated with the Open Door Policy and followed by subsequent programs, including Torch and The Thousand Talents Plan. Chinese political leaders have since called for a nationwide embracing of mass entrepreneurship, while its returnee entrepreneurs say that they no longer need nor desire to follow the technology leadership of the West. Likewise, China's indigenization of innovation strategy in the 2010s reflects its formidable growth in technological and thus economic (and political) power.

Just as ancient China was the original technonationalist pre-nation-state, it has now become the archetype for networked technonationalism. This is predicated on its knowledge and network regime of mitigated openness, in turn enabling China to make simultaneous innovation and entrepreneurial gains, leapfrogging such competitors as Japan in the process. Its large, growing, and increasingly diverse domestic market, coupled with its trained workforce (at least in urban centers), itself rivaling the population size of the entire United States, guarantee that China will continue to be studied in coming years. In contrast, after independence in 1946, India adopted an import-substitution-centered vision of classic technonationalism; it would eventually, some decades behind the pace of China, shift toward a version of NTN.

India: Swadeshi to Videshi

India's devastating experience under British colonialism had a direct effect on its developmental vision as of its independence in 1947. The inward self-reliant Swadeshi Movement inspired by Mahatma Gandhi would remain a guiding force for economic-development policy until as late as 1991. Self-reliance for India meant decades of import substitution and overall decoupling from the international intellectual property rights (IPR) regime. Following a Gandhian vision of self-reliance through policies under its first prime minister, Jawaharlal Nehru, and subsequent postcolonial PMs, India delayed opening its market. Instead, India spent decades on import substitution and other exclusionary policies. Meanwhile, in the aim of improving human health and responding to endemic illnesses common to its climate, India invested in generic drug research and development and production capacity, complemented by advances in information technology.

On humanitarian grounds, India's leaders refused to grant patent protection to Western pharmaceutical companies for medicines needed to heal its ailing populace. India's moist, subtropical climate is a breeding ground for deadly illnesses prevalent in those regions of the world. On this basis, India became a leader in generic medicines, including for HIV/AIDS. This manufacturing capacity would eventually become the foundation for India's biopharmaceutical industry. Complementing this gradual industrial upgrading was the revolution in Indian education initiated by the establishment in 1950 of the independent and autonomous Indian Institutes of Technology (IIT). State-led human-capital development in the IITs initially targeted information technology and by the 2000s focused on biomedicine. It is noteworthy that even though India would delay embracing its diaspora until the turn of the twenty-first century, two of the founders of the IIT concept had engineering degrees from MIT, which became the model for India's IIT system. Expatriate networks of Indian professionals have contributed to the development of innovative capacity and entrepreneurial firms, though decades behind the progress of China.

India's gradual shift from an inward facing and insular CTN variant would take four decades after becoming an independent nation-state. Its Congress Party–led government would initially exclude foreigners from the domestic economy and then gradually allow them in certain industries, including pharmaceuticals. Similar to China's prioritizing of SOEs, India's PSUs (as outlined in table 1.2) would benefit from government protection and subsidies. Likewise, the three key periods of India's developmental process would commence in 1947 with swadeshi, or inward facing policies, which would continue into the 1960s. By the start of that decade, its Ministry of Education would spearhead the creation of a revolutionary new independent government higher-education system of IITs. The institutionalization of the IIT education model would continue to the 1990s, with even greater expansion in the 2010s. The third period, videshi, or outward facing stage, was precipitated by a financial crisis that enabled reformers in the government to circumvent entrenched interests and liberalize the economy.

NTN knowledge and network architecture in place in the IT industry allowed the Indian economy to build competencies beyond call centers, eventually becoming a leading center for software development. These economic clusters were concentrated in urban centers, including Bangalore, upon which the state would further build out capacity via an outwardly oriented knowledge and network architecture to make inroads into biomedicals, especially biopharmaceuticals.

India has aspired to have a knowledge and network regime of mitigated openness, allowing it to make the economic gains of its similarly sized neighbor to the north. However, India lacks the autonomy of a single-party authoritarian state that both China and Japan have had. India's vibrant democracy means that state policy makers have not been insulated from the demands of the populace. Its policies must thus be more inclusive of its citizen stakeholders.

Further, by 2004, in its attempts to catch up to China's economic growth, India had established an entire ministry devoted to engaging with the Indian diaspora. India, though decades behind China in terms of opening its knowledge and network architecture to returnees (NRIs), nonetheless is in a better position than, for example, Japan to reap the benefits of increased tacit-knowledge exchange.

India's joining the World Trade Organization and signing onto the TRIPs in 1995 (with a ten-year grace period for compliance) meant that patent protection would be valid for domestic scientists and entrepreneurs just as it would for foreign pharmaceutical firms. Also lagging twenty-five years behind China, India established SEZs in 2005, having targeted biotechnology in earnest by the five-year plan launched in 2002. Building on infrastructure and academic capacity in India's leading IT cluster cities (Bangalore, Hyderabad, and Mumbai), these regions have also been a center for biomedical entrepreneurship. After the noted accomplishments of the Indian pharmaceutical company CIPLA, Biocon (started in a garage in Bangalore) has become India's leading biopharmaceutical company.

Biocon's founder, Kiran Mazumdar-Shaw, who became the richest self-made woman in India, was able to parlay her training and expertise in enzymes as the daughter of a brewmaster to the helm of the venture firm Biocon in 1978. Under India's then self-reliant and protective policies, foreign ownership was limited, which meant that Mazumdar-Shaw would have a majority stake. As a result, she was able to maintain managerial control over the course of decades, with multiple foreign partners, including Unilever.

Biocon's billion-dollar IPO in 2004 earned Shaw the funds that she used to establish Biocon Park in Bangalore, now the largest dedicated biotechnology R&D facility in India. The success of Biocon reflects India's entrepreneurial ecosystem (despite the red tape of the License Raj bureaucratic culture) and established biopharmaceutical capacity. Now that India's IPR regime tracks with global standards, it may encourage more inward FDI and a higher level of R&D investment from its foreign partners. Singapore has struggled to increase its inward FDI, despite intense effort. Like China, India's large domestic market and rising middle class make it attractive to foreign firms. At the same time, its pluralist innovation and entrepreneurship systems make private-sector–government collaboration more contentious. For example, the missteps of the Indian Patent Office and overcorrection by Ministry of Health prompted by an Indian Supreme Court ruling in 2013 have bottlenecked clinical-trials approvals of biomedical entrepreneurs. Nevertheless, India's knowledge and network architecture demonstrates high levels of labor mobility and institutional flexibility (the upper quadrants of the KNT), which may prove a competitive advantage in the future.

Singapore: Capacity Building to Bureaucratic Reform

Singapore, like India, emerged from the aftermath of World War II as a newly independent nation-state. From the beginning, its developmental model was global in outlook, reflecting its multicultural national identity. Of the cases herein, it has the most globally oriented knowledge and network architecture, the closest in structure to the ideal of technoglobalism. As illustrated in figure 2.3, Singapore is characterized by knowledge and network openness, allowing foreign firms and their capital relatively unfettered access to the domestic economy. As such, the state has attracted foreign investment through an "open for business" transparent regulatory framework. In this regard, MNCs play a key role in the domestic economy. In some ways, state interests became subordinate to the interests of MNCs and even foreign universities. To the extent that Singapore followed more classic technonational strategies, it was in requiring employment of its citizens and the redistribution of foreign capital to the housing and education infrastructure for indigenous Singaporeans.

In an underdeveloped situation when it found itself outside the Malay state on a patch of swamp to the south, Singapore focused at first in the 1960s on building manufacturing capacity. The developmental trajectory of Singapore would be punctuated by personalities, including the technobureaucratic visionaries Yip and Yeo, who served as leaders through decades of industrial-development policies. Small city-states are like small towns: community leaders tend to serve multiple, often overlapping roles. This has made for occasional turf battles in Singapore. The aforementioned leaders of Singapore's biomedical policies and related ministries have been no exception.

The year 1997 would be a turning point for Singapore, with the Asian financial crisis as a crucible for the nation-state. Dwindling capital inflows meant that strategic bets would have to be all chips in for a shorter list of target industries. Like the other countries in this book, Singapore would pin its fortunes on biomedicals. However, despite billions of dollars invested in the hopes of creating an Asian biomedical hub, by the mid-2010s, a series of high-profile MNC departures—most of which had been lured by opportunities in mainland China—would continue despite government reform initiated in 2006.

Singapore's meritocratic Economic Development Board and Agency for Science, Technology and Research targeted MNCs in the biomedical industry early on for inward FDI. Its human-capital development programs contributed to productivity gains through attracting the Asian region's best and brightest STEM youth and offering them citizenship. However, Singapore's small domestic market and tiny population have limited the number of biomedical entrepreneurs. The country has attempted to compensate for its weaknesses with lucrative incentives to encourage talented foreigners to contribute to the domestic economy. While high-skilled foreigners have benefited, a growing disparity in the benefits accrued of openness for the indigenous population has led to calls for more inclusive innovation.

Singapore's activist state, lacking the indigenous human resources and budgets of other countries, placed a huge bet on the biomedical industry. The watchful eye of the national government monitors the progress of universities, technology parks like Biopolis and firms closely. Its nanny-state tendencies were evident in the aptly named MOM (Ministry of Manpower) move in 2017 to impose additional restrictions on the employment of foreign nationals. Its technoentrepreneurs have been dependent on the state for their start-up capital and incubation space, and they even rely on state officials in international business activities, as the case of HistoIndex illustrates. The line between state-owned enterprise and private firm is blurred in the case of Clearbridge and its spin-offs. Invitrocue waxed poetic about the significant state support behind it and biomedical ventures in Singapore in general. The stories of beholden-to-the-state biomedical ventures obscure another concern. That is, Singapore has fallen short of the mark in improving its innovation system, in addition to the lack of scale in its entrepreneurial ecosystem. As alluded to above, the departures in the 2010s of major multinationals' R&D centers, including Novartis to Shanghai and GlaxoSmithKline shutting down its Singapore center, as well as failed international university partnerships, such as with Johns Hopkins University, reflect the underwhelming progress in new product innovations and paltry amount of entrepreneurship.

Conclusion

As the Japan case illustrates, governments have been more effective at creating the ecosystem-level conditions—such as labor mobility and human-capital development—than at creating entrepreneurial business networks by policy fiat. This points to the challenge of developing entrepreneurial ecosystems that free domestic individuals and firms to forge international connections, build social capital, and harness the resources obtained via international networks for investment into the future of their economies.

Both China and India have large domestic markets fueling consumption. Inward FDI has been channeled into upgrading production, absorptivity, and ultimately innovation capacity. Harnessing millions in their global diaspora—via remittances at the low-skill end and science and technology innovation and entrepreneurship at the high-skill end—has resulted in technology leapfrogging in niches of the biomedical industry, such as genomics (China) and biosimilars (India). A Janus-faced mitigated openness to international capital and foreigners reflects a new networked technonational model for innovation and entrepreneurship at the technological frontier. Japan's more limited potential for future domestic market growth (outside of eldercare-related industries) and a minimal diaspora from which to draw human-capital talent present a challenge to the classic technonationalist approach of an insular and closed domestic knowledge and network regime. Further, Japan's limited labor mobility exacerbates weaknesses in its overall knowledge and network architecture.

While Japan has attempted to increase its international connectivity of S&T human capital, through, for example, international collaborations in research and development, it lacks the scale of its new Asian competitors to its west. The manner in which other Asian countries have connected to and utilized their diaspora is illuminating and worthy of more extensive research in the future. China was the first to appeal to the familial (and national) piety of its international sojourners of all walks of life, and serendipitously the communist period liberated many Chinese from preexisting class hierarchies. India was slower to embrace its diaspora, and its caste hierarchies have limited potential synergies. Japan's receptivity to its diaspora has always been tempered by three nested biases: by purity of jus sanguinis, by jus soli, and by class. Returnees are judged by assumptions about their family origins (peasant stock as low, samurai class as high), though their families may have left Japan more than a century ago. Even returnees of so-called pure Japanese heritage have often been excluded from employment and business opportunity as harshly as those of mixed race or foreigners if they have not resided every moment from birth within the borders of Japan.

The temple Janus, open for a time in the heat of the battle, is also a temporal, ephemeral presence. Janus, characterized by battle-ready openness to the outside, while protective of those on the inside, is intended to be fleeting, eventually fading away once its purpose has been served. Likewise, mitigated openness in a country's knowledge and network regime may perhaps be replaced by something else, more suited to the competitive environment of future generations. Perhaps a new, new technonationalism will emerge, Ganesh style, after the Hindu deity of new beginnings and auspicious ventures. With this future view in mind, more questions arise. Does the networked technonationalist framework have generalizable relevance in other countries in or outside of Asia? Are all states inherently technonationalist, with varying will and wherewithal to carry it out? Are there specific countries elsewhere to apply the knowledge and network framework, with or without technonationalist framing?

The Asian region continues to grow economically and is quickly becoming the center of the world's population and its business activity. As such, Asian countries' unique technonational approach to developing their innovation systems and entrepreneurial ecosystems is worthy of further analysis. The knowledge and network typology may provide a basis to compare developmental processes as other countries around the world seek to emulate the successes, while avoiding unintended consequences, of present-day networked technonationalism.

The core lesson of the analysis herein is that developing economies whose state leaders imbibe the economic liberalism on offer by multilateral institutions such as the IMF and WTO, backed by Western countries with a vested (trade, investment) interest, and as a result fully open their doors to unfettered trade, have done so at their own peril. The networked technonational country case studies analyzed here demonstrate that engagement with the global economy is unavoidable in the search for inward FDI and technology gains in the uncertain context of competing at the technological frontier. Nevertheless, a Janus-faced mitigated openness has proven most effective in economic growth that translates into economic development.

ACRONYMS

Acronym	Full term
ABLE	Association of Biotechnology Led Enterprises
AIIMS	All India Institute of Medical Sciences
AIST	National Institute of Advanced Industrial Science and Technology
BGI	Beijing Genomics Institute
BITS	Birla Institute of Technology and Science
BMRC	Biomedical Research Council
BMS	Biomedical Science
BSA	Bank Secrecy Act
BYBP	Beijing Yizhuang Biomedical Park
CCP	Chinese Communist Party
CDI	Cellular Dynamics International
CIPLA	Chemical, Industrial and Pharmaceutical Laboratories
CiRA	Center for iPS Cell Research and Application
CRO	Contract Research Organization
CSC	Committee on Singapore's Competitiveness
CSIR	Council of Scientific and Industrial Research
DAE	Department of Atomic Energy
DBT	Department of Biotechnology
DIET	National Legislature of Japan
DIPP	Department of Industrial Policy and Promotion
DPJ	Democratic Party of Japan
DRDO	Defence Research and Development Organization
EDB	Economic Development Board
EDBI	Economic Development Board Investments
ES	embryonic stem cell

ETPL	Exploit Technologies Pte. Ltd.
FIRM	Forum for Innovative Regenerative Medicine
GCI	Global Competitiveness Index
GEDI	Global Economic Development Index
GEM	Global Entrepreneurship Monitor
GERD	Gross Domestic Expenditure on Research and Development
GII	Global Innovation Index
HAL	Hindustan Antibiotics Ltd.
HDB	Housing and Development Board
IBI	International Business Incubators
iCeMS	Institute for Integrated Cell-Material Sciences
ICI	Innovation and Competitive Index
ICMR	Indian Council of Medical Research
IDMA	Indian Drug Manufacturers Association
IDPL	Indian Drugs and Pharmaceuticals Ltd.
IE	International Enterprise
IIIF	India Inclusive Innovation Fund
IIMs	Indian Institutes of Management
IIT	Indian Institute of Technology
IMCB	Institute of Molecular and Cellular Biology
IMF	International Monetary Fund
INVs	International New Ventures
IPO	initial public offering
IPR	intellectual property rights
iPS	induced pluripotent stem cells
IUSSTF	Indo-U.S. Science and Technology Forum
JETRO	Japan External Trade Organization
JHU	Johns Hopkins University
JVs	joint ventures
KNT	Knowledge and Network Typology
KPIs	key performance indicators
LDP	Liberal Democratic Party
M&A	mergers and acquisitions

METI	Ministry of Economy, Trade and Industry
MEXT	Ministry of Education, Culture, Sports, Science and Technology
MHLW	Ministry of Health, Labour and Welfare
MITI	Ministry of International Trade and Industry
MNC	multinational corporation
MoD	Ministry of Defense
MOF	Ministry of Finance
MOH	Ministry of Health
MTI	Ministry of Trade and Industry
NAIST	Nara Institute of Science and Technology
NASSCOM	National Association of Software Services Companies
NBDS	National Biotechnology Development Strategy
NEDO	National Energy and Industrial Technology Development Organization
NIH	National Institutes of Health
NIP	New Industrial Policy
NIS	national innovation system
NITs	National Institutes of Technology
NLEM	National List of Essential Medicines
NMRC	National Medical Research Council
NPPA	National Pharmaceutical Pricing Authority
NRF	National Research Foundation
NRI	nonresident Indian
NSI	national system of innovation
NSTB	National Science and Technology Board
NSTEDB	National Science and Technology Entrepreneurship Development Board
NTBs	nontariff barriers
NTN	Networked Technonationalism
NTU	Nanyang Technological University
NUS	National University of Singapore
NVCA	National Venture Capital Association
OBOR	One Belt, One Road Initiative

OCAO	Overseas Chinese Affairs Office
OECD	Organisation for Economic Co-operation and Development
OEMs	original equipment manufacturers
PAP	People's Action Party
PCT	Patent Cooperation Treaty
PDMA	Pharmaceuticals and Medical Devices Agency
PM	prime minister
PMO	Prime Minister's Office
PPP	public private partnership
PRC	People's Republic of China
PRICs	public research institutes
PSUs	public sector undertakings
QE	quantitative easing
R&D	research and development
RI	research institute
RIE	Research, Innovation and Enterprise
RIEC	Research, Innovation and Enterprise Council
RMB	renminbi
ROI	return on investment
ROIC	return on invested capital
RSS	Rashtriya Swayamsevak Sangh
S&T	science and technology
SBIR	Small Business Innovation Research
SCI	Science Citation Index
SEZs	special economic zones
SIB	Stanford India Biodesign
SMC	Southwestern Medical Center
SME	small- and medium-sized enterprise
SMU	Singapore Management University
SOE	state-owned enterprise
SPRING	Standards, Productivity and Innovation Board
SRP	Scientific Resolution Policy
STA	Science and Technology Agency
STEM	science, technology, engineering, and mathematics

STEP	Science and Technology Entrepreneurs Park
STIP	Science and Technology Industrial Parks
TBI	Technology Business Incubators
TCM	traditional Chinese medicine
TFP	total factor productivity
TiE	The Indus Entrepreneurs
TIS	Technology Incubation Scheme
TLOs	Technology Licensing Organizations
TN	Technonationalism
TRIPS	Trade-Related Aspects of Intellectual Property Rights
TTOs	Technology Transfer Offices
UNDP	United Nations Development Programme
UNESCO	United Nations Educational, Scientific and Cultural Organization
UNICEF	United Nations Children's Fund
VLSI	Very Large Scale Integration
WEF	World Economic Forum
WIPO	World Intellectual Property Organization
WTO	World Trade Organization

NOTES

Chapter 1

1. In theory, a completely closed economy would not have any imports or exports, and the less open to the outside, the greater control state leaders have over capital and labor within the domestic economy.

2. In the twentieth century, according to Rostow (1960), advanced industrialized countries in a "flying geese" pattern of development served as lead goose in advancing through the stages of development within industries in less developed countries (LDCs) toward higher levels. In this pattern, LDCs would start at low levels (e.g., component manufacturing) of the global value chain in a given product, learning by doing and eventually catching up to the lead goose in a particular technology.

3. I have chosen to use the Roman god Janus as a point of reference as it is likely to be familiar to Western readers. In Asia, the paradox of open-exposed / closed-protective imagery (for example, in Buddhist temple guardian lion-dogs) predates Janus by more than half a millennium.

4. The role of international networks is discussed in detail in Chapter 2. See Freeman (1991) for an overview of innovation networks and Coviello and Munro (1995) for reviews of the internationalization of entrepreneurial firms.

5. Joseph Schumpeter (1942) coined the term *creative destruction* to describe the transformation within economies from mature and declining sectors to new and emerging in which the role of entrepreneurs is paramount.

6. In contrast to earlier periods in which rapid home-country economic development occurred via colonization in politically suppressed and economically exploited host country colonies, national governments have since been constrained in their access to outside resources (Chang 2002; D'Costa 2012).

7. For example, as discussed in Chapter 5, from the 1930s, India had invested in generic pharmaceuticals, but until the late 1990s, it relied on technology importing.

8. In the Deloitte study, the life-science industry was comprised of biotechnology, pharmaceuticals, and medical technology segments.

9. Patents filed under the PCT, administered by the World Intellectual Property Organization (WIPO), allow applicants to have intellectual property protections across

a large number of countries simultaneously. As of 2017, there were 152 PCT member countries (WIPO n.d.).

10. The OECD revealed technological advantage index is determined by the share of country (or economy) in biotechnology patents relative to the share of total patents in that country (or economy). OECD statistics include countries with greater than five hundred biotechnology patents (OECD 2014).

11. Overall competitiveness in these economies mirrors the global trends outlined above in the biomedical industry. The World Economic Forum, known for its annual convening in Davos, Switzerland, of the economic literati and moneyed, publishes the Global Competitiveness Report. Its rankings of 144 world economies are based on a composite of twelve measures, including institutional capacity, technological readiness education and training, and overall macroeconomic environment. The 2014–2015 edition places Switzerland at the top, followed by Singapore, the United States, Finland, and Germany. The top three in Asia are Singapore, Japan, and Hong Kong SAR. China places eleventh in Asia with a global rank of twenty-eighth, while India ranks seventy-first (Sala-i-Martin et al. 2014). The 2017–2018 edition places Switzerland in first place, followed by the United States, and Singapore in third place. Furthermore, Japan is ranked in ninth place, China in twenty-seventh place, and India in fortieth place (World Economic Forum 2017a). The Global Innovation Index (GII), published jointly by Cornell University, INSEAD, and the World Intellectual Property Organization is a composite of seven indices (five input, two output). Input measures include such human capital as scientists and engineers, research, infrastructure, policy, and knowledge absorption. Knowledge, technology, and creative outputs complement input measures. The 2018 GII ranks the top ten innovation economies as follows: Switzerland, Netherlands, Sweden, United Kingdom, Singapore, United States, Finland, Denmark, Germany, and Ireland. Japan ranks thirteenth; China, seventeenth; and India, fifty-seventh. In the GII 2014 report, China was noted in the report for its significant improvements in developing institutions to support innovation. India lags due to declines in manufacturing output and a slide in input capacity (Dutta 2014, Lanvin, and Wunsch-Vincent 2018).

12. Nakamura refers to a special issue—*kurashisu*, クラシス (crisis)—in 1983 in which he introduced the concept as "techno-nationalism" in English.

13. See J. Wong (2011) for an analysis of the limits of developmental state policies in the biotechnology industry in Singapore, South Korea, and Taiwan.

14. See Mazzucato (2013, 2014) for a discussion of the role of public finance in innovation.

Chapter 2

1. The news media in China and Japan are either explicitly censored by the central state (China) or engage in self-censorship as a prerequisite for access to government officials and corporate executives (Japan) (Reporters without Borders 2016c). Among

Asian countries, Singapore and China are considered "Not Free," India is "Partly Free," and Japan is considered to be "Free" (Freedom House 2017). The use of violence against the media in India has been rising (Reporters without Borders 2016a; Seshu 2017).

2. It should be noted that this represents an anomaly in Japan, in that these international linkages have heretofore been few and far between.

3. For example, in the United States the majority of new technology start-ups in Silicon Valley are led by either Chinese or Indian entrepreneurs (Wadhwa et al. 2009).

4. Definitions and measures of "diaspora" vary across countries. Chinese diaspora includes the Han ethnicity and 56 other ethnic minority groups; the number excludes 1.4 million returned students. Japanese diaspora is also known as *nikkei*. According to the Association of Nikkei and Japanese Abroad, nikkei are "Japanese people who have relocated overseas on a permanent basis, as well as their second, third and fourth generation descendants, irrespective of current nationality and degree of Japanese ethnicity." Indian diaspora comprises expatriate Indians and people of Indian origin.

5. The KNT might be applied, for the purposes of international comparison, within other (nontechnonationalist) contexts.

6. Temple (1999), referencing Kuznets on how small N country case studies limit generalizability in growth theory and Gershenkron on the importance of a historical (institutional) view, notes that the former type of analyses provide possible hypotheses of probable causal explanations. The contribution of econometrics is that it can test these grounded hypotheses more broadly, to yield generalizations across many cases.

7. While international composite indices are a useful starting point for comparative analysis, care should be taken in assessing the quality and reliability of the original country-level data sets upon which these indices are based. For example, national-level data is often provided by national governments with an interest in promoting their international brand, not to mention downplaying negative data.

8. See also Powell (2003) for a review of the literature on networks as an alternative to markets and hierarchies in accomplishing firm-, industry-, and regional-level economic goals. The Chicago Vienna hot dog mystery is a classic example of the import to organizations of tacit knowledge, the cost of losing it, and the difficulty of identifying and reestablishing its mechanism after it is lost (*This American Life* 2003).

9. Leydesdorff has developed a number of mapping algorithms to measure international intellectual capacity networks. (See Leydesdorff, Carley, and Rafols 2013, 7–8, for map link.)

10. Chinese Taipei was excluded from the Chinese data, with a growth of 423 percent in copatents and an overall patent growth of 863 percent.

11. Other countries in the top ten in terms of percentage growth included Chile, Lithuania, Malta, Turkey, Korea, and Poland.

12. An English-language ProQuest search (1990–2016 data) using keywords "technonational" and "techno-national," excluding review articles, resulted in 145

publications. China led in the country foci (22), followed by the United States (19), Japan (16), India (11), and other Asia (5). Various countries from around the world were the foci of a single article or perhaps two, such as Argentina, Bangladesh, Hong Kong, and Vietnam (ProQuest, www.proQuest.com, accessed January 4, 2017).

13. See also Samuels (2003) on Italy and Japan.

14. During his lifetime, Qin built a very large and extravagant mausoleum for himself, home to the Terra-Cotta Warriors, in Xi'an, China.

15. Until the year 2000, Ministry of Economy, Trade and Industry (METI) was named Ministry of International Trade and Industry (MITI).

16. After 1945, *zaibatsu*, family-held industrial holding companies that controlled entire sectors of the economy, were broken up and replaced by a structure of keiretsu, or large firms characterized by cross-shareholding across sectors. Well-known zaibatsu-turned-keiretsu include Mitsui, Mitsubishi, and Sumitomo. Noteworthy is that many of these firms were established by entrepreneurs in the pre-Meiji period, in regions outside of Tokyo (then Edo).

17. For example, the pursuit of technology independence was led also by industrial capitalists and entrepreneurs, including Eichi Shibusawa, 渋沢栄一 (1840–1931). As a young man, Shibusawa studied Confucius and is said to have led the creation of hundreds of new companies, including the first joint stock company in Japan (*shōhō kaisho*, 商法会所), the first banks, Sapporo Beer, and early private railroads. Shibusawa often stated that he saw new firm establishment and growth as a national and moral duty. Shibusawa, whose vast business empire extended to mainland China, observing how the Chinese had been exploited by the British, at home in Japan promoted economic nationalism as a way to stimulate and protect the development of domestic industry (Sagers 2014).

18. Recent advances in the mathematical modeling of the location of innovation in the "adjacent possible" interplay between the actual and the possible (e.g., the formal models of Vittorio Loreto and Stuart Kauffman, cited in Emerging Technology 2017), as well as with social network theories of innovation finding that breakthrough scientific discoveries occur between previously disconnected areas of knowledge (Chen et al. 2009), may help national governments in mapping innovation and entrepreneurship potential in the unknown territory of frontier science.

19. Articulations of nationalist rhetoric by enterprising individuals may have been a way to appeal to government leaders for preferential treatment.

20. The structure of *Betting on Biotech* comparing countries side by side within thematically organized chapters is stylistically different than that of the present work. The structure here is to present the theory and methods and then apply the framework in succession across countries, allowing a depth within each country, while referring back to the conceptual framing when appropriate.

21. It should be noted that a country's power to set international standards does not necessarily mean that the concomitant technology itself is the best quality. An ex-

ample is the eventual market dominance of American-made VHS video technology over the higher quality Japanese Betamax in the 1980s.

22. For example, Lazonick and Tulum (2011) note "without [the hundreds of billions of dollars in] NIH funding to create the indispensable knowledge base, venture capital and public equity funds would not have flowed into biotech" (1176).

23. Breznitz and Murphree (2010, 2011) argue that China's competitive advantage is in its second-mover process innovations on foreign technologies, in products for the large domestic market, and see as foolhardy national government attempts to become a first-mover in high-technology industries.

24. Hall and Soskice (2001) outline varieties of capitalism on a continuum from economic liberal to developmental approaches, highlighting differences in Germany, Japan, the United Kingdom, and the United States. In the varieties of capitalism typology characterizing countries by the dominant state-/private-sector institutional forms, countries pursuing liberal policies become "liberal market economies" while developmental-state approaches would be "coordinated market economies."

25. In Japan, university faculty were incentivized in the 2000s by the Ministry of Education, Culture, Sports, Science and Technology (MEXT) to establish "university ventures." While this has led to the creation of more than one thousand "on paper" companies, to date only a handful have products or services that have reached the market (Ibata-Arens 2014).

Chapter 3

1. Other positive signs that Japan is considering new directions include a government-sponsored report, "Anxious individuals, nation at a standstill," which in unprecedented fashion featured perspectives from junior bureaucrats across ministries and agencies (Tsuji 2017).

2. In the 1990s, a series of bailouts backed by the Japanese government of "zombie" firms such as Sharp is indicative of the refusal of Japan to create an institutional space for Schumpeterian gales of creative destruction (see Caballero, Hoshi, and Kashyap 2008).

3. Japan's technocracy colluded with the militarists in the occupation of Manchuria, as part of Japan's imperial ideology of "comprehensive" technology development for Asia (Moore 2013).

4. Beason and Weinstein (1996) in an article critical overall about the impact of Japanese government policies on high-growth sectors (arguing instead that the Japanese government gave more to low-growth sectors) cite research by Marcus Noland (1993) finding that R&D subsidies did increase exports in targeted sectors.

5. The founder and then chairman of Sony, Akio Morita, and longtime governor of Tokyo Shintaro Ishihara published a book in 1989 called *The Japan That Can Say*

No in a proverbial thumbing of the Japanese nose at the United States, which had lobbied Japan to open its borders to foreign imports.

6. It is customary in English to list Japanese names in first name, last name order. Chinese names follow the custom of appearing in English in last name, first name order.

7. As defined in Chapter 2, *business network* here refers to inter-firm connections not limited to the cross-shareholding corporations (keiretsu) but instead inter-firm relations more broadly.

8. See Samuels (1994, 2003) for an intellectual and policy history of nationalism and technology leadership in Japan.

9. Japan's electoral bias toward senior voters is considered the most severe among industrialized countries.

10. See Noble (2011) for a discussion of the organizational and political context of lifetime (permanent) employment and low labor mobility.

11. Pekkanen and Tsai (2005), highlighting the experiences of China and Japan, show how states reconfigure themselves in the context of changing conditions in the world economy.

12. In Asia, Japan and Korea are full members of the OECD, while in 2007 China, India, and Indonesia became part of data collection via the organization's Enhanced Engagement programmes (OECD 2015).

13. The OECD Revealed Technological Advantage Index is calculated as the share of country (or economy) in biotechnology patents relative to the share of country (or economy) in total patents. Only countries and economies with more than five hundred patents in 2010–2013 are included in the figure (OECD 2016a).

14. "Cost-down" refers to unilateral top-down reductions in the prices large companies were willing to pay subcontractors for their products. Just-in-time production meant that large companies could compel suppliers to have their components ready, i.e., parked nearby in trucks, for purchase and delivery just hours before they would be used in production. This placed the burden of holding inventories on suppliers. Ibata-Arens (2005) analyzes how such big business practices related to innovation and entrepreneurship activity in high technology Japanese firms during the recessionary 1990s.

15. Japan is also burdened by a high debt load with related debt service costs (OECD 2015).

16. It should be noted that informal investment often rests on noncontractual "handshake" agreements between investors and entrepreneurs, so these transactions rarely appear in official statistics.

17. Though Japan repatriated an estimated 6 million returnees between 1945 and 1950, and later experimented with importing Brazilian Japanese migrant labor, the economic impact of these returnees is unclear. It is clear, however, that these groups faced widespread discrimination at the time of their return (Watt 2010; Tsuda 1999).

18. The 2.5 million Japanese diaspora noted in Chapter 2 is inclusive of nationals and also persons of Japanese descent.

19. In the United States, 38.5 million of 307 million persons are foreign-born immigrants. This represents 12.5 percent of the population (Adogame 2013).

20. Data excludes finance, insurance, and real estate (METI 2010). The number of foreign firms departing Japan each year exceeded the number of new foreign entries through 2016, the latest year for which data are available. For example, in the 2016 survey data, Japan had 27 new entrants, while 149 foreign entities had departed (METI 2017b).

21. In 2009, METI suspended providing public data tracking inward FDI.

22. Since the Fukushima nuclear crisis, energy policy has become a major focus of national policy.

23. The U.S. SBIR program provides grants to small firms for the purpose of research and development.

24. See also Kneller (2007b, 133–37), for a summary of legal changes in Japan in this regard.

25. An entrepreneur in a southern city of China noted that there is a similar sentiment about the central state bureaucrats in Beijing, referring to an old Chinese saying: "the mountains are tall, and the emperor is far away."

26. Some progress was indicated in a 2017 announcement by the Justice Ministry that for certain "highly skilled professionals" the wait time for granting permanent residency could be as short as one year, down from a minimum five-year wait (*Japan Times* 2017).

Chapter 4

1. Han Fei was an aristocrat of the state of Han during the Warring State Period of China (Xing 1993).

2. Breznitz and Murphree (2011) are critical of China's attempts to indigenize innovation and instead argue that there should be no urgency to engage in first-mover radical product innovations, as sustained economic growth is to be had via second followership.

3. Data includes Hong Kong and Macau.

4. For research on China's science and technology policy beyond the Deng period, see Temple and Needham (1986).

5. See Serger and Breidne (2007) for an outline of key agencies and bureaucrats.

6. Japanese business executives and entrepreneurs with experience in both countries often complain that Japan is more communist in practice than communist China.

7. The National Center for Biotechnology Development was established in 1983, a part of the (later to be named) Ministry of Science and Technology.

8. Cao (2004), in a review of China's so-called techno-warriors, notes that the 863 Program underdelivered on its aims of indigenizing technology, given the substantial funds invested at the time (5.9 billion RMB in the first fifteen years).

9. The data were indicated originally on the Chinese government 863 Program website, but the site has since been removed.

10. Z-Park is massive in size, covering 488 square kilometers.

11. This impact is similar to that of the post–Opium War (1842) response of the Qing government. One part modernization, one part an attempt to revitalize ancient civilizational technology leadership, the Qing government sent thousands of students overseas to study (Nastro 2015; Greenwood 2013).

12. Chinese government statistics have been criticized for overstating positive outcomes and understating negative ones (Koch-Weser 2013).

13. These also include Torch Program Specialized Industrial Bases and Productivity Promotion Centers.

14. It should be noted that politics is less unified in China than appears from the outside. In addition to an urban-rural divide, where the rural poor are left behind in the march toward modernization, the Communist Party itself is said to be fractured into three competing factions (the Sons of the Revolution, the Shanghai group, and the Princelings). Crackdowns on corruption often reflect a tit-for-tat jostling for power and control at the top by the leaders of these three factions, whereby second-tier bureaucrats and their private-sector partners are targeted. By 2015, this had led to large-scale capital flight by Chinese businessmen—sending their money and families to safer countries, including Canada and the United States. For example, in Canada, a whole generation of multilingual and wealthy young Chinese has been raised entirely outside China in this fashion. Whether or not these young professionals will take their place as part of the returnees from the diaspora is unclear.

15. Other research argues that the use of TCM remains on par with Western medical treatments (Griffiths, Chung, and Tang 2010).

16. According to a 2011 article in the *Economist*, 22 million ethnic Indians resided outside of India. The number for China was 61 million in that year (*Economist* 2011a).

17. At the same time, China lags in the creation of a transparent regulatory system, for example, within which inter-firm disputes, such as those over IP rights, can be adjudicated impartially.

18. Other industries included advanced materials, alternative energy, information technology, and equipment manufacturing (Xinhua News 2013).

19. The fourth industrial revolution was understood as the application of cyber-physical systems—generally the application of "connected industry," such as intelligent machines and cloud computing. The first three industrial revolutions are mechanization (1780s), electrification (1900s), and digitalization (1970s) (Drath and Horch 2014).

20. With the intent in part on developing export opportunities and the international transport infrastructure to support it, the One Belt, One Road Plan (OBOR), first announced in 2013 and launched officially in 2015, is comprised of the Asian Infrastructure Investment Bank and the Silk Road Fund. These programs have two aims.

First, OBOR extends China's trading infrastructure across Eurasia to Europe. The Silk Road Fund, eponymous for the ancient trading route, its Western side connecting China via South and Central Asia to European markets, earmarks government investment for OBOR projects. Second, building up infrastructure in recipient economies absorbs domestic overcapacity in materials, including steel and cement, in massive multicountry rail, seaport, and airport construction projects. The Chinese government stated in 2015 that it intended to employ primarily Chinese nationals in these megaprojects (Rowley 2015).

21. Some government officials have expressed concern that this is part of China's dual economy problem whereby a small number of internationally connected, high-technology elites operate independently from a billion unskilled, left-behind Chinese citizens.

22. It should be noted that the Western, allopathic approach is antithetical to the holistic healing philosophy of the discipline of traditional Chinese medicine, which diagnoses and treats the body system as a whole. Research on natural herb- and plant-derived compounds and treatments has been identified in scientific documents from as far back as 3000 B.C.E.

23. See also CCID Consulting 2011.

24. This adversity has created a niche market opportunity for small-scale credit guarantors, many of which are led by female entrepreneurs (Ibata-Arens 2014).

25. Even giant Huawei was said to avoid accepting government money and the oversight that comes with it. According to the former chief of the National Energy Administration, Guobao Zhang (张国宝), in 1987, Huawei refused an offer of 300 million RMB financial support from the Chinese government. The lore behind this decision is that the military and Communist Party member background of the founder and CEO of Huawei, Ren Zhengfei (任正非), might raise concerns with potential international partners and their governments (Wu 2013). Even so, its founder, Ren, faced suspicion about Huawei's presumed government ties when he sought partners abroad.

26. See also Z. Wang 2016.

27. Observers have noted that BGI, as of 2016, a decade and a half after its founding, has yet to move from genomic-testing services to higher value-added products. (To protect informant confidentiality, the names and date of interviewees are withheld per the request of the informant. Interview conducted in 2016.)

28. Sadly, founder Wang would not see this success, having resigned in 2012 for health reasons, passing in 2015 at the age of sixty-nine. Wang would be succeeded by Chen Chen and then Lim Li, also a returnee.

29. In 2016, the company was accused of financial improprieties in China, though the basis of these accusations is unknown. It should be noted that according to international news reports, the former head of the China agency regulating drug approvals, who was in charge at the time of the Gendicine approval, was later sentenced to death for taking bribes (Cha 2007).

Chapter 5

1. The word *swadeshi* derives from Sanskrit and is a conjunction of two Sanskrit words: *swa* means "self" or "own," and *desh* means "country." Thus, *swadeshi* means "of one's own country." The opposite of *swadeshi* in Sanskrit is *videshi*, "not of one's country," or foreign (*Oxford English Dictionary* 2008).

2. Aggarwal (2001) identifies the 1970s as a restrictive phase as self-reliance policies continued into this period, limiting technology imports, and sees the 1980s as part of the liberalization period, as some restrictions on foreign trade were lifted. See also Sibal 2012.

3. For a time, the government built capacity in defense and space technologies.

4. Under Prime Minister Modi, Hindu nationalism had a resurgence, for example, in the expansion of activities of the "national volunteer organization" Rashtriya Swayamsevak Sangh (RSS), a citizen's group with historical ties to violent Hindu nationalist movements (Basu 1996; Varshney 1993, 2014).

5. See A. Sen (2011) for a discussion of regional variations within India in human-capital development.

6. S. Sen (2017) explores the electoral and party politics behind bank nationalization in India. For a historical view of the Indian banking sector, see Khanna and Kaushal 2013.

7. Citing Credit Suisse's wealth-based estimates, Salve (2015) found that the actual size of the Indian middle class was 24 million. By the same criteria, China's was 108.7 million. OECD data are more optimistic (Kharas 2010).

8. The 1947 Partition divided majority Hindu India from then mostly Muslim Pakistan, now further divided into Pakistan and Bangladesh.

9. An inward-oriented closed market was considered necessary to protect fledgling (PSU) firms from competition from foreign firms. The international context also played a role in this inward orientation, since India's anticolonial distancing from the United Kingdom put it in an awkward position, as the two sides of the Cold War quickly solidified into the U.S.-Soviet poles (Waterbury 1999; Chibber 2003; Bruton 1970, 1978, 1998). The ongoing emphasis on technology-absorption-based innovation through the 1980s led to the announcement of the Technology Policy Statement in 1983, which underlined yet additional protective measures.

10. The author's ignorance of deities of Indian civilization limits the reference herein to analogous entities elsewhere.

11. Scholars, including D'Costa, note that foreign investors still complain that India is not sufficiently (liberal and) open.

12. Japanese reformers use *gaiatsu* (external pressure) in a similar manner.

13. The Bombay Stock Exchange determines top, or "Group A," firm listings based on a number of corporate governance and performance criteria (Bombay Stock Exchange 2018).

14. The Ministry of Chemicals and Fertilizers oversees traditional (chemical) pharmaceuticals; the Ministry of Science and Technology looks after biopharmaceuticals.

15. A five-year plan outlines the economic growth targets by sector, made by the national government, and the policy measures and funds that will support plan goals.

16. Transparency International is an international nongovernmental organization that monitors corruption in over one hundred countries.

17. For a global overview of Indian labor mobility, see D'Costa 2008.

18. At the time, the commission relied heavily on the inputs on such industrial organizations as the Federation of Indian Chambers of Commerce and Industry, the Confederation of Indian Industry, and the Indian Institute of Foreign Trade to produce its report, reflecting the economic logic of targeting the resource- and talent-rich diaspora population.

19. Only 475 billion rupees were expended in the Eleventh Five-Year Plan.

20. To protect informant confidentiality, the names and dates of interviewees are withheld per the request of the informant. Interview conducted in 2016.

21. Brahmins, estimated at 5 percent of India's total population of 1.3 billion people, are considered the highest of the four major castes of traditional Indian society (which are, in order of social prestige, Brahmins, Kshatriyas, Vaishyas, and Shudras). It should be noted that high social status does not necessarily mean high economic wealth.

22. Eventually, Shantha Biotech was acquired by the French Pharmaceutical firm Sanofi Pasteur for 550 million euros.

Chapter 6

1. The compulsory retirement age in the Singaporean military for most officers, fifty-five, means that a number go on to serve in high-ranking positions in the economic agencies. One interviewee noted that the high level of focus and discipline of high-ranking officials in Singapore's meritocracy on the task of economic development is due in part to this postmilitary-service pipeline.

2. This was contrasted with the *bumiputraism* of Malaysia in which indigenous Malays received preferential treatment.

3. For an overview of Singapore's position as global city-state, see Calder 2016.

4. See Hobday (1995) for an overview of technological learning from MNCs, supported by education policies in South Korea, Singapore, Hong Kong, and Taiwan.

5. To protect informant confidentiality, the names and dates of interviewees are withheld per the request of the informant. Interview conducted in 2017.

6. In Japan this is called the *bara maki* problem, in reference to spreading budget dollars too thinly across many groups. It is like cutting a roll of sushi too thinly: it all falls apart.

7. Around the same time that India opened its borders to inward FDI, EDB Investments (EDBI) was established (1991) to serve as the EDB's investment arm (National Library Board, Singapore 2018). Bio*One Capital, established in 2001, is EDBI's private equity and biomedical venture fund manager that invests primarily in biomedicals. One challenge that EDBI has faced is that in its attempt to strengthen biomedical industry in Singapore, it has found that due to Singapore's limited domestic market, most EDBI investees operate outside of Singapore, limiting domestic return on capital.

8. Japanese banks alone withdrew US$235 billion from Asia during the crisis years, mostly from Hong Kong and Singapore, even though Singapore had been regarded at the time as a disciplined and sound financial system (Sheng 2009).

9. This focus on the biomedical sector corresponded with the earlier emphasis on developing education capacity and the forward-looking need to promote a knowledge economy, which merged government, industry, and university in accordance with a triple-helix framework (discussed below).

10. The Raffles Institution Lecture Series takes place in the Raffles Institute, the oldest school in Singapore, and is named after the lieutenant governor of British Java (1811–1815) Stamford Raffles, who took the territory as a trading post for the British Crown.

11. Singapore is located a degree north of the equator.

12. Coincidentally, this echoes a friendly rivalry between top universities in the small town of Cambridge, Massachusetts, in the United States. Tan has a scientific graduate degree from MIT and Yeo an MBA from Harvard.

13. In Singapore, the term *infocomm* refers to the information technology and telecommunications industries jointly.

14. Companies with fewer than twenty-four employees or positions, which pay a fixed monthly salary of $12,000 and above are exempt.

15. Another pertinent statistic concerns Singapore's strength of IPR. It has been ranked by the World Economic Forum as number two overall and number one in Asia for strength of intellectual property laws (World Economic Forum 2013).

16. Some political risk analysts believe the ripple effect of this loosening of control over the economy and academic institutions with a new focus on innovative start-ups may spill over in the political sphere. As Singapore's government ventures into start-ups as a basis for growth, it risks compromising its monopoly on economic leadership, a key instrument used to maintain its legitimacy (Luedi 2015).

17. According to the 2016 Medical Tourism Index, Singapore continues to be a choice destination for medical tourism. With a focus on service and specialists, in 2016, and a score of 73.56, Singapore ranked fourth, while India ranked fifth with a score of 72.10. Canada (76.62) topped the ranking while Japan was twelfth with a score of 68.0, and China placed twenty-fourth with 64.78 (International Healthcare Research Center and Global Healthcare Resources 2016). However, with a strong currency and

high prices for similar services, other Asian countries, including India and Indonesia, are catching up to Singapore (*International Medical Travel Journal* 2017). Singapore Tourism Board (STB) data show medical tourism receipts fell to S$832 million in 2013, down from S$1.1 billion the year before. They rose to S$994 million in 2014, after which time the STB stopped publicizing the figure in a move reminiscent of when Japan's data are less than laudatory (Lai 2017). This decline is due in part to improved medical services in Indonesia, the largest source of Singapore's medical tourists, and Malaysia and Thailand. As a result, the Singapore private sector is providing luxury services along with specialized care in an effort to beat growing competition.

18. Series B round investments represent a second round of funding, after a venture has first received Series A. Firms seek Series B rounds of funding after meeting initial growth targets, such as in product development or sales, as well as forecasts anticipating increasing revenue.

19. According to QS Top Universities, the QS scale, the Times Higher Education World University rankings, and the Academic Ranking of World Universities (ARWU) are the three best-known world university ranking systems. The QS scale in particular aims to examine six categories: academic reputation, employer reputation, student-to-faculty ratio, research citations per faculty member, proportion of international faculty, and proportion of international students (Bridgestock 2017).

20. Ho Kwon Ping, the executive chairman of Banyan Tree Holdings, quoted in the *Malay Mail Online* (2015).

REFERENCES

Ács, Zoltán J. 2012. Global Entrepreneurship and Development Index 2012. Northampton, MA: Edward Elgar Publishing.

Ács, Zoltán J., and Laszlo Szerb. 2010. "Global Entrepreneurship and the United States." Small Business Administration. Accessed September, 2010. Archive.sba.gov/advo/research/rs370tot.pdf.

Ács, Zoltán J., and Attila Varga. 2005. "Entrepreneurship, Agglomeration and Technological Change." *Small Business Economics* 24 (3): 323–34. Accessed September 2014. https://link.springer.com/content/pdf/10.1007%2Fs11187-005-1998-4.pdf.

Adogame, Afe. 2013. *The African Christian Diaspora: New Currents and Emerging Trends in World Christianity.* New York: Bloomsbury Academic.

Agarwal, Manmohan, Jing Wang, and John Whalley. 2017. *The Economies of China and India.* Hackensack, NJ: World Scientific Publishing Company.

Agency for Science, Technology and Research (A*STAR). 2010. "20 Years of Science and Technology in Singapore." Last modified November 2010. Accessed December 11, 2014. http://www.astar.edu.sg/Portals/0/aboutastar/2012_Commemorative_Pub_Webv6.pdf.

Agency for Science, Technology and Research (A*STAR). 2011a. "Asia's Innovation Capital Stepping Up: Yearbook 2011/12." Singapore: Agency for Science, Technology and Research.

Agency for Science, Technology and Research (A*STAR). 2011b. "Science, Technology & Enterprise Plan 2015." Last modified May 2011. Accessed October 11, 2017. http://www.a-star.edu.sg/portals/0/media/otherpubs/step2015_1jun.pdf.

Agency for Science, Technology and Research (A*STAR). 2013. "Singapore's Biopolis: A Success Story." October 16, 2013. Accessed September 25, 2017. https://www.a-star.edu.sg/News-and-Events/News/Press-releases/ID/1893/Singapores-Biopolis-A-Success-Story.aspx.

Agency for Science, Technology and Research (A*STAR). 2016. "National Survey of Research and Development in Singapore 2015. National Survey, Singapore: Agency for Science, Technology and Research." Accessed August 20, 2018. https://www.a-star.edu.sg/News-and-Events/Publications/National-Survey-of-R-D.

Agency for Science, Technology and Research (A*STAR). n.d.a. "About-IMCB, Overview." Accessed September 5, 2018. https://www.a-star.edu.sg/imcb/About-IMCB/Overview.

Agency for Science, Technology and Research (A*STAR). n.d.b. "Biomedical Research Council Overview." Accessed October 30, 2017. https://www.a-star.edu.sg/About-A-STAR/Biomedical-Research-Council/Overview.aspx.

Agency for Science, Technology and Research (A*STAR). n.d.c. "New Biomedical Sciences Executive Committee established to lead Phase 2 of Singapore's Biomedical Sciences initiative." Accessed January 2018. https://www.a-star.edu.sg/News-and-Events/News/Press-Releases/ID/222.

Aggarwal, A. Vikas, Nicolaj Siggelkow, and Harbir Singh. 2011. "Governing Collaborative Activity: Interdependence and the Impact of Coordination and Exploration." *Strategic Management Journal* 32 (7): 705–30.

Aggarwal, Aradhna. 2001. "Technology Policies and Acquisition of Technological Capabilities in the Industrial Sector: A Comparative Analysis of the Indian and Korean Experiences." *Science, Technology and Society* 6 (2): 255–304.

Ahearne, Alan G., and Naoki Shinada. 2005. "Zombie Firms and Economic Stagnation in Japan." *International Economics and Economic Policy* 2 (4): 363–81.

Ajay, Dara, and Abhay T. Sangamwar. 2014. "Identifying the Patent Trend, Licensing Pattern and Geographical Landscape Analysis of the Council for Scientific & Industrial Research (CSIR) of India Between 2000 and 2011." *World Patent Information* 38: 42–49.

Alfant, Michael, interview, 2012.

Altbach, Philip G. 1993a. "The Dilemma of Change in Indian Higher Education." *Higher Education* 26 (1): 3–20.

Altbach, Philip G. 1993b. "Gigantic Peripheries: India and China in World Knowledge System." *Economic and Political Weekly* 28 (24): 1220–25.

Altenburg, Tilman, Hubert Schmitz, and Andreas Stamm. 2008. "Breakthrough? China's and India's Transition from Production to Innovation." *World Development* 36 (2): 325–344.

Amsden, Alice H. 1994. "Why Isn't the Whole World Experimenting with the East Asian Model to Develop? Review of the East Asian Miracle." *World Development* 22 (4): 627–33.

Amsden, Alice Hoffenberg. 1992. *Asia's Next Giant: South Korea and Late Industrialization.* New York: Oxford University Press.

Amsden, Alice Hoffenberg. 2001. *The Rise of "the Rest": Challenges to the West from Late-Industrializing Economies.* New York: Oxford University Press.

Anadon, Laura Diaz. 2012. "Missions-Oriented R&D Institutions in Energy Between 2000 and 2010: A Comparative Analysis of China, the United Kingdom, and the United States." *Research Policy* 41 (10): 1742–56.

Anchordoguy, Marie. 1989. *Computers Inc: Japan's Challenge to IBM*. Cambridge, MA: Harvard University Press.

Anchordoguy, Marie. 2005. "Japan's Technology Policies and Their Limitations." In *Japan and China in the World Political Economy*, ed. Saadia Pekkanen and Kellee Tsai, 189–204. New York: Routledge.

Anderson, Benedict. 1983. *Imagined Communities: Reflections on the Growth and Spread of Nationalism*. New York: Verso.

Ang, James S., Yingmei Cheng, and Chaopeng Wu. 2014. "Does Enforcement of Intellectual Property Rights Matter in China? Evidence from Financing and Investment Choices in the High-Tech Industry." *Review of Economics and Statistics* 96 (2): 332–48.

Aspalter, Christian. n.d. "The Welfare State in Emerging-Market Economies: With Case Studies from Latin America, Eastern-Central Europe, and Asia (April 1, 2003)." Unpublished paper. http://dx.doi.org/10.2139/ssrn.2665500.

Association of Nikkei and Japanese Abroad. 2015. About Us. Accessed August 1, 2015. http://www.jadesas.or.jp/en/about/.

Atkinson, Robert D., Stephen J. Ezell, L. V. Giddings, Luke A. Stewart, and Scott M. Andes. 2012. "Leadership in Decline: Assessing US International Competitiveness in Biomedical research." Washington, DC: The Information Technology and Innovation Foundation and United for Medical Research, vol. 78.

Audretsch, David B. 2001. "The Role of Small Firms in US Biotechnology Clusters." *Small Business Economics* 17 (1–2): 3–15.

Audretsch, David B., and Maryann P. Feldman. 2004. "Knowledge Spillovers and the Geography of Innovation." *Handbook of Regional and Urban Economics* 4: 2713–39.

Bagchi, Amiya Kumar, Parthasarathi Banerjee, and Uttam Kumar Bhattacharya. 1984. "Indian Patents Act and Its Relation to Technological Development in India: A Preliminary Investigation." *Economic and Political Weekly* 19 (7): 287–304.

Bagchi-Sen, Sharmistha, Helen Lawton Smith, and Linda Hall. 2004. "The US Biotechnology Industry: Industry Dynamics and Policy." *Environment and Planning C: Government and Policy* 22 (2): 199–216.

Basu, Amrita. 1996. "Mass Movement or Elite Conspiracy? The Puzzle of Hindu Nationalism." In *Contesting the Nation: Religion, Community and the Politics of Democracy in India*, ed. David Ludden, 81–97. Philadelphia: University of Pennsylvania Press.

Beason, Richard, and David E. Weinstein. 1996. "Growth, Economies of Scale, and Targeting in Japan (1955–1990)." *Review of Economics and Statistics* 78 (2): 286–95.

Beech, Hannah. 2016. "China's Great Firewall Is Harming Innovation, Scholars Say." *Time* (online). Last modified June 1, 2016. Accessed July 19, 2017. http://time.com/4354665/china-great-firewall-innovation-online-censorship/.

Beeson, Mark. 2009. "Developmental States in East Asia: A Comparison of the Japanese and Chinese Experiences." *Asian Perspective* 33 (2): 5–39.

Beijing.gov. n.d. "Bei Jing Ji Shu Chuang Xin Xing Dong Ji Hua (2014–2017 Nian)" 北京技术创新行动计划 (2014–2017年) (Beijing Technological Innovation Action Plan [2014–2017]). Accessed September 27, 2017. http://zhengwu.beijing.gov.cn/ghxx/qtgh/t1352269.htm (Chinese).

Berger, Mark T., and Mark Beeson. 1998. "Lineages of Liberalism and Miracles of Modernisation: The World Bank, the East Asian Trajectory and the International Development Debate." *Third World Quarterly* 19 (3): 487–504.

Besen, Stanley M., and Joseph Farrell. 1994. "Choosing How to Compete: Strategies and Tactics in Standardization." *Journal of Economic Perspectives* 8 (2): 117–31.

Bhatt, Kaushal A., and Kinjal Bhatt. 2012. "Effects of Investor Occupation and Education on Choice of Investment: An Empirical Study in India." *International Journal of Management* 29 (4): 439.

Bhattacharya, Ananya. 2017. "Singapore First: Quietly Shutting the Door on Indian Techies and Other Foreign Workers." *Quartz India*, April 12, 2017. Accessed August 2017. https://qz.com/950172/the-us-isnt-the-only-country-shutting-the-door-on-indian-techies/.

Biomedical Research Council. 2013. "The Biopolis Story: Commemorating Ten Years of Excellence." Singapore: A*STAR and Jurong Town Corporation.

Biotech Connection Singapore. 2016. "Insight to InvitroCue's Success: From Invention to IPO." Biotech Connection Singapore, February 23, 2016. Accessed August 8, 2018. http://www.biotechconnection-sg.org/insight-to-invitrocues-success-from-invention-to-ipo/.

Biswas, Radha Roy. 2014. "Reverse Migrant Entrepreneurs in India: Motivations, Trajectories and Realities." In *Indian Skilled Migration and Development: Dynamics of Asian Development*, ed. U. Bhattacharya, B. Khadria, and G. Tejada, 285–307. New Delhi: Springer.

Bloomberg. 2015. "Pharma Foods International Co Ltd 2929: JP." Bloomberg Markets. Accessed September 21, 2015. http://www.bloomberg.com/research/stocks/financials/financials.asp?ticker=2929:JP.

Bloomberg Equity Screening. 2017a. Result of Bloomberg Biotech IPO. October 18, 2017.

Bloomberg Equity Screening. 2017b. Result of Bloomberg Biotech Publicly-Traded. October 18, 2017.

Boermans, Martijn Adriaan, and Hein Roelfsema. 2013. "The Effects of Managerial Capabilities on Export, FDI and Innovation: Evidence from Indian Firms." *Asian Business and Management* 12 (4): 387–408.

Bombay Stock Exchange. n.d. *Guidelines for Selection of "A" Group Companies*. Accessed August 8, 2018. https://www.bseindia.com/downloads1/Guidelines_Group_A_Companies.pdf.

Bradford, Annette. 2015. "Changing Trends in Japanese Students Studying Abroad." *International Higher Education* 83: 22–23.

Bray, Thomas M., and Wing On Lee, eds. 2001. *Education and Political Transition: Themes and Experiences in East Asia.* Hong Kong: Comparative Education Research Centre, Hong Kong University.

Breznitz, Dan, and Michael Murphree. 2010. "Run of the Red Queen." *China Economic Quarterly* (September): 21–25. http://www.theairnet.org/files/research/breznitz /Run_of_the_Red_Queen_Article.pdf.

Breznitz, Dan, and Michael Murphree. 2011. *Run of the Red Queen: Government, Innovation, Globalization, and Economic Growth in China.* New Haven, CT: Yale University Press.

Bridgestock, Laura. 2017. *World University Ranking Methodologies.* QS Top Universities, June 7, 2017. Last Modified September 5, 2016. Accessed August 17, 2018. https://www.topuniversities.com/qs-world-university-rankings/methodology.

Bruche, Gert. 2009. "The Emergence of China and India as New Competitors in MNCs' Innovation Networks." *Competition and Change* 13 (3): 267–88.

Bruderl, Josef, and Peter Preisendorfer. 1998. "Network Support and the Success of Newly Founded Business." *Small Business Economics* 10 (3): 213–25.

Bruton, Henry J. 1970. "The Import-Substitution Strategy of Economic Development: A Survey." *Pakistan Development Review* 10 (2): 123–46.

Bruton, Henry J. 1978. "Unemployment Problems and Policies in Less Developed Countries." *American Economic Review* 68 (2): 51–55.

Bruton, Henry J. 1998. "A Reconsideration of Import Substitution." *Journal of Economic Literature* 36 (2): 903–36.

Bu, Ruiwei. 2015. "The Great Firewall of China." Accessed July 31, 2017. http://campus .murraystate.edu/academic/faculty/wlyle/540/2013/Bu.pdf.

Burk, Dan L. 2008. "The Role of Patent Law in Knowledge Codification." *Berkeley Technology Law Journal* 23 (3): 1009.

Burrill Media. 2014. "Accelerating Growth: Forging India's Bioeconomy." https://www .bio.org/sites/default/files/files/Burrill_AcceleratingGrowth_India-6-9-final.pdf.

Burris, Scott, Peter Drahos, and Clifford Shearing. 2005. "Nodal Governance." *Australian Journal of Legal Philosophy* 30: 30.

Caballero, Ricardo J., Takeo Hoshi, and Anil K. Kashyap. 2008. "Zombie Lending and Depressed Restructuring in Japan." *American Economic Review* 98 (5): 1943–77.

Cabinet Office (Japan). 2001a. "Points of Science and Technology Basic Plan." Last modified March 2001. Accessed October 2, 2017. http://www8.cao.go.jp/cstp/english /basic/2nd-PlanPoints.pdf.

Cabinet Office (Japan). 2001b. "The 2nd Science and Technology Basic Plan (FY2001–FY2005)." Last modified March 30, 2001. Accessed October 2, 2017. http://www8 .cao.go.jp/cstp/english/basic/2nd-BasicPlan_01-05.html.

Cabinet Office (Japan). n.d. "Dai 2-ki kagaku gijutsu kihon keikaku Honbun" 第2期科学技術基本計画本文 (The second science and technology basic plan text). Accessed October 6, 2017. http://www8.cao.go.jp/cstp/kihonkeikaku/honbun.html (Japanese).

Cabinet Secretariat. 2007. "Industrial Technology Enhancement Act (Act No.44 of 2000)." August 6, 2007. Accessed October 2, 2017. http://www.cas.go.jp/jp/seisaku/hourei/data/itea.pdf.

Cabinet Secretariat. 2013. "The Rule of Establishment of Health and Medical Care Nation Policy Unit." Last modified February 22, 2013. Accessed August 7, 2013. http://www.kantei.go.jp/jp/singi/kenkouiryou/konkyo.pdf.

Calder, Kent. 2016. *Singapore: Smart City, Smart State*. Washington, DC: Brookings Institution Press.

Campbell, Charlie. 2016. "The Architect of China's Great Firewall Was Himself Blocked by the Firewall." *Time* (online). Last modified April 5, 2016. Accessed September 20, 2017. http://time.com/4354665/china-great-firewall-innovation-online-censorship/.

Campos, J. Edgardo, and Donald Lien. 1999. "The Impact of Corruption on Investment: Predictability Matters." *World Development* 27 (6): 1059–67.

Cao, Cong. 2004. "Chinese Technonationalism." *Metascience* 13 (1): 71–74.

Cao, Cong. 2012. "Biotechnology in China." In *The Interface of Sciences, Technology and Security: Areas of Most Concern, Now and Ahead*, ed. Virginia Bacay Watson, 99–109. Honolulu, HI: Asian-Pacific Center for Security Studies.

Cao, Cong, Feng-chao Liu, Denis Fred Simon, and Yu-tao Sun. 2011. "China's Innovation Policies: Evolution, Institutional Structure, and Trajectory." *Research Policy* 40 (7): 917–31.

Casper, Steven, and Hannah Kettler. 2001. "National Institutional Frameworks and the Hybridization of Entrepreneurial Business Models: The German and UK Biotechnology Sectors." *Industry and Innovation* 8 (1): 5–30.

CBS News. 2001. "AIDS Drug: $1 a Day." February 7, 2001. Accessed August 15, 2018. https://www.cbsnews.com/news/aids-drug-1-a-day/.

CCID Consulting. 2011. "中国生物医药产业地图白皮书(2011年)" (China Biotechnology Industry Map 2011). CCID Consulting, April 29, 2011. Accessed August 10, 2018. http://cubeimg.zhongsou.com/1/3292155753986673283749762971.pdf (Chinese).

Central Committee of the Communist Party of China 中共中央. 2015. "Zhong Gong Zhong Yang Guan Yu Zhi Ding Guo Ming Jing Ji He She Hui Fa Zhan Di Shi San Ge Wu Nian Gui Hua De Jian Yi" 中共中央关于制定国民经济和社会发展第十三个五年规划的建议 (Suggestions on making the Thirteenth Five-Year Plan, from CPC Central Committee). Last modified November 3, 2015. Accessed September 27, 2017. http://www.gov.cn/xinwen/2015-11/03/content_5004093.htm (Chinese).

Central Intelligence Agency. n.d. "Singapore." World Factbook. Accessed March 1, 2017. https://www.cia.gov/library/publications/the-world-factbook/geos/sn.html.

CGTN. "Live: Opening session of CPC National Congress 中国共产党第十九次全国代表大会开幕会." Youtube.com, October 17, 2017. https://www.youtube.com/watch?v=wEn8AZqAAf4.

Cha, Ariana Eunjung. 2007. "To China for a U.S. Cancer Drug." *Washington Post*, July 5, 2007. Accessed October 15, 2017. http://www.washingtonpost.com/wp-dyn/content/article/2007/07/04/AR2007070401402.html.

Chakma, Justin, Hassan Masum, Kumar Perampaladas, Jennifer Heys, and Peter A. Singer. 2011. "Indian Vaccine Innovation: The Case of Shantha Biotechnics." *Globalization and Health* 7 (9). http://www.ncbi.nlm.nih.gov/pmc/articles/PMC3110116/.

Chand, Smriti. n.d. "Major Objectives of India's New Industrial Policy 1991." Accessed September 29, 2017. http://www.yourarticlelibrary.com/policies/major-objectives-of-indias-new-industrial-policy-1991/23441/.

Chandler, Alfred D., Franco Amatori, and Takashi Hikino. 1997. *Big Business and the Wealth of Nations*. New York: Cambridge University Press.

Chang, Ha-Joon. 2002. *Kicking Away the Ladder: Development Strategy in Historical Perspective*. New York: Anthem Press.

Chaturvedi, C., and Joanna Chataway. 2009. "The Indian Pharmaceutical Industry: Firm Strategy and Policy Interactions." In *The New Innovation Dynamics: China and India in Perspective*, ed. Govindan Parayil and Anthony P. D'Costa, 138–69. Basingstoke, UK: Palgrave Macmillan.

Chaudhri, Guljit, interview, 2016.

Chaundru, Vijay, interview, 2016.

Chen, Andrew. 2010. "Biotechnology in China." *Insight*, January/February. Accessed August 10, 2013. https://www.amcham-shanghai.org/en/taxonomy/term/1161.

Chen, Chaomei, Yue Chen, Mark Horowitz, Haiyan Hou, Zeyuan Liu, and Donald Pellegrino. 2009. "Towards an Explanatory and Computational Theory of Scientific Discovery." *Journal of Informetrics* 3 (3): 191–209.

Chen, Jin, Yufen Chen, and Wim Vanhaverbeke. 2011. "The Influence of Scope, Depth, and Orientation of External Technology Sources on the Innovative Performance of Chinese Firms." *Technovation* 31 (8): 362–73.

Chernyshenko, Olexander S., Marilyn A. Uy, Weiting Jiang, Moon-ho R. Ho, Seong Per Lee, Kim Yin Chan, and Trevor K. Y. Yu. 2015. "Global Entrepreneurship Monitor 2014 Singapore Report." Singapore: Nanyang Technological University.

Chervenak, Matthew. 2005. "China: Moving Towards Innovation in Pharma." *Drug Discovery Today* 10 (17): 1127–30.

Chew, Soon Beng, and Rosalind Chew. 2003. "Promoting Innovation in Singapore: Changing the Mindset." *International Journal of Entrepreneurship and Innovation Management* 3 (3): 249–66.

Chibber, Vivek. 2003. *Locked in Place: State-Building and Late Industrialization in India*. Princeton, NJ: Princeton University Press.

China Education News 中国教育新闻网. 2012. "42% De Jiu Ye De 2008 Jie Da Xue Bi Ye Sheng Bi Ye San Nian Nei Zhuan Huan Le Zhi Ye" 42%的就业的2008届大学毕业生毕业三年内转换了职业(42% of the class of 2008 graduates changed their professions within 3 years of graduation). Last modified June 11, 2012. Accessed July 17, 2016. http://job.jyb.cn/jysx/201206/t20120611_497827.html (Chinese).

Chong, Alan. 2012. "Disciplining Globalization for Local Purposes? The Peculiarity of Contending Singaporean Economic Nationalisms." In *Globalization and Economic Nationalism in Asia*, ed. Anthony P. D'Costa, 177. Oxford, UK: Oxford University Press.

Chopra, K. L., and P. B. Sharma. 2009. "Higher Technical Education in India—Profile of Growth and Future Perspectives." ADP sponsored RETA Project Report. New Delhi: NAM Centre for Science and Technology.

Chung, Vincent C. H., Sheila Hillier, Chun Hong Lau, Samuel Y. S. Wong, Eng Kiong Yeoh, and Sian M. Griffiths. 2011. "Referral to and Attitude Towards Traditional Chinese Medicine Amongst Western Medical Doctors in Postcolonial Hong Kong." *Social Science and Medicine* 72 (2): 247–55.

Chuong, Sum Chee, and James Ang. 2008. "Supply Chain Management and Logistics in Southeast Asia." In *Production Networks and Industrial Clusters: Integrating Economies in Southeast Asia*, ed. Ikuo Kuroiwa and Toh Mun Heng, 161. Singapore: ISEAS Publishing.

CIPLA. 2014. "Cipla Annual Report 2013–2014." Mumbai.

CiRA. 2017. "Setsuritsu shushi・enkaku" 設立趣旨・沿革 (Establishment mission・history). Accessed July 2017. http://www.cira.kyoto-u.ac.jp/j/about/mission.html (Japanese).

Cohen, Wesley M., and Daniel A. Levinthal. "Absorptive Capacity: A New Perspective on Learning and Innovation." *Administrative Science Quarterly* (1990): 128–52.

Cole, Matthew A., Robert J. R. Elliott, and Jiang Zhang. 2009. "Corruption, Governance and FDI Location in China: A Province-Level Analysis." *Journal of Development Studies* 45 (9): 1494–512.

Colignon, Richard, and Chikako Usui. 2001. "The Resilience of Japan's Iron Triangle." *Asian Survey* 41 (5): 865–95.

Compass.co. 2015. "The Global Startup Ecosystem Ranking 2015." The Startup Ecosystem Report Series. https://goo.gl/7QJY2r.

Cooke, Philip. 2002. "Regional Innovation Systems: General Findings and Some New Evidence from Biotechnology Clusters." *Journal of Technology Transfer* 27 (1): 133–45.

Cornell University, INSEAD, and WIPO. 2017. "The Global Innovation Index 2017: Innovation Feeding the World." Ithaca, Fontainebleau, and Geneva.

Corning, Gregory P. 2004. *Japan and the Politics of Techno-globalism*. New York: M. E. Sharpe.

Corning, Gregory P. 2016. *Japan and the Politics of Techno-globalism*. New York: Routledge.

Council of Scientific and Industrial Research, Ministry of Science and Technology (India). 1996. "CSIR Mission Archival." Last modified January 1996. Accessed October 9, 2017. http://www.csir.res.in/csir-mission-archival.

Coviello, Nicole E., and Hugh J. Munro. 1995. "Growing the Entrepreneurial Firm: Networking for International Market Development." *European Journal of Marketing* 29 (7): 49–61.

Coviello, Nicole, and Hugh Munro. 1997. "Network Relationships and the Internationalisation Process of Small Software Firms." *International Business Review* 6 (4): 361–86.

Cpc.people.com 人民网 (Ren Min Wang). 1984. "Zhong Gong Zhong Yang Guan Yu Jing Ji Ti Zhi Gai Ge De Jue Ding" 中共中央关于经济体制改革的决定 (Central Committee of the Communist Party of China presented the decisions of the reform of the Economic System). Last modified October 20, 1984. Accessed September 27, 2017. http://cpc.people.com.cn/GB/64162/64168/64565/65378/4429522.html (Chinese).

Cumings, Bruce. 1984. "The Origins and Development of the Northeast Asian Political Economy: Industrial Sectors, Product Cycles, and Political Consequences." *International Organization* 38 (1): 1–40.

D'Costa, Anthony P. 2005. *The Long March to Capitalism*. Basingstoke, UK: Palgrave Macmillan.

D'Costa, Anthony P. 2008. "The International Mobility of Technical Talent: Trends and Development Implications." In *International Mobility of Talent and Development Impact*, 44–83. Tokyo: United Nations University.

D'Costa, Anthony P. 2009. "Economic Nationalism in Motion: Steel, Auto, and Software Industries in India." *Review of International Political Economy* 16 (4): 620–48.

D'Costa, Anthony P. 2010. *A New India? Critical Reflections in the Long Twentieth Century*. London: Anthem Press.

D'Costa, Anthony P. 2012. *Globalization and Economic Nationalism in Asia*. Oxford, UK: Oxford University Press.

Dahl, Michael S., and Toke Reichstein. 2007. "Are You Experienced? Prior Experience and the Survival of New Organizations." *Industry and Innovation* 14 (5): 497–511.

Dang, Jianwei, and Kazuyuki Motohashi. 2015. "Patent Statistics: A Good Indicator for Innovation in China? Patent Subsidy Program Impacts on Patent Quality." *China Economic Review* 35: 137–55.

Das, Gurcharan. 2006. "The India Model." *Foreign Affairs* 85 (4): 2–16.

Dasgupta, Gaurab. 2016. "Key Projects Announced under Make in India." *Business Standard*, February 12, 2016. Accessed September 12, 2017. http://www.business -standard.com/article/economy-policy/key-projects-announced-under-make-in -india-116021200853_1.html.

Daverman, Richard, and Tracy Yeo. 2012. *China Life Science: From Local to Global.* ChinaBio LLC White Paper, March 20, 2012. Accessed July 1, 2016. http://www .chinabio.com/.

Dawra, Preeti. 2015. "Singapore's Success Is an Inspiration for India: Narendra Modi." HT Media Ltd. November 25, 2015. Accessed October 22, 2017. http://www.livemint .com/Politics/za5IXunZlr8lBD2AKIW4yI/Singapores-success-is-an-inspiration -for-India-Narendra-Mo.html.

De La Tour, Arnaud, Matthieu Glachant, and Yann Ménière. 2011. "Innovation and International Technology Transfer: The Case of the Chinese Photovoltaic Industry." *Energy Policy* 39 (2): 761–70.

Deloitte. "2015 Global Life Sciences Outlook: Adapting in an Era of Transformation." Deloitte.com. Last modified 2014. Accessed August 29, 2016. https://www2.deloitte .com/content/dam/Deloitte/global/Documents/Life-Sciences-Health-Care/gx -lshc-2015-life-sciences-report.pdf.

Department of Industrial Policy and Promotion. 2003. Patent Amendment Act 2002. Government of India, Ipindia.nic.in. Accessed August 18, 2016. http://ipindia.nic .in/ipr/patent/patent_re_03.pdf.

Department of Industrial Policy and Promotion. 2014. Make in India, September 2014. Accessed July 21, 2017. http://www.makeinindia.com/about.

Department of Industrial Policy and Promotion. 2017. "Fact Sheet on Foreign Direct Investment (FDI)." New Delhi: Government of India. Accessed March 5, 2018. http://dipp.nic.in/sites/default/files/FDI_FactSheet_Updated_September2017.pdf.

Department of Industrial Policy and Promotion and Department of Biotechnology. 2017. "Biotechnology Sector: Achievement Report." New Delhi: Government of India. Accessed March 5, 2018. http://www.makeinindia.com/documents/10281 /114126/Biotechnology+Achievement+Report.pdf.

Department of Science and Technology. 2006. "Research and Development Statistics at a Glance 2004–05." New Delhi: Government of India, 3.

Department of Science and Technology. n.d. "Welcome to Department of Science and Technology." New Delhi: Government of India. http://www.dst.gov.in/stsysindia /stp2013.htm.

Department of Statistics Singapore. 2010. "Census of Population 2010 Advance Census Release." Singapore, v. Accessed October 30, 2017. http://www.singstat.gov.sg /docs/default-source/default-document-library/publications/publications_and _papers/cop2010/census_2010_advance_census_release/c2010acr.pdf.

Department of Statistics Singapore. 2017. *Yearbook of Statistics 2017*. Singapore: Department of Statistics Singapore. Accessed September 6, 2018. https://www.singstat.gov.sg/-/media/files/publications/reference/yearbook_2017/yos2017.pdf.

Desilver, Drew. 2014. "5 Facts About Indian Americans." Pew Research Center, September 30, 2014. Accessed August 16, 2017. http://www.pewresearch.org/fact-tank/2014/09/30/5-facts-about-indian-americans/.

Development and Reform Commission 发展改革委 (Fa Zhan Gai Ge Wei). 2007. "Sheng Wu Chan Ye Fa Zhan 'Shi Yi Wu' Gui Hua (Quan Wen)" 生物产业发展"十一五"规划（全文） (Eleventh Five-Year Plan for the biology industry). Last modified April 28, 2007. Accessed October 9, 2017. http://www.china.com.cn/policy/txt/2007-04/28/content_8185296.htm (Chinese).

Diamond Online. 2014. "Nihon zanpai' wa W-hai dakede wanai keizai demo Doitsu, Oranda ni zettai katenai riyū" "日本惨敗"はW 杯だけではない経済でもドイツ、オランダに絶対勝てない理由 ("Japan defeat" is not only about the World Cup. reasons why way Japan can never win against Germany and Holland [The Netherlands] economically). July 11, 2014. Accessed July 29, 2014. https://mail.google.com/mail/u/0/#inbox/15fa746051524789 (Japanese).

Dodgson, Mark, John Mathews, Tim Kastelle, and Mei-Chih Hu. 2008. "The Evolving Nature of Taiwan's National Innovation System: The Case of Biotechnology Innovation Networks." *Research Policy* 37 (3): 430–45.

Dohrmann, Jona Aravind. 2008, "Special Economic Zones in India—an Introduction." *Asien* 106: 60–80.

Dore, Ronald Philip. 1986. *Flexible Rigidities: Industrial Policy and Structural Adjustment in the Japanese Economy, 1970–80*. Redwood City, CA: Stanford University Press.

Drahos, Peter. 2002. "Developing Countries and International Intellectual Property Standard-Setting." *Journal of World Intellectual Property* 5 (5): 765–89.

Drath, Rainer, and Alexander Horch. 2014. "Industrie 4.0: Hit or Hype?" *IEEE Industrial Electronics Magazine* 8 (2): 56–58.

Dutta, Soumitra, Bruno Lanvin, and Sacha Wunsch-Vincent, eds. 2014. "The Global Innovation Index: The Human Factor in Innovation 2014." Accessed July 1, 2016. http://www.wipo.int/econ_stat/en/eco-nomics/gii.

Dutta, Soumitra, Bruno Lanvin, and Sacha Wunsch-Vincent, eds. 2017. "The Global Innovation Index: The Human Factor in Innovation 2017." Accessed December 1, 2017. https://www.globalinnovationindex.org/gii-2017-report.

Dutta, Soumitra, Bruno Lanvin, and Sacha Wunsch-Vincent, eds. 2018. *The Global Innovation Index 2018: Energizing the World with Innovation*. 11th ed. Ithaca, NY, Fontainebleau France, and Geneva, Switzerland: Cornell University, INSEAD, and WIPO.

Ebner, Alexander. 2007. "Public Policy, Governance and Innovation: Entrepreneurial States in East Asian Economic Development." *International Journal of Technology and Globalisation* 3 (1): 103–24.

Ebner, Alexander. 2013. "Cluster Policies and Entrepreneurial States in East Asia." In *Clusters and Economic Growth in Asia*, ed. Soren Eriksson, 1–20. Northampton, MA: Edward Elgar Publishing.

Economic and Political Weekly. 1954. "Pharmaceuticals Manufacture Not Processing." *Economic and Political Weekly* 6 (49). http://www.epw.in/system/files/pdf/1954_6/49/pharmaceuticals_manufacture_not_processing.pdf.

Economist. 2010. "Patents, Yes; Ideas, Maybe." Last modified October 14, 2010. Accessed April 8, 2016. http://www.economist.com/node/17257940.

Economist. 2011a. "Diasporas: Mapping Migration." Last modified November 17, 2011. Accessed March 6, 2017. http://www.economist.com/blogs/dailychart/2011/11/diasporas.

Economist. 2011b. "The Half-Finished Revolution." January 21, 2011. http://www.economist.com/node/18986387.

Economist Intelligence Unit (EIU). 2014. *World Industry Outlook: Healthcare and Pharmaceuticals.* London: Economist Intelligence Unit.

Edgerton, David E. H. 2007. "The Contradictions of Techno-Nationalism and Techno-Globalism: A Historical Perspective." *New Global Studies* 1 (1): 1–32.

Edvinsson, Leif, and Patrick Sullivan. 1996. "Developing a Model for Managing Intellectual Capital." *European Management Journal* 14 (4): 356–64.

863 Program Document. 1986. "863 Program." SiteUrl.Org. Last modified 2013. Accessed February 20, 2017. http://www.most.gov.cn/eng/programmes1/.

Elliot, Simon, and Antoinette F. Konski. 2013. "Induced Pluripotent Stem Cells: A U.S. Patent Landscape Analysis." *Genetic Engineering and Biotechnology News*, May 14, 2013. Accessed November 28, 2016. http://www.genengnews.com/gen-articles/induced-pluripotent-stem-cells-a-u-s-patent-landscape-analysis/4877.

Emerging Technology. 2017. "Mathematical Model Reveals the Patterns of How Innovations Arise." MIT Technology Review, January 13, 2017. Accessed 13 January 2017. https://www.technologyreview.com/s/603366/mathematical-model-reveals-the-patterns-of-how-innovations-arise/.

Epps, Heather L. Van. 2006. "Singapore's Multibillion Dollar Gamble." *Journal of Experimental Medicine* 203 (5): 1139–42.

Etienne, Gilbert. 2009. "India's 11th Five Year Plan 2007–12: Challenges and Constraints." *Mainstream Weekly* 47 (37). Accessed August 31, 2009. https://www.mainstreamweekly.net/article1600.html.

Etzkowitz, Henry. 1993. "Technology Transfer: The Second Academic Revolution." Technology Access Report, 7–9.

Etzkowitz, Henry, and Loet Leydesdorff. 2000. "The Dynamics of Innovation: From National Systems and 'Mode 2' to a Triple Helix of University-Industry-Government Relations." *Research policy* 29 (2): 109–23.

Evalueserve. 2006. "Is the Venture Capital Market in India Getting Overheated?" Whitepaper, Schaffhausen: Evalueserve.

Evans, Peter, and James E. Rauch. 1999. "Bureaucracy and Growth: A Cross-National Analysis of the Effects of" Weberian" State Structures on Economic Growth." *American Sociological Review* 64 (5): 748–65.

Export.gov. 2017. "China—Medical Devices." Last modified July 25, 2017. Accessed September 22, 2017. https://www.export.gov/article?id=China-Medical-Devices.

Fan, Peilei, and Chihiro Watanabe. 2006. "Promoting Industrial Development Through Technology Policy: Lessons from Japan and China." *Technology in Society* 28 (3): 303–20.

Feigenbaum, Evan A. 1999. "Soldiers, Weapons and Chinese Development Strategy: The Mao Era Military in China's Economic and Institutional Debate" *China Quarterly* 158:285–313.

Feigenbaum, Evan A. 2003. *China's Techno-Warriors: National Security and Strategic Competition from the Nuclear to the Information Age*. Redwood City, CA: Stanford University Press.

Feng Kaidong, interview, 2016.

Fialka, John J. 1999. *War by Other Means: Economic Espionage in America*. New York: W. W. Norton & Company.

Finegold, David, Poh-Kam Wong, and Tsui-Chern Cheah. 2004. "Adapting a Foreign Direct Investment Strategy to the Knowledge Economy: The Case of Singapore's Emerging Biotechnology Cluster." *European Planning Studies* 12 (7): 922. Accessed December 4, 2014. http://dx.doi.org/10.1080/0965431042000267830.

Forbes. 2016. "Forbes Announces 13th Annual World's Most Powerful Women List." June 6, 2016. Accessed July 17, 2016. https://www.forbes.com/sites/forbespr/2016/06/06/forbes-announces-13th-annual-worlds-most-powerful-women-list/?ss=power-women#13c0271437a1.

———. 2017. "Asia's 200 Best Under a Billion List." Accessed October 23, 2017. https://www.forbes.com/asia200/list/#tab:overall.

Francis, Sabil. 2011. *The IITs in India: Symbols of an Emerging Nation*. Sudasien-Chronik/South Asia Chronicle. Last modified January 2011. Accessed August 17, 2018. https://edoc.hu-berlin.de/bitstream/handle/18452/18602/293.pdf?sequence=1.

Freedom House. 2017. "Press Freedom's Dark Horizon." Accessed September 8, 2017. https://freedomhouse.org/report/freedom-press/freedom-press-2017.

Freeman, Chris. 1995. "The 'National System of Innovation' in Historical Perspective." *Cambridge Journal of Economics* 19 (1): 5–24.

Freeman, Chris. 2002. "Continental, National and Sub-national Innovation Systems—Complementarity and Economic Growth." *Research Policy* 31 (2): 191–211.

Freeman, Christopher. 1991. "Networks of Innovators: A Synthesis of Research Issues." *Research Policy* 20 (5): 499–514.

Freeman, Christopher, and Luc Soete. 1997. *The Economics of Industrial Innovation.* Abingdon, UK: Routledge.

French, Howard W. 2000 "Japan Unsettles Returnees, Who Yearn to Leave Again." *New York Times.* Last modified May 3, 2000. Accessed February 26, 2017. http://www.nytimes.com/2000/05/03/world/japan-unsettles-returnees-who-yearn-to-leave-again.html.

Frew, Sarah E., Stephen M. Sammut, Alysha F. Shore, Joshua K. Ramjist, Sara Al-Bader, Rahim Rezaie, Abdallah S. Daar, and Peter A. Singer. 2008. "Chinese Health Biotech and the Billion-Patient Market." *Nature Biotechnology* 26 (1): 37–53.

Friedberg, Errol C. 2010. *Sydney Brenner: A Biography.* New York: Cold Spring Harbor Laboratory Press.

Fujisue, Kenzo. 1998. "Promotion of Academia-Industry Cooperation in Japan—Establishing the 'Law of Promoting Technology Transfer from University to Industry' in Japan." *Technocation* 18 (6–7): 371–81. http://www.sciencedirect.com/science/article/pii/S0166497298000558#.

Fukao, Kyoji 深尾京司, and Hyeog Ug Kwon 権赫旭. 2004. "Nippon no Seisansei to Keizai Seicho: Sangyo Reberu Kigyo Reberu Deta niyoru Jissho Bunseki" 日本の生産性と経済成長：産業レベル・企業レベルデータによる実証分析 (The productivity and economic growth of Japan: empirical analysis based on industry-level and firm-level data). *Keizai Kenkyu* 55 (3): 261–81.

Fukao, Kyoji 深尾京司, and Hyeog Ug Kwon 権赫旭. 2012. "Dono yona kigyo ga koyo o umidashite iru ka: Jigyosho kigyo tokei chosa mikurodēta ni yoru jissho bunseki" どのような企業が雇用を生み出しているか：事業所・企業統計調査ミクロデータによる実証分析 (Who creates jobs in Japan—an empirical analysis based on the establishment and enterprise census). *Economic Research* 経済研究63 (1): 70–93.

Gelfert, Axel. 2013. "Before Biopolis: Representations of the Biotechnology Discourse in Singapore." *East Asian Science, Technology and Society* 7 (1): 103–23.

Gerschenkron, Alexander. 1962. *Economic Backwardness in Historical Perspective: A Book of Essays.* Cambridge, MA: Belknap Press.

Gerschenkron, Alexander. 1966. *Economic Backwardness in Historical Perspective.* Cambridge, MA: Belknap Press.

Gerth, Jeff. 1982. "Japanese Executives Charged in I.B.M. Theft Case." *New York Times,* June 23, 1982. Accessed August 21, 2018. http://www.nytimes.com/1982/06/23/business/japanese-executives-charged-in-ibm-theft-case.html?mcubz=0.

Gerth, Karl. 2012. "Consumption and Nationalism: China." In *The Oxford Handbook of the History of Consumption*, ed. Frank Trentmann, 418–32. New York: Oxford University Press.

Giesecke, Susanne. 2000. "The Contrasting Roles of Government in the Development of Biotechnology Industry in the US and Germany." *Research Policy* 29 (2): 205–23.

Ginsburgh, Victor, and Shlomo Weber. 2011. *How Many Languages Do We Need? The Economics of Linguistic Diversity*. Princeton, NJ: Princeton University Press.

Global Entrepreneurship Development Index (GEDI). 2014. Accessed May 19, 2014. http://www.thegedi.org/research/gedi-index/.

Global Entrepreneurship Development Index (GEDI). 2018. Accessed March 7, 2018. http://thegedi.org/global-entrepreneurship-and-development-index/.

Global Entrepreneurship Monitor (GEM). 2015. "Japan Profile." Accessed October 30, 2017. http://www.gemconsortium.org/country-profile/76.

Global Entrepreneurship Monitor (GEM). 2017. "Global Report 2016/17." Accessed February 4, 2017. http://www.gemconsortium.org/report/49812.

Goh Chok Tong. 2001. Speech at the Inaugural Raffles Institution Lecture on National Issues, April 12, 2001. Accessed August 18, 2018. http://www.nas.gov.sg/archivesonline/speeches/view-html?filename=2001041201.htm.

Goldsmith, Jack, and Tim Wu. 2006. *Who Controls the Internet?* Oxford, UK: Oxford University Press.

Gopinathan, S. L. M. H., and Michael H. Lee. 2011. "Challenging and Co-opting Globalisation: Singapore's Strategies in Higher Education." *Journal of Higher Education Policy and Management* 33 (3): 287–99.

Gopinathan, Saravanan. 2001. "Globalisation, the State and Education Policy in Singapore." In *Education and Political Transition: Themes and Experiences in East Asia*, ed. Thomas M. Bray and Wing On Lee, 21–36. Hong Kong: Comparative Education Research Centre (CERC), the University of Hong Kong, and Springer.

Gore, Charles. 2000. "The Rise and Fall of the Washington Consensus as a Paradigm for Developing Countries." *World Development* 28 (5): 789–804.

Görg, Holger, and Eric Strobl. 2005. "Spillovers from Foreign Firms Through Worker Mobility: An Empirical Investigation." *Scandinavian Journal of Economics* 107 (4): 693–709.

Government of Japan. 1996. "Science and Technology Basic Plan." July 2, 1996. Accessed October 2, 2017. http://www8.cao.go.jp/cstp/english/basic/1st-BasicPlan_96-00.pdf.

Government of Japan. 2006. "Science and Technology Basic Plan." Last modified March 28, 2006. Accessed October 4, 2017. http://www8.cao.go.jp/cstp/english/basic/3rd-Basic-Plan-rev.pdf.

Granovetter, Mark. 1973. "The Strength of Weak Ties." *American Journal of Sociology* 78 (6): 1360–80.

Granovetter, Mark. 1983. "The Strength of Weak Ties: A Network Theory Revisited." *Sociological Theory* 1: 201–33.

Granovetter, Mark. 1985. "Economic Action and Social Structure: The Problem of Embeddedness." *American Journal of Sociology* 91 (3): 481–510.

Greater Pacific Capital. 2013. "The Indian Diaspora: A Unique Untapped Global Asset for India." Greaterpacificcapital.com. Last modified March 2013. Accessed January 4, 2017. http://greaterpacificcapital.com/march-2013/.

Greenwood, James C. 2013. "Biotech in China." Last modified January 2013. Accessed March 6, 2017. https://www.bio.org/sites/default/files/Biotechnology-Industry-Pg62-64.pdf.

Griffiths, Sian M., Vincent C. H. Chung, and Jin Ling Tang. 2010. "Integrating Traditional Chinese Medicine: Experiences from China." *Australasian Medical Journal* 3 (7): 385–96.

Guha, Ramachandra. 2014. "How the Congress Lost the Diaspora." *Hindustan Times.* Last modified September 28, 2014. Accessed August 14, 2017. http://www.hindustantimes.com/columns/how-the-congress-lost-the-diaspora/storyK8hIXsz1D7dzZFFjr41fbO.html.

Gupta, Deepti, and Navneet Gupta. 2012. "Higher Education in India: Structure, Statistics and Challenges." *Journal of Education and Practice* 3 (2): 17–24.

Gurpur, Shashi, interview, 2016.

Guruz, Kemal. 2011. *Higher Education and International Student Mobility in the Global Knowledge Economy.* Revised and updated 2nd ed. Albany, NY: SUNY Press.

Haas, Benjamin. 2017. "China Moves to Block Internet VPNs from 2018." *Guardian.* Last modified July 11, 2017. Accessed July 24, 2017. https://www.theguardian.com/world/2017/jul/11/china-moves-to-block-internet-vpns-from-2018.

Hall, Peter A., and David Soskice, eds. 2001. *Varieties of Capitalism: The Institutional Foundations of Comparative Advantage.* Oxford, UK: Oxford University Press.

Hao, Jie, and Anthony Welch. 2012. "A Tale of Sea Turtles: Job-Seeking Experiences of 'Hai Gui' (High-Skilled Returnees) in China." *Higher Education Policy* 25 (2): 243–60.

Hao, Xian Feng, Yun Sun, Wan Tan Tian, and Zhe Yu Pan. 2015. "Analysis of Innovation Incentive Policy in China." Atlantis Press: 5th International Conference on Education, Management, Information and Medicine. doi:10.2991/emim-15.2015.114.

Harayama, Y. 2004. "Japanese Technology Policy on Technology Transfer: Development of Technology Licensing Organizations and Incubators." *Tech Monitor* 6: 30–36.

Hart, David M., ed. 2003. *The Emergence of Entrepreneurship Policy: Governance, Start-Ups, and Growth in the US Knowledge Economy.* New York: Cambridge University Press.

Hayashi, Fumio, and Edward C. Prescott. 2002. "The 1990s in Japan: A Lost Decade." *Review of Economic Dynamics* 5 (1): 206–35.

Heller, Michael A., and Rebecca S. Eisenberg. 1998. "Can Patents Deter Innovation? The Anticommons in Biomedical Research." *Science* 280 (5364): 698–701.

Henderson, Rebecca, Luigi Orsenigo, and Gary P. Pisano. 1999. "The Pharmaceutical Industry and the Revolution in Molecular Biology: Interactions Among Scientific, Institutional, and Organizational Change." In *Sources of Industrial Leadership: Studies of Seven Industries*, ed. David C. Mowery and Richard R. Nelon, 267–311. New York: Cambridge University Press.

Hildreth, Cade. 2015. "5 Market Leaders in iPS Cell Therapy Development You Need to Know." *BioInformant*. Last modified July 16, 2015. http://www.bio informant.com/five-companies-developing-induced-pluripotent-stem-cell -therapies/.

Hindustan Times. 2017. "PM Modi Asks Diaspora to Invest in India, Work Towards Its Development." January 8, 2017. Accessed July 23, 2017. http://www.hindustan times.com/india-news/pm-modi-asks-diaspora-to-invest-in-india-work-towards -its-development/story-aMECWo9WWDqEcoMb9wI2LK.html.

Ho, Elaine Lynn-Ee, and Mark Boyle. 2015. "Migration as Development Repackaged? The Globalising Imperative of the Singaporean State's Diaspora Strategies." *Singapore Journal of Tropical Geography* 36 (2): 164–82.

Hoang, Ha, and Bostjan Antoncic. 2003. "Network-Based Research in Entrepreneurship: A Critical Review." *Journal of Business Venturing* 18 (2): 165–87.

Hobday, Mike. 1995. "East Asian Latecomer Firms: Learning the Technology of Electronics." *World Development* 23 (7): 1171–93.

Hodgson, An. 2016. "Top 5 Developed Markets with the Best Middle Class Potential." *Euromonitor International*, April 26, 2016. Accessed August 19, 2018. http://blog .euromonitor.com/2016/04/top-5-developed-markets-with-the-best-middle-class -potential.html.

Holden, Kerry, and David Demeritt. 2008. "Democratising Science? The Politics of Promoting Biomedicine in Singapore's Developmental State." *Environment and Planning D: Society and Space* 26 (1): 68–86.

Hong, Yu. 2011. "Reading the Twelfth Five-Year Plan: China's Communication-Driven Mode of Economic Restructuring." *International Journal of Communication* 5:1045–57.

Huang, Yanping. 2015. "A Study on the Relationship Between Entrepreneurial Environment and Entrepreneurial Activities—Take Entrepreneurial Activities of Returned Overseas Students in Zhongguancun as an Example." *International Business and Management* 11 (3): 107–11.

Huang, Zheping. 2017. "What China's 'New Era' Looks Like, in Xi Jinping's Own Words." October 19, 2017. Accessed August 17, 2018. https://qz.com/1106365/chinas -19th-party-congress-speech-text-what-xi-jinping-said-on-climate-south-china -sea-taiwan-technology/.

Hudson Global Resources. 2016. "The Hudson Report: Today's Workforce Demands Tomorrow's Skills Singapore." Annual report, Hudson Global Resources (Singapore) Pte Ltd.

Hughes, Christopher W. 2011. "The Slow Death of Japanese Techno-nationalism? Emerging Comparative Lessons for China's Defense Production." *Journal of Strategic Studies* 34 (3): 451–79.

Humphrey, John, and Hubert Schmitz. 2002. "How Does Insertion in Global Value Chains Affect Upgrading in Industrial Clusters?" *Regional Studies* 36 (9): 1017–27.

Hvistendahl, Mara. 2014. "Show Me the Money." *Science* 346 (6208): 411–15. doi:10.1126/science.346.6208.411.

Ibata-Arens, Kathryn. 2005. *Innovation and Entrepreneurship in Japan: Politics, Organizations and High Technology Firms.* Cambridge: Cambridge University Press.

Ibata-Arens, Kathryn. 2008. "The Kyoto Model of Innovation and Entrepreneurship: Regional Innovation Systems and Cluster Culture." *Prometheus* 26 (1): 89–109.

Ibata-Arens, Kathryn C. 2012. "Race to the Future: Innovations in Gifted and Enrichment Education in Asia, and Implications for the United States." *Administrative Sciences* 2 (1): 1–25.

Ibata-Arens, Kathryn C. 2014. "Japan's New Business Incubation Revolution." In *Handbook on East Asian Entrepreneurship*, ed. Tony Fu-lai Yu and Ho don Yan, 145–56. London: Routledge.

Ikeno, Fumiaki. "Changing the World Through Japan's Scientific Endeavors." Presentation to the Japan-US Science Forum in Boston, Japan's Rapidly Aging Society: How to Innovate for This? Japan Society for the Promotion of Science (JSPS), Harvard University, Boston, MA, November 12, 2016.

Imai, Kenichi 今井 賢一. 1992. *Shihon-Syugi no System kan Kyoso* 資本主義のシステム間競争 (Competition among different systems in capitalism). Tokyo東京: Chikuma Shobo 筑摩書房.

India Brand Equity Foundation (IBEF). 2016. "Indian Pharmaceutical Industry." Accessed August 19, 2018. http://www.ibef.org/industry/pharmaceutical-india.aspx.

Indian Institute of Technology. 1961. "The Institutes of Technology Act, 1961." Indian Institute of Technology, Powai, Bombay. Accessed October 1, 2017. http://www.iitb.ac.in/sites/default/files/IITsAct_1.pdf.

Indian Institute of Technology. 1963. "The Institutes of Technology (Amendment) Act, 1963." Accessed August 20, 2018. http://www.iitb.ac.in/sites/default/files/IITsAct_1.pdf.

Industrial Cluster Study Group 産業クラスター研究会. 2005. "Sangyo kurasutā kenkyūkai hōkoku" 産業クラスター研究会報告 (Industrial Cluster Study Group report). Accessed September 6, 2018. http://warp.da.ndl.go.jp/info:ndljp/pid/286890/www.meti.go.jp/press/20050524002/4-monitoring-houkokusho-set.pdf (Japanese).

Industrial Revitalization Division, Ministry of Economy, Trade and Industry. 2010. "Turnover ADR (Alternative Dispute Resolution)." Last modified January 2010. Accessed October 2, 2017. http://www.meti.go.jp/policy/jigyou_saisei/ADR%20HP _E-virsion_100126.pdf.

Innovation Fund for Technology Based Firms. n.d. Accessed July 28, 2013. http://www .innofund.gov.cn.

Institute of International Education. 2011. *Open Doors 2011: Report on International Educational Exchange.* Washington DC: National Press Club.

INTER-CEP. n.d. "National Framework for Research, Innovation and Enterprise: Schemes, Grants and Programmes—Singapore." Accessed October 11, 2017. http:// www.inter-cep.com/case-studies/national-framework-for-research-innovation -and-enterprise-schemes-grants-and-programmes-singapore/.

International Healthcare Research Center and Global Healthcare Resources. 2016. "2016 Medical Tourism Index." Palm Beach Gradens, FL: International Healthcare Research Center.

International Medical Travel Journal. 2017. "The Decline of Singapore Medical Tourism." Last modified February 2017. Accessed September 11, 2017. https://www.imtj .com/news/decline-singapore-medical-tourism/.

Iwata, Kikuo 岩田規久男, and Tsutomu Miyagawa 宮川努. 2003. "Ushinawareta 10 toshi no shinin wa nanika?" 失われた 10 年の真因は何か ("What are the true reasons for Japan's lost decade?"). *Economics Series*エコノミックス・シリーズ. Kyoto: Toyokeizaishin-housha東洋経済新報社.

Jansson, Hans, Martin Johanson, and Joachim Ramstrom. 2007. "Institutions and Business Networks: A Comparative Analysis of the Chinese, Russian, and West European Markets." *Industrial Marketing Management* 36 (7): 955–67.

Japan Bioindustry Association. 2011. "Bio-venture Statistics and Trend Survey Report 2011," p. 3. Last modified January 1, 2011. Accessed June 5, 2012. http://www.jba .or.jp/report/industry/document/pdf/bv/2011_bv_summary.pdf.

Japan Bioindustry Association. 2015. バイオインダストリー協会. "Nisenjūgonen bio bencha-tōkei dōkō hōkokusho" 2015 年バイオベンチャー統計・動向調査報告書 ("2015 bio-venture statistics and activity report"). Last modified October 2015. Accessed July 10, 2016. http://www.jba.or.jp/pc/activitie/open_innovation/info /001981.html (Japanese).

Japan Times. 2014. "More Japanese Living Abroad Than Ever, Ministry Says." Last modified August 15, 2014. Accessed February 26, 2017. https://www.japantimes.co.jp /news/2014/08/15/national/more-japanese-living-abroad-than-ever-ministry-says/.

Japan Times. 2017. "Japan Set to Fast-Track Permanent Residency for Skilled Foreign Professional." Last modified January 18, 2017. Accessed February 26, 2017. http:// www.japantimes.co.jp/news/2017/01/18/national/crime-legal/japan-set-fast-track -permanent-residency-skilled-foreigners/#.WLJ6GbHMz-Y.

JETRO. 2008. "Japan Attractiveness Survey." Invest Japan Division, Invest Japan Department. Accessed July 25, 2012. https://www.jetro.go.jp/switzerland/topics/20080731142-topics/japan_attractiveness_survey.pdf.

JETRO. 2013. *Global Trade and Investment Report—Revitalizing Japan Through Global Business.* Accessed September 6, 2018. https://www.jetro.go.jp/en/news/releases/2013/20130808148-news.html.

Jiang, Bin, and Timothy Koller. 2006. "A Long-Term Look at ROIC." *McKinsey Quarterly.* Last modified February 2006. Accessed November 16, 2016. http://www.mckinsey.com/business-functions/strategy-and-corporate-finance/our-insights/a-long-term-look-at-roic.

Jiang, Ting, and Huihua Nie. 2014. "The Stained China Miracle: Corruption, Regulation, and Firm Performance." *Economics Letters* 123 (3): 366–69.

Johnson, Bjorn, Edward Lorenz, and Bengt-Ake Lundvall. 2002. "Why All This Fuss About Codified and Tacit Knowledge?" *Industrial and Corporate Change* 11 (2): 245–62.

Johnson, Chalmers. 1982. *MITI and the Japanese Miracle: The Growth of Industrial Policy; 1925–1975.* Redwood City, CA: Stanford University Press.

Johnson, Chalmers. 1987. "Political Institutions and Economic Performance: The Government-Business Relationship in Japan, South Korea, and Taiwan." In *The Political Economy of the New Asian Industrialism*, ed. Frederic C. Deyo, 136–64. Ithaca, New York: Cornell University Press.

Johnson, Chalmers A. 1995. *Japan, Who Governs? The Rise of the Developmental State.* New York: W. W. Norton & Company.

Jozuka, Emiko, and Junko Ogura. 2017. "Can Japan Survive Without Immigrants?" CNN, August 1, 2017. Accessed April 11, 2018. https://www.cnn.com/2017/08/01/asia/japan-migrants-immigration/index.html.

JTC Corporation. 2007. "Biopolis @ One-North." Accessed March 1, 2017. https://web.archive.org/web/20071031043114/http://www.biomed-singapore.com/etc/medialib/bms_downloads/newsroom/media_kit.Par.0013.File.tmp/Fact%20Sheet%20-%20Biopolis%20(September%202007).pdf.

Junn, Loh Chuan. 2017. "Singapore Firms Tapping 3D Printing Tech for New Growth Opportunities." *Channel News Asia*, January 23, 2017. Accessed January 10, 2018. http://www.channelnewsasia.com/news/singapore/singapore-firms-tapping-3d-printing-tech-for-new-growth-opportun-7576708.

Kalegaonkar, Archana, Richard Locke, and Jonathan Lehrich. 2008. "The Biocon India Group." Last modified November 4, 2008. Accessed January 10, 2018. https://mitsloan.mit.edu/LearningEdge/CaseDocs/08081%20Biocon%20India%20Group%20Case.pdf.

Kaplinsky, Raphael, and Dirk Messner. 2008. "Introduction: The Impact of Asian Drivers on the Developing World." *World Development* 36 (2): 197–209.

Kapur, Devesh. 2003. "Indian Diaspora as a Strategic Asset." *Economic and Political Weekly* 38 (5): 445–48.

Katz, Richard. 2003. "Japan's Phoenix Economy." *Foreign Affairs* 82 (1): 114–29.

Kaufmann, Dan. 2013. "The Influence of Causation and Effectuation Logics on Targeted Policies: The Cases of Singapore and Israel." *Technology Analysis and Strategic Management* 25 (7): 853–70.

Kavlekar, Poornima. 2012. "The Biocon Story." *The Smart CEO*, February 25, 2012. Accessed October 10, 2017. http://www.thesmartceo.in/magazine/cover-story/the-biocon-story.html. See also http://startup50.in/the-biocon-story/.

Keidanren, internal report, 2011.

Kennedy, Scott. 2015. "Made in China 2025." Center for Strategic and International Studies. Last modified June 1, 2015. Accessed August 12, 2017. https://www.csis.org/analysis/made-china-2025.

Kenney, Martin, and Urs Von Burg. 1999. "Technology, Entrepreneurship and Path Dependence: Industrial Clustering in Silicon Valley and Route 128." *Industrial and Corporate Change* 8 (1): 67–103.

Khadria, Binod. 2006. "India: Skilled Migration to Developed Countries, Labour Migration to the Gulf." *Migración y Desarrollo* (7): 4–37. Accessed August 20, 2018. http://www.redalyc.org/html/660/66000702/.

Khanna, Manish, and Saurabh Kaushal. 2013. "Growth of Banking Sector in India: A Collective Study of History and Its Operations." *Asian Journal of Advanced Basic Science* 2 (1): 36–45.

Khanna, Tarun. 2007. *Billions of Enterpreneurs: How.* New Delhi: Penguin Books India.

Kharas, Homi. 2010. "The Emerging Middle Class in Developing Countries." Working paper, OECD Development Centre, OECD.

Khorsheed, Mohammad S. 2016. "Learning from Global Pacesetters to Build the Country Innovation Ecosystem." *Journal of the Knowledge Economy* 8 (1): 1–20.

Kim, Mirei, interview, 2012.

Kim, Mujo, interview, 2004.

Kim, Mujo, interview, 2010.

Kim, Mujo, interview, 2012.

King, Gary, Jennifer Pan, and Margaret E. Roberts. 2013. "How Censorship in China Allows Government Criticism but Silences Collective Expression." *American Political Science Review* 107 (2): 326–43. http://www.jstor.org/stable/43654017.

King, Kenneth. 1984. "Science, Technology and Education in the Development of Indigenous Technological Capability." In *Technological Capability in the Third World*, ed. Martin Fransman and Kenneth King, 31–63. London: Palgrave Macmillan.

Kitanaka, Anna, and Satoshi Kawano. 2013. "ReproCell Poised to Jump Fivefold from IPO After Debut." *Bloomberg News.* Last modified June 27, 2013. Accessed

February 27, 2017. https://www.bloomberg.com/news/articles/2013-06-27/reprocell-set-to-quadruple-from-ipo-on-stem-cell-optimis.

Kneller Robert. 1999. "Intellectual Property Rights and University-Industry Technology Transfer in Japan." Last modified September 20, 1999. Guildford, UK: Beech Tree Publishing. Accessed October 2, 2017. https://www.nsf.gov/od/oise/tokyo/reports/trm/rm99-08.html.

Kneller, Robert. 2007a. "The Beginning of University Entrepreneurship in Japan: TLOs and Bioventures Lead the Way." *Journal of Technology Transfer* 32 (4): 435–56.

Kneller, Robert. 2007b. *Bridging Islands: Venture Companies and the Future of Japanese and American Industry.* Oxford, UK: Oxford University Press.

Kneller, Robert. 2010. "The Importance of New Companies for Drug Discovery: Origins of a Decade of New Drugs." *Nature Reviews Drug Discovery* 9 (11): 867–82. Academic Search Complete, EBSCOhost. Accessed November 29, 2016. https://www.ncbi.nlm.nih.gov/pubmed/21031002.

Kneller, Robert. 2013. "The Japanese Pharmaceutical Industry: Its Evolution and Current Challenges (Review)." *Journal of Japanese Studies* 39 (1): 235–40.

Kochhar, Rakesh. 2015. "China's Middle Class Surges, While India's Lags Behind." Pew Research Center, July 15, 2015. Accessed July 24, 2016. http://www.pewresearch.org/fact-tank/2015/07/15/china-india-middle-class/.

Koch-Weser, Iacob N. 2013. *The Reliability of China's Economic Data: An Analysis of National Output.* US-China Economic and Security Review Commission. Last modified January 30, 2013. Accessed August 17, 2018. https://www.uscc.gov/Research/reliability-chinas-economic-data-analysis-national-output.

Koh, Winston T. H., and Poh Kam Wong. 2005. "Competing at the Frontier: The Changing Role of Technology Policy in Singapore's Economic Strategy." *Technological Forecasting and Social Change* 72 (3): 255–85.

Kohli, Atul. 2006. "Politics of Economic Growth in India, 1980–2005: Part I: The 1980s." *Economic and Political Weekly* 41 (13): 1251–59.

Kōno, Osami 河野修己. 2013. "IPS saibō de shinfuzen o chiryō, Kyōdai CiRA-hatsu benchā no iHeart Japan ga shidō, 4-nen-go no rinshō shiken kaishi o mezasu." iPS 細胞で心不全を治療、京大CiRA発ベンチャーのiHeart Japanが始動、4年後の臨床試験開始を目指す (Treating heart failure with iPS cells, Kyoto University CiRA venture iHeart Japan starts, aiming to be in clinical trials within four years). *Nikkei Biotechnology and Business* 日経バイオテ. Last modified May 23, 2013. Accessed August 7, 2013. https://bio.nikkeibp.co.jp/article/news/20130523/168498/ (Japanese).

Kuhn, Thomas S. 1970. *The Structure of Scientific Revolutions.* Chicago: University of Chicago Press.

Kumar, Sanjay, and Deepa Kachroo Tiku. 2009. "The Conservative Path to Biotech Protection." *Managing Intellectual Property* 192: 91–94.

Kurup, Anitha, S. Chandrashekar, and K. Muralidharan. 2011. "Woman Power in Corporate India: In Conversation with Kiran Mazumdar Shaw, Chairperson & MD, Biocon ltd." *2011 IIMB Management Review* 23 (4): 223–33.

Kuznetsov, Yevgeny. 2006. *Diaspora Networks and the International Migration of Skills: How Countries Can Draw on their Talent Abroad.* Washington, DC: World Bank Institute.

Lai, Linette. 2017. "Singapore Tops for Medical Tourism, but Rivals Catching Up Quickly." *Straits Times,* June 6, 2017. Accessed September 11, 2017. http://www.straitstimes.com/singapore/health/spore-tops-for-medical-tourism-but-rivals-catching-up-quickly.

Lakhan, Shaheen Emmanuel. 2006. "The Emergence of Modern Biotechnology in China." *Issues in Informing Science and Information Technology* 3: 333–53.

Lall, Sanjaya. 1992. "Technological Capabilities and Industrialization." *World Development* 20 (2): 165–86.

Lall, Sanjaya. 2004. "Selective Industrial and Trade Policies in Developing Countries: Theoretical and Empirical Issues." In *The Politics of Trade and Industrial Policy in Africa: Forced Consensus,* ed. Charles Chukwuma Soludo, Michael Osita Ogbu, and Ha-Joon Chang, 4–14. Fento, MO: World Press.

Laurell, Hélène, Svante Andersson, and Leona Achtenhagen. 2013. "The Importance of Industry Context for New Venture Internationalisation: A Case Study from the Life Sciences." *Journal of International Entrepreneurship* 11 (4): 297–319.

Lazonick, W., and O. Tulum. 2011. "US Biopharmaceutical Finance and the Sustainability of the Biotech Business Model." *Research Policy* 40 (9): 1170–87.

LD Investment. 2017. "China's Medical Device Sector Growth Prospects." *Seeking Alpha.* Last modified January 27, 2017. Accessed September 22, 2017. https://seekingalpha.com/article/4040254-chinas-medical-device-sector-growth-prospects.

Lee, Jong-Wha. 1996. "Government Interventions and Productivity Growth." *Journal of Economic Growth* 1 (3): 391–414.

Lee, Terence. 2017. "The Rare Startup That Wants to Put Singapore on the Medical Robotics Map." *Tech in Asia,* September 1, 2017. Accessed January 15, 2018. https://www.techinasia.com/rare-startup-put-singapore-medical-robotics-map.

Lee, Yong-Sook, Ying-Chian Tee, and Dong-wan Kim. 2009. "Endogenous versus Exogenous Development: A Comparative Study of Biotechnology Industry Cluster Policies in South Korea and Singapore." *Environment and Planning C: Government and Policy* 27 (4): 612–31.

Lee Kuan Yu. 1998. *The Singapore Story: Memoirs of Lee Kuan Yew.* Singapore: Singapore Press Holdings.

Lessig, Lawrence. 2002. "The Architecture of Innovation." *Duke Law Journal* 51 (6): 1783–801.

Levitt, Steven D., and Stephen J. Dubner. 2005. *Freakonomics: A Rogue Economist Explores the Hidden Side of Everything*. New York: William Morrow.

Lew, Christopher R., and Edwin Pak-wah Leung. 2013. *Historical Dictionary of the Chinese Civil War*. London: Scarecrow Press, Rowman and Littlefield.

Lew, Yong Kyu, and Rudolf R. Sinkovics. 2013. "Crossing Borders and Industry Sectors: Behavioral Governance in Strategic Alliances and Product Innovation for Competitive Advantage." *Long Range Planning* 46 (1): 13–38.

Leydesdorff, L., and O. Persson. 2010. "Mapping the Geography of Science: Distribution Patterns and Networks of Relations Among Cities and Institutes." *Journal of the American Society for Information Science and Technology* 61:1622–34.

Leydesdorff, Loet. 2013. *Triple Helix of University-Industry-Government Relations*. New York: Springer.

Leydesdorff, Loet, Stephen Carley, and Ismael Rafols. 2013. "Global Maps of Science Based on the New Web-of-Science Categories." *Scientometrics* 94 (2): 589–93.

Leydesdorff, Loet, and Henry Etzkowitz. 1996. "Emergence of a Triple Helix of University-Industry-Government Relations." *Science and Public Policy* 23 (5): 279–86.

Leydesdorff, Loet, and Martin Meyer. 2006. "Triple Helix Indicators of Knowledge-Based Innovation Systems: Introduction to the Special Issue." *Research Policy* 35 (10): 1441–49.

Li, Cheng. 2004. "Bringing China's Best and Brightest Back Home: Regional Disparities and Political Tensions." *China Leadership Monitor* 11: 1–19.

Li, Xibao. 2012. "Behind the Recent Surge of Chinese Patenting: An Institutional View." *Research Policy* 41 (1): 236–49.

Libertas Consulting. 2006. "Heisei 17-nendo sangyo kurasutā keikaku monitaringu-to chosa hokoku-sho" 平成17 年度産業クラスター計画モニタリング等調査報告書 (Survey of the Industrial Cluster Plan monitoring 2005). Industrial Cluster Study Group 産業クラスター研究会. Last modified March 2006. Accessed July 18, 2016. http://www.cluster.gr.jp/relation/data/pdf/17y_cluster_moni_houkoku.pdf (Japanese).

Life Science World. n.d. "The Human Care Company." Accessed April 10, 2018. http://lifescienceworld.in/.

Li Keqiang. 2015. "Chinese Premier Li Keqiang's Speech at Davos 2015." World Economic Forum. Last modified January 23, 2015. Accessed March 6, 2017. http://www.weforum.org/agenda/2015/01/chinese-premier-li-keqiangs-speech-at-davos-2015/.

Lim, Benjamin Kang, and Simon Rabinovitch. 2010. "China Mulls $1.5 Trillion Strategic Industries Boost: Sources." Reuters. Last modified December 3, 2010. Accessed July 8, 2017. http://www.reuters.com/article/us-china-economy-investment-idUSTR E6B16U920101203.

Lim, Louisa. 2011. "China's Great Science Gamble: Plagiarism Plague Hinders China's Scientific Ambition." National Public Radio. Last modified August 3, 2011. Accessed July 8, 2017. http://www.npr.org/2011/08/03/138937778/plagiarism-plague -hinders-chinas-scientific-ambition.

Lin, Yi-min. 2001. *Between Politics and Markets: Firms, Competition, and Institutional Change in Post-Mao China.* Cambridge: Cambridge University Press.

Lincoln, Edward J. 2004. *Arthritic Japan: The Slow Pace of Economic Reform.* JPRI Working Paper, vol. 81. Washington, DC: Brookings Institution Press.

List, Friedrich. 1841. *The National System of Political Economy.* Trans. S. Lloyd. 1909 ed. London: Green and Company.

Liu, Hong, and Els Van Dongen. 2016. "China's Diaspora Policies as a New Mode of Transnational Governance." *Journal of Contemporary China* 25 (102): 805–21.

Liu, Yipeng. 2012. "High-Tech Start-Up Innovation in Wuxi and Shanghai, PR. China Embedded in the Institutional Environments." In *Proceedings of the 5th European Conference on Innovation and Entrepreneurship,* ed. Alexandros Kakouris, 371–79. Abingdon, UK: Routledge. Last modified, June 2012. Accessed August 17, 2018. https://s3.amazonaws.com/academia.edu.documents/54894912/eciel0-cd.pdf ?AWSAccessKeyId=AKIAIWOWYYGZ2Y53UL3A&Expires=1534799774&Signature=BfP6L3vCpDiU3GOxtMJAX6sPNlA%3D&response-content-disposition =inline%3B%20filename%3DProceedings_of_the_5th_EurExploring_Unde .pdf#page=393.

López-Claros, Augusto. 2009. *The Innovation for Development Report 2009–2010.* New York: Palgrave Macmillan.

Lucas, R. B. E. 2001. *Diaspora and Development: Highly Skilled Migrants from East Asia.* Washington, DC: World Bank.

Luedi, Jeremy. 2015. "Start-Ups Poised to Change Politics in Singapore." *Global Risk Insights,* August 28, 2015. Accessed September 12, 2017. http://globalriskinsights .com/2015/08/start-ups-poised-to-change-politics-in-singapore/.

Lundstrom, Anders, and Lois Stevenson. 2005. *Entrepreneurship Policy: Theory and Practice.* International Studies in Entrepreneurship, vol. 9. New York: Springer.

Lundvall, Bengt-Ake. 1992. *National Systems of Innovation: An Analytical Framework.* London: Pinter.

Lundvall, Bengt-Ake. 2005. "National Innovation Systems—Analytical Concept and Development Tool." 10th Danish Research Unit for Industrial Dynamics (DRUID) Conference, Copenhagen, Denmark. Published subsequently as Lundvall, Bengt-Åke. 2007. "National Innovation Systems—Analytical Concept and Development Tool." *Industry and Innovation* 14 (1): 95–119. http://www.druid.dk/conferences /summer2005/papers/ds2005-603.pdf.

Mahley, Robert W., interview, November 2016.

Mahmood, Ishtiaq P., and Jasjit Singh. 2003. "Technological Dynamism in Asia." *Research Policy* 32 (6): 1031–54.

Make in India. 2017. "Sectors." Last modified June 2017. Accessed September 20, 2017. http://www.makeinindia.com/sectors.

Malay Mail Online. 2015. "Entrepreneurship Is Not a Silver Bullet for the Singapore Economy." July 11, 2015. https://www.todayonline.com/singapore/size-lack-access -markets-barriers-entrepreneurship-here.

Manpower Research and Statistics Department. 2016. "Labour Force in Singapore 2016" (survey). Singapore: Ministry of Manpower.

Martin, Alexander. 2016. "Line, a Japanese Messaging App, Raises over $1 Billion in IPO." *Wall Street Journal*, July 11, 2016. Accessed October 15, 2017. https://www .wsj.com/articles/japanese-messaging-app-line-raises-over-1-billion-in-ipo -1468199800.

Masterson, Nola, and Nandhini Tandon. 2014. "Beer to Pharmaceuticals: Biocon's Kiran Mazumdar-Shaw." *LSF Magazine*, Fall 2014, 48–57. Accessed March 4, 2017. http://www.sciencefuturesinc.com/docs/LSF_Beer_to_Pharm.pdf.

Matsumoto, Toshiro 橋本寿朗. 2001. "Sengonihon keizai no seichō kōzō: Kigyō shisutemu to sangyō seisaku no bunseki" 戦後日本経済の成長構造: 企業システムと産業政策の分析 (Growth structure of postwar Japan economy: analysis of enterprise system and industrial policy). Tokyo: Yūhikaku 東京:有斐閣.

Mattli, Walter, and Tim Buthe. 2003. "Setting International Standards: Technological Rationality or Primacy of Power?" *World Politics* 56 (1): 1–42.

Mazumdar, Mainak. 2012. *Performance of Pharmaceutical Companies in India: A Critical Analysis of Industrial Structure, Firm Specific Resources, and Emerging Strategies*. New York: Springer Science & Business Media.

Mazzucato, M., and G. Dosi, eds. 2006. *Knowledge Accumulation and Industry Evolution: Pharma-biotech*. Cambridge: Cambridge University Press.

Mazzucato, Mariana. 2011. "The Entrepreneurial State." *Soundings* 49 (49): 131–42.

Mazzucato, Mariana. 2013. "Financing Innovation: Creative Destruction vs. Destructive Creation." *Industrial and Corporate Change* 22 (4): 851–67.

Mazzucato, Mariana. 2015. *Entrepreneurial State: Debunking Public vs. Private Sector Myths*. New York: Perseus Books (Ingram).

Mazzucato, Mariana. 2016. "From Market Fixing to Market-Creating: A New Framework for Innovation Policy." *Industry and Innovation* 23 (2): 140–56.

Mazzucato, Mariana, and Carlota Perez. 2014. "Innovation as Growth Policy: The Challenge for Europe." Science Policy Research Unit (SPRU) Working Paper Series, July. Oxford Scholarship Online. Accessed August 21, 2018. https://www.sussex .ac.uk/webteam/gateway/file.php?name=2014-13-swps-mazzucato-perez .pdf&site=25.

McKelvey, Maureen, and Sharmistha Bagchi-Sen, eds. 2015. *Innovation Spaces in Asia: Entrepreneurs, Multinational Enterprises and Policy.* Northampton, MA: Edward Elgar Publishing.

McMillan, G. Steven, Francis Narin, and David L. Deeds. 2000. "An Analysis of the Critical Role of Public Science in Innovation: The Case of Biotechnology." *Research Policy* 29 (1): 1–8.

Min, Chia Yan. 2016. "Novartis Moving Research Facility out of Singapore." *Straits Times*, October 5, 2016. Accessed March 8, 2017. http://www.straitstimes.com /business/economy/novartis-moving-research-facility-out-of-singapore.

Ministry of Economy, Trade and Industry (METI). 2001. "Biotech Industry Creation Basic Investigation 2000," p. 8. Accessed June 5, 2012. Heisei juuninendo. Baiosan gyōsōzōkisochōsahōkokusho. Heiseijūsannnensangatsu. 平成12 年度. バイオ産業 創造基礎調査報告書. 平成13 年3 月. http://www.meti.go.jp/statistics/sei/bio/result /pdf/12FYBioIndustryStatistics.pdf.

Ministry of Economy, Trade and Industry (METI). 2006. "Sangyo kurasutā dai ni-ki chūki keikaku" 産業クラスター第二期中期計画 (Industrial Cluster Project, second period mid-term plan). METI Regional Economic and Policy Group. Last modified April 1, 2006. Accessed July 2, 2017. http://www.meti.go.jp/policy/local _economy/tiikiinnovation/source/2nd_middle_project.pdf (Japanese).

Ministry of Economy, Trade and Industry (METI). 2009. "S&T Policies." Last modified Dec 27, 2009. Accessed October 11, 2017. http://www.meti.go.jp/english/apec /apec-isti/IST/abridge/sgz/sgzpol00.htm.

Ministry of Economy, Trade and Industry (METI). 2010. "Summary of the 2010 (44th) Survey of Trends in Business Activities of Foreign Affiliates (Total Asia)," Oceania Regional Headquarters (Total), 2009. Accessed April 3, 2012. http://www.meti.go .jp/english/statistics/tyo/gaisikei/index.html.

Ministry of Economy, Trade and Industry (METI). 2011. "The Summary of Managing a New Drug Bio Venture." Last modified March 2011. Accessed August 7, 2013. http://www.meti.go.jp/policy/mono_info_service/mono/bio/Bioventure/bioven turehoukokusyo.pdf.

Ministry of Economy, Trade and Industry (METI). 2013. "Regarding Bio Related Budget." Last modified July 29, 2013. Accessed August 7, 2013. http://www.meti.go.jp /policy/mono_info_service/mono/bio/Yosan/index.html.

Ministry of Economy, Trade and Industry (METI). 2016. "Second Term Medium-Range Industrial Cluster Plan." METI Regional Economic and Policy Group. Last modified April 1, 2016. Accessed October 2, 2017. http://www.meti.go.jp/policy/local _economy/tiikiinnovation/source/2ndplan_outline_eng.pdf.

Ministry of Economy, Trade and Industry (METI). 2017a. "Horei" 法令 (Regulation). Last modified August 25, 2017. Accessed October 6, 2017. http://www.meti.go.jp /intro/law/index.html (Japanese).

Ministry of Economy, Trade and Industry (METI). 2017b. "Summary of the 2017 (51st) Survey of Trends in Business Activities of Foreign Affiliates (Total Asia)," Oceania Regional Headquarters (Total), 2016. Accessed September 6, 2018. http://www.meti .go.jp/english/statistics/tyo/gaisikei/index.html.

Ministry of Economy, Trade and Industry (METI). n.d. "Industrial Cluster Project 2009." Regional Economic and Industrial Policy Group, Regional Technology Division. Accessed October 2, 2017. http://www.meti.go.jp/policy/local_economy /tiikiinnovation/source/2009Cluster(E).pdf.

Ministry of Economy, Trade and Industry (METI). n.d. "Sangyo kurasuta seisaku ni tsuite" 産業クラスター政策について (Industrial Cluster Plan [Innovation Cluster]). Accessed October 6, 2017. http://www.meti.go.jp/policy/local_economy/tiikiinno vation/industrial_cluster.html (Japanese).

Ministry of Economy, Trade and Industry (METI). n.d. "Technological Innovation and Its Transfer to Industry." Accessed October 2, 2017. http://www.meti.go.jp/english /information/data/cIP9972e.html.

Ministry of Education Culture, Sports, Science and Technology (MEXT). 2000. "Sangyo gijutsu-ryoku kyōka-hō ni okeru tokkyo-ryo oyobi shinsa seikyū-ryō no keigen so- chi ni tsuite" 産業技術力強化法における特許料及び審査請求料の軽減措置について (Measures to reduce patent fee and examine in the law to strengthen industrial technology capability). July 2, 2000. Accessed October 2, 2017. http://www.mext .go.jp/a_menu/shinkou/sangaku/sangakuc/sangakuc6_3.htm.

Ministry of Education Culture, Sports, Science and Technology (MEXT). 2001. "Daigakunado ni okeru gijutsu ni kansuru kenkyū seika no minkan jigyō-sha e no iten no sokushin ni kansuru hōritsu" 大学等における技術に関する研究成果の民 間事業者への移転の促進に関する法律 (Law for promotion of university-industry technology transfer and promotion to private business operators). MEXT Research Promotion Department Environment Research, Industry Cooperation Division 研究振興局研究環境・産業連携課 (kenkyūshinkōkyokukenkyūkankyō・ sangyōrenrakuka). Last modified May 6, 2001. Accessed October 2, 2017. http:// www.mext.go.jp/a_menu/shinkou/sangaku/sangakuc/sangakuc10_1.htm (Japanese).

Ministry of Education, Culture, Sports, Science and Technology (MEXT). 2004. "Kuni- tachidaigaku hojin-ho no gaiyo" 国立大学法人法の概要 (Outline of national uni- versity law). Last modified April 1, 2004. Accessed October 2, 2017. http://www .mext.go.jp/a_menu/koutou/houjin/03052704.htm.

Ministry of Education Culture, Sports, Science and Technology (MEXT). 2005. "Ki- hon keikaku tokubetsu iinkai (dai 3-ki kagaku gijutsu kihon keikaku) no jūyō sei- saku (chūkan torimatome)" 基本計画特別委員会（第3期科学技術基本計画）の重要 政策（中間とりまとめ） (Science and Technology Basic Plan Special Committee [Third Science and Technology Basic Plan] important policies [interim summary]). Last modified April 2005. Accessed October 2, 2017. http://www.mext.go.jp/b_menu /shingi/gijyutu/gijyutu11/houkoku/05042301.htm (Japanese).

Ministry of Education Culture, Sports, Science, and Technology (MEXT). n.d. "Kagaku gijutsu kihon-ho no pointo" 科学技術基本法のポイント (Points of science and technology basic law). Accessed October 6, 2017. http://www.mext.go.jp/b_menu/shingi /kagaku/kihonkei/kihonhou/point.htm (Japanese).

Ministry of Education Culture, Sports, Science, and Technology (MEXT). n.d. "Kagaku gijutsu kihon-hō teian riyū setsumei" 科学技術基本法提案理由説明 (Explanation of rationale for proposed science and technology basic law). Accessed October 6, 2017. http://www.mext.go.jp/b_menu/shingi/kagaku/kihonkei/kihonhou/riyuu .htm (Japanese).

Ministry of Education Culture, Sports, Science, and Technology (MEXT). n.d. "Kagaku gijutsu kihon keikaku dai 1-shō kihon rinen 5. Dai 1-ki kagaku gijutsu kihon kei- kaku no seika to kadai" 科学技術基本計画 第1章 基本理念5. 第1期科学技術基本計 画の成果と課題 (Science and technology basic law Chapter 1 Basic philosophy 5. Re- sults and issues of the first science and technology basic plan). Accessed October 6, 2017. http://www.mext.go.jp/a_menu/kagaku/kihon/honbun/006.htm (Japanese).

Ministry of Education, Culture, Sports, Science and Technology (MEXT), Ministry of Health, Labour and Welfare (MHLW), Ministry of Economy, Trade and Industry (METI). 2007. "5-Year strategy for the creation of innovative pharmaceuticals and medical devices." Last modified April 26, 2007. Accessed October 4, 2017. http:// www.mhlw.go.jp/bunya/iryou/shinkou/dl/03.pdf.

Ministry of Education, Singapore. n.d. "Our Vision." Accessed August 8, 2018. https:// www.moe.gov.sg/about.

Ministry of Health. 2012. "Annex D: Achievements of the Biomedical Sciences (BMS) Iniative." Accessed August 22, 2017. https://www.moh.gov.sg/content/dam/moh _web/PressRoom/Articles/2012/Annex%20D%20-%20Achievements%20of%20 the%20Biomedical%20Sciences%20(BMS)%20Iniative.pdf.

Ministry of Health, Labour and Welfare厚生労働省 (Kosei Rōdōshō). 2007. "Kakush- inteki iyakuhin iryokki soshutsu no tame 5-nen senryaku ni tsuite" 革新的医薬品・ 医療機器創出のための5か年戦略」について (Regarding the 5-year strategy for the creation of innovative pharmaceuticals and medical devices). Last modified April 7, 2007. Accessed October 6, 2017. http://www.mhlw.go.jp/houdou/2007/04/h0427-3 .html (Japanese).

Ministry of Health, Labour and Welfare. 2013. "Institutional Framework for Promot- ing the Future Implementation of Regenerative Medicine." Last modified May 10, 2013. Accessed October 4, 2017. http://www.mhlw.go.jp/english/policy/health -medical/medical-care/dl/150407-01.pdf.

Ministry of Health, Labour and Welfare厚生労働省 (Kosei Rōdōshō). n.d. "Saisei iryo ni tsuite" 再生医療について (Regarding regenerative medicine). Accessed October 6,

2017. http://www.mhlw.go.jp/stf/seisakunitsuite/bunya/kenkou_iryou/iryou/saisei
_iryou/ (Japanese).

Ministry of Law, Justice and Company Affairs. 1999. "The Patents (Amendment) Act."
Last modified March 26, 1999. Accessed October 9, 2017. http://www.ipindia.nic
.in/writereaddata/Portal/IPOAct/1_34_1_patents-amendment-act-1999.PDF.

Ministry of Law, Justice and Company Affairs. 2002. "The Patents (Amendment) Act,
2002." Last modified June 25, 2002. Accessed October 20, 2017. http://www.wipo
.int/edocs/lexdocs/laws/en/in/in028en.pdf.

Ministry of Manpower. 1999. "Manpower 21: Vision of a Talent Capital." Committee
report. Singapore: Ministry of Manpower.

Ministry of Science and Technology of the People's Republic of China 科学技术部 (Ke
Xue Ji Shu Bu). 2003. "Zhong Guo Ke Ji Tong Ji Shu Ju (2003)" 中国科技统计数据
(China Science and Technology Statistics Data Book [2003]). Accessed July 26, 2013.
http://www.most.gov.cn/eng/statistics/2003/index.htm (Chinese and English).

Ministry of Science and Technology of the People's Republic of China 科学技术部 (Ke
Xue Ji Shu Bu). 2004. "Zhong Guo Ke Ji Tong Ji Shu Ju (2004)" 中国科技统计数据
(2004) (China Science and Technology Statistics Data Book [2004]). Accessed
July 26, 2013. http://www.most.gov.cn/eng/statistics/2004/index.htm (Chinese and
English).

Ministry of Science and Technology of the People's Republic of China 科学技术部 (Ke
Xue Ji Shu Bu). 2005. "Zhong Guo Ke Ji Tong Ji Shu Ju (2005)" 中国科技统计数据
(2005) (China Science and Technology Statistics Data Book [2005]). Accessed
July 26, 2013. http://www.most.gov.cn/eng/statistics/2005/index.htm (Chinese and
English).

Ministry of Science and Technology of the People's Republic of China 科学技术部 (Ke
Xue Ji Shu Bu). 2006a. "Guan Yu Yin Fa《Guo Jia Ke Ji Zhi Cheng Ji Hua "Shi Yi
Wu" Fa Zhan Gang Yao》De Tong Zhi" 关于印发《国家科技支撑计划"十一五"发展
纲要》的通知 (The notification for issuing the "Eleventh Five-Year Plan" for the National Science and Technology Support Program). Last modified September 19,
2006. Accessed September 27, 2017. http://www.most.gov.cn/mostinfo/xinxifenlei
/gjkjgh/200811/t20081129_65772.htm (Chinese).

Ministry of Science and Technology of the People's Republic of China 科学技术部 (Ke
Xue Ji Shu Bu). 2006b. "Shi Yi Wu Ke Ji Fa Zhan Gui Hua" "十一五"科技发展规划
("Eleventh Five-Year Plan" for the biotechnology industry). Accessed September 27,
2017. http://www.most.gov.cn/kjgh/kjfzgh/ (Chinese).

Ministry of Science and Technology of the People's Republic of China 科学技术部 (Ke
Xue Ji Shu Bu). 2006c. "Zhong Guo Ke Ji Tong Ji Shu Ju (2006)" 中国科技统计数据
(2006) (China Science and Technology Statistics Data Book [2006]). Accessed
July 26, 2013. http://www.most.gov.cn/eng/statistics/2006/index.htm (Chinese and
English).

Ministry of Science and Technology of the People's Republic of China 科学技术部 (Ke Xue Ji Shu Bu). 2007a. "863 Ji Hua Sheng Wu He Yi Yao Ji Shu Ling Yu 2007 Nian Du Zhong Dian Xiang Mu Sheng Qing Zhi Nan" 863计划生物和医药技术领域2007年度重点项目申请指南 (Guidelines for key projects of the 863 Biology and Medical Technology Applications in 2007). Last modified March 29, 2007. Accessed September 27, 2017. http://www.most.gov.cn/tztg/200703/t20070329_42451.htm (Chinese).

Ministry of Science and Technology of the People's Republic of China 科学技术部 (Ke Xue Ji Shu Bu). 2007b. "Zhong Guo Ke Ji Tong Ji Shu Ju (2007)" 中国科技统计数据 (2007) (China Science and Technology Statistics Data Book [2007]). Accessed July 26, 2013. http://www.most.gov.cn/eng/statistics/2007/index.htm (Chinese and English).

Ministry of Science and Technology of the People's Republic of China 科学技术部 (Ke Xue Ji Shu Bu). 2011. "Guo Jia 'Shi Er Wu' Ke Xue He Ji Shu Fa Zhan Gui Hua" 国家"十二五"科学和技术发展规划 (The "Twelfth Five-Year Plan" for the National Science and Technology Development Program). Last modified July 4, 2011. Accessed September 27, 2017. http://www.most.gov.cn/kjzc/gjkjzc/gjkjzczh/201308/P0201308 23574943757592.pdf (Chinese).

Ministry of Science and Technology of the People's Republic of China 科学技术部 (Ke Xue Ji Shu Bu). 2015. "Guan Yu Zhen Xie Shi Er Jie Quan Guo Wei Yuan Hui Di San Ci Hui Yi Di 0592 Hao (Ke Xue Ji Shu Lei 022 Hao) Ti An Da Fu De Han " 关于政协十二届全国委员会第三次会议第0592号(科学技术类022号)提案答复的函 (The letter to address the answer to the proposal No. 0592 [S&T No. 022] from the third meeting of the CPPCC twelfth session). Last modified August 25, 2015. Accessed February 23, 2016. http://www.most.gov.cn/mostinfo/xinxifenlei/qgzxtafwgk /201603/t20160307_124503.htm (Chinese).

Ministry of Science and Technology of the People's Republic of China 科学技术部 (Ke Xue Ji Shu Bu). n.d. "National High-Tech R&D Program (863 Program)." Accessed September 22, 2017. http://www.most.gov.cn/eng/programmes1/.

Ministry of Trade and Industry Singapore. 1998. "Committee on Singapore's Competitiveness Report: 1998." November 1, 1998. Singapore: Singapore Government Press Release.

Ministry of Trade and Industry Singapore. 2006. "Science and Technology Plan 2010: Sustaining Innovation-Driven Growth." Last modified February 2006. Accessed August 20, 2018. https://www.mti.gov.sg/ResearchRoom/Documents/app.mti.gov .sg/data/pages/885/doc/S%20And%20T%20Plan%202010.pdf.

Ministry of Trade and Industry Singapore. 2011. "Research, Innovation and Enterprise (RIE) 2015." November 1, 2011. Accessed September 25, 2017. https://www.mti.gov .sg/ResearchRoom/Pages/Research,-Innovation-and-Enterprise-(RIE)-2015 .aspx.

Mitsubishi Research Institute 三菱総合研究所. 2005. "Sangyo kurasutā keikaku moni-taringu chōsa hōkoku-sho" 産業クラスター計画モニタリング調査報告書 (The report for industrial cluster monitoring research). Cluster Study Group クラスター研究会. Last modified March 2005. Accessed July 2, 2016. http://www.cluster.gr.jp/relation/data/pdf/Cluster_Moni_houkoku.pdf (Japanese).

Miura, Mari. 2012. *Welfare Through Work: Conservative Ideas, Partisan Dynamics, and Social Protection in Japan*. New York: Cornell University Press.

Modi, Narendra. 2014. "An Invitation to 'Make in India.'" *Wall Street Journal*, September 26, 2014. Accessed July 29, 2017. https://www.wsj.com/articles/narendra-modi-an-invitation-to-make-in-india1411687511.

Mok, Ka Ho. 2013. *The Quest for Entrepreneurial Universities in East Asia*. New York: Palgrave Macmillan.

Momma, Maki. Mar. 2017. "Middle Class Perception—a Dozen Years Later." *Economic Review of Toyo University* 42 (2): 189–201.

Montresor, Sandro. 1998. *Techno-globalism and Techno-nationalism: An Interpretative Framework*. Bologna: Dipartimento di Scienze economiche.

Montresor, Sandro. 2001. "Techno-globalism, Techno-nationalism and Technological Systems: Organizing the Evidence." *Technovation* 21 (7): 399–412.

Moore, Aaron Stephen. 2013. *Constructing East Asia: Technology, Ideology, and Empire in Japan's Wartime Era, 1931–1945*. Redwood City, CA: Stanford University Press.

Morita, Akio, and Shintaro Ishihara. 1989. "The Japan That Can Say No." In *The New US-Japan Relations Card*, ed. Akio Morita and Shintaro Ishihara, 4–62. New York: Simon & Schuster.

Morris-Suzuki, Tessa. 1994. *The Technological Transformation of Japan: From the Seventeenth to the Twenty-First Century*. New York: Cambridge University Press.

Motoyama Yasuyuki. 2012. *Global Companies, Local Innovations: Why the Engineering Aspects of Innovation Making Require Co-location*. Farnham, UK: Ashgate Publishing.

Mowrey, David, and Richard Nelson. 1999. "Defining Industrial Leadership." In *Sources of Industrial Leadership: Studies of Seven Industries*, ed. David Mowrey and Richard Nelson, 1–18. Cambridge: Cambridge University Press.

Mowery, David C., Richard R. Nelson, Bhaven N. Sampat, and Arvids A. Ziedonis. 2001. "The Growth of Patenting and Licensing by US Universities: An Assessment of the Effects of the Bayh–Dole Act of 1980." *Research Policy* 30 (1): 99–119.

MSME. 2017. "India's Industrial Policy from 1948 to 1991." Last modified October 23, 2017. Accessed October 23, 2017. http://www.dcmsme.gov.in/policies/iip.htm#Indus5.

Mukherji, Rahul. 2008. "The Political Economy of India's Economic Reforms." *Asian Economic Policy Review* 3 (2): 315–31.

Mukherji, Rahul. 2009. "The State, Economic Growth, and Development in India." *India Review* 8 (1): 81–106.

Murphy, Kevin M., Andrei M. Shleifer, and W. V. Robert. 1991. "The Allocation of Talent: Implications for Growth." *Quarterly Journal of Economics* 106: 503–30.

Myers, Robert A. 2005. *Challenges for Japanese Universities' Technology Licensing Offices: What Technology Transfer in the United States Can Tell Us.* New York: Center of Japanese Economy and Business Graduate School of Business, Columbia University.

Nagayya, D., and T. V. Rao. 2010. "Special Economic Zones for Rapid Industrialization and Regional Development: Progress and Concerns." *IUP Journal of Managerial Economics* 8 (1/2): 93–111.

Nakamura, Masao. 2012. "Japanese Corporate Governance Reform, Globalization and Selective Adaptation." *Journal of Asian Business* 25: 1–34.

Nakamura, Yoshiaki 中村吉明 and Hiroyuki Odagiri 小田切宏之. 2002. "Nihon no baio benchā kigyō sono igi to jittai" 日本のバイオ・ベンチャー企業その意義と実態 (Biotechnology-related startup firms in Japan: lessons from a survey study). Last modified June 1, 2002. Accessed June 18, 2016. http://www.nistep.go.jp/index-j .html. (Japanese).

Nakatsuji, Norio. 2007. "Irrational Japanese Regulations Hinder Human Embryonic Stem Cell Research." *Nature Reports Stem Cells*, August 9, 2007. doi:10.1038/ stemcells.2007.66.

Nakatsuji, Norio. 2012. "Interview with Biomaterials Science Editor-in-Chief Professor Norio Nakatsuji." Interviewed by Russell Johnson. Last modified May 21, 2012. Accessed August 20, 2018. http://blogs.rsc.org/bm/2012/05/21/interview-with -biomaterials-science-editor-in-chief-professor-norio-nakatsuji/#more-216.

Nakayama, Shigeru. 1983. "Science in Japan." *Nature* 305:214–20.

Nakayama, Shigeru. 1991. *Science, Technology and Society in Postwar Japan.* New York: Routledge.

Nakayama, Shigeru. 2012. "Techno-nationalism Versus Techno-globalism." *East Asian Science, Technology and Society* 6 (1): 9–15.

Nanyang Technological University. 2010. *Nanyang Technological University Annual Report 2010*, p. 113. Singapore: Board of Trustees. Accessed March 20, 2017. http:// www.ntu.edu.sg/AboutNTU/Documents/AR10%2020110221%20-%20AR%20 (without%20financial).pdf.

Nanyang Technological University. 2011. "Research Report 2010/2011." Singapore: Nanyang Technological University. Accessed March 12, 2017. http://www.ntu.edu.sg /AboutNTU/Documents/120801_NTUAR2011(FINAL).pdf.

Nanyang Technological University. 2017. *Annual Report 2017.* Singapore: Board of Trustees. Accessed March 12, 2017. http://www.ntu.edu.sg/AboutNTU/University Publications/Documents/NTUAR2017.pdf.

Nanyang Technological University News Release. 2017. "NTU ranks 11th in world rankings, highest position ever by a Singapore or Asian University." June 8, 2017.

Naruse, Cheryl Narumi. 2013. "Singapore, State Nationalism, and the Production of Diaspora." *CLCWeb: Comparative Literature and Culture* 15 (2): 2–9.

Nastro, Barbara. 2015. "Enter the Dragon, China's Biopharmaceutical Clusters, Biotech in China." Undated report, modified October 2015. Accessed August 17, 2018. https://www.researchgate.net/publication/282575400_China'sbiopharma cluster2012.

National Institute of Advanced Industrial Science and Technology. 2017. "Biomedical Research Institute." Accessed February 26, 2017. https://unit.aist.go.jp/bmd/en /about/outline.html.

National Library Board, Singapore. 2018. "Economic Development Board." Accessed August 17, 2018. http://eresources.nlb.gov.sg/infopedia/articles/SIP_2018-01-08 _135544.html.

National Research Foundation. 2016. *Research Innovation Enterprise 2020 Plan: Winning the Future Through Science and Technology.* Accessed August 8, 2018. https:// www.nrf.gov.sg/docs/default-source/default-document-library/rie2020 -publication-(final-web).pdf.

National Research Foundation. 2017. "Research, Innovation and Enterprise 2020 Plan." RIE2020 Plan. Last modified July 11, 2017. Accessed October 11, 2017. https://www .nrf.gov.sg/rie2020.

National University of Singapore. 2010. *Change Reaction: National University of Singapore Annual Report 2010.* Accessed August 19, 2018. http://www.nus.edu.sg /annualreport/pdf/nus-annualreport-2010.pdf.

National University of Singapore. 2017. *#weareNUS: National University of Singapore Annual Report 2017.* Accessed September 5, 2018. http://www.nus.edu.sg/annual report/pdf/nus-annualreport-2017.pdf.

National Venture Capital Association. 2005. *National Venture Capital Association— Yearbook 2005.* New York: Thomson Venture Economics.

Nee, Victor, and Sonja Opper. 2012. *Capitalism from Below: Markets and Institutional Change in China.* Cambridge, MA: Harvard University Press.

Nelson, Richard. 2004. "The Challenge of Building an Effective Innovation System for Catch-Up." *Oxford Development Studies* 32 (3): 365–74.

Nelson, Richard R., ed. 1993. *National Innovation Systems: A Comparative Analysis.* New York: Oxford University Press.

Nelson, Richard R., and Sylvia Ostry. 1995. *Techno-nationalism and Techno-globalism.* Washington, DC: The Brookings Institution.

Nelson, Richard R., and Nathan Rosenberg. 1993. "Technical Innovation and National Systems." In *National Innovation Systems: A Comparative Analysis*, ed. Richard R. Nelson, 3–28. New York: Oxford University Press.

Nightingale, Paul, and Paul Martin. 2004. "The Myth of the Biotech Revolution." *Trends in Biotechnology* 22 (11): 564–69.

Nikkei Asian Review. 2017. "Japan's Gender Wage Gap Persists Despite Progress." February 23, 2017. Accessed August 18, 2018. https://asia.nikkei.com/Politics-Economy/Economy/Japan-s-gender-wage-gap-persists-despite-progress.

Nikkei Business Publications. 2012. *Nikkei Bio-yearbook: The 2012 Editions of Research and Development, and a Market and Industry Performance.* New York: Nikkei Business Publications Publication Center, 13.

Nikkei Business Publications. 2014. Nikkei bioteku henshū Nikkei bio nenkan 2014 kenkyūkaihatsu to shijo sangyōdōkō 日経バイオテク編集日経バイオ年鑑2014 研究開発と市場・産業動向 (Nikkei bio-yearbook: The 2014 edition of research and development and market and industry performance). Tokyo: Nikkei BP Company日経BP社.

Nilsson, Anna S. 2006. "Commercialization of Life-Science Research at Universities in the United States, Japan and China." Östersund, Sweden: Swedish Institute for Growth Policy Studies.

Noble, Gregory W. 2011. "Changing Politics of Japanese Corporate Governance: Party Dynamics and the Myth of the Myth of Permanent Employment." In *Joint Conference of the Association for Asian Studies and International Convention of Asia Scholars.* Honolulu. Unpublished paper.

Noland, Marcus. 1993. "The Impact of Industrial Policy on Japan's Trade Specialization." *Review of Economics and Statistics* 75 (2): 241–48.

NPO Kinki Bio-Industry Development Organization. *Industrial Cluster Planning, Kansai Bio Cluster Project—The Second Period.* March 2006. Sangyou kurasutākeikaku, Kansai Baiokurasutā purojekuto Bio Cluster ~ Dai ni-ki Keikaku. NPO hōjinkinki baioindasutorīshinkōkaigi. Heiseijūhachinensangatsu 産業クラスター計画. 関西バイオクラスタープロジェクト Bio Cluster~ 第II期計画 NPO法人近畿バイオインダストリー振興会議, 平成18年3月 (Japanese).

NUS Enterprise. 2014. "Clearbridge Healthcare Solutions: From Lab to Market." Accessed February 22, 2018. http://enterprise.nus.edu.sg/success-stories/detail/11.

Oba, Jun. 2006. "Incorporation of National Universities in Japan and Its Impact upon Institutional Governance." Last modified January 16, 2006. Accessed October 2, 2017. http://home.hiroshima-u.ac.jp/oba/docs/incorporation2006.pdf.

Odagiri, H. 2004. "Advance of Science-Based Industries and the Changing Innovation System of Japan." In *Asian's Innovation Systems in Transition*, ed. Edward Elgar, 200–26. Tokyo: Hitotsubashi University.

OECD. 2010a. "Measuring Innovation: A New Perspective." Accessed February 12, 2017. https://doi.org/10.1787/9789264059474-en.

OECD. 2010b. "Singapore: Rapid Improvement Followed by Strong Performance." In *Strong Performers and Successful Reformers in Education: Lessons from PISA for the United States*, by OECD, 159–76. Paris: OECD Publishing.

OECD. 2013. "OECD Factbook 2013: Economic, Environmental and Social Statistics." Last modified 2013. Accessed April 7, 2016. http://www.oecd-ilibrary.org/sites

/factbook-2013-en/08/01/03/index.html?itemId=%2Fcontent%2Fchapter%2Ffact-book-2013-62-en&containerItemId=%2Fcontent%2Fserial%2F18147364&mimeTy pe=text%2Fhtml.

OECD. 2014. "Revealed Technological Advantage in Biotechnologies, Based on the New Biotech Definition, 2002–05 and 2012–15." OECD Key Biotech Indicators. Last modified November 2011. Accessed August 17, 2018. http://www.oecd.org/sti /keybiotechnologyindicators.htm.

OECD. 2015. "OECD Economic Surveys Japan Overview." Accessed June 17, 2016. http://www.oecd.org/eco/surveys/Japan-2015-overview.pdf.

OECD. 2016a. "KBI 12 Revealed Technological Advantage in Biotechnologies, 2000– 03 and 2010–13, STI Micro-data Lab: Intellectual Property Database." Accessed October 15, 2016. http://oe.cd/ipstats.

OECD. 2016b. "Key Biotechnology Indicators." Last modified October 2016. Accessed February 23, 2017. http://www.oecd.org/sti/inno/keybiotechnologyindicators.htm.

OECD. 2016c. "OECD Factbook 2015–2016: Economic, Environmental and Social Statistics." Last modified April 8, 2016. Accessed September 20, 2017. http://www .oecd-ilibrary.org/docserver/download/3015041e.pdf?expires=1505945724&id =id&accname=guest&checksum=5138348418A8D4A968B7CEE5003F4819.

OECD. 2017. "OECD Economic Outlook." 2017 (1). http://www.oecd.org/eco/outlook /economic-forecast-summary-japan-oecd-economic-outlook-june-2017.pdf.

OECD. 2018. "FDI Flows (Indicator)." Accessed March 5, 2018. doi:10.1787/99f6e393-en.

OECD. n.d.a. "GERD, % of GDP." Accessed July 16, 2016. http://stats.oecd.org/.

OECD. n.d.b. "International Coauthorship, Percentage of Total Scientific Articles." Accessed May 18, 2016. https://stats.oecd.org/.

OECD. n.d.c. "Patents by Technology: Triadic Patent Families." Accessed July 16, 2016. http://stats.oecd.org/.

Office of the Prime Minister of Japan. 2002. "Baiotekunorojī senryaku taiko," バイオテクノロジー戦略大綱 (Biotechnology strategy fundamental principles). December 6, 2002. Accessed June 5, 2014. http://www.kantei.go.jp/jp/singi/bt/kettei/021206 /taikou.html (Japanese).

Office of the Prime Minister of Japan. 2012. "Iryōinobeshon kaigi: Iryō inobeshon 5-kanen senryaku" 医療イノベーション会議 医療イノベーション5 か年戦略 (Medical innovation meeting: Medical innovation 5-year strategy). Last modified June 6, 2012. Accessed October 6, 2017. http://www.kantei.go.jp/jp/singi/iryou/5senryaku /siryou01.pdf (Japanese).

Office of the Prime Minister of Japan. n.d. "Basic Law on Intellectual Property (Law No. 122 of 2002)." Accessed October 2, 2017. http://japan.kantei.go.jp/policy/titeki /hourei/021204kihon_e.pdf.

Oikawa, Yuta 及川雄太. 2012. "Sōyaku o chūshin to shita iyakuhin sangyō no genjō to baiobenchā hatten ni mukete" 創薬を中心とした医薬品産業の現状とバイオベンチャー

発展に向けて (The present situation in mainly drug industry and a prospect of bio ventures' growth). Nihonseisakutōshiginkō 日本政策投資銀行. Development Bank of Japan. Last modified July 2012. Accessed August 7, 2013. http://www.dbj.jp/pdf /investigate/area/kansai/pdf_all/kansai1207_01.pdf (Japanese).

Okada, Yoshitaka. 2006. *Struggles for Survival Institutional and Organizational Changes in Japan's High-Tech Industries.* Tokyo: Springer. http://public.eblib.com/choice /publicfullrecord.aspx?p=337642.

Ono, Hiroshi. 2007. "Careers in Foreign-Owned Firms in Japan." *American Sociological Review* 72 (2): 267–90.

Orser, B., M. Cedzynski, and R. Thomas. 2007. "Modeling Ownership Experience: Linking Theory with Practice." *Journal of Small Business and Entrepreneurship* 20 (4): 387–408.

Ostry, Sylvia, and Richard R. Nelson. 2000. *Techno-nationalism and Techno-globalism: Conflict and Cooperation.* Washington, DC: Brookings Institution Press.

Oxford English Dictionary. 2008. Retrieved May 30, 2008. Accessed August 10, 2018. http://www.oed.com/.

Oye, K. A., H. G. Eichler, A. Hoos, Y. Mori, T. M. Mullin, and M. Pearson. 2016. "Pharmaceuticals Licensing and Reimbursement in the European Union, United States, and Japan." *Clinical Pharmacology and Therapeutics* 100 (6): 626–32.

Ozaki, Toshiya. 2012. "Open Trade, Closed Industry: The Japanese Aerospace Industry in the Evolution of Economic Nationalism and Implications for Globalization." In *Globalization and Economic Nationalism in Asia*, ed. Anthony P. D'Costa, 109–34. Oxford, UK: Oxford University Press.

Palatino, Mong. 2013. "Don't Let the Flames of Nationalism Engulf Southeast Asia." *Diplomat*, April 6, 2013. Accessed August 7, 2017. http://thediplomat.com/2013 /04/dont-let-the-flames-of-nationalism-engulf-southeast-asia/.

Panchal, Manish, Charu Kapoor, and Mansi Mahajan. 2014. "Success Strategies for Indian Pharma Industry in an Uncertain World." *Business Standard.* Last modified February 17, 2014. Accessed October 20, 2017. http://www.business-standard.com /content/b2b-chemicals/success-strategies-for-indian-pharma-industry-in-an -uncertain-world-114021701557_1.html.

Pandey, Abhishek, Alok Aggarwal, Richard Devane, and Yevgeny Kuznetsov. 2006. "The Indian Diaspora: A Unique Case?" In *Diaspora Networks and the International Migration of Skills: How Countries Can Draw on Their Talent Abroad*, ed. Yevgeny Kuznetsov, 71–98. Washington, DC: World Bank.

Parayil, Govindan. 2005. "From 'Silicon Island' to 'Biopolis of Asia': Innovation Policy and Shifting Competitive Strategy in Singapore." *California Management Review* 47 (2): 50–73.

Parayil, Govindan, and Anthony P. D'Costa, eds. 2009. *The New Asian Innovation Dynamics: China and India in Perspective.* Basingstoke, UK: Palgrave Macmillan.

Parthiban, David, Jonathan P. O'Brien, Toru Yoshikawa, and Andrew Delios. 2010. "Do Shareholders or Stakeholders Appropriate the Rents from Corporate Diversification? The Influence of Ownership Structure." *Academy of Management Journal* 53 (3): 636–54.

Patel, Pankaj C., Stephanie A. Fernhaber, Patricia P. McDougall-Covin, and Robert P. van der Have. 2014. "Beating Competitors to International Markets: The Value of Geographically Balanced Networks for Innovation." *Strategic Management Journal* 35 (5): 691–711.

Payne, William H. 2004. "Angels Shine Brightly for Start-up Entrepreneurs." Kauffman Foundation. Last modified 2004. Accessed May 29, 2012. http://www.kauffman.org/entrepreneurship/angels-shine-brightly.aspx.

Pekkanen, Saadia, and Kellee Tsai. 2005. *Japan and China in the World Political Economy.* New York: Routledge.

Pempel, T. J. 1987. "The Unbundling of 'Japan, Inc.': The Changing Dynamics of Japanese Policy Formation." *Journal of Japanese Studies* 13 (2): 271–306.

Pempel, T. J. 1998. *Regime Shift.* Ithaca, NY: Cornell University Press.

Pempel, T. J. 2005. "Revisiting the Japanese Economic Model." In *Japan and China in the World Political Economy*, ed. Saadia Pekkanen and Kellee Tsai, 29–44. New York: Routledge.

Peng, Li. 1996. "Report on the Outline of the Ninth Five-Year Plan (1996–2000) for National Economic and Social Development and the Long-range Objectives to the Year 2010 (Excerpts)." China.org. Last modified March 5, 1996. Accessed September 27, 2017. http://www.china.org.cn/95e/95-english1/2.htm.

Pesek, William. 2017. "Why Singapore Is Struggling to Reinvent Itself." *Nikkei Asian Review.* July 11, 2017. Accessed August 7, 2017. https://asia.nikkei.com/Viewpoints/William-Pesek/Why-Singapore-is-struggling-to-reinvent-itself?page=1.

Pharmaceutical-technology.com. n.d. "Biopolis Biomedical Research Hub, Buona Vista, Singapore." Accessed September 25, 2017. http://www.pharmaceutical-technology.com/projects/biopolis/.

Philippidis, Alex. 2016. "Top Eight Asia Biopharma Clusters 2016." *Genetic Engineering and Biotechnology News.* Last modified May 30, 2016. Access February 13, 2017. http://www.genengnews.com/the-lists/top-eight-asia-biopharma-clusters-2016/77900669.

Pisano G. P. 2006. "Can Science Be a Business? Lessons from Biotech." *Harvard Business Review* 84 (10): 1–12.

Planning Commission (Government of India). 2013. *Twelfth Five Year Plan (2012–2017): Faster, More Inclusive and Sustainable Growth.* New Delhi: Sage Publications. Accessed August 17, 2018. http://planningcommission.nic.in/plans/planrel/fiveyr/11th/11_v1/11v1_ch1.pdf.

Planningcommission.gov. 2014. "Five Year Plan." Last modified September 18, 2014. Accessed September 29, 2017. http://planningcommission.gov.in/plans/planrel/index.php?state=planbody.htm.

Planningcommission.gov. n.d. "Twelfth Five Year Plan 2012–17." Accessed September 29, 2017. http://planningcommission.gov.in/plans/planrel/fiveyr/welcome.html.

Poh, Lim Chuan. 2016. "From Research to Innovation to Enterprise: The Case of Singapore, Chapter 10." *The Global Competitiveness Index 2016*, pp. 133–39. World Intellectual Property Organization. Accessed August 17, 2018. http://www.wipo.int/edocs/pubdocs/en/wipo_pub_gii_2016-chapter10.pdf.

Porter, Michael E. 1990. "The Competitive Advantage of Nations." *Harvard Business Review* 68 (2): 73–93.

Powell, Walter. 2003. "Neither Market nor Hierarchy." *The Sociology of Organizations: Classic, Contemporary, and Critical Readings* 315: 104–17.

Powell, Walter W. 1998. "Learning from Collaboration: Knowledge and Networks in the Biotechnology and Pharmaceutical Industries." *California Management Review* 40 (3): 228–40.

Powell, Walter W., and Stine Grodal. 2005. "Networks of Innovators." *The Oxford Handbook of Innovation*, ed. Jan Fagerberg, David C. Mowery, and Richard R. Nelson, 56–85. Oxford, UK: Oxford University Press.

Powell, Walter W., Kenneth W. Koput, James I. Bowie, and Laurel Smith-Doerr. 2002. "The Spatial Clustering of Science and Capital: Accounting for Biotech Firm-Venture Capital Relationships." *Regional Studies* 36 (3): 291–305.

PR Newswire. 2010. "Singapore Draws Biomedical Companies' First-in-Asia Manufacturing and Headquarters Offices." May 3, 2010. Accessed December 1, 2014. https://www.fiercebiotech.com/biotech/singapore-draws-biomedical-companies-first-asia-manufacturing-and-headquarters-offices.

Prahalad, C. K., and R. A. Mashelkar. 2010. "Innovation's Holy Grail." *Harvard Business Review.* Last modified July–August, 2010. Accessed August 20, 2018. https://hbr.org/2010/07/innovations-holy-grail.

Prashantham, Shameen. 2011. "Social Capital and Indian Micromultinationals." *British Journal of Management* 22 (1): 4–20.

Press Information Bureau. 2013. "Achievements of the Ministry of Science and Technology During 2013." Last modified December 31, 2013. Accessed September 29, 2017. http://pib.nic.in/newsite/PrintRelease.aspx?relid=102231.

Press Information Bureau. 2016. "Major Impetus to Job Creation and Infrastructure: Radical Changes in FDI Policy Regime; Most Sectors on Automatic Route for FDI." Press Information Bureau, June 20, 2016. Accessed March 14, 2018. http://pib.nic.in/newsite/PrintRelease.aspx?relid=146338

Press Information Bureau. 2017. "Launch of National Biopharma Mission." Press Information Bureau, June 28, 2017. Accessed September 28, 2017. http://pib.nic.in/newsite/PrintRelease.aspx?relid=166951.

Price Waterhouse Coopers. 2015. "Global Health's New Entrants: Meeting the World's Consumer." PWC.com. Last modified March 2015. Accessed February 13, 2017. http://www.pwc.com/gx/en/healthcare/publications/assets/pwc-global-new-entrants-healthcare.pdf.

Prime Minister of Japan and His Cabinet. n.d. "Chiteki zaisan kihon-hō (heisei [jūyo nnenhōritsudaihyakunijūnigō])" 知的財産基本法(平成14年法律第122号 (Basic law on intellectual property [law no.122 of 2002]). Accessed October 6, 2017. http://www.kantei.go.jp/jp/singi/titeki/hourei/021204kihon.html (Japanese).

Pring, Coralie. 2017. "People and Corruption: Asia Pacific-Global Corruption Barometer." Report, Transparency International. Berlin: Transparency International.

Pruthi, Sarika. 2014. "Social Ties and Venture Creation by Returnee Entrepreneurs." *International Business Review* 23 (6): 1139–52.

QS World University Rankings Asia. 2018. Accessed August 15, 2018. https://www.topuniversities.com/university-rankings/asian-university-rankings/2018.

Rajan, Ramkishen S., and Rahul Sen. 2002. "A Decade of Economic Liberalization in India." *World Economics* 3 (4): 1–14.

Rajan, S. Irudaya, V. Kurusu, and C. K. Saramma Panicker. 2013. "Return of Diasporas: India's Growth Story vs. Global Crisis." Ministry of Overseas Indian Affairs Research Unit on International Migration Centre for Development Studies. Accessed August 10, 2016. http://www.solutionexchange-un-gen-gym.net/wp-content/uploads/2015/11/Return-of-Diaspora.pdf.

Ramani, Shyama V., and Augustin Maria. 2005. "TRIPS: Its Possible Impacts on the Biotech Segment of the Indian Pharmaceutical Industry." *Economic and Political Weekly*, February 12, 2005. Online February 22, 2011. Accessed August 11, 2016. https://www.jstor.org/stable/4416206?seq=1#page_scan_tab_contents.

Ranga, Marina, and Henry Etzkowitz. 2015. "Triple Helix Systems: An Analytical Framework for Innovation Policy and Practice in the Knowledge Society." In *Entrepreneurship and Knowledge Exchange*, ed. Jay Mitra and John Edmondson, 117–58. New York: Routledge.

Rao, Yi, Bai Lu, and Chen-Lu Tsou. 2004. "Zhong guo ke ji xu yao de gen ben zhuan bian: cong chuan tong ren zhi dao jing zheng you sheng ti zhi—zhong chang qi gui hua jiang liu xia you xiu yi chan, hai shi cuo guo liang ji" 中国科技需要的根本转变：从传统人治到竞争优胜体制—中长期规划将留下优秀遗产、还是错失良机. (Fundamental transition from rule-by-man to rule-by-merit: What will be the legacy of the medium to long-term plan of science and technology?). *Nature* 432: A12–A17.

Rasmussen, Bruce. 2004. *Innovation and Industry Structure in the Biomedical Industry: Some Preliminary Results.* Melbourne City, Australia: Victoria University of Techonology.

Rauch, James E., and Vitor Trindade. 2002. "Ethnic Chinese Networks in International Trade." *Review of Economics and Statistics* 84 (1): 116–30.

Reiche, B. Sebastian. 2009. "To Quit or Not to Quit: Organizational Determinants of Voluntary Turnover in MNC Subsidiaries in Singapore." *International Journal of Human Resource Management* 20 (6): 1362–80.

Reporters without Borders. 2016a. "India." Reporters without Borders. January 20, 2016. Accessed September 17, 2017. https://rsf.org/en/news/india-0.

Reporters without Borders. 2016b. "Intolerant Government, Self-Censorship." Reporters without Borders. January 20, 2016. Accessed September 20, 2017. https://rsf .org/en/singapore.

Reporters without Borders. 2016c. "RSF Concerned About Declining Media Freedom in Japan." July 16, 2016. Accessed September 8, 2017. https://rsf.org/en/news/rsf -concerned-about-declining-media-freedom-japan.

Reserve Bank of India. 2017a. "Foreign Direct Investment Flows to India: Country-Wise and Industry-Wise." Annual report. New Delhi: Reserve Bank of India. Accessed August 17, 2018. https://rbidocs.rbi.org.in/rdocs/AnnualReport/PDFs/9T57F1837 83E274EB08097EB8351349AF6.PDF.

Reserve Bank of India. 2017b. "Frequently Asked Questions." Last modified February 13, 2017. Accessed August 14, 2017. https://www.rbi.org.in/scripts/FAQView .aspx?Id=26#Q25.

Rialp, Alex, Josep Rialp, and Gary A. Knight. 2005. "The Phenomenon of Early Internationalizing Firms: What Do We Know After a Decade (1993–2003) of Scientific Inquiry?" *International Business Review* 14 (2): 147–66.

Richardson, Pikay. 2002. *New Science, Technology and Innovation Developments in India.* European Commission Directorate—General for Research, Brussels.

Robson, Paul J. A., and Robert J. Bennett. 2000. "SME Growth: The Relationship with Business Advice and External Collaboration." *Small Business Economics* 15 (3): 193–208.

Rogers, F. Halsey. 2005. "Missing in Action: Teacher and Medical Provider Absence in Developing Countries." Research brief, World Bank, September 26, 2005. Accessed March 4, 2017. http://www.worldbank.org/.

Rostow, Walt Whitman. 1960. *The Stages of Growth: A Non-Communist Manifesto.* New York: Cambridge University Press.

Rowley, Anthony. 2015. "Xi Jinping's One Belt, One Road: An Antidote to China's Slowdown, Say Critics, CLSA." *Global Capital: Global Market.* Last modified October 9, 2015. Accessed March 6, 2017. http://www.globalcapital.com/article

/yvxxk1zsv73h/xi-jinpings-one-belt-one-road-an-antidote-to-chinas-slowdown
-say-citic-clsa.

Sagers, John. 2014. "Shibusawa Eiichi, Dai Ichi Bank, and the Spirit of Japanese Capitalism, 1860–1930." *Shashi: The Journal of Japanese Business and Company History* 3 (1): 3–12.

Sakakibara, Eisuke. 2003. *Structural Reform in Japan: Breaking the Iron Triangle*. Washington, DC: Brookings Institution Press.

Sala-i-Martin, Xavier, Benat Bilbao-Osorio, Attilio Di Battista, M. Drzeniek Hanouz, T. Geiger, and C. Galvan. 2014. "The Global Competitiveness Index 2014–2015: Accelerating a Robust Recovery to Create Productive Jobs and Support Inclusive Growth." World Economic Forum. Accessed August 19, 2018. http://reports.weforum.org/global-competitiveness-report-2014-2015/introduction/.

Salve, Prachi. 2015. "Not 264 Million, Middle Class Is 24 Million: Report." *India Spend*, October 29, 2015. Accessed October 20, 2017. http://www.indiaspend.com/cover-story/not-264-million-middle-class-is-24-million-report-37317.

Sampat, Preeti. 2008. "Special Economic Zones in India." *Economic and Political Weekly* 43 (28): 25–29.

Sampat, Preeti. 2010. "Special Economic Zones in India: Reconfiguring Displacement in a Neoliberal Order." *City and Society* 22 (2): 166–82.

Samuels, Richard J. 1994. *Rich Nation, Strong Army: National Security and the Technological Transformation of Japan*. Ithaca, NY: Cornell University Press.

Samuels, Richard J. 2003. *Machiavelli's Children: Leaders and Their Legacies in Italy and Japan*. Ithaca, NY: Cornell University Press.

Sandelin, J. 2005. "Japan's Industry-Academic-Government Collaboration and Technology Transfer Practices: A Comparison with United States Practices." *Journal of Industry-Academia-Government* 1 (3): 1–4.

Sandra Rotman Centre for Global Health. 2008. "China's Biotech Industry: An Asian Dragon Is Growing." American Association for the Advancement of Science. Last modified January 7, 2008. Accessed March 6, 2017. https://www.eurekalert.org/.

Sankei (newspaper). 2013. "Regarding a Draft Budget of Fiscal Year 2013." *Sankei*, January 29, 2013. Accessed August 7, 2013. http://sankei.jp.msn.com/economy/news/130129/biz13012920130030-n1.htm.

Saravia, Nancy Gore, and Juan Francisco Miranda. 2004. "Plumbing the Brain Drain." *Bulletin of the World Health Organization* 82 (8): 608–15.

Saxenian, Anna Lee. 1999. "Silicon Valley's New Immigrant Entrepreneurs." Vol. 32. San Francisco: Public Policy Institute of California.

Saxenian, Anna Lee. 2006. *The New Argonauts: Regional Advantage in a Global Economy*. Cambridge, MA: Harvard University Press.

Saxonhouse, G. 1985. *Japanese Cooperative House R&D Ventures: A Market Evaluation*. Discussion paper no. 156, Department of Economics, University of Michigan.

Scharfe, Hartmut. 1999. "The Doctrine of the Three Humors in Traditional Indian Medicine and the Alleged Antiquity of Tamil Siddha Medicine." *Journal of the American Oriental Society* 119 (4): 609–29.

Schiller, Bradley R., and Philip E. Crewson. 1997. "Entrepreneurial Origins: A Longitudinal Inquiry." *Economic Inquiry* 35 (3): 523–31.

Schoppa, Leonard J. 2006. *Race for Exits: The Understanding of Japan's System of Social Protection.* Ithaca, NY: Cornell University Press.

Schumpeter, Joseph. 1942. "Creative Destruction." In *Capitalism, Socialism and Democracy*, 82–85. New York: Harper Collins Publisher.

Segerstrom, Paul S. 1991. "Innovation, Imitation, and Economic Growth." *Journal of Political Economy* 99 (4): 807–27.

Sen, Amartya. 2011. "Radical Needs and Moderate Reforms." In *Perspectives on Modern South Asia: A Reader in Culture, History, and Representation*, ed. Kamala Visweswaran, 328–53. Malden, MA: Wiley-Blackwell.

Sen, Nirupa. 2003. "Science and Technology Policy—2003." *Current Science* 84 (1). Accessed September 29, 2017. http://www.iisc.ernet.in/currsci/jan102003/13.pdf.

Sen, Suhit K. 2017. "The Politics of Bank Nationalization in India." In *Accumulation in Post-Colonial Capitalism*, ed. Iman Kumar Mitra, Samita Sen, and Ranabir Samaddar, 125–45. Singapore: Springer.

Sender, Henny. 2015. "Including: Chinese Innovation: BGI's Code for Success." *Financial Times*, February 16, 2015. Accessed October 15, 2017. https://www.ft.com/content/9c2407f4-b5d9-11e4-a577-00144feab7de.

Sengupta, Devina, and Kala Vijayraghavan. 2016. "1991–2016: 25 Years of Reforms, Children of the Open Era." *Economic Times*. Last modified July 29, 2016. Accessed July 29, 2016. http://epaperbeta.timesofindia.com/Article.aspx?eid=31818&articlexml=1991-2016-25-YEARS-OF-REFORMS-Children-of-29072016019021.

Serger, Sylvia Schwaag, and Magnus Breidne. 2007. "China's Fifteen-Year Plan for Science and Technology: An Assessment." *Asia Policy* 4 (1): 135–64.

Seshu, Geeta. 2017. "India 2016–17: The Silencing of Journalists." *The Hoot*, April 30, 2017. Accessed September 2017. http://www.thehoot.org/free-speech/media-freedom/india-2016-17-the-silencing-of-journalists-10070.

Shane, Scott, and D. Cable. 2002. "Network Ties, Reputation, and the Financing of New Ventures." *Management Science* 48 (3): 364–81.

Shapiro, Carl. 2001. "Navigating the Patent Thicket: Cross Licenses, Patent Pools, and Standard Setting." In *Innovation Policy and the Economy* 1:119–50. Cambridge, MA: MIT Press.

Shapiro, Robert J., and Aparna Mathur. 2014. "How India Can Attract More Foreign Direct Investment, Create Jobs and Increase GDP: The Benefits of Respecting the Intellectual Property Rights of Foreign Pharmaceutical Producers." Georgetown McDonough School of Business, research paper no. 2540591.

Sharma, Anishka, Garg Amrita, and Kumar Ankush. 2012. "Role of Entrepreneurship in Economic Development in Shaping India as a Developed Country." Tmu.ac.in. Accessed August 18, 2108. http://www.tmu.ac.in/management/page344-591.pdf.

Sharma, Pankaj, Srinivasa B. S. Nookala, and Anubhav Sharma. 2012 "India's National and Regional Innovation Systems: Challenges, Opportunities and Recommendations for Policy Makers." *Industry and Innovation* 19 (6): 517–37. Accessed August 2016. http://www.tandfonline.com/doi/abs/10.1080/13662716.2012.718878.

Sharma, Yojana. 2011. "China: Cronyism Outrage After Science Title Is Denied." *University World News*. Last modified October 23, 2011. Accessed August 7, 2017. http://www.universityworldnews.com/article.php?story=20111021220014567.

Sheng, Andrew. 2009. *From Asian to Global Financial Crisis: An Asian Regulator's View of Unfettered Finance in the 1990s and 2000s*. New York: Cambridge University Press.

Shi, Yigong, and Yi Rao. 2010. "Editorial: China's Research Culture." *Science* 329 (5996): 1128. http://www.jstor.org/stable/40803025.

Shim, Yongwoon, and Dong-Hee Shin. 2016. "Neo-techno Nationalism: The Case of China's Handset Industry." *Telecommunications Policy* 40 (2): 197–209.

Shimizu (Miyazono), Yumi 清水(宮園)由美. 2013. "Nihon no baiobenchā seicho e no ayumi" 日本のバイオベンチャー成長への歩み (Steps towards success for Japan's bioventures). *The Society of Biotechnology* 生物工学会誌 91 (3): 171–73 (Japanese).

Shirai, Sayuri. 2016. "Bank of Japan Monetary Easing Policy and Abenomics." Presentation to the Japan America Society of Chicago, Chicago, IL, November 7, 2016.

Sibal, D. Rajeev. 2012. "The Untold Story of India's Economy." In *India: The Next Superpower*, ed. D. Rajeev Sibal, 17–22. LSE Research Online. Last modified May 2012. Accessed August 17, 2018. http://eprints.lse.ac.uk/43443/1/India_the%20untold%20story%20of%20India%27s%20economy%28lsero%29.pdf.

Sidhu, Ravinder, K.-C. Ho, and Brenda Yeoh. 2011. "Emerging Education Hubs: The Case of Singapore." *Higher Education* 61 (1): 23–40.

Sigfusson, Thor, and Sylvie Chetty. 2013. "Building International Entrepreneurial Virtual Networks in Cyberspace." *Journal of World Business* 48 (2): 260–70.

Sigfusson, Thor, and Simon Harris. 2013. "Domestic Market Context and International Entrepreneurs' Relationship Portfolios." *International Business Review* 22 (1): 243–58.

Silverman, Ed. 2015. "Price Controls for Drugs in India Fail to Improve Access for Patients: Report." *Wall Street Journal*, July 20, 2015.

Singapore EDB. 2014. "Incentives for Businesses." Last modified October 29, 2014. Accessed December 24, 2014. http://www.edb.gov.sg/content/edb/en/why-singapore/ready-to-invest/incentives-for-businesses.html. See also http://www.edb.gov.sg/content/dam/edb/en/resources/pdfs/financing-and-incentives/International%20or%20Regional%20Headquarters%20(HQ)%20Leaflet.pdf.

Singh, Manmohan. 2013. "PM's Address to Japan-India Association." Japan-India Parliamentary Friendship League and International Friendship Exchange Council, National Informatics Centre. May 28, 2013. Accessed October 20, 2017. http://archivepmo.nic.in/drmanmohansingh/speech-details.php?nodeid=1319.

Singh, Seema. 2012. "YK Hamied: Cipla's One-Man Army." *Forbes India*, October 2012. http://forbesindia.com/printcontent/33881.

Singh, Seema. 2016. *Mythbreaker: Kiran Mazumdar-Shaw and the Story of Indian Biotech*. Uttar Pradesh, India: Collins Business.

Sinha, Aseema. 2004. "The Changing Political Economy of Federalism in India: A Historical Institutionalist Approach." *India Review* 3 (1): 25–63.

Skilldevelopment.gov. n.d. "National Skill Development Mission." Accessed September 29, 2017. http://www.skilldevelopment.gov.in/nationalskillmission.html.

Skocpol, Theda, Peter Evans, and Dietrich Rueschemeyer. 1999. *Bringing the State Back In*. New York: Cambridge University Press.

Sleeboom-Faulkner, Margaret, and Prasanna Kumar Patra. 2008. "The Bioethical Vacuum: National Policies on Human Embryonic Stem Cell Research in India and China." *Journal of International Biotechnology Law* 5 (6): 221–34.

Smit, Soo Hyung. 2016. "Singapore Moves to Protect Its Labor Force—What This Means for You." *Relocate Magazine*, June 13, 2016. Accessed August 22, 2017. https://www.relocatemagazine.com/articles/editorial-pro-link-global-singapore-moves-to-protect-its-labour-force-what-this-means-for-you.

Söderqvist, Anette, and Sylvie Kamala Chetty. 2013. "Strength of Ties Involved in International New Ventures." *European Business Review* 25 (6): 536–52.

South China Morning Post. 2008. "Sinopharm, Citic Pharmaceutical to raise US$950m." *South China Morning Post (SCMP)*, August 18, 2008. Accessed April 3, 2018. http://www.scmp.com/article/649461/sinopharm-citic-pharmaceutical-raise-us950m.

Specter, Michael. 2014. "The Gene Factory: A Chinese Firm's Bid to Crack Hunger, Illness, Evolution—and the Genetics of Human Intelligence." *New Yorker*. Last modified January 6, 2014. Accessed March 6, 2017. http://www.newyorker.com/magazine/2014/01/06/the-gene-factory.

SPRING. 2016. "Making the Leap from Lab to Market." *SPRINGnews*. March 16–17, 2016. Accessed October 14, 2016. https://goo.gl/yeI00N.

Sridharan, Eswaran. 2004. "The Growth and Sectoral Composition of India's Middle Class: Its Impact on the Politics of Economic Liberalization." *India Review* 3 (4): 405–28.

Stanford Biodesign. 2013. "Biodesign Global Sourcebook: China Overview." Biodesign.stanford.edu. Last modified March 14, 2013. Accessed September 3, 2016. http://biodesign.stanford.edu/bdn/global/sourcebook/China-Overview.pdf.

Startupindia.gov. n.d. "Action Plan." Accessed September 29, 2017. http://startupindia.gov.in/actionplan.php.

State Council of the People's Republic of China 中华人民共和国国务院 (Zhong Hua Ren Min Gong He Guo Guo Wu Yuan). 1990. "Guo Wu Yuan Guan Yu Zuo Hao Yi Jiu Jiu Ling Nian Gao Deng Xue Xiao Bi Ye Sheng Fen Pei Gong Zuo De Tong Zhi" 国务院关于做好一九九〇年高等学校毕业生分配工作的通知 (Notification on the job assigning of college graduates in 1990). Last modified April 14, 1990. Accessed August 22, 2016. http://www.gov.cn/xxgk/pub/govpublic/mrlm/201012/t20101217_63151.html.

State Council of the People's Republic of China 中华人民共和国国务院 (Zhong Hua Ren Min Gong He Guo Guo Wu Yuan). 2006. "Guo Jia Zhong Chang Qi Ke Xue He Ji Shu Fa Zhan Gui Hua Gang Yao (2006–2020)" 国家中长期科学和技术发展规划纲要 (National Long-Term Science and Technology Development Plan [2006–2020]). Last modified February 9, 2006. Accessed September 27, 2017. http://www.most.gov .cn/mostinfo/xinxifenlei/gjkjgh/200811/t20081129_65774.htm (Chinese).

State Council of the People's Republic of China 中华人民共和国国务院 (Zhong Hua Ren Min Gong He Guo Guo Wu Yuan). 2009. "Cu Jin Sheng Wu Chan Ye Jia Kuai Fa Zhan De Ruo Gan Zheng Ce" 促进生物产业加快发展的若干政策 (Policies on promoting the development of biotechnology industry). Last modified June 2, 2009. Accessed August 22, 2016. http://www.gov.cn/zwgk/2009-06/05/content_1332777 .htm (Chinese).

State Council of the People's Republic of China 中华人民共和国国务院 (Zhong Hua Ren Min Gong He Guo Guo Wu Yuan). 2012. "Guan Yu Shen Hua Ke Ji Ti Zhi Gai Ge Jia Kuai Guo Jia Chuang Xin Ti Xi Jian She De Yi Jian" 关于深化科技体制改革加快国家创新体系建设的意见 (Opinions on the science and technology system reform to improve the construction of innovation system). Last modified September 23, 2012. Accessed September 27, 2017. http://www.most.gov.cn/kjzc/gjkjzc/gjkjzczh /201308/t20130823_108132.htm (Chinese).

State Council of the People's Republic of China 中华人民共和国国务院 (Zhong Hua Ren Min Gong He Guo Guo Wu Yuan). 2013. "Guo Wu Yuan Guan Yu Yin Fa 'Shi Er Wu' Guo Jia Zi Zhu Chuang Xin Neng Li Jian She Gui Hua De Tong Zhi" 国务院关于印发"十二五"国家自主创新能力建设规划的通知 (The notification for issuing "Twelfth Five-Year Plan" national indigenous innovation capability construction plan). Last modified May 29, 2013. Accessed September 27, 2017. http://www.gov .cn/zwgk/2013-05/29/content_2414100.htm (Chinese).

State Council of the People's Republic of China 中华人民共和国国务院 (Zhong Hua Ren Min Gong He Guo Guo Wu Yuan). 2015a. "Guo Wu Yuan Ban Gong Ting Guan Yu Yin Fa Guo Jia Biao Zhun Hua Ti Xi Jian She Fa Zhan Gui Hua (2016–2020 Nian) De Tong Zhi" 国务院办公厅关于印发国家标准化体系建设发展规划（2016–2020年）的通知 (The notification of issuing the development plan of national standardization system construction [2016–2020]). Last modified May 16, 2015. Accessed September 27, 2017. http://www.gov.cn/zhengce/content/2015-12/30/content_10523.htm (Chinese).

State Council of the People's Republic of China 中华人民共和国国务院 (Zhong Hua Ren Min Gong He Guo Guo Wu Yuan). 2015b. "Guo Wu Yuan Ban Gong Ting Guan Yu Zhuan Fa Zhi Shi Chan Quan Ju Deng Dan Wei Shen Ru Shi Shi Guo Jia Zhi Shi Chan Quan Zhan Lve Xing Dong Ji Hua" 国务院办公厅关于转发知识产权局等单位深入实施国家知识产权战略行动计划（2014–2020年）的通知 (The strategic action plan of in-depth implementation of the national intellectual property [2014–2020]). Last modified January 4, 2015. Accessed September 27, 2017. http://www.gov.cn /zhengce/content/2015-01/04/content_9375.htm (Chinese).

State Council of the People's Republic of China 中华人民共和国国务院 (Zhong Hua Ren Min Gong He Guo Guo Wu Yuan). 2015c. "Guo Wu Yuan Guan Yu Da Li Tui Jin Da Zhong Chuang Ye Wan Zhong Chuang Xin Ruo Gan Zheng Ce Cuo Shi De Yi Jian" 国务院关于大力推进大众创业万众创新若干政策措施的意见 (The State Council suggestion on mass entrepreneur and innovation policies and measures). Last modified May 16, 2015. Accessed September 27, 2017. http://www.gov.cn/zhengce /content/2015-06/16/content_9855.htm (Chinese).

State Council of the People's Republic of China 中华人民共和国国务院 (Zhong Hua Ren Min Gong He Guo Guo Wu Yuan). 2015d. "Guo Wu Yuan Guan Yu Yin Fa <Zhong Guo Zhi Zao 2025> De Tong Zhi" 国务院关于印发《中国制造2025》的通知 (The notification for issuing "Made in China 2025"). Last modified May 19, 2015. Accessed September 27, 2017. http://www.gov.cn/zhengce/content/2015-05/19/content_9784 .htm (Chinese).

State Council of the People's Republic of China 中华人民共和国国务院 (Zhong Hua Ren Min Gong He Guo Guo Wu Yuan). 2015e. "Wo Guo Liu Xue Hui Guo Ren Yuan Zong Shu Da 180.96 Wan Ren, 2014 Nian Hui Guo 36.48 Wan Ren" 我国留学回国人员总数达180.96万人 2014年回国36.48万人 (The total number of the Chinese international student returnees reached 1,809,600; there are 364,800 people retuned in 2014). Gov.cn 中华人民共和国国务院 (Zhong Hua Ren Min Gong He Guo Guo Wu Yuan). Last modified May 29, 2015. Accessed March 8, 2017. http://www.gov .cn/xinwen/2015-05/29/content_2870295.htm (Chinese).

Street, Christopher T., and Ann-Frances Cameron. 2007. "External Relationships and the Small Business: A Review of Small Business Alliance and Network Research." *Journal of Small Business Management* 45 (2): 239–66.

Studyinchina.com. n.d. "Why Overseas Chinese Students Return?" Accessed October 30, 2017. http://www.studyinchina.com.my/web/page/why-overseas-chinese -students-return/.

Su, Yu-Shan, and Ling-Chun Hung. 2009. "Spontaneous vs. Policy-Driven: The Origin and Evolution of the Biotechnology Cluster." *Technological Forecasting and Social Change* 76 (5): 608–19.

Sugii, Shigeki, interview, 2017.

Suttmeier, Richard P. 2004. "Review Essay: China's Techno-Warriors, Another View." *China Quarterly*, 804–10. Accessed August 20, 2018. https://china-us.uoregon.edu /pdf/China's%20techno-warriors%20another%20view.pdf.

Suttmeier, Richard P. 2005. "A New Technonationalism? China and the Development of Technical Standards." *Communications of the ACM* 48 (4): 35–37.

Suttmeier, Richard P., and Xiangkui Yao. 2004. *China's Post-WTO Technology Policy: Standards, Software, and the Changing Nature of Techno-nationalism.* Seattle: National Bureau of Asian Research.

Suzuki, Sasaki 佐々木聡. 2001. "Nihon no sengo kigyōya-shi: Hankotsu no keifu" 日本 の戦後企業家史: 反骨の系譜 (History of entrepreneurs in postwar Japan: genealogy of rebels). Yūhikaku 有斐閣. December.

Suzuki, Tadaaki. 2012. "Globalization, Finance, and Economic Nationalism: The Changing Role of the State in Japan." In *Globalization and Economic Nationalism in Asia*, ed. Anthony P. D'Costa, 109–34. Oxford, UK: Oxford University Press.

Syed, Murtaza H., and Jinsook Lee. 2010. "Japan's Quest for Growth: Exploring the Role of Capital and Innovation." International Monetary Fund Working Paper 10/294. Accessed August 20, 2018. https://msuweb.montclair.edu/~lebelp/IMF2010JapanC apitalInnovationwp10294.pdf.

Tabuchi, Hiroko. 2012. "Young and Global Need Not Apply in Japan." *New York Times*, May 29, 2012. Accessed June 1, 2012. http://www.nytimes.com/2012/05/30/business /global/as-global-rivals-gain-ground-corporate-japan-clings-to-cautious-ways .html?pagewanted=1.

Taipei Times. 2004. "'Techno-Nationalism' Drives Iffy Innovation in China." Last modified May 26, 2004. Accessed January 19, 2016. http://www.taipeitimes.com/News /worldbiz/archives/2004/05/26/2003157047/.

Tamura, Norihisa 田村憲久. 2014. "Kosei rōdō shōrei dai hachijūhachigō" 厚生労働省令 第八十八号 (The ordinance no. 88 of Ministry of Health, Labour and Welfare). Kosei rōdō daijin 厚生労働大臣 (Minister for Health, Labour and Welfare). Last modified July 30, 2014. Accessed October 6, 2017. http://www.kantei.go.jp/jp/singi/iryou /5senryaku/siryou01.pdf, page archived at http://warp.ndl.go.jp/info:ndljp/pid /11065479/www.jil.go.jp/kokunai/mm/hourei/syourei/20140724a.html (Japanese).

Tan, Cheng Yong, and Clive Dimmock. 2015. "Principals' Contribution to Educational Inequity: An Analysis of the Structure-Agency Relationship in the Centrally Controlled Education System of Singapore." Asia Leadership Roundtable, Bangkok 2015. Accessed March 10, 2017. http://www.ied.edu.hk/apclc/roundtable 2015/paper.html.

Tan, David. 2013. "Biotech in Singapore: A Perspective." Singapore Oxbridge Biotech Roundtable, September 19, 2013. Accessed December 15, 2015. http://www .oxbridgebiotech.com/review/featured/biotech-singapore-perspective/.

Tan, Jason, and S. Gopinathan. 2000. "Education Reform in Singapore: Towards Greater Creativity and Innovation?" *National Institute for Research Advancement Review* 7 (3): 5–10.

Tan, Kenneth Paul. 2017. *Governing Global City Singapore: Legecies and Future After Lee Kuan Yew.* New York: Routledge.

Tao, Wenzhao 陶文昭. 2006. "Jishu minzu zhuyi yu zhongguode zizhu chuangxin" 技術民族主義与中国的自主創新 (Techno-nationalism and Chinese autonomous creation). *Gao xiao li lun zhan xian*高校理论战线 5: 43–48 (Chinese).

Tassey, Gregory. 2000. "Standardization in Technology-Based Markets." *Research Policy* 29 (4): 587–602.

Taylor, Lance. 1997. "Editorial: The Revival of the Liberal Creed—the IMF and the World Bank in a Globalized Economy." *World Development* 25 (2): 145–52.

Temple, Jonathan. 1999. "The New Growth Evidence." *Journal of Economic Literature* 37 (1): 112–56.

Temple, Robert K. G., and Joseph Needham. 1986. *The Genius of China: 3,000 Years of Science, Discovery, and Invention.* New York: Simon & Schuster.

Thakral, Karen, interview, 2010.

Thakur, Harish. 2010. *Gandhi Nehru and Globalization.* New Delhi: Concept Publishing Company.

This American Life. 2003. "Episode 241: 20 Acts in 60 Minutes, Act Fourteen. Call in Colonel Mustard for Questioning, Transcript." Originally aired July 11, 2003. Accessed November 17, 2016. https://www.thisamericanlife.org/241/20-acts-in-60-minutes.

Times of India. 2016. "Biocon Bets on Biosimilars for Global Ascendancy." July 1, 2016. Accessed August 10, 2016. https://timesofindia.indiatimes.com/city/delhi/Biocon -bets-on-biosimilars-for-global-ascendancy/articleshow/53009328.cms.

Today Online. "More S'poreans Overseas, but Brain Drain Concerns Dissipate." March 6, 2015. Last modified July 3, 2017. Accessed August 10, 2017. https://www .todayonline.com/singapore/more-sporeans-overseas-brain-drain-concerns -dissipate.

Torch High Technology Industry Development Center. 2013. "Building an Innovative Environment." Accessed July 28, 2013. http://www.ctp.gov.cn/ctp-eng/areas_three .htm.

Tsuda, Takeyuki. 1999. "The Permanence of 'Temporary' Migration: The 'Structural Embeddedness' of Japanese-Brazilian Immigrant Workers in Japan." *Journal of Asian Studies* 58 (3): 687–722.

Tsuda, Takeyuki. 2012. "Global Inequities and Diasporic Return: Japanese American and Brazilian Encounters with the Ethnic Homeland." Discover Nikkei. Last modified July 2, 2012. Accessed March 8, 2017. http://www.discovernikkei.org/en /journal/2012/7/2/diasporic-return-2/.

Tsuji Takashi. 2017. "Young Japanese Bureaucrats Drop a Bombshell on Old Habits." *Nikkei Asian Review*, August 27, 2017. Accessed March 14, 2018. https://asia.nikkei .com/Politics-Economy/Policy-Politics/Young-Japanese-bureaucrats-drop-a -bombshell-on-old-habits.

UNESCO. 2018. "Gross Domestic Expenditure on R&D (GERD), Definition." UNESCO Institute of Statistics. Accessed September 11, 2018. http://uis.unesco.org/node /334882.

UNESCO. n.d.a. "Education: Outbound Internationally Mobile Student by Host Region." Accessed April 13, 2018. http://data.uis.unesco.org/Index.aspx?queryid =172#.

UNESCO. n.d.b. "Global Flow of Tertiary-Level Students." UNESCO.org. Accessed March 12, 2018. http://uis.unesco.org/en/uis-student-flow.

UNICEF. 2012. "Supply Chains for Children: Annual Report 2012." Unicef.org. Accessed August 18, 2016. http://www.unicef.org/supply/files/UNICEF_Supply _Annual_Report_2012_web.pdf.

University of Pennsylvania, Wharton School. 2012. "How India's Liberalization Shaped a Generation of Entrepreneurs." Knowledge@Wharton, February 15, 2012. Accessed July 5, 2016. http://knowledge.wharton.upenn.edu/article/how-indias-liberali zation-shaped-a-generation-of-entrepreneurs/.

U.S. Chamber of Commerce. 2017. "ASEAN Business Outlook Survey 2017" (survey). Washington, DC.

Vaidya, Ashok D. B. 2014. "Reverse Pharmacology—A Paradigm Shift for Drug Discovery and Development." *Current Research in Drug Discovery* 1 (2): 39–44.

Vajpayee, K. C. Pant, Jaswant Singh, Yashwant Sinha, Vasundhara Raje, S. P. Gupta, D. N. Tewari, K. Venkatasubramanian, Som Pal, Kamaluddin Ahmed, and N. K. Singh. 2002. *Planning Commission, Republic of India; 5 Year Plans; Tenth Five Year Plan 2002–07*, by Atal Bihari. New Delhi: Oxford University Press.

Vallas, Steven P., Daniel Lee Kleinman, and Dina Biscotti. 2015. "Political Structures and the Making of US Biotechnology." In *State of Innovation: The U.S. Government's Role in Technology Development*, ed. Fred Block and Matthew Keller, 57–76. Boulder, CO: Paradigm Publishers.

Van Praag, C. Mirjam, and Peter H. Versloot. 2007. "What Is the Value of Entrepreneurship? A Review of Recent Research." *Small Business Economics* 29 (4): 351–82.

Varma, Sujith. 2009. "An Overview of Biopharmaceutical Industry in India." Saffron .pharmabiz.com. Last modified December 10, 2009. http://saffron.pharmabiz.com /article/detnews.asp?articleid=53092&sectionid=50.

Varshney, Ashutosh. 1993. "Contested Meanings: India's National Identity, Hindu Nationalism, and the Politics of Anxiety." *Daedalus* 122 (3): 227–61.

Varshney, Ashutosh. 2014. "Hindu Nationalism in Power?" *Journal of Democracy* 25 (4): 34–45.

Vogel, Ezra F. 2011. *Deng Xiaoping and the Transformation of China*. Cambridge, MA: Belknap Press.

Waarden, Frans van, and Steven Casper, eds. 2005. *Innovation and Institutions: A Multidisciplinary Review of the Study of Innovation System*. Northampton, MA: Edward Elgar.

Wade, Robert. 1990. *Governing the Market: Economic Theory and the Role of Government in East Asian Industrialization*. Princeton, NJ: Princeton University Press.

Wadhwa, Vivek, Gary Gereffi, Ben Rissing, and Ryan Ong. 2007. "Where the Engineers Are." *Issues in Science and Technology* 23 (3): 73–84.

Wadhwa, Vivek, Sonali Jain, Anna Lee Saxenian, Gary Geref, and Huiyao Wang. 2011. "The Grass Is Indeed Greener in India and China for Returnee Entrepreneurs: America's New Immigrant Entrepreneurs, Part VI." Kauffman Foundation. Last modified April 2011. Accessed March 8, 2017. http://www.kauffman.org/~/media/kauffman_org/research%20reports%20and%20covers/2011/04/grassisgreenerforrreturneeentrepreneurs.pdf.

Wadhwa, Vivek, Anna Lee Saxenian, Richard B. Freeman, and Alex Salkever. 2009. *Losing the World's Best and Brightest: America's New Immigrant Entrepreneurs, Part V*. Last modified March 15, 2009. Accessed August 17, 2018. https://www.kauffman.org/what-we-do/research/immigration-and-the-american-economy/losing-the-worlds-best-and-brightest-americas-new-immigrant-entrepreneurs-part-v.

Wadhwa, Vivek, Anna Lee Saxenian, Ben Rissing, and Gary Gereffi. 2007. *America's New Immigrant Entrepreneurs*. Last modified January 4, 2007. Accessed August 17, 2018. http://people.ischool.berkeley.edu/~anno/Papers/Americas_new_immigrant_entrepreneurs_I.pdf.

Waldby, Catherine. 2009. "Singapore Biopolis: Bare Life in the City-State." *East Asian Science, Technology and Society* 3 (2–3): 372. Accessed December 14, 2014. http://dx.doi.org/ 10.1007/s12280-009-9089-2.

Wang, Huiyao, David Zweig, and Xiaohua Lin. 2011. "Returnee Entrepreneurs: Impact on China's Globalization Process." *Journal of Contemporary China* 20 (70): 413–31.

Wang, Zhen 王真. 2016. "Guo Jia Ji Yin Ku Wei Shen Me Hui Xuan Ze Hua Da Ji Yin Lai Cheng Jian He Yun Ying" 国家基因库为什么会选择华大基因来承建和运营 (Why BGI would be chosen to operate the National Gene Bank). Last modified September 12, 2016. Accessed September 22, 2017. http://tech.163.com/16/0912/02/C0NR3EHC00097U81.html (Chinese).

Wang Jian 汪建. 2015. [Kai jiang la] 20150516 Wang Jian: "Yi bai sui de meng xiang"《开讲啦》20150516 汪建：一百岁的梦想 (Lecture on May 16, 2015, Wang Jian: "The One Hundred Years Old Dream"). CCTV—1 Zong he pin dao CCTV-1综合频道 (CCTV-1 [China Central Television] channel). Last modified May 17, 2015. Accessed August 19, 2018. http://tv.cctv.com/2015/05/17/VIDE1431795258217395.shtml (Chinese).

Ward, Andrew, and Patti Waldmeir. 2016. "Fundraisings Highlight the Rise in Chinese Pharma R&D" *Financial Times*, February 18, 2016. Accessed September 30, 2017. https://www.ft.com/content/6fd26e06-d564-11e5-8887-98e7feb46f27.

Warner, Eric. 2015. *Patenting and Innovation in China: Incentives, Policy, and Outcomes*. Santa Monica, CA: Rand Graduate School.

Watanabe, Yasuko, interview, 2014.

Waterbury, John. 1999. "The Long Gestation and Brief Triumph of Import-Substituting Industrialization." *World Development* 27 (2): 323–41.

Watt, Lori. 2010. *When Empire Comes Home: Repatriation and Reintegration in Postwar Japan*. Harvard East Asian Monographs, vol. 317. Cambridge, MA: Harvard University Press.

Wee, Sui-lee. 2018. "Made in China: New and Potentially Lifesaving Drugs." *New York Times*, January 3, 2018. Accessed September 5, 2018. https://www.nytimes.com /2018/01/03/business/china-drugs-health-care.html.

Weede, Erich. 2010. "The Rise of India: Overcoming Caste Society and Permit-License-Quota Raj, Implementing Some Economic Freedom." *Asian Journal of Political Science* 18 (2): 129–53.

Wei, Chunjuan Nancy, and Darryl E. Brock. 2013. *Mr. Science and Chairman Mao's Cultural Revolution: Science and Technology in Modern China*. Lanham, MD: Lexington Books.

Whalley, John. 2017. *The Economies of China and India*. Ed. Manmohan Agarwal and Jing Wang. Hackensack, NJ: World Scientific Publishing.

Whiting, Michael D. 2008. "The Great Firewall of China a Critical Analysis." Wright-Patterson Air Force Base, Ohio: Department of the Air Force, Air University.

Wilsdon, James. 2007. "China: The Next Science Superpower?" *Engineering and Technology* 2 (3): 28–31.

WIPO. 2016. "U.S. Extends Lead in International Patent and Trademark Filings." WIPO. Last modified March 16, 2016. Accessed November 16, 2016. http://www .wipo.int/pressroom/en/articles/2016/article_0002.html.

———. n.d. "PCT Contracting States." Accessed November 1, 2017. http://www.wipo .int/pct/en/pct_contracting_states.html.

Wolf, Charles, Jr., Siddhartha Dalal, Julie DaVanzo, Eric V. Larson, Alisher Akhmedjonov, Harun Dogo, Meilinda Huang, and Silvia Montoya. 2011. "China and India, 2025: A Comparative Assessment." Santa Monica, CA: RAND Corporation. Accessed August 20, 2018. https://www.rand.org/pubs/monographs/MG1009.html. Also available in print form.

Wong, Catherine Mei Ling. 2012. "The Developmental State in Ecological Modernization and the Politics of Environmental Framings: The Case of Singapore and Implications for East Asia." *Nature and Culture* 7 (1): 95–119.

Wong, Joseph. 2005. "Re-Making the Developmental State in Taiwan: The Challenges of Biotechnology." *International Political Science Review* 26 (2): 169–91.

Wong, Joseph. 2011. *Betting on Biotech: Innovation and the Limits of Asia's Developmental State*. Ithaca, NY: Cornell University Press.

Wong, Poh-Kam. 2007. "Commercializing Biomedical Science in a Rapidly Changing 'Triple-Helix' Nexus: The Experience of National University of Singapore." *Journal of Technology Transfer* 32 (4): 371. Accessed December 9, 2014. http://dx.doi.org /10.1007/s10961-006-9020-0.

Wong, Poh Kam, interview, 2010.

Wong, Poh Kam, Yuen Ping Ho, and Annette Singh. 2005. "Singapore as an Innovative City in East Asia: An Explorative Study of the Perspectives of Innovative Industries." World Bank Policy Working Paper, April 2005. Accessed August 17, 2018. http://documents.worldbank.org/curated/en/432221468102872101/Singapore-as -an-innovative-city-in-East-Asia-an-explorative-study-of-the-perspectives-of -innovative-industries.

Wong, Poh-Kam, Yuen-Ping Ho, and Annette Singh. 2007. "Towards an 'Entrepreneurial University' Model to Support Knowledge-Based Economic Development: The Case of the National University of Singapore." *World Development* 35 (6): 941–58.

Worden, Robert L., Andrea Matles Savada, and Ronald E. Dolan. 1988. *China: A Country Study*. Washington, DC: Federal Research Division, Library of Congress.

World Bank. 2016. "Doing Business 2017: Equal Opportunity for All." Washington, DC: World Bank. Accessed July 23, 2017. http://www.doingbusiness.org/rankings.

World Bank. 2017. "Doing Business 2018: Reforming to Create Jobs." Report. Washington, DC: World Bank. Accessed November 1, 2017. http://www.doingbusiness .org/reports/global-reports/doing-business-2018.

World Economic Forum, Klaus Schwab, ed. 2013. "The Global Competitiveness Report 2013–2014: Full Data Edition." Geneva: Global Competitiveness and Benchmarking Network. Accessed December 9, 2014. http://www.weforum.org/gcr.

World Economic Forum, Klaus Schwab, ed. 2017a. "The Global Competitiveness Report 2017–2018." Geneva: Global Competitiveness and Benchmarking Network. Accessed October 30, 2017. http://www3.weforum.org/docs/WEF_GlobalCom petitivenessReport_2013-14.pdf.

World Economic Forum, Klaus Schwab, ed. 2017b. "The Global Competitiveness Report 2016–2017." Accessed March 30, 2018. http://www3.weforum.org/docs/GCR20162017 /05FullReport/TheGlobalCompetitivenessReport2016-2017_FINAL.pdf.

Worsley, Oliver. 2013. "Singapore: Searching for 'Follow-On' Venture Capital Funding in a Steadily Growing Biotech Industry." Singapore Oxbridge Biotech Roundtable, November 6, 2013. Accessed December 20, 2014. http://www.oxbridgebiotech.com

/review/business-development/singapore-searching-follow-venture-capital
-funding-steadily-growing-biotech-industry/.

Wu, Lin lin 吴琳琳. 2013. "Huawei ceng ju 3 yi guo jia zi jin zhi chi" 华为曾拒3亿国家资
金支持 (Huawei refused 300 million RMB in national funding). Beijing Youth Daily
北京青年报. Last modified December 26, 2013. Accessed August 7, 2017. http://
epaper.ynet.com/html/2013-12/26/content_32456.htm?div=-1.

Wübbeke, Jost, and Bjorn Conrad. 2015 *Industrie 4.0: Will German Technology Help
China Catch Up with the West?* Mercator Institute for China Studies, April 14, 2015.

Xiang, Biao. 2016. "Emigration Trends and Policies in China." In *Spotlight on China*,
247–267. Rotterdam: SensePublishers.

Xie, Gaofeng. 2010. "Clusters in Europe II, Mobilizing Clusters for Competitiveness."
China Torch Program for Industrial Clusters. Last modified 2010. Accessed
August 7, 2013. http://www.bioin.or.kr/upload/policy/1313543807453.pdf.

Xie, Yu, Chunni Zhang, and Qing Lai. 2014. "China's Rise as a Major Contributor to
Science and Technology." *Proceedings of the National Academy of Sciences* 111 (26):
9437–42.

Xi Jinping. 2017. "President Xi's Speech to Davos in Full." World Economic Forum.
Last modified January 17, 2017. Accessed March 6, 2017. https://www.weforum.org
/agenda/2017/01/full-text-of-xi-jinping-keynote-at-the-world-economic-forum.

Xing, Lu. 1993. "The Theory of Persuasion in Han Fei Tzu and Its Impact on Chinese
Communication Behaviors." *Howard Journal of Communications* 5 (1/2): 108–22.

Xinhua News. 2013. "China to Boost Biotech Industry." Xinhuanet. Last modified January 6, 2013. Accessed March 6, 2017. http://news.xinhuanet.com/english/sci
/2013-01/06/c_132084198.htm.

Xinhua News. 2015. "'Made in China 2025 Plan Unveiled to Boost Manufacturing."
Xinhuanet. Last modified May 19, 2015. Accessed March 6, 2017. http://news
.xinhuanet.com/english/2015-05/19/c_134252230.htm.

Xinhua News. 2016. "Xi Sets Targets for China's Science, Technology Mastery." Xinhuanet. Last modified May 30, 2016. Accessed July 24, 2017. http://news.xinhuanet
.com/english/2016-05/30/c_135399691.htm.

Xu, Judy, and Yue Yang. 2009. "Traditional Chinese Medicine in the Chinese Health
Care System." *Health Policy* 90 (2–3): 133–39.

Yamada, Atsushi. 2000. "Neo-techno-nationalism: How and Why It Grows." Columbia International Affairs Online. Accessed July 15, 2016. http://www.ciaonet.org/isa
/yaa01/.

Yamamoto, Kiyoshi. n.d. "Corporation of National Universities in Japan: An Analysis
of the Impact on Governance and Finance." Center for National University Finance
and Management, University of Tokyo. Accessed October 2, 2017. http://ump.p.u
-tokyo.ac.jp/crump/resource/crump_wp_no3.pdf.

Yamanaka, Shinya. 2013. "Dr. Shinya Yamanaka's Keynote Address—2013 Annual Conference." Presentation to Annual Meeting of the U.S.-Japan Council, Washington, DC, October 4, 2013.

Yasuda, Satoko 安田聡子. 2007. "Gaikoku hito kōdo jinzai no gurobaru idō to inobēshon—brain circulation (zunō junkan) no sekai-teki chōryū ni wagakuni chūshōkigyō wa do mukiau ka" 外国人高度人材のグローバル移動とイノベーション—brain circulation (頭脳循環) の世界的潮流にわが国中小企業はどう向き合うか (The global movement of foreign high-skill talent—how should our country's small and medium sized enterprises face global [brain circulation] flows?). *Research for Small and Medium Enterprises*中小企業総合研究 6:21–42 (Japanese).

Yates, Ronald. 1990. "Japan's 'Returnees' Face Rejection, Find That Coming Home Isn't Easy." *Chicago Tribune*, September 23, 1990.

Yeo, Phillip, interview, 2010.

Yeung, Henry Wai-chung, and W. Chung. 1999. "The Political Economy of Singapore Investments in China." East Asian Institute, National University of Singapore, March 31, 1999.

Yu, Xiaoyu, and Steven Si. 2012. "Innovation, Internationalization and Entrepreneurship: A New Venture Research Perspective." *Innovation: Management, Policy and Practice* 14 (4): 524–39.

Yusuf, Shahid, and Kaoru Nabeshima, eds. 2007. *How Universities Promote Economic Growth*. Washington, DC: World Bank Publications.

Zaharia, Marius, and Fathin Ungku. 2017. "In the Hunt for New Ideas, Singapore Eases Obsession with Grades." Reuters, January 8, 2017. Accessed September 19, 2017. http://www.reuters.com/article/singapore-education/in-the-hunt-for-new-ideas -singapore-eases-obsession-with-grades-idUSL5N1E905B.

Zeng Xiaodong, interview, 2016.

Zhang, Shengen 张神根. 2008. "Gai Ge Kai Fang 30 Nian Shu Xi: Gai Ge Kai Fang 30 Nian Zhong Da Jue Ce Shi Mo" 改革开放30年书系:改革开放30年重大决策始末 (Chinese economic reform 30 years book series: the beginning and ending of Chinese economic reform 30 years important decision making). Sichuan, China: Sichuan People Publishing House.

Zhang, Sufang, and Yongxiu He. 2013. "Analysis on the Development and Policy of Solar PV Power in China." *Renewable and Sustainable Energy Reviews* 21: 393–401.

Zhao, Wei, and Frank La Pira. 2013. "Chinese Entrepreneurship: Institutions, Ecosystems and Growth Limits." *Advances in Economics and Business* 1 (2): 72–88.

Zhao, Yongxin 赵永新. 2015. "Zuo quan qiu zui hao de kang ai xin yao" 做全球最好的抗癌新药 (Produce the world's best new anticancer drug). Last modified May 27, 2015. Accessed August 20, 2018. http://scitech.people.com.cn/n/2015/0527/c1007 -27062530.html (Chinese).

Zheng, Yongnian, and Rongfang Pan. 2012. "From Defensive to Aggressive Strategies: The Evolution of Economic Nationalism in China." In *Globalization and Economic Nationalism in Asia*, ed. Anthony P. D'Costa, 84–108. Oxford, UK: Oxford University Press.

INDEX

Page numbers in italics refer to figures and tables.